The Book No Pope Would Want You To Read

Tim C. Leedom
and
Maryjane Churchville

EWORLD INC.

Buffalo, New York
14208
eeworldinc@yahoo.com

COVER DESIGN: *Abigail Huchel*

First Edition

Published by *EWorld Inc.*

ISBN: 978-1-61759-029-0

www.nopope.com

EWorld Inc.
Buffalo, New York 14208
eeworldinc@yahoo.com

11 12 13 14   6 5 4 3 2 1
Printed in Canada

DEDICATION

Mary Ellen Leedom,
who set the stage for discernment and inquiry

TABLE OF CONTENTS

Preface   ix

Section I — The Basis: Dogma And Practices   1

Catholic Dogma   3
•Dogma   3
    No interpretation tolerated
•Some Papal Bulls   6
    God's first team – assembled by the Church of course
•Papal Infallibility   7
•Is The Catholic Church A Cult?   7
•Behavioral Patterns Commonly Found in Cultic Environments   8
    By Janja Lalich, PhD. and Michael D. Langone, PhD

Catholic Practices   11
•Beatification   11
•Controversial Candidates for Sainthood   12
    The good, the bad, the ugly
•The Catholic Exorcist   16
    The 14th century alive and well in the Catholic Church
•How to Perform an Exorcism   16
    Don't try this at home
•Legatus   18
    21st century elite crusaders
•Josémarie Escriva   19
    A product of Franco's Spain
•Opus Dei   21
    Catholic henchmen: Was Dan Brown right?

Section II — A Historical View Of The Church **23**

Early History of the Catholic Church 25
•What Does The Word "Vatican" Mean? 25
   Before it was a country and the center of Catholicism
•The Pope 26
   Origin, Vicar of God? Infallible? Holy?
•Built Upon Lies: The Vatican's False Foundations *by Paul Tice* 28
•Hus: Example of a Martyr 38
   Fiction recorded as Fact
   By Daante
•The Council of Nicaea 43
   One vote that changed history
•Christ: A Composite Character *by Acharya S* 45
   Man, myth, legend, nothing new under the sun
•The Fish Story: Another Borrowed Icon 49

Section III — The Popes **53**

Criminal History of The Papacy 55
•Antipopes 55
•Black Popes 55
•Pope Joan 55
   Hidden woman undeniable
•Dirty Dozen 61
   Not a saint among them
•Pope John Paul II *by Tony Bushby* 62
•Pope Benedict XVI 64
   A Nazi youth, non-discloser of molestation and espouser of
   Dark Age doctrine

The Dark Ages 67
•Let the Crimes Begin 67
   No country, no army, no ideology has committed more crime
   than the Roman Catholic Church
•Onward Christian Soldiers 68
   The blood spilled in the Name of the Prince of Peace
•The Crusades 77
   700 years of Roman Catholic Jihad

•Joan of Arc   81
   Military leader burned at the stake then canonized by the
   Vatican 400 years later
•Spanish Inquisition   81
   Roman Catholic terrorists of old in the dark age of western
   civilization
•The Fig Leaf Campaign   86
•Roman Catholic Imperialism   88

World War II and the Roman Catholic Church   95
•Pope Pius XII: The "Nazi Pope"   97
•German Soldiers Rallied by the Church 104
   The Roman Catholic Church marches lock step with the
   Nazis
•Yugoslavia Holocaust 108
   Released documents prove Church's complicity
•An All Telling Case Study *by Tim C. Leedom* 111
   Croatian mass murderer escapes through Roman Catholic
   Ratline and finds home in California Catholic Church
•Ratlines Map: The Vatican Safety Net 133
   Highway to freedom for thousands of war criminals and
   their gold
•A Ratline Not Well Traveled . . . . , , , , .
   Connecting the dots from death camps to abbeys to
   cathedrals to South America
•The Rats: Notorious Nazis – killers, executioners, murderers,
   and Catholics 138
•Adolph Eichmann: Godless executioner was issued a Roman
   Catholic passport 142
•The Power and the Glory *by Tim C. Leedom* 148
   The Teflon Pope exposed

Section IV — Issues Of The Church **149**

Vatican Finances 151
•Money Laundering by Dr. Jonathan Levy 151
•The Brimstone Report 152
•Cardinal John Patrick Cody: Poster Child for Corruption 157
   Corrupt Chicago Cardinal was the lynch pin for crime in the U.S.

•Mea Culpa 158
    Vatican Denies it Held Stock in Maker of the Pill
    September 2010 Heist

The Church and Science 161
•The Galileo Affair 161
    Get away from that telescope – imprisoned for his
    discoveries
•The "Lucifer" Telescope *by Greg Szymanski, JD* 163
    The Catholic hope to ignorant souls in space
•The Catholic Church and Evolution 169
    Science, reason, knowledge – always threats to Catholic Dogma
•Church Warns Cell Scientists 170
    A morality plan to derail scientists
•Vatican Document on Bioethics 170
    Control has slipped away from the Church
•Catholic Alternative to Condoms 171
    While thousands die the Church closes its eyes to prevention

Banning 173
•Ten Books Banned by the Catholic Church 175
    No thinking allowed
•Notable Authors Who Made the List 176
    Award winning authors and Nobel Prize winners banned
•Dead Sea Scrolls Cover-up *by Tim C. Leedom* 176
    Semi-successful campaign to hide the truth
•No Holy Communion 177
    If you're not on your knees – you're out
•Free Speech is Free Speech 178
    Another tenant of Jefferson ignored
•After Ted Kennedy's Death: 179
    America's first Catholic family snubbed
•Vatican Denounces the Film "AVATAR" 179
    Nature, God's creation became reason for banning
•Italian Comedienne Faced Possible Imprisonment 180
    No laughing matter, this is serious
•Father, May I? 180
    A precursor to Orwellian thinking
•*America's* Editor Resigns 181
    Balanced Catholic reporting axed

•Archbishop Bans Music 182
  Rock of Ages – Australian down under edict
•The Lady and the Pit-bull *by Tim C. Leedom* 182
  Lady Gaga under attack by fellow Catholics

Women and the Church 183
•Ordination of Women 183
  A sin branded with heresy and molestation
•Woman Priest Excommunicated 184
  When the Church says "no" it means "no"
•Timeline of world Religions' Acceptance of Woman 184
  Absent on the list? One guess
•The Catholic Church's War on Nuns *by Tom Henheffer* 186
  Less than second-class citizens of heaven

Celibacy 187
•Timeline of Celibacy in the Catholic Church 187
•Popes Who Were Married 189
  Rules are made for others
•Popes Who Had Illegitimate Children 189
  Say it isn't so
•Widows Walk 190
  The bottom line on priest marriage
•Belgian Bishops Question Mandatory Celibacy 190
  Speaking up after 2000 years

Catholic Insurance: In Good Hands? 191

Section V — Crimes Of The Church **193**

Let Us Not Confuse The Difference Between
"Sins" and "Crimes" 195

The Murdered Pope: John Paul I *by Tim C. Leedom* 213
The smiling Pope John I – the light of reform too dangerous to live

Popes Murdered and Alleged Murdered 219

Child Molestation: The Crime of the Millennium 221
•Tell It Like It Is *by Tim C. Leedom* 221
•Murder and Molestation in Hometown, U.S.A.: 222
    The Unspeakable Is Happening Right Around the Corner
•Bishop Accountability 223
•Letters from Father Thomas Doyle 238
    No good deed goes unpunished
•Crimen Sollitationis 243
•Catholic Sex Abuse Scandals 255
    Beyond words and thought
•The John Jay Report: The geographic solution 256
•The Holy See's Reaction by Matt Taibbi 257
•Cries Not Heard Round the World *by Maryjane Churchville* 260
    The global village soiled
•The Canadian Holocaust *by Kevin D. Annett, MA, MDiv.* 263
    Covered up – out of sight, out of mind
•The Native American Holocaust *by Ken Bear Chief* 273
    A crime so outrageous
•Belgian Abuse 275
•Pedophiles and Priests *by Michael Parenti, PhD.* 276
•Tod D. Brown *by Tim C. Leedom* 280
•Pope Accused of Letting Truth Lay Dormant 280
    A blind eye to their beloved priests
•Settlements in Catholic Sex Abuse Cases 281
    The numbers don't lie
•Boston College Fallout *by Tim C. Leedom* 283
    The ripple effect of crimes against children
•SNAP Press Release 284
•Nuns Too 284
    The molestation culture unknown
•OC Diocese Lawyers Seek to Seal Deposition 285
    by Gustavo Arellano
        Justice under lock and key
•Accused Priest's Plaque Removed 286
    Citizen's action at work
•The Pedophiles of Orange County and Los Angeles 287
    The Billion Dollar Men:
        Bishop Tod D. Brown & Cardinal Roger Mahony
•The Report on Claudy 287
•The Same Modus Operandi 289
• An Open Letter to Pope Benedict XVI *by Sinead O'Connor* 290

•Priest Charged in U.S. Still Serving In India 292
•Supreme Court Allows sex-abuse case to proceed against the Vatican . 293
  Holy See vs. Doe
•Making Distinctions: A Bishop Defends His Actions 294
•Pope Protected Criminals from Law 296
•Get Out Of Jail Free Card 299
  Go Directly to Club Ped
•Bernard Francis Law 300
  Sexual Abuse Scandal in the Archdiocese of Boston
•Victim Justice 302
•Make My Day 302
•Vatican Fails to File Report on Children's Rights: 303
  What would Jesus say?

Section VI — The Church Today 305

Priest Admits He's Gay 307
  Don't Ask, Don't Tell

Sample Rants from Different Slants *by Tim C. Leedom* 307

CNN Asks "What the Pope Knew" 308

Come Home Again: Branding for Catholics 308

The Catholic League 309

Dignity USA 310

Luigi Cascioli Lawsuit 310

List of Ex-Catholics 311

Daily Missal Ipad 312

People Speak but the Church Hears Not 312

St. Christopher *by Maryjane Churchville* 313

Vatican Secret Archives 313

The Future of The Roman Catholic Church 314

Section VII — What They Are Saying On The Street **317**

The EVIL Catholic Church *by Karl Frank* 319

The Pope's New Clothes *by Brian Burkhart* 321

The Mass *from Y.* 321

No Answers *from B.* 321

My Experience *from J.* 322

I Would Like to See the Church *from K.* 323

Rants and Raves *from H.* 324

Musings of a Catholic School Girl *by Maryjane Churchville* 325

The Pew Forum: Catholics Rank Last 326

No Wiggle Room: "Virtus" A First Step 327

POSTSCRIPT: AND NOW.... 329

In Memoriam: Steve Allen 333

Contributors 339

About the Authors 343

Acknowledgements 345

Illustrations and Photos 347

Index 351

PREFACE

" The Catholic Church is organized crime...a proverbial crime wave through history"...

Steve Allen

Is it the crimes themselves – or the eternal denials that are worse? Actually the combination makes them both more hideous thus unforgivable.

The Vatican, the Church, the Holy See, and the Pope.... a day doesn't go by that The Roman Catholic Church is not heard about in one form or another. For close to 2000 years, the "Mother Church" has been a major factor shaping the world's history. As we know, history is not always joyous and inspiring. Quite to the contrary, history has been dark with wars, greed, poverty, suppression and inequity. No one force or element can be blamed for all the evils, nor be credited with progress, light and humanity.

However, one institution, the Roman Catholic Church, more than any other historical influence has lead to more crime, corruption and pain throughout modern history.. As Steve Allen, the consummate Renaissance man of the arts, comedy and literature, said in an interview with me in 1994, "the Catholic Church is organized crime...a proverbial crime wave throughout history."

The Book No Pope Would Want You to Read will walk you through the destructive historical path of the Roman Catholic Church, starting with Emperor Constantine's hijacking of higher truths; to the church's two-century killing spree christened the "Holy Crusades"; the Spanish Inquisition; the witch trials; the Native American Holocaust; the imprisonment of scientists and philosophers (Galileo, Copernicus and Bruno); the ruthless elimination of other followers of the Prince of Peace; and the liquidation of rival factions in the Church itself. Any thing, idea or person not in conformity with the Roman Catholic hierarchy's interpretation of "truth" became sinful, the work of the Devil and heretical.

The crimes of the Church spanned the globe, and they still do. The 20th and 21st century rap sheet includes, but is not limited to, shady land and money deals with Mussolini, Franco and Hitler; an alliance with the brutal Croatian Ustashe; the Ratlines for escaping Nazi war criminals; the theft of gold and spoils of World War II; the molestations, cover-ups for predator priests; and the most hidden holocaust of all, the Canadian Holocaust, where 50,000 Canadian children died as a result of abuse, medical experiments, and neglect at the hands of the Roman Catholic Church of Canada.

Today, the Roman Catholic Church is still employing the strategy of denial which it always has in regard to past crimes. And it boldly beatifies and promotes sainthood for Father Sierra, Nazi priests, the founder of Opus Dei and criminals of the past while keeping one of history's greatest scientists: Copernicus, in purgatory for his declaration that the earth is not the center of the universe. Galileo was just forgiven in 1983 by John Paul II – only 300 years after his unprecedented and lasting scientific discoveries were determined to be crimes by the Roman Catholic Church..

Meanwhile, the Vatican's financial dealings are riddled with scandal: such as the Vatican Bank scandal, costing investors billions; the Mafia connections; the looting of foreign accounts by the Vatican through mafia connections; and the support of right-wing dictators and military juntas.

Any progressive social agendas of humanitarian legislation have been crushed by the Roman Catholic Church stance on birth control, planned parenthood, women's equality, sexual orientation, and euthanasia. The Roman Catholic Church still clings to its exclusive dictatorial dogma despite historical, archeological and anthropological evidence, which have suggested change and progress.

In this book, we offer nothing but the facts for your consideration – not the fictions that have been passively accepted by many as truth. As with our best-selling anthology *The Book Your Church Doesn't Want You to Read*, we invite you to take a hard look at the past and the present to see the truth and what the Church's top leadership is doing to perpetuate itself at any cost.

During our research, we were appalled and surprised to discover the depth of deceit and damage done by this dinosaur that lumbers across the human landscape. We are struck by the uniformity of the Roman Catholic Church Leaders' strategy of elimination of opposition and attitude of arrogant superiority, giving it the right to lie, deny facts, cover-up atrocities, and attack anyone who dares to draw attention to the obvious contradictions between what the Church says and what it does.

The process of our discovery began with our observations of -- and opposition to -- the predator crimes in the Orange County, California and Los Angeles dioceses. The arrogance was shocking! The sociopathic defenses and mind-sets hailed back to the ultimate and long aged-out premise that the Leadership of the Church is **_Infallible_**, i.e. It Can Do No Wrong. If you are willing to accept that premise, then read no further, because you will discount every fact in this book as the Church has discounted facts for centuries.

We are only the messengers. What you do with this information is your decision. Millions of Roman Catholics have deserted the fold in recognition of the contradiction between fact and The Church's fiction. Others have remained in the fold, ignorant of what has been going on behind the scenes, and what has been done to keep things behind the scenes. Unsuspecting parents in the 21st century parishioners remain in their pews while their children are being molested and their Sunday donations go to attorneys and a corrupt Vatican as it has for the last 2,000 years. If this spell is not broken, the Roman Catholic Church will continue unchecked in its recessive criminal habits and the rest of the world will continue to pay for its damage.

We, the editors, want to state and emphasize the following:

1. The intent of this book is not to cast aspersion in any way on the Roman Catholic faith, or on Christianity, or on those believers who practice their beliefs.

2. Our intent **_is_**, however, to expose how the men in Leadership positions of the Roman Catholic Church – especially the Popes – have created power and wealth for themselves and have abused that power and wealth vested in them to commit what can only be called "Crimes," in any definition of the word, against those whom they have been "anointed" to serve.

Section I

THE BASIS –
DOGMA AND
PRACTICES

CATHOLIC DOGMA

"I will not attack your doctrines or creeds if they accord me ...if they hold thought to be dangerous...if they aver thoughts to be criminal then I attack them all, because they enslave men's liberty."

Robert Ingersoll

"Theology...induces a dogmatic belief that we have knowledge where in fact we have ignorance, and by doing so generates a kind of impertinent insolence towards the universe. Uncertainty, in the presence of vivid hopes and fears, is painful, but must be endured if we wish to live without the support of comforting fairy tales."

Bertrand Russell

DOGMA

Dogma, in the Roman Catholic lexicon, refers to an article of faith revealed by God.

Dogma consists of two elements:
- The Revelation
- The Announcement

The Revelation must have its origin in either scripture or tradition. The Announcement comes either ex-cathedra by the Pope (in the form of a "Papal Bull") or from Ecumenical Council, after which the revelation becomes binding on the faithful.

There have been 21 Ecumenical Councils. They were the settings for denouncing heretics and defining dogma, with the exception of the twenty-first council, which was a call for peace.

The First Ecumenical Council at Nicaea
This council condemned the heresy of Arias, who held that God the Father and God the son were separate. The Council confirmed that God the Father and God the Son are of the same substance and not separate.

The Second Ecumenical Council at Constantinople
The Emperor called this council. Pope St. Damascus I did not attend. The council defined the divinity of the Holy Ghost and the Divine Trinity.

The Third Ecumenical Council at Ephesus
Defined the Divine Maternity of the Blessed Virgin Mary, as the mother of the one person, Christ, who has two natures – Divine and Human. She is the mother of the one person with two natures.

The Fourth Ecumenical Council
Reaffirmed the dogma of one Christ with two natures.

The Fifth Ecumenical Council at Constantinople II
Condemned the writing of heretics against original sin.

The sixth Ecumenical Council at Constantinople III
Condemned the heresy attributing only One Will to Christ, instead of two wills, divine and human.

The Seventh Ecumenical Council at Nice II
Condemned Iconoclasm.

The Eighth Ecumenical Council at Constantinople IV
Condemned Photius, the patriarch of Constantinople and author of the Greek Schism. This council ended the Eastern Councils.

The Ninth Ecumenical Council at Lateran I
Set forth the format for the election of bishops and declared that once a priest was ordained he may not marry.

The Tenth Ecumenical Council at Lateran II
This Council was called by Pope Innocent II. It condemned the heresies of Peter

Bruys, who denounced the Mass, opposed the Eucharist, marriage and the baptism of children; and Arnold Brescia, who declared the Church should not own any property.

The Eleventh Ecumenical Council at Lateran III
Called for by Pope Alexander III, this Council regulated the election of the Pope.

The Twelfth Ecumenical Council at Lateran IV
Called for by Pope Innocent III, this Council proclaimed "There is but one Universal Church of the faithful, outside which no one at all is saved;" set forth mandatory annual confession and communion; and introduced the word "Transubstantiation" to assert that, in the Eucharist, the wine and the bread are changed into the blood and body of Christ.

The Thirteenth Ecumenical Council at Lyons I
This Council was called by Pope Innocent IV to excommunicate Emperor Frederick II for his attempt to reduce the position of the Church to a mere department of state. The 6th Crusade was called for at this council.

The Fourteenth Ecumenical Council
Called for by Pope Gregory X, this Council declared the procession of the Holy Ghost from the Father and the Son.

The Fifteenth Ecumenical Council at Vienne
Called for by Pope Clement V, this Council suppressed the Knights Templars.

The Sixteenth Ecumenical Council at Constance
Called for by Pope Gregory XII, this Council ended the confusion of the Western Schism and condemned the heresies of John Wycliffe, who rejected the Holy Sacrifice of the Mass, declared scripture as the sole rule of faith, and asserted the Pope is not the head of the Church.

The Seventeenth Ecumenical Council at Florence
This council was dissolved by Pope Eugene IV, angering bishops, who began to assert that it was heresy to hold "a general council superior to the pope."

The Eighteenth Ecumenical Council at Lateran
Called for by Pope Julius II, this Council condemned the edict of King Charles, which declared a general council superior to the Pope and denied the right of the Pope to nominate bishops in France.

The Nineteenth Ecumenical Council at Trent
Called for by Pope Paul III but not ratified until eighteen years later by Pope Pius IV, the council condemned the heresies of Luther and Calvin and issued decrees on the Eucharist, the Mass, the Sacraments of Baptism and Holy Orders, the teachings on marriage, purgatory, indulgences and the use of images.

The Twentieth Ecumenical Council at Vatican I
Called for by Pope Pius IX, this Council asserted the infallibility of the Pope when he speaks from the Seat of St. Peter (ex-cathedra) on matters of faith and morality, pronouncing a doctrine to be believed by the faithful.

The Twenty-First Ecumenical Council at Vatican II
Called for by Pope John XXIII, this Council was ratified by Pope Paul VI. It is not considered a "dogmatic" council but a "Pastoral Council." Pope John XXIII called for a religious fellowship rather than a Catholic missionary for the conversion to the Faith. Pope Paul VI issued his encyclical *Humanae Vitae* against artificial contraception.

Source: Jordan Maxwell, Catholic Encyclopedia; inspired by Wikipedia (Retrieved August 16, 2010)

SOME PAPAL BULLS

1216 Honorius III established the Dominican Order
1218 Honorius III demanded that Jews wear clothing to distinguish themselves and pay the tithe to local churches
1219 Honorius closed law schools in Paris and forbid the study of civil law
1244 Innocent IV called for the burning of the Talmud
1252 Innocent IV called for the use of torture for eliciting confessions from heretics
1302 Boniface VIII declared there is no salvation outside the Church
1312 Clement V disbands the Knights Templar
1435 Eugene IV forbid the slavery of black natives in the Canary Islands
1478 Sixtus IV appointed Ferdinand and Isabella to initiate the Spanish Inquisition
1513 Leo X declared the immortality of the soul
1521 Leo X excommunicated Martin Luther
1540 Paul III approved the formation of the Society of Jesus
1559 Paul IV confirmed that only Catholics can be elected Pope

1570   Pius X declared Elizabeth I of England a heretic
1586   Sixtus V condemned judicial astrology as superstitious
1738   Clement XII bans Catholics from becoming Freemasons
1871   Pius IX declares papal infallibility
1950   Pius XII declared the dogma of the Assumption of Mary

"God found out about the Trinity in 325A.D."
Rocco Errico

PAPAL INFALLIBILITY

Papal Infallibility is dogma in the Roman Catholic Church. Catholics are to believe that the Pope, through the actions of the Holy Spirit, is without error when he speaks on theological issues of faith and morals. The dogma very clearly DOES NOT state that the Pope is without sin in his own personal life.

IS THE CATHOLIC CHURCH A CULT?

Characteristics Associated with Cultic Groups - Revised
By Janja Lalich, Ph.D. & Michael D. Langone, Ph.D.

Concerted efforts at influence and control lie at the core of cultic groups, programs, and relationships. Many members, former members, and supporters of cults are not fully aware of the extent to which members may have been manipulated, exploited, even abused. The following list of social-structural, social-psychological, and interpersonal behavioral patterns commonly found in cultic environments may be helpful in assessing a particular group or relationship.

Compare these patterns to the situation you were in (or in which you, a family member, or friend is currently involved). This list may help you determine if there is cause for concern. Bear in mind that this list is not meant to be a "cult scale" or a definitive checklist to determine if a specific group is a cult. This is not so much a diagnostic instrument as it is an analytical tool.

7

BEHAVIORAL PATTERNS
COMMONLY FOUND IN CULTIC ENVIRONMENTS:

•The group displays excessively zealous and unquestioning commitment to its leader and (whether he is alive or dead) regards his belief system, ideology, and practices as the Truth, as law.

•Questioning, doubt and dissent are discouraged or even punished.

•Mind-altering practices (such as meditation, chanting, speaking in tongues, denunciation sessions, use of drugs, and debilitating work routines) are used in excess and serve to suppress doubts about the group and its leader(s).

•The cult's leadership dictates how members should think, act, and feel (for example, members must get permission to date, change jobs, marry – or leaders prescribe what types of clothes to wear, where to live, whether or not to have children, how to discipline children, and so forth).

•The group is elitist, claiming a special exalted status for itself, its leader(s) and members (for example, the leader is considered the Messiah, a special being, an avatar – or the group and/or the leader is on a special mission to save humanity).

•The group has a polarized us versus them mentality, which may cause conflict with the wider society.

•The leader is not accountable to any authorities (unlike, for example, teachers, military commanders or ministers, priests, monks, and rabbis of mainstream religious denominations).

•The group teaches or implies that its supposedly exalted ends justify whatever means it deems necessary. This may result in members participating in behaviors or activities they would have considered reprehensible or unethical before joining the group (for example lying to family or friends, or collecting money for bogus charities).

•The leadership induces feelings of shame and/or guilt in order to influence or control members. Often this is done through peer pressure and coercive forms of persuasion.

•Subservience to the leader or group requires members to cut ties with family and friends, and radically alter the personal goals and activities they had before joining the group.

•The group is preoccupied with bringing in new members.

•The group is preoccupied with making money.

•Members are expected to devote inordinate amounts of time to the group and group-related activities.

• Members are encouraged or required to live and/or socialize only with other group members.

•The most loyal members (the "true believers") feel there can be no life outside the context of the group. They believe there is no other way to be, and often fear reprisals to themselves or others if they leave (or even consider leaving) the group.

This checklist will be published in the new book, Take Back Your Life: Recovering from Cults and Abusive Relationships by Janja Lalich and Madeleine Tobias (Berkley Bay Tree Publishing, 2006). It was adapted from a checklist originally developed by Michael Langone.

CATHOLIC PRACTICES

BEATIFICATION

"Saint n. A dead sinner revised and edited."
Ambrose Bierce, 1842-1914

"Beatification" is a recognition accorded by the Catholic Church of a dead person's accession to Heaven and capacity to intercede on behalf of individuals who pray in his or her name (intercession of the saints).

Beatification is the third step in the four-step canonization process. The person who is beatified is given the title "Blessed."

Since the Canon Law Reform of 1983, one miracle must be proven to have taken place through the intercession of the person to be beatified unless the person died as a martyr.

In the early ages, the recognition was entirely local and passed from one local diocese to another with the permission of its bishop.

During the Middle Ages, some beatifications were scandalous. Charlemagne was beatified by a local court bishop. He was never canonized, his veneration has been widely suppressed, and he has been denied the title "Blessed."

Pope John Paul II (1978-2005) markedly changed the previous Catholic practice of beatification. By October 2004 he had beatified 1,340 people, more than the sum of all his predecessors since Pope Pius V (d.1590) who established a beatification process similar to that used today.

Today's Pope Benedict XVI removed the custom of holding beatification rites in the Vatican with the Pope presiding. They can now be held in the location where the subject lived with a Cardinal designated to preside over the ceremony.

Source: Catholic Encyclopedia; Inspired by Wikipedia (Retrieved August 16, 2010)

LIST OF AMERICAN SAINTS:

St. Damian of Molokai (2009), leper priest of Molokai.
St. Mother Theodore Guerin (2006), founder of The Sisters of Providence of Saint Mary-of-the Woods.
St. Katherine Drexel (2000), benefactor and school builder.
St. Rose Philippine Duchesne (1988), missionary to Native Americans.
St. John Neumann (1977), missionary and bishop of Philadelphia.
St. Elizabeth Ann Seton (1975), founder of the Sisters of Charity of St. Joseph.
St. Frances Xavier Cabrini (1946), worked among immigrants in New York City.
St. Isaac Jogues (1930), missionary to the Hurons.
St. Rene Goupil (1930), missionary to the Hurons.
St. Jean de Lalande (1930), missionary to the Hurons.

LIST OF AMERICANS BEATIFIED:

Blessed Carlos Manuel Rodriguez, lay minister in Puerto Rico.
Blessed Francis Xavier Seelos, missionary preacher.
Blessed Junipero Serra, founder of the Spanish missions in California.
Blessed Marianne Cope, worked among the lepers of Hawaii.

Source: Catholic Encyclopedia; Inspired by Wikipedia (Retrieved July 23, 2010)

CONTROVERSIAL CANDIDATES: FOR SAINTHOOD:

1. Blessed Junipero Serra, founder of the Spanish missions in California, born in Mallorca in 1713. Junipero Serra was directly involved with the Inquisition and committed to defending its main causes: defending and enforcing accepted Catholic decrees, dogma, liturgy and beliefs.
    Serra was appointed Father President of the Franciscan missions and a commissary of the Inquisition in the Sierra Gorda region, 20 miles north of Mexico City. In his capacity as Commissary of the Inquisition he presided over cases of Indians accused of witchcraft and devil worship. There is little or no historical accounting of Serra's activities during this period of his career except for the Maria Pasquala witchcraft case, leading to her eventual murder while imprisoned by the Inquisition led by Serra.

To the indigenous people of the Sierra Gordo and Alta California areas, the missions were nothing but forced labor camps. They formed the major part of colonization in those regions and amounted to what some historians define as cultural genocide. Between 1769 and 1821, the Indian population dropped from 300,000 to 200,000. Serra's plan was to convert all the Indians to Catholicism. By law, all baptized Indians were under the authority of the Franciscans. The converts were given Spanish names and became slaves of the mission farms. Disobedience was punished by whipping, branding, mutilation or execution. If they fled the grounds there were hunted down.

Life expectancy in the missions was about 10 years. As one Friar noted, the Indians "...live well when free but as soon as we reduce them to a Christian and community life...they fatten, sicken and die." *[Junipero Serra-Wikipedia]*.

Many Indians, historians and academics have condemned the decision of Pope John Paul II to beatify Junipero Serra. They point to the harsh conditions of mission life and Serra's justification of beatings. Serra wrote in 1775 "...that spiritual fathers should punish their sons, the Indians, with blows, appears to be as old as the conquest of America; so general, in fact, that the saints do not seem to be any exception to the rule." *[http://www.pbs.org/weta/thewest/people/s_serra.htm]*

2. Blessed Alojzije Stepinac , Croatian Cardinal beatified by Pope John Paul II on October 2, 1988. Stepinac himself headed the committee responsible for forcible "conversions" to Roman Catholicism under threat of death. He was the Supreme Military Apostolic Vicar of the Utashi Army, which effectuated the slaughter of those who failed to convert.

    In May 1941, Stepinac used a Pastoral Letter ordering Croatian clergy to support the new Ustashe State. Stepinac recorded in his diary on August 3, 1941 that "... the Holy See recognized *de facto* the independent State of Croatia". In the same year he wrote "God, who directs the destiny of nations and controls the hearts of Kings, has given us Andre Pavelic and moved the leader of a friendly and allied people, Adolf Hitler, to use his victorious troops to disperse our oppressors...Glory be to God, our gratitude to Adolf Hitler and loyalty to our Poglavik, Andre Pavelic."

3. Pope Pius XII, nominated by present Pope Benedict XVI for beatification, "Hitler's Pope."

4. Pope John Paul II, who did nearly nothing during his thirty year reign to rid the Church of its predator priests or enablers. He sat idly by as the Church orchestrated a cover-up and never met with one molested Catholic.

Source: Catholic Encyclopedia; Inspired by Wikipedia (Retrieved July 23, 2010)

Father Edward Coughlin
"Heretics, let them burn"

> *"The true believer is an archenemy to three things, all for the same reason. He believes totally in what he totally believes in; thus he is an enemy to himself and all that cross his path."*
> **Eric Hoffer**

List of Heretics

Stephen Hawking	Rachel Carson
Joseph Campbell	Clarence Darrow
Albert Einstein	Charles Robert Darwin
Steve Allen	Benjamin Franklin
Isaac Asimov	Katherine Hepburn
Clara Barton	Thomas Hobbs
Alexander Graham Bell	Aldous Huxley
Giordano Bruno	Immanuel Kant
Luther Burbank	Ayn Rand
Albert Camus	Carl Sagan
B.F. Skinner	Mark Twain

Heresy:
An opinion or doctrine at variance with the orthodox or accepted doctrine, especially of a church or a religious system.

"Give me a child at seven and I will give you a man."
The quote attributed to Jesuit founder, St. Ignatius of Loyola, has many variations, such as *"Give me a child at seven and I will have him for the rest of his life."*

THE CATHOLIC EXORCIST

Father Gabriele Amorth is the chief exorcist of the Roman Catholic Church whose job is to expel the devil from someone who is possessed. He has served as Vatican exorcist for over 25 years. He is the founder of the International Association of Exorcists and estimates to have performed over 70,000 exorcisms.

In an interview with CNN he said: "It's not my opinion, I'm saying that if you believe in the Gospels, you believe in the existence of the devil, in the devil's power to possess people."

HOW TO PERFORM AN EXORCISM
Don't Try This At Home…..

1. The exorcist begins the rite with the sign of the cross and the sprinkling of holy water.

2. A litany of the Saints is recited asking for God's mercy.

3. One or more selections of Psalms are read.

4. The Psalm-prayer is said.

5. The Gospel is read aloud.

6. An imposition of hands upon the possessed.

7. An invocation of the Holy Ghost (aka Holy spirit) is recited.

8. The insufflation is performed (blowing on the face of the possessed by the exorcist).

9. The Creed is recited.

10. The Lord's Prayer is recited.

11. The Sign of the Cross is traced on the possessed's forehead in front of a Cross of the Lord.

12. A prayer to God is recited.

13. The imperative command is made to the devil to leave the possessed person.

Source: Official Catholic Procedure

Pope John Paul II,
himself, performed an unsuccessful exorcism during his reign as Pope.

LEGATUS

To study, live and spread the Faith in our business, professional and personal lives.

According to its website, Legatus has a three fold purpose:

•Study: Ongoing education is at the heart of Legatus. We are matching members, who have a thirst for knowledge, with the most profound and convincing body of religious knowledge in the history of human thought.

•Live: Translating the teachings of Christ and the social teaching of the Church into practical applications helps our members become eminently pragmatic about their faith.

•Spread: Legatus is the Latin word for "ambassador". Our members don't typically wear their faith on their shirtsleeves. They spread the faith through good example, good deeds and high ethical standards.

Criteria for membership in Legatus:

Executive Membership: Primary membership for the top ranking Catholic in a business. Must be titled in the firm as a Chairman, President, CEO, Owner, Managing Director, Managing Partner or Publisher. Must employ 30 employees or ten employees with a one million dollar payroll and demonstrate 100 million dollars in assets.

Division Head Membership: The top ranking Catholic in a qualifying division or subsidiary. Must be titled in the firm the same as an Executive Member or Vice-President. Must demonstrate the same employees and assets as Executive Member.

Intermediate Membership: Adjusted criteria for applicants under the age of 40. Must be titled as Executive Member, must employ 22 employees or $750,000 annual payroll and demonstrate 3.75 million dollars worth of assets.

Legatus was the inspiration of Domino's Pizza King, Tom Monaghan, following his audience with Pope Paul II in 1987. Its membership has spread across the United States, Canada and Ireland.

The website does not elaborate on the organization's inclusion of John Birch Society tenants or its ultra conservative ideology that prompts critics to describe the organization as rich Catholics using their money to staff the branches of government to impose their beliefs on society.

As George Carlin once said: "Religion is like a cereal box, it looks great on the shelf when you can only see the label, but when you turn it around and see the contents, you're in for a big surprise."

Source: Legatus website and personal interviews

JOSEMARIA ESCRIVA

Saint Josemaria Escriva was a Roman Catholic priest and founder of Opus Dei. He was canonized by Pope John Paul II.

His principal work was the foundation, government and expansion of Opus Dei. His best-known book, *The Way*, has sold more than 5 million copies in 50 languages.

Escriva and his organization Opus Dei are polarizing subjects among members of the Catholic Church.

The Controversy:

Monsignor Vladimir Felzmann, a former Opus Dei priest, claims to have heard this statement from Escriva: "Vlad, Hitler couldn't have been such a bad person. He couldn't have killed six million. It couldn't have been more than four million." And "Hitler against the Jews, Hitler against the Slavs, this means Hitler against Communism".

The following concerns surfaced during Escriva's nomination for sainthood:
- His ill-tempered behavior
- His cruelty
- His vanity
- His close relationship with dictator Francisco Franco
- His pro-Nazi position
- His activities supporting Fascist regimes of Franco and Pinochet in Chile

On May 23, 1958, Escriva sent a letter to General Francisco Franco of Spain, which said:

"Although a stranger to any political activity, I cannot help but rejoice as a priest and Spaniard that the Chief of State's authoritative voice should proclaim that, 'The Spanish nation considers it a badge of honor to accept the law of God according to the one and true doctrine of the Holy Catholic Church, inseparable faith of the national conscience which will inspire its legislation'".

This statement as been interpreted by critics as support for Franco, but supporters deny this.

A Newsweek article by Kenneth L. Woodward claimed that, of the nine judges of the Congregation for the Causes of Saints presiding over Escriva's nomination for sainthood, two requested a suspension of the proceedings and did not approve the cause. The two judges were said to be Archbishop Luigi de Magistris, deputy head of the Vatican's Sacred Penitentiary and Monsignor Justo Fernandez Alonso, rector of the Spanish National Church in Rome. However, Jose Saravia Martins, Cardinal Prefect of the Congregation for the Causes of Saints, denied that there was a dissenting vote.

The Opus Dei Awareness Network (ODAN), a collaboration of former members of Opus Dei has taken a strong position against Opus Dei and its alleged violent practices. Former members of Opus Dei were refused a hearing during the nomination for sainthood of Escriva.

"No ideal becomes a reality without sacrifice. Deny yourself. It is so beautiful to be a victim." (From *The Way*, Josemaria Escriva)

Source: ODAN, R. and Catholic Encyclopedia, Inspired by Wikipedia (Retrieved August 16, 2010)

Opus Dei

"Blessed be pain. Loved be pain. Sanctified be pain... Glorified be pain!"
*From: The Way by **Josemaria Escriva***

OPUS DEI

Opus Dei is an organization founded in Spain by Catholic priest, Josemaria Escriva de Balaguer. The mission of Opus Dei is "to spread throughout society a profound awareness of the universal call to holiness and apostolate through one's professional work carried out with freedom and personal responsibility. (*From the Encyclopedia of Associations*) and has offices in the Vatican.

Final approval for the organization was granted in 1950 by Pope Pius XII.

There are an estimated 87,000 members from 90 countries throughout the world.

Opus Dei is made up of lay members and priests. All Opus Dei members follow the "plan of life" made up of spiritual practices such as daily Mass, the rosary, spiritual readings and prayer.

There are different classes of membership:

Numerary members pledge to remain celibate and generally live in Opus Dei houses. They commit their entire salaries to Opus Dei, submit incoming and outgoing mail to their directors and practice various forms of corporal mortification.

Supernumerary members may be married and live with their families. They contribute large portions of their income to Opus Dei.

Numerary priests join Opus Dei as lay members, but are then handpicked by Opus Dei superiors to become priests. Numerary priests hold the top government positions in Opus Dei. Many hold important positions in the Vatican.

Associate Opus Dei members pledge celibacy, but generally do not live in Opus Dei houses.

Numerary assistants are women who pledge celibacy and are responsible for the care and cleaning of all Opus Dei residences.

Cooperators of Opus Dei provide financial support but are not considered members of Opus Dei.

OPUS DEI QUESTIONABLE PRACTICES:

The following practices of Opus Dei are not common knowledge and need to be examined and questioned. The serious issues ODAN raises are based on a collection of first-hand experiences:

- •Corporal mortification (self-inflicting pain and deprivation)
- •Aggressive recruitment/undue pressure to join
- •Lack of informed consent and control of environment
- •Alienation from families

Source: R and Opus Dei website and ODAN website

Jose Escriva

Section II

AN HISTORICAL VIEW OF THE CHURCH

THE EARLY HISTORY
OF
THE ROMAN CATHOLIC CHURCH

WHAT DOES THE WORD *VATICAN* MEAN?
According to the Catholic Encyclopedia Online

The origin of the name Vatican is uncertain; some claim that the name comes from a vanished Etruscan town called Vaticum. Others claim the Vatican Hill takes its name from the Latin word *Vaticinus ferendis*, an allusion to Etruscan oracles (Vaticinus), which were anciently believed to be delivered there.

The Vatican

Research on the word *Vatican* in Latin-English /English-Latin dictionaries yields a definition that Vatican City and St Peter's Basilica of the Roman Catholic Church were built upon what was called in Latin *vaticanus mons* or *vaticanus collis*. The words *mons* and *collis* mean hill or mountain.

Source: Catholic Encyclopedia

THE POPE

The word "Pope" comes from the Latin "pappas," an affectionate word for father.

The Pope is the Bishop of Rome, the position that makes him the leader of the entire Roman Catholic Church.

The office of the pope is called "the papacy" and his jurisdiction is the "Holy See." The Pope is also head of state of Vatican City, an independent, sovereign city-state within the city of Rome, Italy.

Catholics recognize the Pope as a successor to Saint Peter; however, Saint Peter never used the title "pope." The study of the New Testament, in fact, shows no evidence that Jesus established the papacy.

In early times the popes were responsible for the spread of Christianity and the resolution of doctrinal disputes. They allied themselves closely with the Roman Emperors, eventually making claims of political supremacy. At times there were more than one Pope. Emperor Constantine gave the Christian religion imperial sanction at the Council of Nicaea and confirmed papal authority under the Donations of Constantine, which is considered one of the most persuasive and lasting concoctions in the history of the West.

In medieval times the popes played powerful roles in struggles with monarchs over affairs of both church and state. The papacy became a position of secular and financial power (at one time even having its own navy) to be protected at all costs.

During the Middle Ages the papacy moved from Rome to Avignon, France, and descended into reigns of greed and corruption. Between 1378-1417 various "anti-popes" challenged the papal office when it officially returned to Rome.

During the Protestant Reformation of the 1500's, the papacy was forced to give up its secular powers and concentrated all efforts in establishing its spiritual authority.

In 1870, at the First Vatican Council, the dogma of "papal infallibility" was decreed.

In 1929, the Lateran Treaty between Mussolini and Pope Pius XI established the Vatican as an independent state free from secular rule.

The Pope is elected by the cardinal electors, comprised of those cardinals under the age of 80. The cardinal electors must meet in the Sistine Chapel within ten days of the death of the Pope and remain in seclusion until a new pope is elected by a full ballot vote. Each ballot is read aloud by the presiding Cardinal, who pierces each ballot with a needle and thread, tying the ends of the thread to ensure accuracy and honesty. Balloting continues until a Pope is elected by a two-thirds majority.

The results of the vote are announced to the world by burning the ballots in a special stove erected in the Sistine Chapel, sending white smoke through a small chimney visible from St. Peter's Square.

The Dean of the College of Cardinals then asks the newly elected pontiff two questions:

"Do you freely accept your election?" If the pope replies "*Accepto*," his reign begins immediately, not at the inauguration ceremony days later. The Dean then asks "By what name shall you be called?" The new Pope announces the name he will use.

The new Pope is then led through the "Door of Tears" to a dressing room where three sets of papal vestments await –small, medium and large. The Pope dons his new vestments and emerges into the Sistine Chapel where he is given his "Fisherman's Ring".

The Senior Cardinal announces from the Balcony over St. Peter's Square "I announce to you a great joy! We have a Pope!" He then announces the new Pope's name.

The time between the pope's death and election of a new pope is known as "*sede vacante*" (vacant seat). Any decision that requires the assent of the pope must wait until a new Pope is elected. Upon the death of a pope, his Fisherman's Ring is cut into two pieces in front of all the Cardinals and his seal is defaced to prevent it from ever being used again. His body lies in state for several days and then interred in the crypt of a leading church or cathedral. A nine-day period of mourning follows the internment.

By the Editors, inspired by Wikipedia (Retrieved May 13,2010) and Catholic Encyclopedia

As many have observed, the last two Popes have spent much time apologizing for their holy Church. The list of recipients of these apologies includes American Natives, Jews, South American indigenous people, women, children, Canadian Indians, Protestant Reformers and Galileo. People are beginning to see that, in many instances, the Roman Catholic Church has been in many ways no worse than the present day terrorists and extremists of Islam.

Editor

BUILT UPON LIES
The Vatican's False Foundations

It is a strong accusation to claim that the seat of Vatican power and authority is based upon lies. But hard and clear evidence is there for those wishing to find it. If you disbelieve it and lean toward the idea that this is just another unfounded attack against the Church, you are asked to read what follows and do your own independent research. Thousands of scholars have done this, and have agreed with these findings – often quietly, due to their faith.

The Papacy has had a long and dysfunctional history. It has struggled to establish and maintain its domination through forgery, fear and violence. It has gone to almost any length to achieve its aim, as documented by numerous credible sources.

These unscrupulous tactics formed a pattern that lasted for centuries, with many an individual or opposing group coming forward to expose corruption or challenge what they perceived to be an unrighteous and unholy organization.

Despite their opposition, the Papacy has held its power throughout the centuries. This power allowed them the ability to exert "damage control" over the most corrupt events they engaged in. Even so, enough embarrassing information has leaked through to create such massive volumes of "dirt" on the Vatican that it cannot be swept under the rug. But because of its longstanding position as a holy institution, many people today still choose to look the other way and keep their holy illusions intact in spite of the evidence to the contrary.

Large numbers of Roman Catholics, however, have awakened in recent years and left the Church. Record numbers of churches have closed their doors, and it has become increasingly difficult to recruit new priests to occupy their pulpits. As far as Christianity is concerned, we are truly at the end of an age. Any kind of revival at this stage seems rather remote, at best, despite the desperate, fundamentalist fevor from those who find no place else to go.

Although Christianity may be fading, spirituality is on the rise. Rather than turning away from religion and becoming atheists, people understand that more meaningful answers can be found through spiritual avenues that have nothing to do with dogmatic, narrow mindsets. Many believe that if the kingdom of God is within you (LUKE 17:21), then who needs the Vatican or the pope to represent it? Many Christian groups oppose the Vatican, citing Jesus' proclamation, "My kingdom is not of this world." (JOHN 18:36)

Beyond scripture itself, we are finding new ways to reach this inner kingdom in a modern world replete with advanced scientific breakthroughs and deeper spiritual insights. We are moving beyond primitive religious structures – structures that still manage to cling to their survival. We have been through these realizations in the past, with one major difference. The Church was previously more powerful – ready and willing to crush anyone brazen enough to question their authority.

The Vatican has enjoyed a long history of success. This success has been in direct proportion to the level of ignorance it has managed to propagate among the masses. Being caught with a Bible at certain times in history often meant instant death. After it became legal to have one, it was not allowed to be in a language the everyday person could understand. An educated, logical reading of the Bible raised too many questions to be ignored. Now that we have moved beyond our imposed ignorance, we are asking these questions, and are beginning to grow up and out of our dogmatic confines.

There have been times throughout western history when we became aware of the problems of our ignorance. The church was powerful and violent. But we asked questions, learned a great deal, made bold moves to become spiritually free, but we were brutally defeated by the religious powers of the time. The papacy was often involved, either directly or indirectly.

The Mitre & Vatican Flag

The Mitre, the Keys to Heaven on the Vatican Flag all come from Babylon. Many other symbols were borrowed (stolen) from Babylon.

Papal Origins

There were no official popes during the first two centuries after Jesus. The word "pope" only began to be used at the beginning of the third century. In the mid 250's Cyprian began being called "bishop of bishops" and "the blessed pope." He took offense to this and scoffed at the idea that such a position "holds the succession from Peter." It was common knowledge at the time that this idea was false, but if you extend a lie with the weight of authority, people will often believe it.

From the third to the fifth centuries, the term "pope" applied to *all* bishops and the title did not become reserved for the bishops of Rome until the sixth century. Finally, in the year 1073 a Roman Council officially banned anyone else from using the title and officially assigned it to the bishop of Rome.

One of the best reasons to contest Vatican authority is to examine the very "foundation" it uses to base its so-called authority upon. We will take it step by step, and completely dismantle the entire foundation of papal authority once and for all. There should be no good reason to recognize this authority in your life after reading the facts.

The False Decretals

According to Will Durand in *The Age of Faith*, a collection of documents called the "False Decretals" was written by a French cleric named Isodorus Mercator and put together at Metz sometime around the year 842. Along with numerous authentic decrees by councils or popes, it also included a set of 60 letters attributed to pontiffs, ranging from Clement I (91-100) to Melchiades (311-314), of which 58 were forgeries. The purpose of this collection was to show that the earliest traditions of the Church relied upon the power of the pope, specifically in matters of convening councils, deposing bishops, or deciding upon any major issue. It attempted to support a claim of the early pontiffs as vicars of Christ, with absolute and universal authority over the Faith.

It wasn't until the 17th century that the "False Decretals" were also found to be false by Blondel, and more thoroughly in the following century by the brothers Ballerini. It was shown that many of the unauthentic documents in the "False Decretals" had quoted from St. Jerome's Scriptural translation. St. Jerome was not born until 26 years *after the death* of Melchiades (311-314). Melchiades was the last so-called "pope" in line concerning the claims of these documents. All of the questionable Decretals were post-Melchiades documents. There is no possible way that he or anyone before him could have made the claims attributed to them.

31

By the time the fraud was discovered, the Vatican had already used it to full advantage and created, with smoke and mirrors, its lofty state of holy acceptance, power, great wealth, military influence and land holdings.

The Donation of Constantine

"The Donation of Constantine" also worked along these lines and was created even earlier, about 754. It falsely represented Pope Sylvester I (314-335) as having full religious and secular authority over all of Western Europe. This is based on the claim that Jesus had founded the Church, made Peter the first in charge, and that the Roman bishops had continued to inherit this power over the centuries.

So was Peter the first "pope?" No. He was just another bishop, and Cyprian was correct by stating quite bluntly, back in the year 250, that the succession from Peter was a sham. Some will argue this proven fact and point to the Bible for its long accepted "proof."

He sayeth unto thee, "But whom say ye that I am?"
And Simon Peter answered and said, "Thou art the Christ, the Son of the living God."
And Jesus answered and said to him, "Blessed art thou, Simon Bar-Jona: for flesh and blood has not revealed it to thee, but my Father which is in heaven."
And I say also to thee, "That thou art Peter, and upon this rock I will build my church:
And the gates of hell shall not prevail against it."
- Matthew 16:15-18

People often quote Matthew 16:18 ("upon this rock...") for support and leave out the three previous verses. Read them carefully. We should remember that after meeting Jesus, Simon Bar-Jona had changed his name to Peter (or Cephas, meaning "rock,") due to his strong faith.

The main point is that Jesus was not referring to Peter when he spoke of building his "church." Jesus spoke Aramaic. In Aramaic "upon this rock" can also mean "upon this truth." The *Geneva Bible* translates "rock" as "true faith, which confesses Christ." Although the words for "Peter" and "rock" are the same in the original language, Jesus reminds Peter what his name is *first*, then says that "upon this truth" he will build his Church. He is complimenting Peter for having confessed this truth in verse 16. The Church will not be built upon Peter, it will be built upon "truth." It is now agreed by not only many Protestants, but by many Roman Catholics that this is the more likely interpretation (for example, see *The Bishops of Rome*, by Jean Tillard).

Jesus often used a play on words in his teachings. This was a pun, of sorts, and a compliment as well. The two words were the same, but used differently by Jesus in a rather nice gesture toward Peter.

When these two words/verses were translated into the Greek, they were also translated as two distinct and separate words, bringing into question Peter's authority. Jesus himself rebuked Peter only five verses later. This resulted after Peter had reproached Jesus for predicting to his disciples his own suffering and death. Peter insisted that it would not happen. Jesus told him:

> *Get thee behind me, Satan: thou art an offense unto me; for thou*
> *savourest not the things that be of God, but those that be of men.*
>
> *- Matthew 16:23*

It is unlikely that Jesus would entrust the future of his church to a man whom he has just addressed in this way.

Returning to verse 18, we should always be aware that in the Aramaic language there was no word for "church" at the time. Jesus repeatedly told his followers that they must not have temples, priests, synagogues, or services. The Greek word, *ecclesie* or *ekklesai*, was used since it was the closest to the Aramaic, and meant, at that time, a "public meeting." So Jesus approved of public meetings, but did not desire temples, priests, or services. He knew that he was building a following, but clearly had no intention of founding a church," as we know it today. A great number of scholars repeatedly tell us that Jesus never intend to found a church, with only the church itself making this claim.

In order to legitimize the papacy, one must prove that Peter not only lived in Rome, but was also a bishop there. This is the Catholic claim. Most authorities today state there is no reason to believe that Peter was ever in Rome, much less being a bishop there. More than 20 different references from respected scholars affirm this. For instance, Charles Du Moulin was an ecclesiastical lawyer from the mid 1500's who was considered a faithful and steadfast Roman Catholic. He said, "Even when, after the breaking up of the empire, the Bishops of Rome began to extend their authority over other Churches, they never alleged or put forth this story of Peter's being in Rome, the story, I supposed, not having yet been invented."

From *The Popular and Critical Bible Encyclopedia*, vol. 3, from 1908, we find,

1. **Peter in Rome**. The most thorough investigation of noted scholars has shown – that there is not even a remote tradition (after Peter's death) for the first century -- to prove that Peter was ever in Rome. In fact there is no such assertion in any document of authentic note until after the beginning of the third century.

Yet modern Catholic literature continues to defend it. With Peter never being in Rome, how could he possibly pass down any papal authority? In 1440 Lorenzo Valla proved beyond any doubt that the "Donation of Constantine" was a fraud. The papacy was *never* put in charge of the Church or its empire by Constantine.

To this day, the papacy has no rightful authority to the position it claims to hold other than the fact that it is exercising "squatter's rights" in Rome and the people blindly accept it. Other scriptural "proofs" of support beyond Matthew 16:18 (which is the strongest) hold little water so we will not entertain them here. The point has been made and it makes no sense to continue beating a dead horse.

The Pope Becomes Infallible

With such a checkered history and, being still in power, it was decided in 1870 by Pope Pius IX to declare the Pope to be infallible. The reasoning, it seems, would be to keep people from asking difficult questions, and thereby prevent past misdeeds from surfacing. If those most reverent to the Pope, including the most religious of followers, would accept this decree and hold to it faithfully, it would preserve the papacy. Otherwise, exposure and scrutiny of such a corrupt office could one day bring it tumbling down. A less conspiratorial reason could be that Pope Pius IX had epilepsy, and harbored the obsessive belief that he had a divine mission to make himself, and the subsequent holders of his office "infallible."

The First Vatican Council officially enacted this decree in 1870, despite much opposition and debate. After the Council, much of the archival material of the opposition was burned by Bishop Joseph Hefele, Cardinal Charles Phillip Place, Episcopal secretary Gustav Genosi, Benedictine Archabbot Krisosztom Kruesz and Archbishop of Paris Georges Darboy. When Archbishop Georges Darboy was arrested during the siege of Paris, he instructed his sister to burn all related documents (although a small portion was spared).

These were people who were likely afraid of what could happen if their opposing views were ever known. Darboy and Bishop Hefele were, among others, outspoken opponents of the validity of the Council and exposed the tremendous lack of freedom they had to debate the issue and control what they were trying to agree upon. This same lack of freedom was experienced at the Council of Nicaea in 325 when it was decided that Jesus, (rather than the pope) was infallible as a divine personage. Constantine had threatened banishment to a remote island for those who would not change their votes to agree with him. With the First Vatican Council of 1870, the bishops chose a form of voluntary banishment of their own. Fifty-five bishops left in protest the day before the final vote, joining numerous others who were already gone. Those 535 remaining were convinced to vote "yes" except for two dissenting voters who were never informed of the "deal" they made.

There was once a previous movement to make the Pope infallible. In 1279 the Franciscans were trying to enforce the idea that the communal renunciation of property was a possible way to salvation. Pope Nicholas III supported the idea because the Church could receive many charitable "payoffs" in exchange for the blessing of salvation. In 1280 a man named Peter Olivi tried to enforce this decision as being irreversible, based on the "infallibility of the pope" on questions of faith and morals.

The next Pope, John XXII, disagreed and drafted a bull in 1324 called *Qui quorundam*. In it he condemned the Franciscan doctrine of papal infallibility as "the work of the devil." The Franciscans appealed this decision, but lost.

JOHN XXII was a forward thinking man. The implications of infallibility limit the powers of the individual pope. All declarations of their predecessors cannot be changed because perfect decisions by an infallible judge cannot be reversed. This is what we are stuck with today. For example, let us use the example of abortion. It is prohibited for Catholics by decree of the Pope, and the decision must be viewed as "final." However, some interesting studies have been done. It was found in the 1990's that a tremendous drop in crime had occurred in U.S. inner cities and no one could figure out why.

Abortions had become legal throughout the United States in 1973. When inner city women who had been unable to financially afford to have a child chose to have an abortion instead, it relieved the community of having young unattended, poor, desperate people who had no place to turn except to drugs, criminal activity, and gangs to commit murders, rapes, robberies and more. Suddenly, we had far less of these problems in the 1990s and a direct connection was made between a major drop in crime and the advent of abortions in the inner cities. Extensive studies were done to show the direct link, as outlined by economics professor Steven Leavitt with Stephen Dubner in their book, *Freakonimics: a Rogue Economist Explores the Hidden side of Everything.*

Should we, with this new information, continue to view the pope as infallible when he has supported a previous creation of desperate criminals? Can the pope, with this new information, ever make a concession to reduce these terrible crimes by admitting that the lack of abortions was the cause? No, because new information doesn't matter. All popes are "infallible." If abortion remained illegal, how many more of us would have been murdered, robbed, raped, beaten or shot, because "life," no matter what the circumstances, is more important to the Church that protecting us as a society? Thousands of us would have been victimized, based on credible studies. It could have been any of us including you.

So much for infallibility. It has been said that the only thing certain in this world is change. We are always learning and evolving, so we need to *adapt*. Living in the dark ages because we must bow down in servitude to an imagined "infallible" human being is an absolute travesty. If followed, such a doctrine will continue to thwart our progress and cause problems for generations to come. Hans Kung was a major critic of papal infallibility and was stripped of his license to teach as a Roman Catholic theologian in 1979. He points out that the idea never came from God, but is man-made and can be reversed. This was once done in 1324, but don't hold your breath. Kung once remarked in a 2009 interview with *Le Monde* that the Pope's theology has remained unchanged since the Council of Nicaea in 325.

The Waning Years

There is a price to pay for insisting we live in the Dark Ages. The waning years of the Vatican have arrived. It still has such vast wealth and holdings that it would stun the public if their books were ever opened to reveal its extent. But things have changed in the eyes of the public, and how we perceive the institution, mainly because of the continuing corruption and abuse that has been exposed. For many of us, our trust is gone. Generally speaking, instead of following others to make our decisions for us, concerning faith, we have chosen to examine the evidence and make such choices for ourselves.

The waning years began when a huge movement surfaced in the U.S. between about 1875 and 1917 called the Free Thought Movement. It was active throughout the world at this time, but it was especially thriving in America. Fueled by intelligent atheists and an explosion of published books, it almost brought modern religion to its knees. But the Vatican refused to go without a fight.

Pope Leo XIII established the Pontifical Biblical Commission in 1903 in order to control Biblical interpretations. The commission decreed that, "at all times the interpreter must cherish a spirit of ready obedience to the Church's teaching authority." In other words, you are free to interpret the Biblical meanings as long as you say exactly what the Church teaches.

In 1907 Pope Pius X wrote his *Lamentabili*. In it he attacked all new interpretations of scripture and Church dogma, telling the world that all truth had already been given to the Church so there was no point in exploring it on your own. These two Papal acts, I believe, were a direct effort to stop the Free Thought Movement in its tracks. Thousands of Free Thought books had flooded the market and people were questioning everything religious. The only thing that stopped it was World

War One. The one thing that brings God back into the lives of people is a good old-fashioned war. Entire nations look to God and claim Him on their side of the battle. The old saw is that "There are no atheists in foxholes." God is on their side. Free Thought took a back seat, resurfacing here and there over the years, only to be displaced with a modern quantum physics-based scientific/mystical view of God that carries even more weight than Free Thought did. The Vatican had met its match in an informed, intelligent populace coupled with scientific backing that puts a new spin on God. The lies of old now hold very little weight.

References and Recommended Reading

•Aarons, Mark and Loftus, John, *Unholy Trinity: The Vatican, the Nazis and Soviet Intelligence, St. Martens Press, 1991.*

•Ambrosini, Luisa with Willis, Mary, *The Secret Archives of the Vatican*, Little, Brown & Co., 1969.

•Bushby, Tony, *The Crucifixion of Truth: The Discovery of Hidden Vatican Scrolls and the Falsehoods They Reveal About Christianity*, Joshua Books, Queensland, Australia, 2004.

•Bushby, Tony, *The Papal Billions: Unknown Facts About the Vatican's Accumulation of Wealth*, Joshua Books, Queensland, Australia, 2008.

•DeRosa, Peter, Vicars of Christ, *The Dark Side of the Papacy*.

•Tice, Paul and Anonymous, *History of the Waldenses: From the Earliest Period to the Present Time*, originally 1892, reprinted by The Book Tree, San Diego, CA, 2005.

•DiFonzo, Luigi, *St. Peter's Banker: Michele Sindona*, Franklin Watts, 1983.

•Hammer, Richard, *The Vatican Connection: The Astonishing Account of a Billion Dollar Counterfeit Stock Deal Between the Mafia and the Church*, Holt, Rinehart and Winston, 1982.

•Hasler, August Bernhard, *How the Pope Became Infallible: Pius IX and Politics of Persuasion*, Doubleday & Co., Inc., New York, 1981.

•Levitt, Steven D. and Dubner, Stephen J., *Freakonimics: A Rogue Economist Explores the Hidden Side of Everything*, William Morrow/HarperCollins, New York, NY, 2005.

•Manhattan, Avro, *The Vatican Billions*, Chick Publications, Chino, CA, 1983.

•Tice, Paul, *Triumph of the Human Spirit: The Greatest Achievements of the Human Soul and How Its Power can Change Your Life*, The Book Tree, San Diego, CA. 1999.

•Williams, Dr. Paul L., *The Vatican Exposed*, Prometheus Books, New York, 2003.

•Yallop, David A., *In God's Name: An Investigation into the Murder of Pope John Paul I*, Bantam Books, 1984.

By Paul Tice, the author of *Shadow of Darkness, Dawning of Light: The Awakening of Human Consciousness in the 21ˢᵗ Century and Beyond; Triumph of the Human Spirit: The Greatest Achievements of the Human Soul and How Its Power Can Change Your Life and Jumpin' Jehovah: Exposing the Atrocities of the Old Testament God.* His work and other interesting books can be found at www.thebooktree.com.

> *"The Catholic Church is no different than any other religion... they made it up as they went along and deemed it holy, sacred and infallible. Just look at the gaps. Paul never knew Jesus. Christianity was an exclusive Jesus cult for 100 years. The four gospels were written 70 to 100 years after the time of Jesus and Jesus wasn't officially deemed the Son of God for at least 400 years at the Council at Nicaea in 325 AD and that was by one vote under extreme pressure by the warrior Emperor Constantine."*
>
> **Jordan Maxwell, Mythologist**

HUS: THE NOBLE HERETIC

At the turn of the century of the Christian era, much of the known world was in great turmoil. Sweeping changes in both government and religion, found Europe, especially, in the throes of labor pains from which would emerge "The Renaissance," "The New World," as well as a whole new church, the Protestant Church, to rival the Roman Catholic Church for European and subsequently Christian world supremacy.

Coming out of the Dark Ages, during which the Christian Church had failed in its attempt to wrest Jerusalem and "The Tomb of Christ" away from the Moslems in the "holy" Crusades. The early fourteenth century saw Pope Clement V, along with Phillip IV, King of France, topple one of the most powerful institutions of its time – The "Poor Knights of Christ at the Temple of Solomon," better known as the Knights Templar, which had become obsolete without the excuse of the crusades.

These complicated issues, among many other socio-political and religious conflicts, led to the eventual Great Schism which left Europe divided – first with two completely different Latin papacies, one in Italy and one in France, and then between Catholic-Roman and Protestant-English Churches, the latter of which had come into being in large parts by the well known efforts of the religious reformist,

Martin Luther in the 16th century.

However, in the time between Wycliffe and Martin Luther, there came a little known Bohemian preacher, called John of Hussineez, a.k.a. Hus, whose poignant story typifies the Roman Catholic Church's black-hearted dealings and powerful ability to not only quash the voice, but the life of an innocent dissident.

The Roman Catholic Church's history has been steeped in controversy from its inception, starting with its disputable claim for the authority to even create a church in the name of Jesus, The Christ.

The Roman Catholic Church has based its claim to "The Keys of Heaven" by claiming that St. Paul, arguably the greatest proselytizer of all time, received that authority from none other that the Disciple Peter, also known in the Holy Bible as *Simon Cephas*, which the Roman Catholic Church to this day claims as the first Pope.

James the Just is historically known to be the new Judeo-Christian Gnostic's Church's first Pope with Jesus' female disciple and perhaps wife, Mary "The Migdal," better known as Mary Magdalene. She followed James as Papess, after angry Jewish scribes and Pharisees stoned James to death for not repudiating the heretical teachings of Jesus.

The Roman Catholic Church has been extremely successful in confiscating or destroying, any and all record or information, which challenges its poser and subsequent control. For example, it is known by some that the apostle Paul went to the leaders of the "true and Gnostic" Christian Church of the mid-first century, who became known as *Ebonites*, ostensibly to gain access to the true teachings of Jesus, but Paul was *hastily* dismissed by the Gnostic church leaders, primarily due to his insistence that Jesus be recognized as divine, instead of human, and as the virgin-born incarnation of the "one and only begotten son of God." However, since many of the Ebonites were directly related to Jesus, including his twin brother Judah, also known as Thomas, or Didymus, which meads twin, they did not agree with Paul's belief that Jesus was the actual physical incarnation of (his beloved) Mithras; a virgin-born sun-cult deity, who is directly related to so many other "Sons of God." The apostle Paul is then known to have approached the Roman authorities, who subsequently gave protection initially to Paul, and began to hunt down, and either exterminate or suppress, the fledging Gnostic Christian Church followers, forcing many to scatter to the four winds and go underground with their teachings and traditions.

Except for perhaps the *Albigensian Crusade*, no actual verifiable historical event is more poignant or more telling of the Roman Catholic Church's power to suppress and eliminate any and all who challenge its authority than the story of Hus, the noble heretic.

Born in Bohemia (now Slovakia) around the year 1369, John of Hussinecz was accepted into the University of Prague as a charity scholar. He then became an ordained priest after which he rose quickly through the ranks at the same university he attended; first as professor, then dean and finally rector of the university in 1401. The following year Hus was appointed to preach at Bethlehem Chapel in Prague, where he soon became widely known as a church reformer who simply wanted what he felt was fir for all people.

Author Paul Tice writes, "At some point, Hus was commissioned to investigate certain reported miracles of the day. He discovered outrageous forgeries instead. He openly protested against Church deceit, including indulgences, and was attempting to restore clergy to its highest ideals rather than change Church doctrines." (page 105, *Hus the Heretic*)

"Indulgences" were one of the Roman Catholic Church's greatest, but shadiest, money-making schemes; basically they were akin to a "get-out-of-jail free-card." If you paid a sufficient amount of money to the Church you could be forgiven almost anything. Just hand your ticket to St. Peter when you get to the Pearly Gates and tell him, "The Pope said it was okay." Wink-wink.

A contemporary church dissident and close friend of Hus, Jerome of Prague, who unlike Hus came from a wealthy family, was also educated at the University of Prague. After going to England and returning with some writings by England's then infamous Wycliffe, Jerome shared these with his friend, Hus, who naturally incorporated the teachings into his sermon. In 1410, a papal decree banned Wycliffe's books, and the archbishop in Prague burned them, and then excommunicated the heretic's supporters, including, eventually, Hus in 1411. Hus, who fortunately was still supported by his Bohemian king, Vaclav, as well as the people of Bohemia, got the attention of the papacy, which was in severe turmoil.

The 15th century Pope John XXIII was eventually deposed at the Council of Constance, where no less than thirty-seven witnesses exposed the arch-criminal, who was convicted of over forty crimes, including the attempted murder of his predecessor by poison, as well as being a thief, liar, adulterer, murderer, fornicator (having seduced over 300 nuns), keeping a personal harem of over 200 sex-slaves at Boulogne, and being guilty of simony, sodomy, incest and other unnatural offenses.

In front of the Council of Constance in 1415, Hus thundered against Pope John XXIII's papal bull, which promised the remission of sins for all those willing to fight against the King of Naples, who was central to John machinations against the other two popes.

Hus had enjoyed his king's support, while preaching against church corruption, and while campaigning for a Bible in the tongue of the people, and even while perpetuating many of Wycliffe's heretical ideologies. But King Vaclav had a vested interest in the indulgence money that was being raised to finance the fighting, and so ruled that no one could speak out against indulgences. Many continued to speak out, including Hus.

Hus was forced out of his home in 1412. A papal decree threatened to forbid all clergy from performing the sacraments unless Hus left Prague. He did leave, but he continued to write and preach against what he knew to be wrong. John Hus did not consider himself a heretic. The word itself has been demonized by the church into having a negative connotation, but it actually means simply, "one who chooses." Hus considered himself to be a good Christian, one who was trying to live the letter and the spirit of the Holy Bible as best he could interpret. One primary way Hus became a grave danger to the Church was in trying to get the Bible written in the language of the people. Hus knew that it was important for everyone to read the Holy Bible for himself or herself, but the church had too much at stake for its parishioners to be thinking and interpreting scripture on their own.

Prior to attending the council of Constance, the twice ex-communicated Hus had the written promise of the Holy Roman Emperor, Sigismund, of safe passage and the empire's protection, if need be. However, Hus was well aware of the dangers as shown by a letter he penned prior to his departure, wherein he writes, "I am departing with a safe-conduct from the king to meet my numerous and mortal enemies..." and then also, "Probably, therefore, you will nevermore behold my face at Prague..." (pg 108 *Hus*)

Before, during, and even after the events at Constance, a group called the "Hussites", due to Hus' influence, had been terrorizing papal clerics and supporters. This campaign was to significantly intensify after what Hus, Jerome and others suffered at the hands of the papal powers, and would last for over eighty years, apparently until all of the first and second-hand witnesses to the travesty had died off.

On the way to Constance, Poggius writes of arriving in Stuttgart, where the people of the city had grown curious, and then agitated upon hearing that Hus was in town, "It was everybody's desire to see the Wycliffian Hus, he who preached a new gospel without fear and ban." (p. 16 *Hus*)

In his second epistle to Nikolai, Poggius writes of the precursor to the council, telling of the crowds being so dense, Hus could hardly squeeze his long body through the masses. Naturally, as Hus was ready for questioning, some felt urged to address the issue of his new teachings, which according to Poggius Hus answered "fittingly and without conceit." Still, Poggius goes on "...these happenings already lines up his preliminary judges against him...(they) reprimanded him furiously, as if he were a demagogue, and an evil-doing renegade, full of malice, and hypocrisy." (p. 25 *Hus*)

Hus tried to continue his eloquent rebuttal, but was quashed by the self-proclaimed "Chief Guardians of the Holy Roman Catholic Church," led by Cardinal Goolve, who yelled so loudly and so angrily, reprimanding Hus for his entreaty, that Poggius was startled. Goolvi commanded Hus to "quiet and silence," granting him permission only to answer their questions, "modestly, without circumspection and useless chatter." But instead of obeying, Hus also raised his voice without fear, " I am sorry for the zeal and rage your lordship, as I am the reason for it and beg your pardon for my manner of speech, if it seems something outside of dutiful servility; but this you gentlemen might grant me, that I only talk, when my conscience urges me and that I always base my words upon the apostle Paul who forcefully says: one must obey God more than man!" Hus continued stating flatly that he had not been called away homeland to be silent.

During Hus' long imprisonment, he was often dragged out of his cell, which was a dank hole right next to the city's sewer and which was making Hus extremely ill, and was questioned as to whether he had relented and changes his convictions. However, Hus stuck to his guns with dignity, and with notable admiration Poggius wrote, "Yet, just like the stone bastions which God's hand had built toweringly upon the shores of the sea, thus firm remained the Bohemian upon the structure of his opinions, which according to his belief, bereft of all sandy foundation, towered above everything else." (pp. 27-68 *Hus*)

After more than three months, Hus was again questioned regarding his beliefs and convictions, and already half-way to death, Hus responded with biblical eloquence, "What else it, that you cardinals, bishops, and judges ask of me than to sin by untruth and deceit, against the Holy Spirit? Do you know what happened, according to testimony of the apostle to the man and woman, who denied their heritage? God punished them with sudden death, for they had thus blasphemed the Holy Spirit. And how much would my soul deserve a terrible end, if I would bury the heritage that you and I have received, deny it and yet unsure with it to the honor of God. You offer me gold, and want thereby to hang a lock on my lips; you want me to give rich revenues, clothe me in soft garment and give me well cooked food, so that I may be lost in everything that is called folly and worldly desire, leading to disaster and damnation. I tell you, that I will not finish in the flesh, like the wavering people of Galatha, what I have begun in the spirit." (p. 28 *Hus*)

Hus then turned against the Church fathers, "Your law is a spoiled structure of sentences, just to no one, resembling stinking, foul water...And all this uncleanliness is to a great extent your, my present preachers, fault. For that, I have the courage to shed light into this desert, you confine me behind dark walls, gruesome bars, and iron-bound doors with heavy bars and locks, grant for my body less foul straw than to a murderer or killer...And these misdeed against me are committed by you...who have not heard my evangelical teachings undistorted...because you believe that it might bring you damage and dishonor, especially to your hypocritical subterfuge." pgs 28-29 *Hus*)

"Truth prevails" was John Hus' most famous saying, and has been used by the Czech people against oppression ever since his death.

by Daante

THE COUNCIL OF NICAEA

The First Council of Nicaea was a council of Christian bishops convened in Nicaea in Bythynia, which is present day Iznik in Turkey, by the Roman Emperor Constantine I in 325 A.D., upon the recommendation of Hosius of Cordoba.

Its main accomplishments were discussions and settlement of the Christological issues of:
- The relationship of Jesus to God the Father
- The construction of the first part of the Nicene Creed
- Settling the calculation of the date of Ester
- Promulgation of early canon law

The First Council of Nicaea is considered to have been the first Ecumenical council of the Christian Church. It resulted in the first uniform Christian doctrine, called the Creed of Nicaea. With the creation of the Creed, a precedent was established for subsequent general ecumenical councils of Bishops (Synods) to create statements of belief and canons of doctrinal orthodoxy – the intent being to define a unity of beliefs for the whole of Christendom.

One purpose of the Council was to resolve the disagreements arising from within the Church of Alexandria over the nature of Jesus in relationship to God the Father; in particular, whether Jesus was literally or figuratively son of God, like the other "sons of God" in other religions.

The teachings of Arius, for example, were considered heretical St. Alexander of Alexandria and Athanasius claimed to take the first position. The popular Arius, from whom the term Aryanism comes, is said to have taken the second. The council decided overwhelmingly against the Arians. His works were seized and burned, and all persons found possessing his works were ordered to be executed.

Another result of the council was an agreement on when to celebrate Easter, the most important feast of the ecclesiastical calendar. The council decided in favor of celebrating the resurrection on the first Sunday after the first full moon following the vernal equinox. It authorized the Bishop of Alexandria to announce annually the exact date to his fellow bishops.

The Council was the first occasion where the technical aspects of Christology were discussed. This council is generally considered the beginning of the period of the First Seven Ecumenical Councils in the history of Christianity.

The council promulgated twenty new church laws called canons (unchanging rules of discipline):

1.   Prohibition of self castration;
2.   Establishment for a minimum terms for persons studying for baptism (catechumens);
3.   Prohibition of the presence in the house of a cleric of a younger woman who might bring him under suspicion;
4.   Ordination of a bishop in the presence of at least three provincial bishops and confirmation by the Metropolitan bishop;
5.   Provision for two provincial synods to be held annually;
6.   Exceptional authority acknowledged for the patriarchs of Alexander and Rome (the Pope) for their respective regions;
7.   Recognition of the honorary rights of the see of Jerusalem;
8.   Provision for agreement with the Novatianists, an early sect;
9-14. Provision for procedures against those lapsed during the persecution under Licinius;
15-16. Prohibition of the removal of priests;
17.   Prohibition of usury among the clergy;
18.   Precedence of bishops and presbyters before deacons in receiving Eucharist;
19.   Declaration of the invalidity of baptism by Paulian heretics;
20.   Prohibition of kneeling during the liturgy on Sundays and during the Pentecost (the fifty days after Easter). Standing was the recognized position for prayer at this time.

The effects of the Council were significant. For the first time, the Emperor played a role, by calling together the bishops under his authority, and using the power of the state to give the Council's order effect.

Source:Religious research documents and inspired by Wikipedia (Retrieved May 13, 2010)

Sol Invictus

CHRIST: A COMPOSITE CHARACTER

Is Christ a Clone of Mithra?

In my book, *The Christ Conspiracy: the Greatest Story Ever Sold*, appears a series of lists in a popular chapter called "*The Characters*." These lists recite characteristics in common with the Jesus figure of the following gods and godmen: Attis, Buddha, Dionysus, Hercules, Horus, Krishna, Mithra, Prometheus and Zoroaster. One of the gods most obviously related to the origins of Christianity is Mithras or Mithra, the Perso-Roman hybrid whose *cultus* was widespread around the Mediterranean during the same period Christianity was being formulated.

Over the centuries, many scholars have pointed out the obvious correspondences between Mithraism and Christianity, based on the remaining evidence, including the writings of early Church fathers who were flummoxed by the similarities. Later writers, however, were not so startled, because they could discern that the Christ character was apparently a rehash of Mithra, among others. Following is a list of the characteristics of Mithra as found in my book *Christ Conspiracy*, p.119:

•Mithra was born of a virgin on December 25th in a cave and shepherds bearing gifts attended his birth.

•He was considered a great traveling teacher.

•He had 12 companions or disciples.

•Mithra's followers were promised immortality.

•He performed miracles.

•As the "great bull of the Sun," Mithra sacrificed himself for world peace.

•He was buried in a tomb and after three days rose again.

•His resurrection was celebrated every year.

•He was called "The Good shepherd" and identified with both the Lamb and the Lion.

•He was considered the "Way, the truth and the Light", and the "Logos", "redeemer," "Savior" and "Messiah."

•His sacred day was Sunday, the Lord's Day," hundreds of years before the appearance of Christ.

•Mithra had his principal festival on what was later to become Easter.

•His religion had a Eucharist or "Lord's Supper," at which Mithra said, "He who shall not eat of my body nor drink of my blood so that he may be one with me and I with him, shall not be saved."

•"His annual sacrifice was the Passover of the Magi, a symbolical atonement of pledge of moral and physical regeneration."

Krishna of India

Nothing unique from Rome to Persia to Egypt to India

By D.M. Murdock/Acharya S., author of the Christ Conspiracy: The Greatest Story Ever Sold.

In discussing the comparisons between Krishna and Christ, it is claimed either that there are no real parallels or that these "exact counterparts" – as the *Catholic Encyclopedia* calls them – rest squarely on the shoulders of the Brahman priesthood, who allegedly copied them from Christianity. Indian and other scholars contend that the story is uninfluenced by Christianity, many averring that any borrowing must have occurred by Christianity from Hinduism.

Krishna shares the following characteristics and motifs with Christ:
- Krishna is an incarnation of the sun god Vishnu, who rises or awakens on the winter solstice, i.e. "December 25th."
- Krishna was born in a stable of the "virgin" Devaki ("Divine One").
- He was of royal descent and was a prince.
- Krishna is the "King of the Yadus."
- Like the cave-born Christ of tradition, Krishna was born in a "cave-like dungeon."
- Great signs and wonders occurred at Krishna's birth, including the appearance of a bright star.
- Angels, wise men, shepherds attended his birth and he was presented with gifts, including gold and incense.
- His foster father was in the city to pay taxes when Krishna was born.
- The hero-god was persecuted by a tyrant who ordered the slaughter of infants.
- As a young boy, he worked miracles and wonders, and was hailed as a divine incarnation.
- He was worshipped by shepherds as a god.
- Krishna was "tempted" in the wilderness by "various fiends," before crushing the serpent's head.
- He raised a child from the dead and healed lepers, the deaf and the blind.
- Krishna preached faith "in God's love to man and in his mercy and forgiveness of sins arising therefrom."
- Krishna miraculously fed the multitudes.
- "He lived poor and he fed the poor," humbly washing the feet of guests.
- He was transfigured in front of his disciples.
- A woman bearing a jar of ointment anointed Krishna with oil.
- Krishna had a beloved disciple named Arjuna or "Ar-jouan."
- After his death he ascended into heaven, where he lives on.
- Krishna descended into to hell to rescue others.
- Krishna is a "personal savior, a messianic deliverer who will bring all men and women salvation is only they choose to give him their devotion."
- Krishna is called the "Shepherd God," "Lord of the god of gods," and "Lord of the lords," and was considered the "Redeemer," "Firstborn," "Sin Bearer," "Liberator," and "Universal Word."

•As Vishnu, he is the second person of the Trinity, considered the "Beginning, the Middle and the End." ["Alpha and Omega"], as well as being omniscient, omnipresent and omnipotent.

•A future incarnation of Vishnu is the Kalki avatar, who will arrive riding a white horse and destroy the wicked.

Sources: D.M. Murdock/Acharya S. and The Book Your Church Doesn't Want You to Read

Jesus from the Deistic Mosaic

HORUS
The Egyptian God

• A star announced Horus' birth; the Star in the East identified Jesus' birthplace.
• Trinity: Atum the Father, Horus the Son and Ra the Holy Spirit;
• God the Father, Jesus, God the Son and God the Holy Ghost (Spirit).
• Horus was Iu-em-Hetep, child teacher in the temple;
• Jesus was the child teacher in the temple
• Horus had twelve followers known as Har-Khutti.
• Jesus had twelve followers called the apostles.
• Horus was called Krst
• Jesus was called Christ
• Horus was baptized with water by Anup, the Baptizer.
• John baptized Jesus with water the Baptist.
• Horus was as the Lamb; Jesus was the Lamb.
• Horus was born in Annu, the place of bread.
• Jesus was born in Bethlehem, the house of bread.

By the Editors and The Book Your Church Doesn't Want You to Read

Albert Schweitzer in his *Search for the Historical Jesus* couldn't find a Jesus.

> *"There is no unique religion. None isolated, nor exclusive, nor one holier than others."*
>
> **Gerald Larue**
> **Professor of Religion**
> **University of Southern California**

THE FISH STORY

The fish in Christian symbols represents Jesus Christ. In the old Roman catacombs, the fish symbol appears frequently. The Greek word for fish is *icthus* and the early Christians saw in the letters of this word a monogram summarizing their faith: "Iesous Christos Theou Uios Soter" (Jesus Christ, Son of God the Savior)

The Christian sign is the same as the sign for the goddess Yoni or Pearly Gate, two crescent moons forming a *vescia piscis*. Sometimes the Christ child was superimposed on Mary's belly representing her womb, just as in the ancient symbol of the Goddess Yoni.

A medieval hymn called Jesus "the little fish which the virgin caught in the fountain." Mary was equated with the virgin Aphrodite-Mari, who brought forth all the fish in the sea.

Source: Mythology Dictionary

The Gnostics were the first Christians and revered the essence of Christ's spirituality without the need of hell-fire. Roman Catholics edited the early bible and turned Christianity into a political power machine, with the threat of eternal damnation to control the empire."
Dr. James Herriott, author and life long student of comparative religion

Pope as Vicar: Holy? Very few. Criminals, liars and thieves. Many."
Jordan Maxwell, Mythologist, Lecturer

The Vision of Constantine
The dictatorial vision that started it all.

Ten Commandments

•I am the Lord, your God: you shall not have false gods before me.
•Thou shalt not take the Lord's name in vain.
•Thou shalt keep holy the Lord's day.
•Thou shalt honor your father and your mother.
•Thou shalt not kill.
•Thou shalt not commit adultery.
•Thou shalt not steal.
•Thou shalt not bear false witness against your neighbor.
•Thou shalt not covet your neighbor's wife.
•Thou shalt not covet your neighbor's goods.

It wasn't long before the Roman Catholic Church and the Popes violated almost all (if not all) of Moses' Laws. It is a habit that has not been broken for 2,000 years.

Crusader

"When smashing monuments, save the pedestals, they come in handy."
Stanislaw Jerzy Lec (1909-1935)

The Vatican has made the survival of the Roman Catholic Church more important than the wisdom and grace of Jesus.

Editor

Section III

THE POPES

CRIMINAL HISTORY OF THE PAPACY

ANTIPOPES

Traditionally, the name "antipope" was given to claimants with a significant following of cardinals due to doctrinal controversy or confusion as to who is the legitimate pope at the time. Briefly during the 1400s, three separate lines of Popes claimed authenticity.

BLACK POPES

Traditionally the name "black pope" was unofficially given to the Superior General of the Society of Jesus (Jesuit) due to their importance within the Church. The name was based on the black cassock worn by the Jesuits and suggested a parallel between the "Black Pope" and the White Pope – since the time of Pope Pius V the Pope's dress is white.

POPE JOAN

Pope Joan is a legendary female Pope who supposedly reigned for a few years sometime during the Middle Ages. The story first appeared in the writings of 13th century chroniclers and subsequently spread throughout Europe. It was widely believed for centuries.

The female Pope is first mention in the chronicles of Dominican Jean de Mailly in his *Chronica Universalis Mettemsis*, written in the early 13th century and Martin of Troppau's *Chronicon Pontificum et Impertorum* later in the 13th century.

Most versions say she was a talented and learned woman who disguised herself as a man. Due to her abilities she advanced through the church hierarchy, eventually being chosen Pope. However, while riding on horseback one day, she gave birth to a child, thus revealing her gender. In most versions she dies shortly thereafter, either by being killed by an angry mob or by natural causes and her memory is shunned by her successors.

According to Jean de Mailly, the female Pope is not named and the events are set in 1099:

"Query. Concerning a certain Pope, or rather female Pope, who is not set down in the list of Popes or Bishops of Rome because she was a woman who disguised herself as a man and became, by her character and talents, a curial secretary, then a Cardinal, and, finally, Pope. One day, while mounting a horse, she gave birth to a child. Immediately, by Roman justice, she was bound by the feet to a horse's tail and dragged and stoned by the people for half a league, and where she died; there she was buried, and at that place is written 'Pietre, Pater Patrum, Papisse Prodito Partum' [Oh Peter, Father of Fathers, Betray the childbearing of the woman Pope]." At the same time the four-day fast called the "fast of the female Pope" was first established.

The female pope legend gained its greatest prominence in the works of Martin of Opava later in the 13th century.

This version was the first to attach a name to the female Pope, indicating she was known as "John Anglicus or Joan of Mainz. According to Martin:

"John Anglicus, born at Mainz, was Pope for two years, seven months and four days, and died in Rome, after which there was a vacancy in the Papacy of one month. It is claimed that this John was a woman, who, as a girl had been led to Athens dressed n the clothes of a man by a certain lover of hers. There she became proficient in a diversity of branches of knowledge, until she had no equal, and afterwards in Rome, she taught the liberal arts and had great masers among her students and audience. A high opinion of her life and learning arose in the city, and she was chosen for pope. While Pope, however, she became pregnant by her companion. Through ignorance of the exact time when the birth was expected, she was delivered of a child while in procession from St. Peter's to the Lateran, in a lane once named Via Sacra (the sacred way) but now known as the "shunned street" between the Coliseum and St. Clement's Church. After her death it is said she was buried in that same place. The Lord Pope always turns aside from the street and it is believed by man that this is done because of abhorrence of the event. Nor is she placed on the list of the Holy Pontiffs, both because of her female sex and on account of the foulness of the matter." (Matin of Opava, *Chronicon Pontificum et Imperatorum*).

One account gives an alternative fate for the female pope: she did not die immediately after her exposure as female, but was confined and deposed, after which she did many years of penance. Her son from the affair eventually became Bishop of Ostia and had her interred in his cathedral when she died.

Other references to the female Pope are attributed to earlier writers, though none appear in manuscripts which predate the *Chronicon*. The one most commonly cited is attached to Anastasius Bibliothecarius (d.886), a compiler of *Liber Pontificalis*, who would have been a contemporary of the female Pope by the *Chronicon* dating. The story is found in only one manuscript of Anastasius. This manuscript, in the Vatican Library, bears the relevant passage inserted as a footnote.

The first mention of the female Pope named Joanna (the earliest source to attach to her the female form of the name is found in Marianus Scous's *Chronicle of the Popes*, a text written in the 11th century.

From the 13th century onwards, the legend was widely disseminated and believed. Joan was used as an "exemplum in Dominican preaching." Bartolomeo Platina, the scholar who was prefect of the Vatican Library, wrote his Vitae *Pontificum Platine Historici Liber de Vita Christi ac Omnium Pontificum Quihactenus Ducenti Fuere et XX* in 1479, at the request of Pope Sixtus IV. The book contains the following account of the female Pope:

"Pope John VII: John, of English extraction, was born a Mentz (Mainz) and is said to have arrived at Popedom by evil art; for disguising herself like a man, whereas she was a woman, she went when young with her paramour, a learned man, to Athens, and made such progress in learning under the professors there that, coming to Rome, she met with few that could equal, much less go beyond her, even in the knowledge of the scriptures; and by her learned and ingenious readings and disputations, she acquired so great respect and authority that upon the death of Pope Leo IV by common consent she was chosen Pope in his room. As she was going to Lateran Church between Colossian Theatre (so called from Nero's Colossus) and St. Clements her travail came upon her, and she died upon the place, having sat two years, one month and four days, and was buried there without any pomp. This story is vulgarly told, but by very uncertain and obscure authors, and therefore I have related it barely and in short, lest I should seem obstinate and pertinacious if I had admitted what is so generally talked. I had better mistake with the rest of the world though it be certain, that what I have related may be thought not altogether incredible."

References to the female Pope abound in the later Middle Ages and Renaissance. Giovanni Boccaccio included a chapter on the female pontiff in his book about famous woman in history (*De Mulierbus Claris* (1353)).

The Welshman, Adam of Usk, traveled to Rome in 1402 and stayed for several years. His *Chronicon*, compiled between 1377 and 1404 includes an account of the coronation of Pope Innocent VII in 1404. The final stages of the Pope's solemn progress to the Lateran are described thus: "After turning aside out of abhorrence of Pope Agnes, whose image in stone with her son stands in the straight road near St. Clements, the Pope, dismounting from his horse, enters the Lateran for his enthronement."

A late 14th century guidebook *Mirabilia Urbis Romae*, tells readers that the female Pope's remains are buried in St. Peter's. It was around this time when a series of busts of past Popes was made for the Duomo of Siena in Tuscany, which included one of the female Popes named "Johannes VII, Foemina de Anglia" and included between Leo IV and Benedict III. The eries of terracotta busts exists today. Anyone looking for Pope Joan will search in vain as her bust was removed about 1600 by Clement VIII.

Stephen Blanck's *Mirabilia* (c. 1500) records a "stone, which is carved with an effigy of the female pope and her child."

Bohemian reformer, Jan Hus, former rector of Prague University, argued at the Council of Constance in 1414 that the only true head of the Catholic Church was Christ Himself and the Church was quite capable of functioning without a terrestrial head on the papal throne. It was for this reason he explained, that the Church had been able to survive even though its members had been "deceived in the Person of Agnes" among others. Hus's opponents at this trial insisted that his argument proved no such thing about the independence of the Church, but they did not dispute that there had been a female pope at all. Hus was eventually condemned as a heretic and burned to death in 1415.

In the 1290s the Dominican Robert of Uzes recounted a vision in which he saw the seat "where it is said, the Pope is proved to be a man". By the 14th century, it was believed that two ancient marble seats, called the *sedia stercoraria* (literally the dung chair) which were used for enthroning the popes in the Basilica of St. John Lateran, had holes in the seats that were used for determining the gender of the new pope. It was said that the pope would have to sit on one of the seats naked while a committee of Cardinals peered through the hole from beneath. Not until the late 15th century was it said that this peculiar practice was instituted in response to the scandal of the female Pope.

In 1587, Florimund de Raemond, a magistrate in the parliament de Bordeaux and an antiquary, published his first attempt to deconstruct the legend of the female Pope in his work "*Erreur Poplulaire de la Papesse Jeanne* (subsequently published under the title "*L'Anti-Papesse*"). He applied humanist techniques of textual criticism to the Pope Joan legend, with the broader intent of supplying sound historical principles to ecclesiastical history, and the legend began to come apart. Raemond's *Erreur Populaire* went through 15 editions as late as 1691.

Pope Clement VIII declared the legend of the female Pope to be untrue. The famous bust of her, inscribed Johannes VIII, Femina ex Anglica, was either destroyed or re-carved and relabeled, replaced by a male figure of Pope Zachary.

The legend of Pope Joan was "effectively demolished" by David Blondel, a mid-17th century Protestant historian, who suggested that the Pope Joan's tale might have originated in a satire against Pope John XI, who died in his early 20s.

The *Catholic Encyclopedia* elaborates on the historical time-lime:

"Between Leo IV and Benedict III, where Martin Polonius places her, she cannot be inserted, because Leo IV died 17 July 855 and immediately after his death Benedict III was elected by the clergy and people of Rome; but owing to the setting up of an Anti Pope, in the person of the deposed Cardinal Anastasias, he was not consecrated until 29 September. Cons exist which bear both the image of Benedict III and of Emperor Lothair I, who died 28 September 855; therefore, Benedict must have been recognized pope before the last mentioned date…All these witnesses prove the correctness of the dates given in the lives of Leo IV and Benedict III, and there is no interregnum between these two Popes, so that at this place there is no room for the alleged Popess [*sic*]."

Sedes Stercoraria

The *sedes stercoraaria*, the thrones with holes at St. John Lateran, did indeed exist and were used in the elevation of Pope Pascal II in 1099 (Boureau 1988). In fact, one is still in the Vatican Museum, another at the Museé du Louvre. They do have a hole in the seat. The reason for the hole is disputed. It has been speculated that they originally were Roman bidets or imperial birthing stools, which because of their age and imperial links were used in ceremonies by the Popes intent on highlighting their own imperial claims.

Alain Boureau quotes the humanist Jacopo d'Angelo de Scarparian who visited Rome in 1406 for the enthronement of Gregory XII in which the Pope sat briefly on two "pierced chairs" at the Lateran…the vulgar tell the insane fable that he is touched to verify that he is indeed a man…" a sign that the Pope Joan legend was still current in Rome.

The Englishman, William Brewyn, compiled his guidebook, *A XVth Century Guide-Book to the Principal Churches of Rome* (1933), wherein he described the Chapel of St. Savior in the Basilica of St. John Lateran:

" …in this chapel are two or more chairs of red marble stone, with apertures carved in them, upon which chairs, as I heard, proof is made as to whether the pope is male or not."

Shunned Street

Medieval Popes, from the 13th century onward, did avoid the direct route between the Lateran and St. Peter's. The origin of the practice is uncertain, but it is quite likely that it was maintained because of widespread belief in the pope Joan legend. The 1375 Mirabilia guidebook describes "…Nigh unto the Coliseum, in the open place, lieth an image which is called the Woman Pope with her child…Moreover in the same place is a Majesty of the Lord, that spake to her as she passed and said, 'In comfort thou shalt not pass,' and when she passed she was taken with pains and cast forth a child from her womb. Wherefore the Pope to this day will not pass by that way'…"

Pope John XX

A problem connected to the Pope Joan legend is the fact that there is no Pope John XX in any official list. It is said that this reflects a renumbering of the Popes to exclude the woman from history even though Louis Duchesne states this renumbering was actually due to a misunderstanding in the textual transmission of the official Papal lists, where in the course of the 11th Century, in the time after John XIX, the entry of John XIV had been misread and by consequence the numbering of Popes John XV through XIX was regarded as being erroneous.

The Tarot which surfaced in the mid-15th Century includes a Papesse with its Pape, called the high Priestess and the Hierophant in English since the 19th century. It is often suggested that this image was inspired by the legend of the female Pope.

Source: Catholic Encyclopedia; inspired by Wikipedia (Retrieved March 24, 2010)

THE DIRTY DOZEN

•Pope Stephen VI (896-897, who had his predecessor Pope Formosus exhumed, tried, de-fingered, and thrown in the Tiber River;

•Pope John XII (955-964), who gave land to a mistress, murdered several people and was killed by a man who caught him in bed with his wife;

•Pope Benedict IX (1032-1044,1045,1047-1048), who "sold" the papacy;

•Pope Boniface VIII (1294-1303), who is lampooned in Dante's Divine Comedy;

•Pope Urban VI (1378-1389), who complained he did not hear enough screaming when Cardinals who had conspired against him were tortured;

•Pope Alexander VI (1492-1503), who was guilty of nepotism;

•Pope Leo X (1513-1521) who was a spendthrift;

•Pope Clement VII (1523-1534) who was responsible for the sacking of Rome;

•Pope Urban II (1035-1099) called for the First Crusade;

•Pope Sergius III (911) ordered the murder of his predecessor and imprisoned ant-Pope Christopher;

•Pope Pius XII (1939-1959) called Hitler's Pope for his silence during World War II atrocities;

•Pope Benedict XVI (2005- present) involved in molestation cover-ups

Source: E.R. Chamberlain, The Bad Popes;

> ***"This myth of Jesus has served us well"***
> ***Pope Leo X***

> *Quote from **THE BAD POPES**
> By E.R. Chamberlain*
>
> *"It is now more than a thousand years since these territories and cities have
> been given to the priest and ever since then the most violent wars have been
> waged on their account, and yet the priests neither now possess them in peace,
> nor will ever be able to possess them. It were in truth better before the eyes
> of God and the world that these pastors should entirely renounce the
> dominium temporal: for since Sylvester's time the consequences of the
> temporal power have been innumerable wars and the overthrow of peoples
> and cities. How is it possible that there has never been any good pope to
> remedy such evil, and that so many wars have been waged for these transient
> possessions? Truly we cannot serve God and Mammon at the same time,
> cannot stand with one foot in Heaven and the other on the Earth."*
>
> ***....Giovanni de'Mussi, Chronicle of Piacenza, c. 1350***

POPE JOHN PAUL II
Pope John Paul II: Zyklon B Salesman

In his book "Behold a Pale Horse", former US Naval Intelligence Officer William
Cooper reveals a story associated the IG Farben Chemical Company.

In the early 1940s, that company employed a Polish chemist and salesman who
sold cyanide gas, Zyklon B and Malathion to the Nazis for extermination of groups
of people in Auschwitz.

After the war, the salesman joined the Catholic Church and was ordained a priest.

In 1958 he became Poland's youngest bishop and after Pope John Paul I's
mysterious death, the ex-cyanide gas salesman, Karol Wojtyla was elected to the
papacy as Pope John Paul II in October 1978.

In March 2000, he publicly apologized not for his war effort, but for the wickedness
of the Christian religion. The plea for forgiveness also sought to pardon the use of
"violence in the service of truth," an often used fragile and troubling reference to

the Inquisition.

The apology read by the Pope was the result of four years of work by a panel of 28 theologians and scholars and was by far the most sweeping act by a leader of a major religion.

On few occasions have ecclesiastical authorities ever acknowledged the faults or abuses of which they themselves were guilty. There was concern that the apology was a major theological miscalculation that could undermine the Pope's weakening authority and the unanswered question posed by the international media was –"In whose name was the Pope asking for forgiveness?" (Excerpted from *The Crucifixion of Truth* by Tony Bushby.

By Tony Bushby, Excerpts from John Paul II: a Political Obituary.

Pope Benedict XVI
The Vatican, like its current Pope, cannot get away from its past.

POPE BENEDICT XVI

Pope Benedict XVI, born, Joseph Alois Ratzinger, was elected Pope of the Roman Catholic Church on April 19, 2005. As Pope, he is Bishop of Rome, rules Vatican City and leads the Roman Catholic Church including Eastern rite Churches in communion with the Holy See.

Joseph Ratzinger was born in Marktl am Inn, Bavaria, Germany, the son of a police officer who was anti-Nazi.

Pope Benedict XVI has a record of controversial remarks on Islam, Buddhism, politics and social issues.

As head of the Congregation for the doctrine of the Faith, Ratzinger waged a campaign against liberation theology, which gained ground in Latin America as a means of involving the Church in social activism and human rights issues.

Benedict XVI –
Hitler Youth

He has described homosexuality as a "tendency" towards an "intrinsic moral evil." However, on November 20, 2010, it was announced by the Vatican, that the same Pope Benedict XVI had approved the use of condoms by homosexual prostitutes, to "prevent the spread of venereal disease." So, in consummate papal logic, Pope Benedict, XVI, has approved the use of a tool to perform acts he has characterized as leading to "intrinsic moral evil."

Ratzinger also spoke out on issues related to politics during the 2004 U.S. presidential election campaign, calling for pro-choice politicians to be denied Holy Communion. He also argued that Turkey should not be admitted into the European Union.

Pope Benedict XVI held the first audience for 25 Jewish leaders from Israel, the United States, Europe and Latin America on June 9, 2005.

On October 27, 2005, Pope Benedict XVI celebrated the 40th anniversary of the Second Vatican Council's "Nostra Aetate" document, which absolved the Jews of collective guilt in the death of Jesus." "This anniversary gives us abundant reason to express gratitude to almighty God," he said, "...in laying the foundations for a renewed relationship between Jewish people and the church, Nostra Aetate stressed the need to overcome past prejudices, misunderstandings, indifference and the language of contempt and hostility...I have expressed my own firm determination to walk in the footsteps traced by my beloved predecessor Pope John Paul II. The Jewish dialogue must continue to enrich and deepen the bonds of friendship which have developed."

Ratzinger's membership in the Hitler Youth raised eyebrows in the Jewish community, but he explained that membership was compulsory in his 1977 book *Salt of the Earth.*

"At first we weren't", he says, speaking of himself and his older brother. "But when the compulsory Hitler Youth was introduced in 1941, my brother was obliged to join. I was still too young, but later, as a seminarian, I was registered in the Hitler Youth. As soon as I was out of the seminary, I never went back. And that was difficult because tuition reduction, which I really needed, was tied to proof of attendance at the Hitler Youth."

In January 2009, Italy's rabbis announced they were pulling out of the Italian Catholic Church's annual celebration of Judaism because of Pope Benedict XVI's decision to restore a prayer in Easter Week services of the old Latin Mass that calls for the conversion of Jews.

Source: CatholicEencyclopedia; Inspired by Wikipedia (Retrieved March 24, 2010)

In January 2009 Italy's rabbis announced they were pulling out of the Italian Catholic Church's annual celebration of Judaism because of Pope Benedict XVI's decision to restore a prayer in Easter Week services that calls for the conversion of Jews.

THE DARK AGES
The Dark Ages were in the shadow of the Church

"There was a time in history when religion ruled the world. It is called the Dark Ages"

Helen Hermence Green
The Born Again Skeptic's Guide to the Bible

LET THE CRIMES BEGIN

It has been recorded that over 200 million people were murdered in the name of Christianity over the past 2,000 years.

"Americans talk about the witch trials in Salem Massachusetts as if they were a great historic horror; only 19 people were killed, and it was all over in a year's time. Europe's witch trials went on for centuries and killed a purported 9,000,000, most of them women – though some scholars consider this to be a low estimate... Scholars have slowly but surely been revising this number for the past few decades, making distinctions between the torture and slaughter of "heretics" over the many centuries of Church domination and the "witches" murdered during the "Burning Times" which defines a much narrower timeframe, with most "tried from 1550 to 1650." ...The records of these evil days have mostly disappeared, 'the Church is working quietly to reduce these figures in order to rewrite is history and absolve itself of massive genocide."

Barbara Walker, Man Made God

"The women who were tortured and burned were accused of crimes ranging from being a midwife, possessing a cat or having intercourse with the devil. Often, the smartest, most outspoken, most beautiful, educated, or wealthy women in the community would be singled out for murder by the female-hating celibate clergy... Almost the entire female population of a town would be immolated in a single day.

In one German city, 900 women were burned in one day...An inquisitor of Como, Italy, was quoted as having burned 1,000 witches in a single year. The murders were not carried out by disorderly mobs, but were well ordered, following a well-defined legal process involving sworn testimony from local citizens, gathering evidence, extraction of confessions and official ecclesiastical judgments."

Dr. James DeMeo

"In 415, the famous female philosopher, Hypatia of Alezandria was torn to pieces with glass fragments, in a church by a hysterical Christian mob led by a priest called Peter. Charlemagne, in 782 had 4,500 Saxons unwilling to convert to Christianity beheaded. In 1096, Pope Urban II (1042-99; pope 1088-1099) sanctioned the first of eight crusades that extended in time to a total of 19, and they continued unabated for 475 years ((1096-1571). "

Tony Bushby, Criminal History of the Papacy

"In this cross you shall conquer"

ONWARD CHRISTIAN SOLDIERS

Things They Don't Tell You about Christianity and Catholicism

•The early fathers of the Church hated Greek civilization and sought its destruction.

"The more a nation looks barbaric and is estranged from Greek culture, the more our teachings shine – this (faithful) barbarian has conquered the entire world and while all Greek culture is extinguished and destroyed, his (the barbarian's) shines brighter every day."...*The philobarbarian attitude of Saint John Chrysostom* [3rd-4th Century]

68

•All over the empire, mobs of Christian monks went about destroying the main Greco-Roman works of art, libraries of antiquity, and pre-Christian temples:

> "The Greek called them "swinish black cloths", because "they looked like men but lived like pigs…armed with clubs or stones and swords they ran to the temples, some without these weapons only with their bare hands and feet."…(*Libanios "Pro temples"*389AD)

•The oldest and most renowned churches are actually built on sites which previously had pre-Christian temples on them – which Christians demolished. This happened all over the Roman Empire, to Syria in the East and North Africa and Palestine in the South.

> **"The cave of the Vatican belonged to Mithras until 376 A.D. when a city prefect suppressed the cult of the rival Savior and seized the shrine in the name of Christ, on the very birthday of the pagan god, December 25."**…*Barbara G. Walker*

•The educated Romans disliked the religion. Some of them wrote books refuting Christianity like the Epicurean Kelsos in his *Alethes Logos*, the last pagan emperor Julian in his *Kata Christianon* and Prophyry's *Against the Christians*. The Church, unable to sufficiently counter their well-reasoned arguments (which it occasionally attempted) "won" the debate by destroying these works when it finally got into power. Even so, some scanty ancient literature against Christianity remains, pieced together from the unsuccessful attempts at responding Christian Church fathers.

•How many Christian persecutions?

Not 10 as Christians claim, but no more than 2 or 3:
Historian Joseph McCabe in his book *The Story of Religious Controversy* states that scholars only recognize 2 general persecutions:
   •The Decian Persecution; no more than 5 or 6 people were martyred in Rome and between 2 and 3 dozen (itself considered dubious) in the entire Roman Empire

   •The Diocletian persecution: The Church claims 40,000 martyrs, many in Rome. However, scholars have shown that there were only 20 "genuine martyrs" – i.e. Christians who decided to die rather than forsake their faith -- in the whole Roman Empire, and none in Rome. A few hundred other Christians were executed. Many of whom perished in jail.

•The *Acta* of the martyrs (records of trials and executions) are entirely from fictitious lives or are forgeries. Pagan deities were sometimes used as martyrs and were turned into Saints. The fraud led to the birth of the profitable <u>relic industry.</u>

•Why and How Did the Pagans of the empire convert?

•"The...undisputed fact is that there was no 'attraction' of the pagans at all. In the extant Theodosian Code, we have ten decrees which the bishops got from the emperors suppressing all rival religions and sects under pain of fine, imprisonment, or death"...*How Christianity Grew Out of Paganism*, by Joseph McCabe.

•"Beginning with Constantine, and under succeeding "Christian" emperors, there is a series of scores of laws which the Christians procured to be enacted for the suppression and persecution to death of Pagans, heretics and Jews. These laws and edicts are to be found in the Codes of Theodosius and of Justinian, the two famous codifications of Roman Law.-*Forgery in Christianity*, by Joseph Wheless.

•Education:

•The Roman municipalities supplied free elementary instruction for the children of all workers. Practically every Roman worker could read and write by the year 380 A.D., when Christianity began to have real power. By 480 nearly every school in the Empire was destroyed.

By 580, and until 1780 at least, from ninety to ninety-five per cent of the people of Europe were illiterate and densely ignorant. That is the undisputed historical record of Christianity as regards education. ---*The Story of Religious Controversy*, by Joseph McCabe.

•"Rome under the Popes had sunk to an illiteracy that has no parallel elsewhere in the history of civilization"---*The Story of Religious History* by Joseph McCabe.

•Intolerance:

•"Unbelievers deserve not only to be separated from the Church, but also...to be exterminated from the world by death."---Saint Thomas Aquinas, *Summa Theological*, 1271

•Crusades:

> •Besides an infamous Children's Crusade, and those against the Jews and Moslems and Easter Orthodox church, there were also Crusades to convert-or-kill the pagans of Eastern Europe and the Balkans.

> •The Balkan Prussians were completely exterminated in a mass genocide, as were the Stedingers of Germany. "Heathens" in Lithuania also faced routine genocide of its population.

> •In Hungary, during the tenth and eleventh centuries, "the new religion was spread by the sword..." – *Forgery in Christianity*, by Joseph Wheless.

> •In the Albigensian Crusade, half of France was exterminated. By the end of the 13th century, one million of the French "heretics" had been murdered.

> •In 1487, Pope Innocent VII called for a Crusade against the French Waldensians, who has already been declared heretics in the 1184 Council of Verona. They were hounded and killed until the 17th century.

•Inquisitions and Witch Hunts:

> •The first Inquisition was against heretics and witches.

> •95% of the victims of the Second Spanish Inquisition were Jews.

> •The Third Inquisition went after Protestants and other heretics as well as witches.

> •At the first Inquisition the victims were only burnt to death, But: "torture of suspects was authorized by Pope Innocent IV in 1252, and thus inquisition chambers were turned into places of abject horror...Torture was not finally removed as a legal option for the church officials until 1917 when the *Codex Juris Canonici* was put into effect."

> •Inquisitors were placed entirely above the law by Pope Innocent IV's bull *Ad extirpanda*. Most of the torturing was performed by members of the Dominican order, while many other inquisitors and torturers were monks of the Franciscan order. The Inquisitors and the Holy church became filthy rich from the assets of their victims.

•The edicts that established the Inquisition have never been repealed. They are officially still part of the Catholic faith, and were used as justification for certain practices as recently as 1969.

•Entire villages and towns were depopulated of their woman. Historian Will Duran, in his *History of Civilization*, puts the number of fatalities of the witch-hunts between 7 and 9 million.

•Reformation:

•The Thirty Year War (1648-48) between the Protestants and Catholics, led to the deaths of more that a quarter of Europe's population *–Ed Babinsky*

•In Germany alone, the war resulted in an estimated drop of its population from 18 million to 4 million.

•In Bohemia its 30,000 villages were reduced to 6,000 and its 3 million citizens slaughtered down to 780,000. (Joseph McCabe)

•The Catholics butchered 30,000 Huguenots in one day: the Saint Bartholomew's Day Massacre.

•Women:

•Woman was merely man's helpmate, a function which pertains to her alone. She is not the image of God but as far as man is concerned, he is by himself the image of God ---Saint Augustine (354-430).

•The 584 Council of Macon: Bishops gathered to vote on what is a "human". By a narrow vote of 1, women obtained human status in Christianity.

•Convert and Kill in the Americas:

•When in 1530 CE the Pope finally declared that Indians were human, the pious Christians began converting the heathens: "the [Catholic] Spaniards in Mexico and Peru used to baptize Indian infants and then immediately dash their brains out; by this means they secured that these infants went to heaven" *---Bertrand Russell*

•The Indian Chief Hatuey fled with his people but was captured and burned alive. As they were tying him to the stake a Franciscan friar urged him to take Jesus to his heart so that his soul might go to heaven, rather than descend into hell. Hautey replied "... if heaven was where the Christians went, he would rather go to hell."---*American Holocaust*, by D. Stannard

•60 million Native Americans had been exterminated by the end of the 16th century itself. For instance, good Christians from Spain "hanged thirteen [natives] at a time in honor of Christ Our Savior and the twelve Apostles…then straw was wrapped around their torn bodies and they were burned alive."---*American Holocaust*, by D. Stannard

•19th century Christian missionaries exterminated the Californian Indians in the most gruesome manner.

•Convert and kill in Africa:

•During the brutal Christian colonization of the Congo, which was defended by the Catholic Church, "As many as 10 million Congolese are estimated to have died as a result of executions, unfamiliar diseases and hunger."(Leopold reigns for a day in Kinshasa , the Guardian, February 4, 2005.)

Source: Freetruth.50webs.org

Hanging Heretics

73

Burning Heretics

The Catholic Cross, Sword, and Bible
A Time when the devil lived on earth in the Vatican

Library at Alexandria
The Great Library at Alexandria, Egypt was torched since the collections were works of heretics.

Crusaders and Children's Crusade

THE CRUSADES
Roman Catholic Jihad

The Crusades were a series of religiously sanctioned military campaigns waged by the Holy Roman Empire for over a period of 200 years between 1085 and 1291. Initially the wars were waged against the Muslims in the effort to recapture Jerusalem and the Holy Land – where the death, resurrection and ascension into heaven of Jesus Christ was to have taken place and Antioch, the first Christian city - from Muslim.

There were nine identified Crusades, each with its own far-reaching political, economic and social impacts. The Sixth Crusade was the first Crusade initiated without the Pope's blessing.

The Crusades were an outlet for an intense religious fervor among the lay people fueled by religious propaganda advocating the "Just War" to retake the Holy Land from the Muslims. A Crusader would take a solemn vow, receive a cloth cross from the hands of the Pope or his legate and be considered a "soldier of the Church." The soldiers believed that by taking Jerusalem they would go straight to heaven.

Pope Gregory VII declared the wars "justified violence." That justification was his own ambition to be the leader of Europe.

The Knights Templar

The Knights Templar trace their origin back to the First Crusade. A French nobleman, Hugues de Payens, organized a small band of knights to defend Christians making pilgrimages to the Holy Land. The Knights were officially sanctioned by the Church at the Council of Troyes. They became the elite fighting force of the times, highly trained, well equipped and highly motivated. But not all the Knights were warriors. The papal office had sanctioned the Knights as a charitable organization and their fundraising tactics matched their military prowess. When a nobleman joined the Crusades he would be away from home for years. He placed his money, land and possessions under the control of the Templars. As the order's financial power grew, they devoted more time to economic pursuits. By 1150 the Knights Templar were guarding the pilgrims and the wealth of the soldiers, innovating practices that have evolved into modern banking.

The Templars shrewd banking practices created loopholes around the church's forbidden practice of lending money in return for interest (usury). The Knights sidestepped this with a stipulation that they retained the rights to the production of mortgaged property. As one Templar scholar summed it up "Since they weren't allowed to charge interest, they charged rent instead."[7]

The Templars political connections and awareness of the essentially urban and commercial needs of the communities led them to a position of significant power, both in Europe and the Holy Land. They owned large tracts of land, built churches and castles, bought farms and vineyards, were involved in manufacturing and import/export trades and had their own fleet of ships. They loaned enormous amounts of money to the kings of France and England.

King Philip IV of France requested a loan and was denied by the Templars prompting the King to initiate a tax on the French clergy and plea to Pope Boniface VIII for the excommunication of the Knights Templar. Boniface refused. At dawn on October 13, 1307, scores of Templars were simultaneously arrested by King Philip and tried as heretics. Pope Clement V issued a Papal Bull *"Pastoralis Praeeminetiae,* instructing all Christian monarchs to arrest the Templars and seize their assets. In 1312 Clement V issued an order officially dissolving the Order. Much of the Templar property was transferred to the Knights Hospitaller. In Portugal the Knights Templar continued the Order under the name "Order of Christ."

In 2002, Barbara Frale found a copy of the Chinon Parchment in the Vatican Secret Archives, a document which indicated that Pope Clement V absolved the leaders of the Order in 1308. She published her findings in the *Journal of Medieval History* in 2004. The document was published under the Vatican imprimatur in 2007.

Source: Catholic Encyclopedia; Inspired by Wikipedia (Retrieved March 24, 2010)

Chronology of the Crusades

The First Crusade: Led by Pope Urban II called upon all Christians to wage war against the Turks to regain the Holy Land, promising all who died in the endeavor would receive immediate remission of their sins.

The Second Crusade: After a period of relative peace in which Christians and Muslims co-existed in the Holy Land, Muslims conquered the City of Edessa. A new crusade was called but failed to when major victories in the Holy Land but of the other side of the Mediterranean, Crusaders conquered Lisbon from the Muslims.

Third Crusade: Pope Gregory VIII called for a crusade in response to the Sultan of Egypt, Saladin, who conquered the city of Jerusalem after nearly a century under Christian rule. The Christians did not recapture the city.

The Fourth Crusade: Initiated by Pope Innocent III with the intent of regaining Jerusalem but their leaders decided to go to Constantinople where they sacked the city in 1204 and established the Latin Empire. This move was the deciding factor in the schism between the Eastern Orthodox Church and the Roman Catholic Church.

The Fifth Crusade: Called for by Pope Honorius III was another failed attempt to recapture the Holy Land.

The Sixth Crusade: Called for by Frederick II, Holy roman Emperor to regain the Holy Land. The Crusade ended in a truce allowing Christians to return to the Holy City, Jerusalem and Muslims control over the Temple Mount.

The Seventh Crusade: The papal interest represented by the Knights Templar, brought on a conflict with Egypt. The crusaders were defeated.

The Eighth Crusade: Led by King Louis IX of France was a failed attempt to capture Syria. Louis IX died after two months fighting in Tunisia and was canonized for his efforts.

The Ninth Crusade: Undertaken by the future king of England, Edward I, was deemed a failure and ended the Crusades in the Middle East.

Sources: Catholic Encyclopedia; inspired by Wikipedia (Retrieved May 5, 2010)

"If there is a God, the phrase that must disgust him is 'holy war'. – Steve Allen

Knights Templar Shield
In This Cross You Shall Conquer

Joan of Arc
A villain, a warrior – burnt at the stake and now a saint

JOAN OF ARC
(1412-1431)

Joan of Arc, named the "Maid of Orleans," was born in Domremy, France, on the border of the provinces of Champagne and Lorraine.

At the young age of 12 she began hearing voices form the saints telling her she had a divine mission from God to rescue her country from the English and help the Dauphin gain the French throne. The voices told her to cut her hair, dress as a man and go into battle.

Joan convinced the Dauphin of her calling and was given troops under her command as captain. At the Battle of Orleans in May 1429, she led her troops to victory over the English.

Charles VII was crowned King of France in July, 1429. At the coronation Joan was given the place of honor next to the new king.

In 1430 during battle outside of Paris, she was captured by the Burgundians and sold to the English. She was handed over to the church and tried for witchcraft and heresy on the grounds that to wear men's clothing was a crime against God.

After a fourteen month trial she was burned at the stake. She was nineteen years old. The French made no attempt to rescue her, nor did the Church.

In 1456 she was retried and found innocent of all charges made against her.

Pope Benedict XV canonized her in 1920.

Source: Catholic Encyclopedia

SPANISH INQUISITION

The Spanish Inquisition was initiated in 1478 by King Ferdinand and Queen Isabella to maintain Catholic orthodoxy in their kingdoms. It was not formally abolished until 1814, during the reign of Isabel II. It surpassed the medieval Inquisition in both scope and intensity. *Conversos* (Secret Jews) and New Christians were targeted.

King Ferdinand and Queen Isabella petitioned the Pope for permission to start an Inquisition in Spain. In 1483 Tomás de Torquemada became the Inquisitor-general for Spain. Also heading the Spanish Inquisition were two Dominican monks, Miguel de Morillo and Juan de San Martín.

The Inquisition, as a tribunal dealing with religious heresy, had jurisdiction only over baptized Christians. During a large part of its history, however, freedom of religion did not exist in Spain or its territories, so, in practice the Inquisition had jurisdiction over all royal subjects. Between 3,000 and 5,000 people died during the Inquisition's 350 years, but debate continues about the extent of and nature of atrocities committed and about the number of victims. Originally politically motivated, it aimed to use religion to foster national unity but later became the object of Protestant anti-Catholic propaganda which "painted Spaniards as barbarians who ravished women and sodomized young boys."

Motives for instituting the Spanish Inquisition:

- To establish political and religious unity.
- To weaken local political opposition to the Catholic Monarchs.
- To do away with the powerful *converso* minority.
- Economic support. Given that one of the measures used with those tried was the confiscation of property, this possibility cannot be discarded.

Extension of the Inquisitions:

Around 1531, Pope Leo X extended the Inquisition to Portugal. The Inquisition spread to the New World and Asia. Spanish tribunals and *auto de fés* were set up in Mexico, the Philippine Islands, Guatemala, Peru, New Granada (where *Moriscos*, converts from Islam) were included), and the Canary Islands.

The Spanish Inquisition first imposed in 1478 and extended by Holy Roman Emperor Charles V to the Netherlands in 1521, promoting the questioning and burning of heretics under government auspices.

Source: Catholic Encyclopedia; Inspired by Wikipedia (Retrieved May 13, 2010)

Giordano Bruno
Like Galileo and Copernicus, victimized because of their knowledge and insight that exposed the Church as ignorant

Copernicus
He was left to rot in purgatory
when Pope John Paul II forgave Galileo.
Ironically Copernicus' statue sits in Poland.

Heresy:
Heresy is an opinion or doctrine at variance with the orthodox or accepted doctrine, especially of a church or a religious system.

John Wycliffe: Heretic
John Wycliffe publicly attacked the Church's doctrine of transubstantiation and claimed that all Godly authority reside in the scriptures and not to any degree in the good offices of the Church.

Even though John Wycliffe died peacefully at home in bed on New Year's Eve, the Church exhumed his body forty-four years later for the crime of translating the Bible into English. They burned his bones and scattered his ashes into a nearby river.

Editor

Galileo Galilei
Another who was too smart for the Church.

THE FIG LEAF CAMPAIGN

Pope Paul IV (1555-1559) declared Michelangelo's painting of the walls of the Sistine Chapel, The Last Judgment, defamatory and had fig leaves painted over the nude figures. Pope Paul IV interpreted the painting to be in direct opposition to Catholic Dogma stating men could not be saved without the intercession of the Catholic Church. The painting portrays Jesus communicating directly to those around him without the Church's presence.
Source: Catholic Encyclopedia

Platform of Jaguars and Eagles
Aztec culture – another victim of Catholic conquistadors. Books and documents disappeared in their Catholic fire.

Dunkin Donuts and the Catholic Church

1600: Pope Clement VIII sanctioned the use of coffee despite petitions by the clergy to ban the Muslim drink as "the devil's drink". The Pope tried a cup and declared it so "delicious that it would be a pity to let the infidels have exclusive use of it. We shall cheat Satan by baptizing it."
By the Editors

The Shroud of Turin

The Shroud of Turin – a 14th Century favorite – has been repeatedly used to bolster the Christ crucifixion story. The question is: How many times does something have to be discredited by historical references and carbon dating.

Tim C. Leedom

ROMAN CATHOLIC IMPERIALISM IN A NEW LAND

Hernando Cortéz brought the Catholic Church to Mexico. His expedition included a friar, Bartolomé de Olmedo and a priest, Juan Díaz. Conversion of the Indians was part of their mandate. In 1492, Pope Alexander VI ordered that natives of the new lands be instructed in Catholicism for the "salvation of their souls." Cortéz accepted this assignment wholeheartedly and acted accordingly. At his first landfall in Cozumel he persuaded the natives to break up their idols and erect crosses and a shrine to the Virgin. He continued these efforts throughout the Conquest. He was also ardent about christening women given to the Spaniards as slaves because it was forbidden for his men to have intercourse with any woman until she was baptized.

It was an effort to destroy Aztec idols and set up Catholic crosses in their place that caused the final break between the Spaniards and the Aztecs. Had the Spanish been less insistent on the conversions of the Aztecs to Christianity and the blood thirsty destruction of their idols, it is possible that Cortéz and Montezuma might have reached a peaceful agreement.

The conflict of interests between Church and State began shortly after the Conquistadors toppled the Aztec Empire. The bone of contention was the treatment of the natives. Between 1519 and 1524 when 12 Franciscan friars arrived in Nueva España, the process of conversion of natives was simple baptism with no follow up. Spaniard settlers claimed that the baptized Indians were not true Christians, had returned to worshipping their old Gods, and could be enslaved. For many years, the "Christianity" of the Indians was a thin veneer barely covering their old pagan beliefs. The Conquistadors, interested only in personal wealth, had seized vast tracts of land. Called *ecomiendas*, the natives who lived within their boundaries, baptized or not, were enslaved.

The first to challenge the treatment of the natives in Nueva España was Bartolomé De Las Casas. He was appointed Bishop of Chiápas in 1544. Twenty-five years earlier he had been expelled from Santo Domingo for protesting the enslavement of Indians. Back in Spain, he drafted new laws that outlawed slavery in the New

World. These "New Laws," signed by the Spanish Emperor, Charles V. in 1542, were ignored and then suspended by those who governed Nueva España. Bishop De Las Casas headed for Chiápas, fully committed to abolishing slavery. Since the entire economy of the colony was based on free native labor, he failed. Ironically, he suggested the importation of black slaves from the Indies or from Africa as a possible solution.

It was the first time that a representative of the Church had challenged the secular authority in Nueva España.

The next Churchman to take up the cause of the Indians was Juan de Zumarraga, appointed Archbishop of Mexico in 1527. Although more moderate in his views than Las Casas, he soon came into conflict with the ruling body of Nueva España headed by Nuño de Guzmán, known as "Bloody Guzman" because of his brutal treatment of both Indians and Spaniards, a clash between the two men was inevitable. When Cortéz, a bitter enemy of Guzmán, returned to the colony as Capitán-General, Bishop Zumarraga excommunicated Guzmán. But Guzmán fled to what is now Jalisco where he continued to wreck havoc among both Spaniards and Indians. Responding to complaints from Zumarraga a new Audiencia was formed under the newly arrived Don Vasco de Quiroga. With the aid of Cortés, a friend of the Indians, and the approval of Don Quiroga and the new Audiancia, Zumarraga established himself and the clergy as "Protector of the Indians." Although they remained slaves, Indians could now turn to the Church with their grievances. Schools for Indians were founded, and the true meaning of Christianity was made clear to those who had converted. There can be little doubt that the firm grip of Catholicism on Mexico can be traced back to the efforts of Archbishop Juan de Zumarraga. It was Zumarraga who confirmed the vision of "Our Lady of Guadalupe." It was he who set up the first shrine, later re-located, that still remains the most popular religious site in Mexico.

Don Vasco de Quiroga, although a layman, had allied himself with Zumarraga. As head of the second Audencia, his punishment of the members of the first Audencia sent a message to the colonists. The Church, with government approval, would monitor the treatment of Indians. When Spanish landowners foiled efforts to force them to grant Indians freedom, De Quiroga started to set up monasteries and community centers in which Indian children could be educated. Manned by friars, they gave instruction in Christianity plus arts and crafts.

Then De Quiroga turned his attention to Michoacán. To repair the damage done by Guzmán, both as head of the first Audencia and on the way to what is now Jalisco, Quiroga established himself in Tzintzuntzan, the ancient Tarascan capital. Here he achieved immediate results. Spaniards who exploited the natives were brought to justice. Indians were given land, housing as provided. Schools and hospitals were run by the church. In essence, a form of socialism, with self-governing Indian communities, was established. In 1538 he was appointed to the newly formed Bishopric of Michoacán despite being a layman. The organization of Catholicism he set up in Michoacán was to set the pattern for the establishment of that religion throughout what is now Mexico.

Now the Church had triumphed and remained in control for the next 250 years. There was an intimate union of church and state. However, with the first stirrings of the drive for independence from Spain things started to change.

In 1749, the Spanish King Ferdinand VI issued an order, transferring mission centers from the control of religious orders to the regular clergy. The order was largely ignored, but in 1767 another royal order expelled the Jesuits. Their property was seized and turned over to the Crown. It is estimated that there were more than 2200 Jesuits in the country, ministering to over 700,000 Indians. Very unpopular, this order stirred up unrest in the country and started protests against Spanish rule.

The government set out to replace the religious infrastructure. Under royal patronage, new secular universities were established. The regular clergy and other orders replaced the Jesuits in their work with the Indians. The mandates were triggered by the unwillingness of the Jesuits to submit to either royal or diocesan authority. They had established what amounted to a Jesuit Republic in Sonora and Lower California. Their expulsion sent a message to Mexicans that they had no voice in the running of their country and fueled Mexican discontent with Spanish rule.

Even after Mexico gained its independence from Spain, no government was strong enough to pay any attention to the activities of the Church. The Plan of Iguala had guaranteed the supremacy of the Catholic Church. Although the new Mexican constitution paid lip service to religious tolerance, only Catholics could be Mexican citizens. Its monopoly established, the Church remained a protector of Indian rights, maintained a good working relationship with civil authorities and solidified its hold on the religious life of the country.

But in 1851, a Zapotecán Indian named Benito Juárez became President of the country. He proclaimed himself an anti-cleric, determined to destroy the power of the church. The "Lerdo Law" was proclaimed which expropriated all property owned by the church or that it had in trust.

Ironically, this act by a party, led by an Indian, stripped his fellow Indians of most of the land they held. Called *"Ejidos"* they were lands granted to Indian tribes, clans, communities or even families. They were owned in common and were farmed communally. But because the majority of the Indians were illiterate, the Church held the lands in trust. Now they were seized along with the convents, monasteries, hospitals and schools. In 1857 a new Constitution was drawn up. Liberty of conscience, religious tolerance and freedom of worship were all professed by the Liberals, but in reality they had deprived the almost 100 percent Catholic population of much of their religious freedom.

Churches remained open, but the country suppressed all religious orders, declared religious vows illegal, prohibited nuns and priests from appearing in public in religious garb. Marriage was made a secular rite and even cemeteries were declared to be secular. In a further blow aimed at Catholicism, Protestants were permitted to establish themselves in the country. Despite the unpopularity of these laws, they remained in effect. But they did not break the allegiance of the Mexican people to Catholicism. Also, it led the clerics and their conservative supporters to appeal to the French, who sent troops and installed Maxmilian as Emperor of Mexico.

During the reign of Emperor Maxmilian, 1864-1867, the Church was able to recover somewhat with the Archbishops of Mexico City and Michoacán and the Bishop of Oaxaca permitted to return to the country. But the hope of a complete restoration of church property and influence never materialized. Some compensation was paid to the Church, but on the instructions of Napoleon III, himself an anti-cleric, the Church remained in disfavor.

When Maxmilian was deposed, Juárez was restored to the presidency and the war against the Church continued. In 1873, a rebellion against the anti-cleric laws, now being enforced by President Lerdo de Tejada, broke out and continued until 1876 when Porfirio Díaz became President. Though not repealed, the laws were not enforced. But later, President Carranza elected in 1917 and Obregón, who came into power in 1920, enforced them selectively. A new Constitution, adopted in 1917, now made it clear that the state was to control the church. President Elias Calles, elected in 1924, was a Socialist, and continued to look on the Church as an enemy. During his presidency, all but Mexican born priests were deported, religious schools were closed. Limits were put on the number of priests in the country and their registration with the Government, required.

In the years that followed, these anti-cleric laws were never repealed but were either enforced or ignored at the pleasure of the ruling PRI and the President. This on again-off again pattern of anti-clericalism finally led to the "Cisteros Wars". It had been brewing since 1925 and in early 1939 the violence escalated as the government moved to crush the rebels. Centered mostly in the northern part of Jalisco called Los Altos, by June of that year, the fighting had ended with a Government victory.

With the election of Lázaro Cardenas to the presidency in1934, a détente between Church and State became a reality. In 1940, Cardenas was succeeded by Ávila Camacho. A devout Catholic, he changed the Constitution to re-affirm religious freedom, but did not succeed in repealing all the anti-cleric provisions it contained. Thus Catholic schools were able to open again but were forced to disguise themselves as private institutions.

Today priests and nuns are free to appear in public in religious garb. There is true freedom of religion. But it is clear that the Catholic Church in Mexico must render unto Caesar the things that are Caesar's unto God the things that are God's.

Source:Iinspired by Wikipedia (Retrieved May 13, 2010)

Preying on - not Praying with – Native Americans

From the beginning, the Catholic Church came into conflict with Native Americans and with their fellow believers in Jesus as Savior of mankind right after the first Thanksgiving in 1621. The Church was in competition to convert the Indians. From Plymouth Massachusetts, led by men such as Miles Standish, who actually stabbed a peaceful Indian leader to death at a meeting, the Catholics systematically set about stealing the Indian lands for their churches throughout the continent. Dissident Indians were often crated up and sent to England and Spain to be sold as slaves. Soon the tribes of Squanto, who saved the desperate Pilgrims and Catholics, were dismantled by disease and victimized by war and land theft. Cities stolen and "bartered land" were incorporated [Duxbury, MA in 1637] and large areas were granted by England to the Church for development...without consulting the native inhabitants who had occupied the lands for centuries.

Tim C. Leedom

> **The Catholic Jesuits were so feared that in 1647 the Massachusetts Bay pilgrims banned Jesuits from the colony under penalty of death. An anti-Catholic coin was circulated throughout the colony picturing the Pope on one side and the devil on the other.**

16th Century Anti-Catholic Coin
Heads (The Pope) and Tails (Satan)

"They came with a Bible and their religion; took our land and crushed our spirit and now they tell us we should be thankful to the Lord for being saved."

Chief Pontiac

"The Church of Rome has made it an article of fact that no man can be saved out of their church and other religious sects approach this dreadful opinion in proportion to their ignorance and the influence of wicked people."

John Adams, Second President of the United States

WORLD WAR II and THE ROMAN CATHOLIC CHURCH

Hypocrisy, Bestiality, Complicity, Denial and Genocidal Crimes at Their Worst

"Germany must become the sword of the Catholic Church."

Wilhelm, II
Emperor of Germany

Flag at Catholic Church in Cologne
An alliance made in heaven or hell

POPE PIUS XII

John Cornwall, the author of ***Hitler's Pope: The Secret History of Pope Pius XII*** writes, "I was convinced that if the full story were told, Pius XII's pontificate would be vindicated." Later Cornwall continues, "The material I had gathered, taking the more extensive view of Pacelli's life, amounted not to exonerate him but to a wider indictment...My research told the story of a bid for unprecedented papal power...His is not a portrait of evil but of fatal moral dislocation – a separation of authority from Christian love." (Preface)

Pope Pius XII

Pacelli, Pope Pius XII, reigned from 1939 to 1958 like a king over a global Catholic fiefdom, and has been in the process of being canonized as a saint since shortly after his death; the process can take centuries. However, a huge black cloud looms over his pontificate. During World War II, atrocities were committed by the Nazis against the Jews and others, and he in effect did nothing, not even condemning them or their actions publicly. Many consider this non-action as complicity, making him an anti-Semitic war criminal.

Another issue threatening to overshadow Pope Pius XII's pontificate is manifesting out of history, one that will likely prevent Pius XII from achieving sainthood, one that shows that the Roman Catholic Church, and by implication, its undisputed ruler, assisted thousand of Nazis to escape from Allied Forces at the end of World War II.

Aiding and abetting war criminals to escape justice is a war crime in and of itself; and Pius XII appears guilty.

In any crime the most important question to answer is "why?" And most of the time the key to the motive is to follow the money.

Born in Rome to an aristocratic family with ties to the "Black Nobility," Eugenio Pacelli was practically born for the papacy as his family boasted such prominent church lawyers as his grandfather, Marcantonio Pacelli, who had been Undersecretary in the Papal Ministry of Finances, and Secretary of the Interior under Pope Pius IX; his father, Fillippo Pacelli, a Franciscan Tertiary, and Dean of the Sacra Roto Romana; and his brother, Francesco Pacelli, a lay canon lawyer, who was financial advisor to Pius IX, and who negotiated the Lateran Treaty of 1929.

It is not often thought of, but throughout human history the priesthood has been a vocation primarily of royalty, as kings and high priests were often intertwined. The Aaronite priesthood which passed down through the tribe of Levi was not permitted to learn a trade, instead the Levites were expected to study and learn the laws and become scribes and clergy. That was their job. The people subsidized the Levite priests directly and through the offerings to the Temple. It has subsequently always been the royal priesthood's duty to understand power, both exoteric and esoteric, in order to support the king, pharaoh, emperor, and together to exercise and maintain control over the masses. Due to this royal connection, the priesthood has always suffered from nepotism and the selfish hoarding of useful information; after all, knowledge is power.

At the age of 23, Eugenio Pacelli was ordained a priest on Easter Sunday, 1899, by a family friend, Bishop Francesco di Paola Cassetta, the vice regent of Rome. Two years later, at the recommendation of another family friend, Cardinal Vincenzo Vannutelli, Pacelli entered the Congregation for Extraordinary Ecclesiastical Affairs, a sub-office of the Vatican Secretariat of State.

With his pedigree, contacts and abilities, Pacelli's swift rise through the Church's hierarchy was assured. Within only five years of his ordination, Pacelli was chosen to assist Cardinal Pietro Gasparri in completely – and secretly – re-writing the

Church's canonical laws. The project would take twelve years to complete.

The fact that Pacelli was chosen personally by Pope Leo XIII to present a letter of condolence to England's King Edward VII due to the death of Queen Victoria in 1908 shows that Pacelli had "already been singled out for the fast track of promotion." (*Hitler's Pope* pg 32.)

Pacelli is further described as a "brilliant young Vatican lawyer, who collaborated in re-drafting the Church's laws in such a way as to grant future popes unchallenged domination from the Roman center." (*Hitler's Pope*, pg 6)

The move toward centralization of papal power had begun shortly before Eugenio Pacelli's birth, as the mid-19th century saw the abolishment of papal sovereignty with a global move toward separation of Church and State. Pope Pius IX called for a General Council, which turned into the Vatican Council of 1870; the largest in the Church's history, with over 700 bishops from all over the world in attendance. One of the main topics was the defense of religion from skepticism and disbelief. This led to the Pope being declared "Infallible," at least in ecclesiastical matters. And then in 1917, the publication of the Code of Canon Law provided the means of establishing, imposing and sustaining remarkable new top-down power relationship." (*Hitler's Pope* pg 6)

It should be remembered that the Roman Catholic Church, like all churches, is ultimately a business, a corporation, and its operation and structure must be viewed as such. It's just business. This is also true of every country and its government, including the Vatican.

The loss of some temporal power in the 19th century forced the Roman papal leadership to find, or create, new ways to maintain and regain the Church's influence globally. These machinations would lead the early 20th century popes into collusion with the rising powers of a new, secular Russia, a burgeoning U.S.A., and the European powers, out of which would explode German Nazism.

It's impossible to understand the rise of Nazism without understanding Hitler and the secret pseudo-religion he and his supporters believed would help them to create the world they envisioned.

Although raised Catholic, Adolph Hitler would eventually conspire to eradicate Christianity in any form, In Hitler Speaks, the author Hermann Raushning, states that "Hitler's goal was to stamp out Christianity in Germany root and branch. One is either a Christian or a German. You can't be both." (p. 55)

The overt causes of World War I are confusing and convoluted. Certainly Archbishop Pacelli did his part in the agitation; the treaty between Serbia and the Austro-Hungarian government that he negotiated in 1914 contributed directly to the tensions which led to the events that became the excuse for the declaration of war, i.e., the assassination of Archduke Ferdinand of Austria.

Through the turbulent 1920's Pacelli remained in Germany where he negotiated the Bavarian Concordat and then seemed to concentrate on humanitarian projects, including negotiating aid in the form of food shipments to Russia where there was no papal nuncio, and where all Christian churches were being persecuted. Additionally Pacelli, whose desire to see a unified Europe with the Roman Catholic Church at its head, pursued secret negotiations with the various countries with his purview.

In December 1929 Pacelli was made a Cardinal-Priest by Pope Pius XI, and a few months later Cardinal Secretary of State, a post he would hold until being named Pontiff in 1939.

The issue of Anti-Semitism, which will likely stain Pope Pius XII's pontificate forever, is an extremely complicated and sensitive one. The horrific manifestation during the early 20th century stemmed from a perverted 19th century social Darwinism, as well as traditional Christian antipathy toward the Jews, born partly out of belief that it was they who murdered the Christ.

Historically, Hitler was born illegitimately with the last name of "Schiklgruber," later changed to Hitler when his mother married Alois Hitler. However, Adolph had suspected (Ashkenazi) Jewish ties through his mother, Klara Poelzl, and also possibly through his supposed biological father, one of the famed Rothschilds, in whose home Adolph's mother had been working when she got pregnant.

Those who would defend Pius XII's pontificate cannot deny the results that the Reich Concordat – which Pacelli negotiated with Hitler in 1933 – had upon the Jewish population in Europe.

The treaty specifically imposed new Church law upon German Catholics, in exchange for generous privileges to Catholic schools and clergy. In return the German Catholic Church withdrew its massive parliamentary political party, clearing the way for the rise of the Nazi Party, and most importantly, giving the perception of papal endorsement of the Nazi's and their policies to the world Catholics. Although Pacelli would categorically deny Hitler's assertions in a two-part article of the papal newsletter that the concordat implied moral approval, Hitler would later state publicly that the door to the "Final Solution" regarding the elimination of the Jews, and other sub-human races, had been flung wide open by the agreement not to interfere.

Both anti-Judaism and anti-Semitism, have been promulgated by Roman Catholic church authorities throughout history, and its complicity during world War II with the Nazi's attempted extermination of all Jews, both Ashkenazi and Sephardic, as well as other people's not filling the Nordic Aryan ideal, is undeniable. However, the Allied forces Command also knew by the middle of 1942 that Jews and others were being systematically murdered and they too are complicit through their non-action.

Nazi International: The Nazi's Postwar Plan to Control Finance, Conflict, Physics and Space by Joseph P. Farrell, details the escape from Nazi Germany of the top Nazi leaders including Reichsleiter Martin Bormann and Gestapo Chief Heinrich Muller as well as Hitler.

The book tells how the Nazis supported Juan Perón in his takeover of Argentina in the 1940's, and in return how Perón, through the Roman Catholic Church helped the Nazis – as many as 30,000 – to escape from Germany at the end of World War II.

However, an older book, The Bunker by James P. O'Donnell, weaves a compelling argument that, in the last days of the war, Hitler and his new bride, Eva Braun, indeed committed suicide together and their bodies were burned in effigy, and then were buried just outside the famous bunker. The new book, *Nazi International*, adds updated information, showing how doubles could have been used to fake his death, and later escape global justice.

Whether the real Hitler escaped or not remains an intriguing question, but he is most certainly dead by now, unless by some feat of magic...? The point remains that the Church appears to be directly complicit in the escape of some of the most notorious criminals in human history, and, since by the 20th century the office of the Pope had become the undisputed master of the Church's hierarchy, due in no small part to Eugenio Pacelli, Pope Pius XII, he too must stand accused.

In the 1964 book *Pius XII and the Third Reich*, the authors, Saul Friedlander and Charles Fullman, conclude that "The Sovereign Pontiff seems to have had a predilection for Germany which does not appear to have diminished by the nature of the Nazi regime and which was not disavowed up to 1944." (p. 376)

Additionally in *Hitler's Pope*, the author also tells of known suppressed documents, including one known as "the Riegner Memorandum," which came from a local

Church priest to a senior Church official, and which described what the Nazis were doing to the Jews in France, Romania, Poland, Slovakia, Croatia, etc.

Conversely, in the same book, Cornwall also mentions a 1967 book by Pinchas E. Lapide, *The Last Three Popes and the Jews*, where the author, an Israeli consul in Milan in the 1960's, claims to have ransacked several Jewish historical archives and found details of Vatican assistance to Jews during World War II. In fact, Lapide "calculated that Pius XII, directly, and indirectly, saved the lives of some 860,000 Jews." (Hitler's Pope p. 378)

There are more dirty little secrets to tell during Pacelli's years with the church that are rarely delved into, including the support from and reciprocation to "organized crime," especially the Italian and Sicilian "Cosa Nostra."

In the early 1900's, the rise of a phenomenon truly began, with several New York City youths, including a Sicilian, and two Jews. Their respective names were Charles "Lucky" Luciano, Benjamin "Bugsy" Seigel, and Meyer Lansky; together these men would go on to create "Murder Incorporated," and the five "New York Mafia Families," effectively taking over organized crime in America.

The New York crime families were known to be very generous to the Catholic Church, so, when Lucky Luciano was convicted for murder and facing prison and then fled U.S. jurisdiction, going to Naples, Italy, where he was fully welcomed by the Roman Catholic Church, no one was surprised.

Perhaps Eugenio Pacelli was a fallible man, who found himself in the extremely bad position of not wanting to anger the Nazis into further atrocities and so he chose not to act.

British historian, Owen Chadwick, in his serious and extended portrait of the wartime Pacelli wrote "so far from being a cool (which I suppose, implies cold-blooded and inhumane) diplomatist, Pius XII was the most warmly humane, kind, generous, sympathetic (and incidentally saintly) character that it has been my privilege to meet in the course of a long life. I know that his sensitive nature was acutely and incessantly alive in the tragic volume of human suffering caused by the war and, without the slightest doubt, he would have been ready and glad to give his life to redeem humanity from its consequences. And this is quite irrespective of nationality or faith. But what could he effectively do?" (*Hitler's Pope* p. 381)

Author Huber Wolf, in *Pope and Devil: The Vatican Archives and the third Reich*, asks, "In the final analysis, was the pact with the Devil, which was motivated primarily by concern for the salvation of the Faithful, responsible for Rome's silence in the face of the persecution and systematic murder of millions of Jews?"

As previously mentioned, Pope Pius XII is being processed for canonization as a Saint of the Roman Catholic church, to which the author of *Hitler's Pope* responds and ends his book with, "I am convinced that the cumulative verdict of history shows him (Pacelli) to be not a saintly exemplar for future generations, but a deeply flawed human being from whom Catholics, and our relations with other religions, can best profit by expressing our sincere regret." (p. 384)

By Daante, a retired Air Force security specialist, author, poet and lyricist.

Nearing the end of an era many Nazi secrets went to the grave with
Pope Pius XII

Hitler with Archbishop
Another inconvenient truth

GERMAN SOLDIERS RALLIED BY CHURCHES

Catholic Churches were reported to have published many articles explaining the duties of German soldiers fighting in the defense of their country and to fight in the spirit of St. Michael for a German victory and a just peace.

During World War II, the archangel Michael was shown brandishing a battle sword and piercing a dragon with a holy lance on the front page of Catholic newspapers.

The Catholic bishops of Germany issued a pastoral letter stating:
"In this decisive hour we admonish our Catholic soldiers to do their duty in obedience to the Fuhrer and be ready to sacrifice their whole individuality..."

If the Catholic Church had problems with Hitler, it could have told its clergy to tell the faithful, in the confessional if not the pulpit, that any participation in the holocaust was immoral. The Church could have stopped issuing glowing recommendations of the administration and prayers for the success of Hitler's war effort.

Instead, the bishops of Germany and the Vatican sent all kinds of signals to the faithful that Hitler was a fellow Roman Catholic leader who was to be respected and obeyed. They celebrated Hitler's birthday with the ringing of bells throughout the country and prayed regularly for God's blessing on Hitler's war.

Source: R. and H.; US State Department documents

Bishops saluting Hitler
Never failing to fall in line

Priests Helping Fascists

Only months after Pope John Paul II apologized for the Catholic Church's silence during the Holocaust, the Vatican was again under scrutiny for its possible role in aiding the escape of pro-Nazi Croatian leaders after the war.

A report by the State Department says Catholic priests in Rome helped Croatian leaders, who sent up to 700,000 Serbs, Jews and others to death camps, to hide in Italy after the war and eventually flee to South America. The Catholic Church lies have been and are continuing to be exposed by INS documents, CIA and state department reports that have been released through the freedom of information actions which cover the Ratlines, hidden gold and collusion with the US government itself. The reports usually validate the accusers and not the apologists.

Source: R. and H. US State Department documents

The Catholic Church and "Kristallnacht"

"The hands off policy of the Church stood out especially in the fateful days of November 1938. The Nazis, in the wake of the assassination of a German embassy official in Paris by a seventeen-year old Jewish boy, unloosed a pogrom that has entered history under the name "Kristallnacht" (the night of glass). During the night of November 9-10 the display windows of Jewish shops over Germany were shattered, about 20,000 male Jews were arrested and herded into concentrations camps, 191 synagogues were set fire and 76 others completely destroyed...thirty six Jews were killed during the well-organized action; a much larger number succumbed to the sadistic treatment meted out to them in Buchenwald and other concentrations camps, where they were imprisoned. (The reaction of the Catholic Church was that) the bishops remained silent in the face of the burning temples and the first round-up of the Jews."

Lewey

By the summer of 1945, we would expect to have seen church proclamations vehemently denouncing Nazism and condemning the murder of the Jews. But we do not. This is one strong indicator of the attitudes held during previous years.

Editor

> *"The hottest places in hell are reserved for those, who in time of great moral crisis, maintain their neutrality"...*
> **Dante**

The Vatican's Triple Crown: control over church, government and state.

Eugenio Pacelli (later became Pope Pius XII) signs Reichsconcordat Concordat with Nazi Germany in 1933. In 1929 Pope Pius XI signed a similar concordat with the fascist Prime Minister of Italy Benito Mussolini known as the Lateran Treaty.

Swastika
The Swastika is actually a form of the Cross.

YUGOSLAVIA HOLOCAUST

1929 – January 6, 1929 in an attempt to hold the federation of multicultural parties together, parliament was dissolved, political parties were banned, local self-government was abolished, and laws were decreed against sedition, terrorism and propagation of communism. A Serb was made premier and the country was officially changed to the "Kingdom of Yugoslavia".

1931 – The Royal dictatorship in Yugoslavia was ended and limited democracy was re-introduced. Croatian discontent grew when the new leader of the Croatian Peasant Party was arrested and jailed for terrorist activities.

1932 – Andre Pavelic, exiled Croatian representative accepted an offer from Mussolini to relocate to Italy, where he began to refashion the Croat Youth Movement into the terrorist group that would come to be known as the Ustase (Insurrection). The Ustase begin a campaign of bombings within Yugoslavia.

1934 – An Ustase agent assassinated King Aleksander of Yugoslavia while visiting in Marseille, France. Italy arrested Pavelic and other leaders of the Ustase but refused to extradite them to face the death sentences passed in absentia in France. Several months later they were released.

1939 – Germany invaded Poland and began the Second World War.

Yugoslavia attempted to remain neutral but succumbed to the mounting pressure of Germany to join the Axis powers (Germany, Italy and Japan).

1941 – March 24th Yugoslavia signed the Tripartie Pact. Two days later junior officers of the Yugoslavia Air Force staged a *coup d'etat* and overthrew the government, unleashing a wave of anti-German demonstrations across Belgrade, the national capital. Germany responds on April 6 in a "blitzkrieg". Axis forces invaded Yugoslavia.

Pavelic called on Croatian soldiers to mutiny. "Use your weapons against the Serbian soldiers and officers, we are fighting shoulder to shoulder with our German and Italian allies."

April 10 – Slavko Kvaternik, the Ustase leader in Croatia proclaimed the "Independent State of Croatia" (Nezavisna Drzava Hrvatska –NDH), which incorporated Croatia, Bosnia-Herzegovina and Syrmia. Pavelic returned to Croatia ending 12 years of exile.

The Germans recognized NDH, occupied most of Serbia and annexed northern Slovenia. Italy took southern Slovia, Dalmatia, joined Kosovo with Albania, and occupied Montenegro. Hungary occupied Vojvodina, Slovenia and Croatian border regions. Bulgaria took Macedonia and part of southern Serbia.

The Germans agreed to establish Pavelic Poglavnik (Chieftan) of NDH. Pavelic immediately declared the primary goal of his government to be the "purification of Croatia" and the elimination of "alien elements." The "ethnic cleansing" of two million Serbs, Jews and Roma began.

Pavelic's Ustase storm troopers employed forced religious conversion, deportation and murder to achieve their goal of an ethnically pure Croatia. Their mantra was "Kill a third, expel a third and convert a third."

Upon joining the Ustase, the novitiate was immediately indoctrinated with its mystery and authority. The initiation rite required that one swear before a crucifix framed by a dagger and a revolver an oath promising total devotion:

"I swear before God and all that I hold sacred that I will observe the laws of this society and will execute without conditions all that I am ordered to do by the poglavnik."

I will scruptously preserve all secrets entrusted to me, and I will beray nothing, no matter what it might be.

I swear to fight in the Ustase army for a free Croat state under the absolute control of the poglavik. Failing in my oath, I shall accept death as the penalty. God help me, Amen"

Pavelic hoped to transfer the intensity of the Croatian Roman Catholic Church to a political movement. The devotion, duty and blood-letting which the Ustase promised, would become a HOLY WAR to create a Croatian State, a state which would be both separate and Roman Catholic.

The Ustase was supported by the Croatian Catholic Church, including the Archbishop of Sarajevo, Ivan Saric. Some Franciscan priests enlisted in the Ustase and participated in the violence.

On New Year's Day 1943 Pope Pius XII gave his blessing to Pavelic:

"Everything you have expressed so warmly in your name and in the name of the Croatian Catholic Church we return gracefully and give you and the whole Croatian people our apostolic blessing." (Dedijer p. 115)

Right from the very beginning, the Vatican knew what was happening in Croatia, and certainly known to Pius XII when he greeted Pavelic in the Vatican – just four days after the genocide at Gline. On this visit, Pavelic had a "devotional" audience with Pus XII, and the Vatican granted de facto recognition of fascist Croatia as a "bastion against communism".

Thus, it can be argued, that the Catholic Cardinals of the Vatican were accomplices of the Holocaust in Yugoslavia and the extermination of the country's Serbs, Jews and other citizens. Many members of the Croatian Catholic clergy took part in the Holocaust.

September 1941: An Ustase run concentration camp was opened in Jasenovac. Up to 200,000 Serbs, Jews, Gypsies and political prisoners were killed in Jasenovac. Along with the Ustase, Catholic clergy staffed the camp and participated in the executions.

1942: British Prime Minister Winston Churchill, US President Franklin Delano Roosevelt, Soviet Leader Joseph Stalin and the King of Yugoslavia agree to give their full support to the Partisans.

1945: The Partisans capture Sarajevo and Ustase leaders flee to Austria. Pavelic moves on to Rome, living in the city under the protection of the Catholic Church and with the knowledge of the Allied Forces who fail to arrest him.

1947: The American Counter-intelligence Corps office in Rome reported the "... Pavelic's contacts are so high and his present position is so compromising to the Vatican that any extradition of Subject would deal a staggering blow to the Roman Catholic Church."

1948: Pavelic moved to a monastery near Castel Gandolfo southeast of Rome, where he lived disguised as a priest until Vatican operatives smuggled him to Buenos Aires, Argentina. In Buenos Aires Pavelic revived the Ustase movement and acted as Security Advisor to Argentine President Juan Peron. An estimated 7,200 members of the Ustase found refuge in Argentina between 1946 and 1948.

Meanwhile in Yugoslavia, the Communists took control. Josip Broz Tito headed the Communist Party, the government and the armed forces.

Over 200 priests and nuns were charged with participating with the Ustase atrocities and were executed by Tito's government.

September, 1946: Archbishop Alojzije Stepinac, head of the Croatian Catholic church, was sentenced to 16 years in jail for complicity with the Pavelic government. He served five years before being released.

"Both the USA and the Vatican…wished to help the flight of war criminals from Europe, each with its own objectives. Whereas the USA wanted to rescue them to carry out political operations against Soviet Russia and the oncoming Cold War, the Vatican wanted to help former political and religious supporters whom it had blessed during the reign of the Nazis. The basic motivation of such strange Vatican-USA fellowship…[was] derived by the necessity…to recruit, as energetically and as quickly as possible, trustworthy anti-Russian, anti-communist battalions ready to fight against Bolshevik Russia. And where could the Vatican and the State Department find such ready, dedicated, anti-communist recruits, if not in the rank and file of…the fleeing war criminals now seeking asylum in the Americas and the USA? The fugitives…were now ready to …help the USA fight Soviet Russia, her former ally.   Baron Avro Mahattan *"The Vatican's Holocaust,"* 1986 Ozark Books, pp139-142.

Source R. and H.; the Editors; US State Department Documents and International Press releases; inspired by Wikipedia (Retrieved August 16, 2010)

AN ALL TELLING CASE STUDY
Andrija Artukovic:
The Highest Ranking Nazi War Criminal to be brought to the U.S. by the Catholic Church

Andrija Artukovic

Sometimes in history there are stories that say it all. Stories that reveal the true nature of the beast – the story of Andrija Artukovic is one such tale that reveals the evil, the complicity, the hypocrisy, the socio-pathetic and self-serving nature of the Catholic Church and its popes, bishops and priests.

111

Andrija Artukovic was described as the "Adolph Eichmann" of Croatia", who boasted he could take care of the "Jewish problem faster than Hitler's Gestapo in Germany." And he was right! He created a river of blood for the Croatian Ustase as the Minister of the Interior. He oversaw the Industry of death for such concentration camps as Jasenovac. Artukovic's interior reign brought destruction to 800,000 Jews, Serbs, Romas and other non-Catholics. He rightly earned the name, while introducing an added "garrotting" (public hanging) to his river of blood.

Artukovic was also known as the "Himmler of the Balkans". Before his death in a Yugoslavian prison, convicted on numerous counts of crimes against humanity, this monster was protected by the Franciscans in Orange County, California, the Knights of Columbus, the bishops of Westminster Church, Vatican henchmen in Orange County, California, and three U.S. Representatives from California, – including Richard M. Nixon. As with many crimes by the Catholic Church throughout history, they are still in denial of their cover-ups, complicity and illegal activities.

The enormity of Artukovic's crimes defies description. From 1941 to 1945 he coordinated mass murder at an unparalleled rate under the watchful eye of Andre Pavelic, Archbishop Stepinac and the Vatican. Stepinac was canonized by the Vatican.

After working hand and glove with the Franciscans and Catholic bishops and priests in their brutal campaign of ethnic cleansing for Hitler, Artukovic, the hunter was suddenly the hunted when the 3rd Reich was defeated. He was on the run with thousands of war criminals aided by Pope Pius XII's Ratlines, who was well on his way to becoming beatified by the Catholic Church.

Unlike many war criminals who went to South America, Artukovic ended up in the United States. He was the highest ranking Nazi war criminal to do so. The Catholic Ratline smuggled him out of Yugoslavia by hiding him in various Catholic churches, monasteries and safe-houses via Austria, Switzerland, Britain and Ireland. He was protected by the Los Angeles cardinal who received the Medal of the Rose from the Fascist Franco, and who continued to write letters of support against his extradition.

He entered the U.S. on July 16, 1948 under a false tourist visa in the name of Alois Anich, a disguised Catholic priest. His false identity was issued by the Catholic Church in 1946. His war partner, Andre Pavelic went on to South America and was institutionalized as a war hero. The war criminal Archbishop Stepinac has streets and schools in Cleveland Ohio are named after him.

Artukovic headed to California where he joined his brother, John, and members of the Radovich construction family in Los Angeles. He was welcomed by a committee of Croatian Catholics, the Franciscans, the right-wing Archbishop of Los Angeles, a coalition of John Birch society U.S. representatives and a future president of the United States. He hid out in Surf Side and Westminster under the auspices of Representatives James Utt and John George Schmitz who raised thousands of dollars to keep him from justice in Yugoslavia.

The Los Angeles Dioceses headed by Cardinal Timothy Manning, who received the Franco fascist Medal of the Rose, wrote letters to the INS and Los Angeles Times in 1986 strongly objecting to his extradition and praising him as a fine man.

At his sentencing Artokovich's words were, "I am innocent, my conscience is clear."

The same words used by other evildoers and enablers in the Mother Church.

It makes one wonder about the dark phenomena of denial and the power of a religious belief system that manifests into death and destruction.

By Tim C. Leedom

Good read: *Wanted: The Search for Nazis in America,* by Howard Blum, Greenwich, CT. Fawcett Books, 1977.

"The only mistake he made was he was on the wrong side."

Mantra repeated many times by Artukovic supporters.

After fighting to liberate Europe from fascism for three and a half years, I am always sickened when I hear of the Ratline and the Church's involvement. It says more to me about the Church that they didn't disavow the Nazis and their involvement, complicity and cover-ups. That's the Church's real nature.

Retired U.S. Army 2nd Lt. European Campaign

The Iron Fist and the Bloody Hands

LETTERS FROM US DEPARTMENT STATE ARCHIVES
Public Domain United States of America State Department; Nixon Library

Letter from Artukovic
Letter from Artukovic's brother
Letter to President Nixon from Rt. Rev Raymond J. O'Flaherty
Letter to President Nixon from Rt. Rev. James E. Dolan
Letter from President Nixon to Rt. Rev. O'Flaherty
Letter from President Nixon to Rt. Rev. James E. Dolan
Letter to President Nixon from Croatian Catholic Union of U.S.A.

P R O   M E M O R I A

Biography.

— Pro —
B y
A. A.

I was born November 29th, 1899 at Klobuk, Hercegovina, Croatia, (Then Austrian-Hungarian Monarchy), where I completed my elementary education.
I attended the Franciscan High School at Sireki Brieg, Hercegovina, through eight years and in the year 1919 I graduated from the State High School at Mostar, Hercegovina, (then already a part of the new state of the Serbs, Croats and Slovenes). From 1919 to 1925 I attended the University of Zagreb, capital of Croatia, studied law and received there my doctors degree. The same year I fulfilled nine months of my military training at Mostar, and after I had passed my examination before a Military Court at Belgrade, I became a Sergeant.
In 1928 after two months more training at the Supreme Military Court at Belgrade I became a military judge as a reservist. After completing my military training I practiced law partially in Zagreb and partially at Gospie, province of Lika, until I had completed my apprenticeship. Then I passed my attorney's examination before the State Board in Zagreb. In 1928 I opened my own offices-of-law as an attorney and remained there until the year 1932 (in Lika, Gospie).

My rearing and education as a youth was based on Catholic principles.
These principles I have believed in and followed throughout my life.

Pending my university studies, I was an organized member of the catholic cultural and educational organization called " Demagoj ".

All the university students of my time were enrolled in one of the three following organixtaions :

(1) The Croatian catholic cultural and educational lodge "Demagoj"(named after the famous Croatian knight, who ruled in Croatia about 865).
The title alone describes the programme.

(2) The Croatian academic lodge " Eugen Quaternik " (named after the Croatian national martyr Dr. Eugen Quaternik). Students with pure national interest were enrolled in this organization.

(3) The Croatian academic lodge " Matija Gubec " (named after the paysant's leader and martyr of the same name). In this lodge students were organized on a basis of class – ideology (class resentments and class prejudice) and panslav ideas were characteristic for their program.

As an attorney in Gospie until 1932 I was a leading member and president of all the Croatian cultural institutions, for example: Napredak, Radica, etc.

The foundation of the new " State of the Serbs, Croats and Slovenes " by the Treaty of Versailles placed the Croatian people in an intolerable situation as it had never happened before. Croatia lost by one single stroke of the pen all the attributes as a state, which she had preserved until then without interruption through 1300 years. The Croatian people are one of the oldest in Europe.

pAvelic
lookup

≈ 2 ≈

These people combatted heroically and victoriously the Huns and Avares and defended through 500 years the whole western civilization from the armies of the huge Ottoman empire, which threatened to overpower Europe. (See Chapter 1 of the enclosed pamphlet "The Tragedy of a Nation"). These Croatian people, which not only for its own sake, but for the sake of Europe bled so long and so much, was pressed by force and against his own will in an unnatural and artificial state in spite of the fourteen points of President Wilson, especially of the point concerning the self-determination of the nations. It is psychologically well to understand that this act terrified the freedom loving Croatian people.

The Croatian people never recognized the state of the Serbs, Croats and Slovenes with the Karageorgevic Dynasty. The constitution was put into force without the consent of the Croatian people

The Croatian people was then organized in two political parties: on the one side the "Croatian Right Party" headed by Dr. Pavelic and on the other side the "Croatian Peasant's Party" headed by Stjepan Radic.

The Croatian Right Party, to which I belonged, was a non-class movement, which included in its program as a main point the restitution of the independent state of Croatia.

The Peasant's Party wanted to establish a Peasant's republic, with class privileges and panslav ideas.

As a result of the growing organized terror from Belgrade the leaders of the two parties consented to write many and many memorandums addressed to the League of Nations in Geneva, but without result. So Stjepan Radic went himself around to all the capitals of Europe trying to secure support of the leading political authorities in obtaining self-determination for the Croatian people. This as well he tried without any success. So, hethought, the only way to come to any result at all would be to go to Belgrade and to fight there before the parliament for the rights of the Croatian people. This was in 1925. But, in 1928 he was deadly wounded in this same parliament, where he wanted to fight honestly for the rights of his people. He was attacked rascally and criminally shot to death by the Serbian Deputy Punisha Rachich. Two other Croatian Deputies, Pavle Radich and Gjure Basrichek were killed on the spot. (See Chapter 11.) The last words of the dying Stjepan Radich were " Don't go any more to Belgrade ". The successor in the leadership of the Peasant's Party was Dr. Macek, who now lives in Washington.

After the assassination in the parliament of Belgrade in defiance of the Treaty of Versailles King Alexander abolished in 1929 the constitution, on which he had sworn himself, annihilated the name of the state, known until then as the State of the Serbs, Croats and Slovenes, and proclaimed his dictatorship and introduced unlawfully the new name of"Yugoslavia". With this infringement he violated an article of the Treaty of Versailles. At this time Dr. Pavelic from the Croatian Right Party and Dr. Krnjevic and Ing. Kosutic from the Croatian Peasant's Party went into exile.

As a lawyer and a patriot I was morally pledged to defend my compatriots

116

3

against the terror raised by the Yugoslav authorities and to try to get honest treatment for them. Already, then, I caused with this attitude the disapproval of the Yugoslav authorities.

The growing oppression led finally in 1932 to a popular insurrection in the province of Lika. The terror which followed the suppression of this popular insurrection was unbearable. I decided to leave my native country and went into exile in the company of the Croatian Deputy Marko Dosen (the last was then 75 years old). After our arrival in Italy we approached Dr. Pavalis and joined his movement, with the aim to contribute to the liberation of our people. I decided then to devote my work to the collecting of documents concerning the history of the Croatian nation. I visited for this purpose from October 1932 to October 1934 different libraries in Italy, Austria and also in England. In Austria, I lived, with the knowledge of the Austrian authorities under the assumed name of David Arnaut. I had to do it to protect my life from the persecutions which the Serbs started to organize even outside of their country against Croatian patriots. (Assassination of Colonel Luich in Karlsbad, etc.). Although I lived under this assumed name, Serbian agents learned of my residence and the Yugoslav government asked the Austrian Government for my extradition, with the statement that I raised the popular insurrection of 1932. The Austrian authorities refused to do that.

October 1934 King Alexander of Yugoslavia was assassinated in Mardeilles. I was then in London. This incident enabled the Yugoslav Government to commit monstrous abuses of the international law. Misrepresenting the true facts and making false accusations the Yugoslav Government persuaded all European Governments to persecute every single Croatian patriot.

Without any other reason the English authorities repealed my permit to stay. When I entered France I was detained in Diappe, later arrested and brought to Paris. There I was detained for three months. The Yugoslav Government got information that the French Government was ready to release me, so they renewed their demand of extradition, repeating their false accusations against me (concerning the popular insurrection of 1932). The French Government complied with the Yugoslav request under certain terms only. The Yugoslav Government gave written promise to keep to these terms (but later they broke it). So I was extradited in January 1935.

I was detained fifteen months in Belgrade. In April 1936 I was brought in a special court for the security of the state, and, after a trial of three days, I was acquitted of any guilt. This acquittal pronounced by the highest possible authority proves that all the false accusations against me, which the Yugoslav Government Spread during two years over Europe, were nothing else than a bunch of malicious, ugly and insulting lies.

I respectfully ask the reader of this to form for himself a judgement as to the amount of super-human sufferings, tortures and humiliations which I had to bear for the only reason that I loved my country and my people.

After being discharged I went back to Gospic, where the Cetniks, Serbian terrorists, (about Cetniks see Chapter V), organized my assassination. Trying

117

— 4 —

to accomplish their plan, they killed instead of me the 73 years old Croatian Deputy Karlo Brkljackich, who had come to visit and welcome me.

After the failure of this attack against my life, I went on the advice of my friends, to Austria into exile for the second time. Invited by my friends Dr. Perač, Dr. Jelic, and Dr. Lorković I came to Germany in 1936 with the purpose to improve my health. There I got in touch with the U. S. Consulate to obtain an immigrant Visa.

At the same time the German Government conducted confidential negotiations with the Yugoslav Government, (see Chapter 111). The consequence of these negotiations we felt, when the illreputed Secret German Police (GESTAPO) detained us. With Dr. Jelic and Dr. Lorkovic I remained six months an internee of the Gestapo until Dr. Lorkovic and I succeeded in escaping in 1937.

From there I came to Hungary where I remained until April 1941, the date of the resurrection of Croatia.

After the Collapse of Yugoslavia and the proclamation of the Independent State of Croatia in April 1941, (see Chapter 111). I returned to my native country. I became a member of the Croatian Government and held the office of the Secretary of Interior, later that of the Secretary of Justice, and finally until May 1945 I became the Keeper of the Privy Seal and President of the State's Council. In spit of the vehement German and Italian oppression against my native country and on our government, I was never a fascist or nazist. I worked only for the welfare of my native country and my people, and fought ardently against communism, which since 1941 became the biggest danger for the biological existence of the Croatian people. I was never sworn in by Hitler or Mussolini, but only by the head of the Croatian State. I respectfully ask to read Chapters lV, V, Vl, Vll and Vlll about the attitude of the Croatian Government during the war. As for the rest, the diaries of Goebbels and Ciano reveal the insubordination of the Croatian Government and people. Besides that, if necessary, the following persons could be asked to testify for my attitude as a member of the Croatian Government:

Mons. Ramino Marcone OFB, Papal Legate, Rome, Vatican.
Dr. Giuseppe Massucchi OFB, Secretary of the Papal Legate, Rome.
Mr. Andre Gailliard, during the war Consul General of France in
    Zagreb, now Consul in Warsaw, Poland.
Dr. Josip Haspudic, my former Secretary, now residing at
    1432 No.20th. Street, Milwaukee 5, Wisconsin
Rev. Mario Matic OFM
Rev. Dr. Ignatius Jurkovic OFM
Rev. Dr. Vendelin Vasilj OFM
Rev. Dr. Ive Sivric OFM
    The four above mentioned priests lived during the war in Croatia
and their residence is now, 4851 Drexel Blvd., Chicago 15, Illinois
Very Rev. Dr. David Zrno OFM, commissary of the Croatian Franciscans
in the U.S.A.

(If necessary more witnesses could be produced.)
                    the
After the fall of/Croatian State in 1945 I had a narrow escape from the
Communists, (see Chapter Vll). I succeeded to fight my way through into Austria,

5

There I was kept by the English Occupation Army in a Detention Camp at Spittal/Drau. After two months of investigations I was discharged. I lived then in Austria until November 1946. From there I went to Switzerland, where I assumed, for my personal security, the name of Alois Anich. I remained in Switzerland until July 15th, 1947. There I obtained, with the knowledge of the Swiss Department of Justice, a certificate of identity for myself and my family, which made it possible for us to travel to Ireland under this assumed name. In Ireland I remained with my family until July 15th, 1949. According to our Swiss certificates of identity, which had expired by then, we obtained Irish Certificates of Identity and received on them visas to enter the U.S.A. as temporary visitors. We entered the U.S.A. on the T. W. A. Flight No. 903 the 16th of July at New York, La Guardia Airport. The 18th of July I came to Los Angeles where I met my brother after eighteen years for the first time again.

I make this application with the aim to become a citizen of this country, because my brother and I wish to remain together for the rest of our lives, considering the well-being of our two families.

Los Angeles, Calif., 27th of December 1949.

Andrija Artukovich

P. & J. ARTUKOVICH, INC.

General Contractors

13305 South San Pedro St.   PLymouth 5-1147 – 5-1148
Los Angeles 61, California

April 17, 1951

Honorable Richard Nixon
United States Senate
Committee on Labor & Public Welfare
Washington, D.C.

Honorable Senator:

I received your letter of February 27th, 1951 and was glad
to know that the organization of the new Congress has been
completed and that you have finally acquired a full secretarial staff.

It is a great pleasure to hear that all of the people of
the United States have been asking you how it was possible
to run up with an overwhelming majority in our state of
California. Please accept my personal congratulations for
your election and secretarial staff.

I hope that I will be visiting in Washington, D.C. during
the month of May. It is not necessary to express my personal
satisfaction if I could see and meet with you at your office
in Washington, D.C.

In the meantime accept my personal regards and I remain,

                    Yours very truly,

                    P. & J. ARTUKOVICH, INC.

                    John M. Artukovich, President

JMA:nk

120

Keep here
plus
+

Detroit, Michigan
September 7, 1951

Hon. Richard Nixon
United States Senate
Washington, D. C.

Dear Sir:

An extradition hearing is to be held in Los Angeles on September 10 to determine whether or not Andrija Artukovich, a Jugoslav displaced person, shall be returned to his native country, under terms of a treaty executed in 1902 between the United States and the then Serbian state.

Mr. Artukovich is in the United States on temporary visitor's status, having entered this country from the Irish Free State at La Guardia Field, New York, on July 16, 1948. His extradition case number is 9-9283-18 U.S.C., Section 3184, Serbian Treaty May 17, 1902.

His situation has been brought to my attention by persons known to me personally to be of sound and discerning judgment and unimpeachable loyalty. In their judgment Mr. Artukovich, as a devoted Catholic and a man who has suffered much in opposing Communism in his native land, is deserving of every consideration. He is of the caliber of man our country needs, and should not be extradited, particularly under the terms of a treaty, the other party of which (viz., the then Serbian state) no longer exists.

His extradition would mean for him a trial similar to those with which we are familiar in communist controlled regimes and certain death by reason of his active opposition to communistic ideologies.

May I request your interest, in justice, in this situation and your efforts in behalf of Mr. Artukovich.

Respectfully yours,

(Rt. Rev.) *Raymond J. O'Flaherty*
Director of Charities, Archdiocese of Los Angeles

STATE OF MICHIGAN)
COUNTY OF WAYNE) SS.

On this 7th day of September 1951, before me, a Notary Public, in and for said county and state, personally appeared *Raymond J. O'Flaherty* who makes oath that the matters set forth in the foregoing statement are true.

[signature]

Notary Public - Wayne County
Michigan

My commission expires: 10-26-54

121

Keep
here +

Detroit, Michigan
September 7, 1951

Hon. Richard Nixon
United States Senate
Washington, D. C.

Dear Sir:

An extradition hearing is to be held in Los Angeles on September 10 to
determine whether or not Andrija Artukovich, a Jugoslav displaced person,
shall be returned to his native country, under terms of a treaty executed
in 1902 between the United States and the then Serbian state.

Mr. Artukovich is in the United States on temporary visitor's status,
having entered this country from the Irish Free State at La Guardia Field,
New York, on July 16, 1948. His extradition case number is 9-9283-18 U.S.C.,
Section 3184, Serbian Treaty May 17, 1902.

His situation has been brought to my attention by persons known to me
personally to be of sound and discerning judgment and unimpeachable
loyalty. In their judgment Mr. Artukovich, as a devoted Catholic and a
man who has suffered much in opposing Communism in his native land, is
deserving of every consideration. He is of the caliber of men our country
needs, and should not be extradited, particularly under the terms of a
treaty, the other party of which (viz., the then Serbian state) no longer
exists.

His extradition would mean for him a trial similar to those with which we
are familiar in communist controlled regimes and certain death by reason
of his active opposition to communistic ideologies.

May I request your interest, in justice, in this situation and your efforts in behalf of Mr. Artukovich.

Respectfully yours,

James E. Dolan

RT. Rev. James E. Dolan
Archdiocesan Director
Los Angeles, St. Vincent De Paul Society

STATE OF MICHIGAN)
COUNTY OF WAYNE) SS.

On this 7th day of September 1951, before me, a Notary Public, in and for
said county and state, personally appeared *James E. Dolan*,
who makes oath that the matters set forth in the foregoing statement
are true.

Notary Public - Wayne County
Michigan

My commission expires: 10-26-54

Nixon

September 11, 1951

Rt. Rev. Raymond J. O'Flaherty
Director of Charities
Archdiocese of Los Angeles
Los Angeles, California

Dear Rev. O'Flaherty:

     I wish to thank you for your letter of September 7 with reference to charges against Andre Artukovich which are presently the subject of investigation by the Immigration and Naturalization Service.

     This case, involving charges of illegal entry, comes entirely within the jurisdiction of the Immigration and Naturalization Service, and consequently does not come within the purview of Congress. However, I wish to assure you that if it appears, upon completion of the investigation, that proper consideration to the merits of Artukovich's case has not been given I shall seek a thorough Congressional review of the matter.

              Sincerely,

              Richard Nixon

RN:mp

123

Nixon

COPY

September 11, 1951

Rt. Rev. James E. Dolan
922 So. Detroit
Los Angeles 5, California

Dear Rev. Dolan:

I wish to acknowledge your letter of September 7 with reference to charges against Andre Artukovich which are presently the subject of investigation by the Immigration and Naturalization Service.

This case, involving charges of illegal entry, comes entirely within the jurisdiction of the Immigration and Naturalization Service, and consequently does not come within the purview of Congress. However, I wish to assure you that if it appears, upon completion of the investigation, that proper consideration to the merit of Artukovich's case has not been given I shall seek a thorough Congressional review of the matter.

Sincerely,

Richard Nixon

RN:mp

124

plus +

Keep

ALL FOR GOD AND PEOPLE

SVE ZA BOGA I NAROD

TELEPHONE GARY 7325

CROATIAN CATHOLIC UNION OF U.S.A.
A Fraternal Benefit Society
HRVATSKA KATOLIČKA ZAJEDNICA U S. D. AMERIKE
225 West 5th Avenue
GARY, INDIANA
Organized October 12, 1921

The Supreme Board of the Croatian Catholic Union of USA gathered at its meeting in Gary, Indiana, October 12th, 1951, on the occasion of its 30th Anniversary celebration, seriously discussed the matter of the demand of the Yugoslav regime of Tito that Dr. Andrija Artukovic, a prominent Croatian opponent of communism, be deported into the custody of Yugoslavia.

In the name of the Croatian Catholic Union of USA and its thousands of members who are loyal citizens of America, prepared to sacrifice everything and even their lives for American freedom and democracy, we protest against such requests of Yugoslavia's communistic regime that Dr. Artukovic be deported to Yugoslavia. We base our protests on the following reasons:

1. Dr. Andrija Artukovic committed no murders and crimes such as he is accused of by the Yugoslav regime; we know positively, that these accusations are purely political means of the Yugoslav communist dictatorship to rid itself of its political opponents in the world who oppose its communistic tactics in Croatia.

2. Dr. Artukovic is well known as an opponent of communism even from his youth.

3. The Yugoslav communist regime, as we know, first demended the deportation of Dr. Artukovic on the basis of political reasons, and when it failed to be successful, it changed the charges against him to murder and criminal action of which he was never guilty.

125

ALL FOR GOD AND PEOPLE

SVE ZA BOGA I NAROD

TELEPHONE GARY 7325

CROATIAN CATHOLIC UNION OF U.S.A.
A Fraternal Benefit Society
HRVATSKA KATOLICKA ZAJEDNICA U S. D. AMERIKE
125 West 5th Avenue
GARY, INDIANA
Organized October 12, 1921

— Page 2 —

4. The law of the kingdom of Serbia of 1902 can in no way be applied
to Dr. Artukovic since he never had been either a citizen or
resident of Serbia.

5. If free and democratic America permits Tito's Communistic
regime to take Dr. Artukovic, it will pave the way for allowing Tito's regime to seek the deportation of ANY and ALL of
its political enemies or opponents who raise their voices in
foreign lands against communism in Yugoslavia and other parts
of the world.

For the above reasons and for the sake of human rights, we appeal to our American
Officials not to deport Dr. Andrija Artukovic to Tito's Communist regime, for in no
case can a political rival deal fairly with his political opponent. If Dr. Artukovic
erred and broke any laws, let the unbiased, democratic American courts decide the
matter.

Holocaust Archive Picture
The war and the work of Andrija Artukovic

Archbishop Saric and Andre Pavelic
One escaped to South America the other to sainthood all with the blessing of the Roman Catholic Church

Archbishop Saric on His Pre-War Meetings with the Ustase

"I was with our Ustase in North and South America. The bishops there, Americans, Germans, Irish, Slovaks and Spaniards with whom I came into contact, all praised the Croat Ustase as good, self-sacrificing believers, as godly and patriotic people...How many times have I heard the Ustase ask where would they be without their priests!...I sang with the Ustase with all my heart and voice and we sang the song of 'Our Beautiful Homeland,' all with big tears in our eyes. And with eager hope in its beautiful, its sweet and its golden freedom, lifting urselves upwards to God, we prayed to the Almighty to guide and protect Andre Pavelic for the liberation of Croatia. The good God heard and, behold, he answered our cries and supplications."

Archbishop Saric

Ivan Saric was born to a Croatian family on September 27, 1871. He was ordained a priest on July 22, 1894.

Saric was a pioneer of Catholic Action and took particular interest in the Catholic press. He was the Archbishop of Sarajevo during World War II and used his Catholic newspapers as an outlet for his politics. He enthusiastically welcomed the new Ustase leadership of Andre Pavelic in 1941; supported the forced conversions of Orthodox Serbs to Roman Catholicism and became the mentor of Father Krunoslav Draganovic, an organizer of post World War II Ratlines.

Professor Robert Lee Wolf, in his book, *The Balkans in Our Times* referred to the Ustase:

"To some they offered the choice between conversion from Orthodoxy to Catholicism or instant death…It must be recorded as a historic fact that certain members of the Croatian hierarchy, notably Archbishop Sharich (Saric) of Sarajevo, endorsed this butchery."

Saric's newspaper published these words by Pitar Pajic:

"Until now God spoke through papal encyclicals, sermons, the Christian press… And they were deaf. Now God has decided to use other methods. He will prepare missions! World missions! They will be upheld not by priests but by army commanders led by Hitler. The sermons will be heard with the help of cannon, machine guns, tanks and bombers."

Source: R. and H.

Catholic bishops giving the Nazi salute
They have eyes but do not see.

129

Door at Auschwitz No 10 Block
The Church opened doors for Hitler his whole life.

"I know nothing"
Sgt. Schultz, Hogan's Heroes

Pope Benedict XVI

Pope Pius XII

Pope John Paul II

**From Nazi complicity to priest molestations
"they knew nothing."**

RATLINES MAP

Ratlines were systems of escape routes for Nazis at the end of World War II. The escape routes led to South America, the United States and Canada.

There were two primary routes: the first went from Germany to Spain then Argentina; the second from Germany to Rome to Genoa to South America. The routes developed independently but eventually came together. [1]

The origins of the first ratlines are connected to various developments in Vatican-Argentine relations before and during World War II. [2] As early as 1942 Monsignor Luigi Maglione contacted Argentine Ambassador Llobet, inquiring as to the "willingness of the government of the Argentine Republic to apply its immigrations law generously, in order to encourage at the opportune moment European Catholic immigrants to seek the necessary land and capital in our country."[3] According to historian Michael Phayer, "this was the innocent origin of what would become the Vatican ratline." [3]

Spain, not Rome, was the "first center of ratline activity that facilitated the escape of Nazis," although the exodus itself was planned within the Vatican. [4]

Charles Lescat, a French Catholic member of the Action Francaise (an organization suppressed by Pius XI and rehabilitated by Pius XII) and Pierre Daye, a Belgian with contacts in the Spanish government, were the first Spanish Ratline organizers. Lescat and Daye were the first to flee Europe with the help of French Cardinal Eugene Tisserant and Argentine Cardinal Antonio Caggiano [5].

According to Phayer, Pius XII "…preferred to see fascist war criminals on board ships to the New World rather than seeing them rotting in POW camps in zonal Germany."[6]

Mark Aarons and John Loftus, in their book *Unholy Trinity*, identify Bishop Alois Hudal as the first Catholic priest dedicated to establishing escape routes. Bishop Hudal was rector of a seminary for Austrian and German priests, and spiritual director of the "German-speaking resident in Italy." At the end of World War II, Hudal became active in ministering to German-speaking prisoners of war held in camps in Italy. In 1944 he was appointed as a representative to "visit the German-speaking civil internees in Italy".

Hudal used this position to aid the escape of wanted Nazi war criminals, including:
- Frantz Stangl, commanding officer at Treblinka
- Gustav Wagner , commanding officer at Sobibor

•Alois Brunner, in charge of deportations to German concentration camps
•Adolf Eichmann, later convicted and put to death for his monstrous crimes against humanity

Some of the war criminals were held in interment camps under false names without identity papers; others were hiding in Italy and sought Hudal out as his reputation for helping war criminals escape became widespread. According to Aarons and Loftus, Hudal supplied his escapees with money and false identity documents issued by the Vatican Refugee Organization.

The Vatican identity documents were not full passports but were the first step in obtaining full passage documents. They could be used to obtain a "displaced person" passport from the International Committee of the Red Cross, ICRC, which could be used to apply for a visa.

THE SAN GIROLAMO RATLINE:

The major Roman Ratline was operated by Franciscan priests under the direction of Father Krunoslav Draganovic headquartered in the San Giralomo Seminary College in Rome. It was a sophisticated operation linking Austria and Genoa as the final debarkation point to South America. This Ratline focused on helping Croatian Ustase members escape, most notably the Croatian dictator, Andre Pavelic. This line included:

•Father Vilim Cecelja, former Deputy Military Vicar to the Ustase
•Father Dragutin Kamder based in San Girolamo
•Father Dominik Mandic, General Economist or treasurer of the Franciscan Order
•Monsignor Karlo Petranovic based in Genoa

Vilim would make contact with those hiding in Austria and help them across the border to Italy. Kamber and Mandic would find lodging for them, and Draganovic would contact Petranovic with the number of berths required on ships to South America.

The San Girolamo Ratline was an open secret among the intelligence and diplomatic communities of Rome. In July, 1946, a U.S. State Department report listed war criminals that "…enjoy Church support and protection." British envoy, Francis Osborne, asked the high-ranking Vatican official, Domenico Tardini, for permission to allow British military police to raid Vatican institutions in Rome. Tardini not only denied that permission, but also denied that the Church sheltered criminals.

In February 1947, CIC Special Agent Robert Clayton Mudd reported that ten members of Dictator Andre Pavelic's cabinet were living in San Girolamo or in the Vatican itself. Mudd infiltrated an agent into the monastery and confirmed that it was "…honeycombed with cells of Ustase operatives" guarded by "armed youths." Mudd also reported:

"It was further established that these Croats travel back and forth from the Vatican several times a week in a car with a chauffeur whose license plate bears the two initial CD, "Corpo Diplomatico." It issues forth from the Vatican and discharges its passengers inside the Monastery of San Girolamo. Since they are subject to diplomatic immunity, it is impossible to stop the car and discover who are its passengers." [8]

MUDD concluded:

"Draganovic's sponsoring of these Croat Ustashes definitely links him up with the plan of the Vatican to shield these ex-Ustashe nationalists until such time as they are able to procure for them the proper documents to enable them to go to South America. The Vatican, undoubtedly banking on the strong anti-Communist feelings of these men, is endeavoring to infiltrate them into South America in any way possible to counteract the spread of Red doctrine. It has been reliably reported for example that Dr. Vrancic has already gone to South America and that Andre Pavelic and General Kren are scheduled for an early departure to South America through Spain. All these operations are said to have been negotiated by Draganovic because of his influence in the Vatican."

A Vatican historian, Father Robert Graham, has confirmed the existence of Draganovic's ratline: "I've no doubt that Draganovic was extremely active in siphoning off his Croatian Ustashe friends." Graham further denies that Dragonovic was not officially sanctioned by his superiors." Just because he is a priest doesn't mean he represents the Vatican. It was his own operation." [9]

On four occasions the Vatican intervened on behalf of Ustasha prisoners.

THE ARGENTINE CONNECTION

Argentine researcher Uki Goni's book, The Real Odessa, describes how Argentine diplomats worked with Draganovic to facilitate the relocation of Nazi and Fascist war criminals to Argentina.

According to Goni, the first Nazi smuggling began in January 1946, when Argentine bishop Antonio Caggiano, leader of the Argentine chapter of Catholic Action, flew to Rome to be anointed cardinal. It was in Rome that the Argentine bishops met with French Cardinal Eugene Tisserant and passed on a message (documented in Argentine archives)

"...The government of the Argentine Republic was willing to receive French persons, whose political attitude during the recent war would expose them, should they return to France, to harsh measures and private revenge."

During the spring of 1946 numerous French war criminals escaped through Italy to Argentina. According to Goni, they were issued passports by the Rome ICRC office; the passports were stamped with Argentine tourist visas. The first documented case of a French war criminal to arrive in Buenos Aires was that of Emil Dewoitine who was later tried and sentenced in absentia to 20 years hard labor. He sailed first class on the same ship back to Argentine with Cardinal Caggiano. [2]

According to Paul Manning in his book, *Martin Bormann: Nazi in Exile*, "... eventually over 10,000 former German military made it to South America along escape routes..."[3]

RATLINE ESCAPEES

- •Adolf Eichmann
- •Franz Stangl
- •Gustav Wagner
- •Erich Priebke
- •Klaus Barbie
- •Eduard Roschmann
- •Aribert Heim
- •Andrija Artukovic
- •Andre Pavelic
- •Walter Rauff
- •Alois Brunner
- •Josef Mengele
- •Johann Feil
- •Among others – there were over 3,500 Nazi war criminals charged – less than 350 were ever convicted – 100s escaped to South America thanks to the Church

[1] Michael Phayer, *The Catholic Church and the Holocaust*, 2008, p.173
[2[Michael Phayer, *The Catholic Church and the Holocaust*, 2008, pp.173-179
[3] Michael Phayer, *The Catholic Church and the Holocaust*, 2008, p.179
[4] Michael Phayer, *The Catholic Church and the Holocaust*, 2008, p. 180
[5] Michael Phayer, *The Catholic Church and the Holocaust*, 2008, p. 182
[6] Michael Phayer, *The Catholic Church and the Holocaust*, 2008, p 187

[7] Aarons and Loftus, *Unholy Trinity: The Vatican, The Nazis and The Swiss Bankers*, (St. Martins Press 1991, revised 1998), p.36

[8] Declassified CIA File: *Background Report on Father Krunoslav Draganovic*, 12 February 1947. Published on the website of the Jasenovic Committee of the Holy Assembly of Bishops of the Serbian Orthodox Church.

[9] Aarons and Loftus, p. 89

[10] Uki Goni, *The Real Odessa: Smuggling the Nazis to Peron's Argentina*, Granta (revised edition) 2003, pp. 96-98

[11] Paul Manning, *Martin Bormann: Nazi in Exile* (Lyle Stuart, Inc., 1980) ISBN 0-8184-0309-8 (p.181

Source: R and H; Editor and inspired by Wikipedia (Retrieved July 23, 2010)

EXCERPT FROM U.S. National Archives:

"The means of escape were the Vatican "Ratlines." Operated with the knowledge and blessing of highly placed US and British government officials, the Ratline guided 30,000 wanted Nazis to sanctuary. Safe haven locations included the US, Britain, Canada, Australia, New Zealand, and the favorite bolt hole of them all: South America.

Those who reached safety in this manner read like a "Who's Who" of the most wanted Nazi war criminals: Klaus Barbie, the cruel Gestapo officer known as the "Butcher of Lyon;" Franz Stangl, Commandant of the notorious Treblinka extermination camp; Gustav Wagner, Commandant of Sorbubor exterminator camp; and Alois Brunner, a brutal official in the Jewish deportation program. Of the most famous to escape along the ratlines were Adolf Eichmann, the chief architect of the "Holocaust' and Dr. Joseph Mengele, the White Angel" of Auschwitz concentration camp. Not least was Deputy Fuhrer Martin Bormann. Incredibly, an entire Waffen SS division – the notorious "Galician Division" – consisting of 8,000 men were smuggled to England"

Excerpt from U.S. National Archives: archives.gov/research-room/holocaust-era-assets/bibliographies/trade-with-third-reich.html

Adolph Hitler paid his Church tax until the end of his life. A tax that is still imposed in several countries, including Italy and Germany.

Bishop Alois Hudal
Protector and enabler of the Nazis during the war and after until his dying day.

One Ratline Route

There was a route that included small inns and hotels next to Catholic Churches which were used as safehouse on the route from Germany through Bavaria and Austria on to Italy. The Catholic part of the escape route was headed up by Bishop Alois Hudal, who handled people like Heinrich Muller and Bormann. Bishop Hudal is buried in Rome's Campo Santo Tentonico cemetery. The route included the Collegio Craotto on Plazza Colonna, a seminary of Yugoslav priests who were adherents of Andre Pavelic, the Nazi dictator of Croatia and the direct boss of Artukovic. The final stage of this route was to meet with the Titular Bishop of Aela, rector of the German Instituto Santa Maria dell'Anima and one of the closest friends of Pope Pius XII (he was the Adjutant at the throne). Remember, this is the same network that guided Artukovic to Westminster, CA and the Catholic Church here in the U.S., as well as other war criminals into Los Angeles, Orange and Santa Barbara counties, California.

Source: R and H.

THE RATS

Andre Pavelic, Croatian dictator, hid out in the Vatican disguised as a monk waiting for arrangements from the Catholic Church for transport to South America.

Klaus Barbie, the infamous "Butcher of Lyons" was smuggled to Bolivia through Father Krunoslav Draganovic's ratline in Genoa, Italy. Draganovic arranged a Red Cross travel permit for him and sponsored his visa.

Franz Stangl, the commandant of the Treblinka death camp was assisted with passport documents by Catholic Bishop Alois Hudal.

The Catholic Church helped Martin Bormann, second in charge of Nazi Germany, escape. It also manufactured the story that he had died in 1945 in Germany, when, in fact, he actually died in the early 1960's in Paraguay.

Adolph Eichmann, in charge of the "Final solution" extermination of all Jews, was smuggled out.

Walter Rauf, the inventor of the "mobile gas chamber," was also a member of this unique travel club.

Andrija Artukovik, Interior Minister of the Nazi puppet state of Croatia under Andre Pavelic, lived in Seal Beach, California until his extradition to Yugoslavia in 1986. He was convicted of war crimes after a one-month trial during which he maintained his innocence. He said he never knew of any killings. The Government postponed his death sentenced on grounds of ill-health and he died in prison.

Dr. Josef Mengele, known as the "Angel of Death" entered South America with false papers arranged by the Catholic Church. In 1959 he returned to Germany for his father's funeral and lived at the Catholic English Institute Convent School. He is also reported to have spent time in Kythnos and Barcelona under the protection of the Catholic Church. Karl Mengele & Sons, a family company, owned 50% of an Argentinean company that assembled German tractors and provided income for Josef Mengele.

Source: H.

Denial

In 2009, Brazilian Archbishop Dadeus Grings joined the ultra-conservative Bishop Richard Williamson of the Society of St. Pius X, in playing down the numbers of Jews who were killed in the Holocaust and insisting that Roman Catholics suffered more than the Jews in World War II.

THE ROGUES GALLERY
No Nazis were disciplined or excommunicated from the Catholic Church; but American priest Thomas Doyle who wrote the famous open letters to Pope John Paul II on the "cancer of molestation" as a warning in the 1980's was rewarded with total banishment and reprimand from The Church.

Klaus Barbie
Another recipient of Catholic
benevolence and protection.

Hermann Goering
Convicted at Nuremberg

Martin Bormann
Second in Command

Catholic Divine Justice?

As for the threat of excommunication or denial of access to the public sacraments, Pope Pius XII declared that any Catholics in Italy who joined the Communist Party, even if they did nothing further, were *ipso facto* excommunicated. Pius XII also used that sledge hammer later to crush the liberal "Worker Priest" movement in France.

At the same time, the Vatican was working underground to get some of the worst Nazi war criminals out of Europe, providing only that they were "Catholics."

When Cardinal Stepinac was convicted on war crimes against innocent non-Catholics in Croatia, largely on the testimony of his Catholic countrymen, Pius XII took no action against Stepinac. On the contrary, those Catholics who testified against him were excommunicated on grounds that a member of the priesthood cannot testify against another priest without permission from the Vatican.

ADOLF EICHMANN
The architect of the "Final Solution"

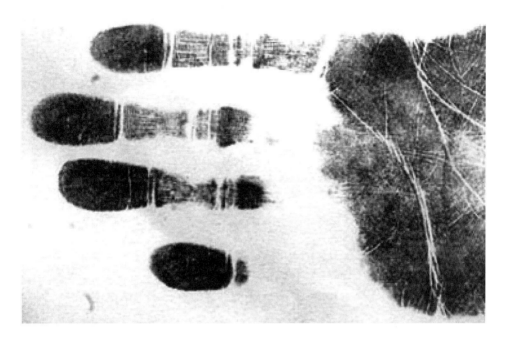

Eichmann's Fingerprints on Passport Provided by the Roman Catholic Church

Eichmann was not the mastermind behind the Eurasian Jewish Holocaust. He was a colonel in the SS working with another colonel Kurt Becher who as later pardoned thanks to the testimony of one of the pope's Court Jews, Rudolf Kastner. However, Eichmann was in charge of the Final Solution for the Jewish people and didn't need anyone's permission to terrorize and kill. In fact, when communication went up the chain of command, they used coded messages so that the people like Himmler and Goebbels could have deniability. The Colonel level was very high in the Nazi Army and was the level that got everything done.

The real mastermind in Germany behind the Holocaust was Munich Archbishop Michael Cardinal von Faulhaber, subject to the Jesuits at the nearby St. Michael's Church. Thus, it was Roman Catholic SS leader Heinrich Himmler who took his orders from von Faulhaber at the direction of his Jesuit advisers.

Eichmann was the apostate Protestant blamed for the Holocaust and who was later sacrificed to the Israelis in 1960 in the Order's successful attempt to save the Ben-Gurion government from complete discrediting due to Kastner's involvement in the deportation of 400,000 Hungarian Jews to Auschwitz in late 1944.

By Brother Eric, and H.

143

Trial at Nuremberg
None of those convicted at the Nuremberg Trials in 1945 were ever excommunicated by Pope Pius XII or subsequent Popes.

Andrija Artukovic
The "Himmler of the Balkans," second in command of the war's river of blood in Croatia, worked closely with Archbishop Alojzije Stepinac and Dictator of Croatia Andre Pavelic.

Benito Mussolini
Puppet master of the Papal State

Adolph Hitler
The reason for it all

Joseph Mengele
"The Angel of Death"
**Mengele was sneaked back into Germany in 1957 with the aid of the
Catholic Church to attend a family funeral.**

Father Thomas Doyle
**His crime: Alerting the Vatican of the sordid predator priests' crimes
and protecting the victims.**

THE POWER AND THE GLORY
A peek at the Roman Catholic version of heaven on earth

There is a dark and "holier than thou" thread that runs through the Catholic Church from top to bottom from ancient times, especially against the Jews. This self-ordained hatred has seeped out in words and actions, overt, like the Nazi Catholics with Archbishop Hudal, Pius XII, Cardinal Stepinac, and the Holocaust denier Bishop Richard Williamson, who was recently welcomed back by Pope Benedict XVI. Policy actions of the Vatican delayed recognition of the State of Israel. Almost more chilling are the attitudes, hypocrisies and actions by the likes of Catholic US Representatives James B. Utt , who introduced in the US Congress a resolution to clear mass murderer Andrija Artukovic of his wartime crimes and saved him from extradition. He made a career out of his campaign to get the United States out of the United Nations. He always voted against all civil rights legislation. His statement that "a large contingent of barefooted Africans are training in Georgia to take over the United States" are legendary.

Utt was followed after his death by John George Schmitz, another "good Catholic."

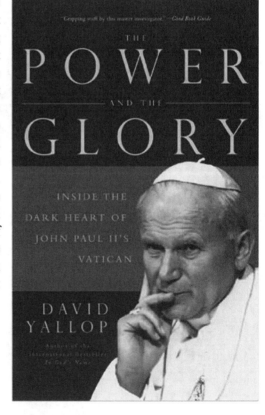

Schmitz fathered at least one illegitimate child. He was kicked out of the John Birch Society for being "too extreme." He ran for President and was a member of George Wallace's American Independent Party. During his tenure as a public servant of the people of Orange County, California, he introduced a bill to investigate any teachers thought to be atheistic communists. Both Utt and Schmitz were in the Diocese of Nazi condoning Cardinal Manning and McIntyre...soon out of his nest flew Cardinal Mahony, the lid keeper of the largest molestation settlement in American history: $650 million.

By Tim C. Leedom

Section IV

ISSUES OF THE CHURCH

PRESERVE THE STATUS QUO.
AT ALL COST

VATICAN FINANCES
The post war crimes continue

MONEY LAUNDERING

Holocaust Survivors Request that the European Central Bank Investigate Vatican Money Laundering of Nazi Gold

Vatican Minted Euros May Contain Concentration Camp Gold

Washington: Former Yugoslavia was a vast killing ground during the Second World War when hundreds of thousands of Orthodox Christians, Jews and Roma were murdered by the Nazis and their Croatian Allies. It has long been known that some of the loot, including a significant amount of gold from concentration camps, ended up at the Vatican Bank, deposited there by Catholic clergy acting on behalf of war criminals.

Although the Holocaust Survivors sued the Vatican Bank in US Federal court, the case was dismissed in March 2010 on grounds of Vatican sovereign immunity from lawsuit in the United States, (Alperin v. Vatican, Ninth Circuit Court of Appeals, Case No. 09-17761, 08-16060).

The Vatican may have breathed a sign of relief after the long running ten years' lawsuit seemed to finally die. However, Holocaust Survivors have now requested the European Central Bank to open a new investigation into Vatican money laundering and possible use of concentration camp gold in the minting of Euro coins by the Vatican.

According to attorney Jonathan Levy who represented the Holocaust Survivors in the US courts, the Vatican, in a rare departure from its usual policy, agreed to place itself under the jurisdiction of the European Union in order to obtain the right to coin Euros. The agreement between in EU and the Vatican expressly contains provisions regarding prevention of money laundering. Further, it is presumed that the beleaguered European Central Bank would frown upon the possibility that concentration camp gold might be used to finance or mint Euro coins.

The Holocaust Survivors are requesting the European Central Bank investigate the allegations and that holders of Vatican Euro coins mail them back to the Vatican and request certification that concentration camp gold was not used in the minting or financing of these coins.

Source: Original message from jonlevy@hargray.com Wed. 30 June, 2010 23.30:46-0400. For more information contact: Dr. Jonathan Levy, Attorney & Solicitor + 1-202-318-2406; info@brimstoneandcompany.com

THE BRIMSTONE REPORT

BRIMSTONE & CO.
ATTORNEYS & SOLICITORS
1629 K STREET NW SUITE 300
WASHINGTON DC 20006 USA
TEL/FAX 1-202-318-2406
CHAMBERS@BRIMSTONEANDCOMPANY.COM
WWW.BRIMSTONEANDCOMPANY.COM

July 1, 2010

European Central Bank
The Governing Council
Kaiserstrasse 29
60311 Frankfurt am Main
Germany

Re: Vatican Money Laundering of Nazi Gold &
Use of Concentration Camp Victim Gold to Mint Vatican Euros

Dear President Trichet:

This is a communication to the European Central Bank by Holocaust Survivors represented by this firm. The Holocaust Survivors request an investigation of the well founded allegations of money laundering and retention of Second World War era concentration camp loot by the Vatican Bank, a self described organ of the The Holy See located in The Vatican City State. Additionally, the Holocaust Survivors request an accounting of concentration camp and victim gold in the possession of the Vatican Bank and/or present in the Vatican City State or controlled by the Holy See that may have been used to mint Vatican Euro coins or to provide financing for their minting.

The ECB has jurisdiction over this matter pursuant to Article 8 of *The Monetary Agreement between the European Union and The Vatican City State* and more specifically at Art. 8(1)(b). The EU-Vatican Monetary Agreement Annex further incorporates by reference Directive 2005/60/EC of the European Parliament and of the Council of 26 October 2005 on the prevention of the use of the financial system for the purpose of money laundering and terrorist financing, OJ L 309, 25.11.2005, p. 15–36, and amended by Directive 2008/20/EC of the European Parliament and of the Council of 11 March 2008 on the prevention of the use of the financial system for the purpose of money laundering and terrorist financing, as regards the implementing powers conferred on the Commission , OJ L 76, 19.3.2008, p. 46–47. Therefore, we believe that these allegations fall under the auspices of the ECB or an EU organization designated by the ECB.

We represent Holocaust Survivors and organizations including Mileva Reljanovic, a citizen of Sweden, and 25 other individuals representing Holocaust Survivors

ATTORNEYS, SOLICITORS, BARRISTERS AND ADVOCATES, PRIMARY LICENSES
WASHINGTON, DC & NIGERIA

153

BRIMSTONE & CO.
ATTORNEYS & SOLICITORS
1629 K STREET NW SUITE 300
WASHINGTON DC 20006 USA
TEL/FAX 1-202-318-2406
CHAMBERS@BRIMSTONEANDCOMPANY.COM
WWW.BRIMSTONEANDCOMPANY.COM

from the United States, Serbia, and Ukraine and The Independent Council of Serbian Roma, The Jasenovac Research Institute, The Republic of Serbian Krajina in Exile, and three other organizations who were all plaintiffs in the lawsuit *Alperin v. Vatican Bank.*

In 1999, the Vatican Bank's then president, Angelo Caloia, was contacted by Holocaust Survivors concerning the 1998 United States State Department Eizenstat/Slany Report entitled *U.S. Concerns About the Fate of the Wartime Ustasha Treasury* which concluded there was evidence pointing to Vatican involvement in laundering concentration camp loot. The Vatican Bank however did not answer Holocaust survivors and litigation in the United States District Court for the Northern District of California ensued. The Vatican Bank was eventually found by the court to be an organ of The Holy See and therefore immune from lawsuit in the United States because there was no evidence that the Ustasha gold controlled by the Vatican Bank was still in the United States. This finding was upheld by the Ninth Circuit Court of Appeals in San Francisco and became final in March 2010.

The Vatican Bank never denied the charges of money laundering or accounted for the concentration camp gold it was accused of receiving. Plaintiffs produced volumes of declassified documents and the transcript of the four day deposition of former US Army Counter Intelligence Special Agent, William Gowen, who investigated the Ustasha Treasury in Rome in 1946-1947 among other evidence.

Mr. Gowen, who resides in New York City, testified under oath that a 10 truck convoy of valuables including concentration camp gold was received at the Vatican Bank in 1946. The value of this loot was estimated to be worth $50 million by US Treasury Agent Emerson Bigelow who also reported contemporaneously to his superiors in Washington about the incident.

Holocaust Survivors are concerned about the following:

1. Gold Vatican Euro coins may contain dental and victim gold from concentration camp victims in former Yugoslavia.

2. Valuables from the Ustasha Treasury or the proceeds of same may have been used by the Vatican City State through accounts at the Vatican Bank to pay for minting of Vatican Euro denominated coins.

ATTORNEYS, SOLICITORS, BARRISTERS AND ADVOCATES, PRIMARY LICENSES
WASHINGTON, DC & NIGERIA

BRIMSTONE & CO.
ATTORNEYS & SOLICITORS
1629 K STREET NW SUITE 300
WASHINGTON DC 20006 USA
TEL/FAX 1-202-318-2406
CHAMBERS@BRIMSTONEANDCOMPANY.COM
WWW.BRIMSTONEANDCOMPANY.COM

3. The Vatican Bank has refused to cooperate in any investigation of laundering the Ustasha Treasury, refused to enter a denial to the allegations of money laundering and chose instead to invoke sovereign immunity in the United States Courts.

The Vatican City State and the state owned or operated financial institutions therein by entering into the *The Monetary Agreement between the European Union and The Vatican City State* have specifically placed themselves under ECB jurisdiction and have waived their sovereign immunity in exchange for the right to coin Euro currency.

Holocaust Survivors request the ECB designate an investigatory committee or agency to which Holocaust Survivors may submit their evidence and that the Vatican Bank and Vatican City State be required to cooperate in the investigation.

Respectfully submitted,

Dr. Jonathan Levy
Attorney & Solicitor for Holocaust Survivors

Nazi Gold
Vatican Bank Top 10 Money Laundering Destination

According to one global source, the Vatican is the main destination for over $55 billion in illegal Italian money laundering, and the number 8 destination worldwide for laundered money, ranked well ahead of such offshore havens as the Bahamas, Switzerland and Liechtenstein.

In a recent report by the London Telegraph and the Inside Fraud Bulletin, the Vatican was named as a top "cut out" country along with offshore banking centers of Nauru, Macao and Mauritius. A "cut out" country is one whose banking secrecy makes it all but impossible to trace laundered funds back to their source.

The Vatican is desperately resisting a legal action for an accounting of stolen World War II assets in a San Francisco Federal court (Alperin v. Vatican Bank) filed by Serb and Jewish Holocaust survivors. Contrary to the above reports, a declaration filed under penalty of perjury by the Vatican Banks' attorney, Franzo Grande Stevens, states that it is part of the Vatican Bank's "fundamental purpose to promote pious acts" and that its depositors "are essentially limited to Vatican state employees, members of the Holy See, religious orders, and persons who deposit money destined, at least in part, for works of piety." Stevens also declared to the court that the Pope controls the Vatican Bank and that bank records are not retained after ten years.

It seems that the Vatican Bank, a major illegal money laundering operation, is hiding behind image of John Paul II. Given the Vatican Bank's alleged involvement with Nazi loot and current links to organized crime, the accumulating evidence points to a more piratical than pious Vatican Bank.

Source: Press Release November 21, 2001 (Easton & Levy Victim Asset Litigation)

Vatican Fights to Keep Nazi Gold Lawsuit Out of US Courts

While the Vatican faces new charges of Holocaust denial over the Pope's pardon of Holocaust denier Bishop Williamson, it has also been fighting a little-known 10-year battle to protect the Vatican Bank from accountability for laundering Nazi loot after the Second World War.

The lawsuit, Alperin v. Vatican Bank (9th Circuit court of Appeals, Case 08-16010), alleges the Vatican Bank and Franciscan Order laundered tens of millions of dollars, including concentration camp gold from former Yugoslavia immediately following the Second World War.

The case against the Vatican Bank (but not the Franciscan Order) was dismissed on grounds the Vatican Bank is or organ of a sovereign entity, the Vatican, which is immune from lawsuits.

The recently filed appeal, however, argues that the Vatican Bank is not sovereign and that it engages in commercial activity in the United States and therefore should be held accountable in a United States Federal Court.

Attorneys for the plaintiffs, Holocaust survivors and their heirs, including Serbs, Jews and Roma, originally filed the lawsuit in 1999. They are seeking an accounting and a return of the loot estimated to have been worth over $50 million dollars in 1946.

Source: Press Release February 3, 2009 (Dr. Jonathan Levy and Tom Easton, Attorneys)

JOHN PATRICK CODY
Cardinal Archbishop of Chicago

"I answer only to the Pope and the Church."

John Cody was born in St. Louis, Missouri, ordained into the priesthood on December 8, 1931, appointed Auxiliary Bishop of St. Louis by Pope Paul XII on May 10, 1947 and archbishop of Chicago on June 16, 1965.

His controversial reign over the Chicago archdiocese included federal investigations of financial improprieties. An estimate of over one million dollars of church funds went missing under Cody, and the National conference of Catholic Bishops lost more than four million dollars in a single year while he was the treasurer.

A Chicago-Sun Times report on the investigations into Cody's activities stated:

"Legally, the investigations by the paper and the federal prosecutors ended inconclusively. In that sense, the legal tactics followed by Cody and his lawyers – chiefly a strategy of delays and stalling – succeed in preventing any indictments. Eight months before his first story was published, the U.S. Attorney's office issued subpoenas to Cody and the archdiocese, but the information that was sought was never turned over to the government. Even after the series was published, the stonewalling continued. A new U.S. Attorney, Dan Webb, had taken the government's investigation and issued new subpoenas, but Frank McGarr, the chief judge of the U.S. District Court for the Northern District of Illinois, did nothing to move the case along. Finally the Cardinal's health became an issue. On April 25, 198, he died. In July 18982, Webb terminated the investigation, stating: "Once the cardinal passed on, the investigation as to the allegations against the cardinal became moot."

Source R. & H.

Cody was a target of wiretaps and an unwitting counter part of a larger drama still playing out.

Cody's arrogance explained: "If I am touched it will blow the lid off the Vatican."

MEA CULPA

A Roman Catholic bank in Germany has apologized after admitting it bought stock in defense, tobacco and birth control companies.

PAX Bank of Germany advertised it participated only in ethical investment funds avoiding arms, tobacco companies and organizations that did not adhere to Catholic beliefs. Yet the bank invested 580,000 euros ($826,675US) in British Arms Company BAE Systems, and another 160,000 euros in Wyeth, an American pharmaceutical company that manufactures birth control pills.

Bank officials told the press it apologized for its behavior "not in keeping with ethical standards...we will rectify the mistakes immediately without negative consequences for our clients. Unfortunately in a few internal reviews, the critical investments in question were overlooked. We deeply regret this."

In a rare departure from Roman Catholic handling affairs upon discovery, the bank official actually thanked the journalists for calling the matter to his attention.

Source: Numerous Press Articles

Vatican Denies it Held Stock in Maker of the Pill

The Vatican denied a German television report that its bank once held shares in a drug company producing birth control pills.

But, a spokesman at the pharmaceutical company, Serono, told the press that the Vatican did hold stock in its Rome Subsidiary in the 1960s and possibly into the early 1970s. The spokesman, however, denied the company made birth control pills.

"We're just the opposite. We are the leader in fertility," treatment, the spokesman said in a telephone interview.

The German report alleged that Serono began producing birth control pills in 1968, the year the Roman Catholic Church laid out its firm opposition to artificial contraceptive methods.

The report said the Vatican bank sold its shares in Serono in 1970 to a Milan-based bank in which it held a 20% stake.

Source: Numerous Press Articles

Vatican Bank facing money-laundering investigation

September 2010 Heist

Italian authorities seized $30 million from a Vatican bank as a result of investigations of the bank's chairman, Ettori Gotte Tedeschi and its general director, Paolo Cipriani, in connection with alleged mistakes made in reports to comply with Italy's anti-money laundering laws.

Tedeschi, an Opus Dei member, told the press he was bitter and humiliated by the probe because he was just implementing new transparency procedures at the bank.

The Bank of Italy, adhering to anti-money laundering directives from the European Union, alerted the authorities of two suspicious transactions from the Vatican bank. One transfer for 26 million euros was to an account held by the bank at the Frankfurt branch of the American Bank JP Morgan; the other transfer was directed to an account it held at the Rome branch of Banco del Fucino.

Evidently, the Vatican bank neglected to explain to authorities where the money had come from. In today's world, international terrorism tops the global agenda

159

and world powers are focused on targeting illicit money.

According to court records, the Vatican has done nothing to comply with Italian banking laws or international regulations to fight money laundering, nor does it seem even possible that it can comply considering the lack of the internal policies and procedures at the Vatican bank.

The Vatican bank isn't a typical bank. It manages assets destined for religious works and works of charity. It also manages ATM machines inside the Vatican. The bank is not opened to the public. Depositors are Vatican employees, religious orders and people who transfer money for the Pope's charities. Five cardinals oversee the bank but the day to day operations are supervised by Tedeschi.

The bank is not on the "white list" of the Organization for Economic Cooperation and Development which monitors the financial transparency on the exchange of tax information. The OECD divides countries into three categories: countries that comply with the rules (white list); countries who say they will comply but are not (gray list) and countries that have not agreed to change their banking secrecy practices (black list).

Currently the Vatican bank is not on any of the OECD lists.

Source: Information releases from the Bank of Italy; the Organization for Economic Cooperation; Court Records

THE CHURCH AND SCIENCE

Our Mind Is Made Up.
Your Facts Must Be Wrong.

THE GALILEO AFFAIR
Get away from that telescope!

Timeline:

1610: Galileo declares that the earth revolves around the sun. He is persecuted for blasphemy.

1983: Catholic Church admits Galileo was correct – the earth does indeed revolve around the sun.

The Galileo Affair unfolded in a sequence of events, beginning around 1610, during which Galileo Galilei came into conflict with the Catholic Church over his discoveries with the new telescope. Problem discoveries
  •Mountains on the moon
  •Lesser moons in orbit around Jupiter
  •Discovery of stars too faint to see without a telescope
  •Phases of Venus
  •Existence of sunspots
  •Reason that objects float or sink in water
  •Heliocentrism - the theory that the earth revolved around the sun
   Support of Copernicus' astronomy theories

He published his observations, which he made with the new telescope, in his book Sidereus Nuncius (Starry Messenger). His discoveries exposed major differences with the understandings of heaven held by the Catholic Church and contradicted the scientific and philosophical ideas of the time.

From antiquity, the majority of people subscribed to the Ptolemaic theory of geocentrism, Ptolemy's theory that all heavenly bodies revolved around the earth. This theory agreed with a literalist interpretation of Scripture in several places: 1 Chronicles 16:30,Psalm 93:10, Psalm 96:10, Ecclesiast 1:5

161

The Church allowed heliocentrism to be taught as a hypothesis and discussed in scientific circles, as long as the faith of the ordinary people was safeguarded, but Galileo argues that his telescopic observations favored the Copernican heliocentric theory as a *physical truth.*

Tommaso Caccini, a Dominican friar, became Galileo's most vicious enemy – reporting Galileo to the Inquisition Office in Rome alleging heresies being spread by Galileo and his pupils.

On February 24, 1616, the Tribunal of the Inquisition's commission of theologians (known as Qualifiers) issued their unanimous report: the idea that the Sun is stationary is "...foolish and absurd in philosophy, and formally heretical since it explicitly contradicts in many places the sense of Holy Scripture..." While the Earth's movement "...receives the same judgment in philosophy and...in regard to theological truth, it is at least erroneous in faith."

The next day, Pope Paul V ordered that Galileo abandon the Copernican opinions and should he resist, stronger action would be taken. On March 5, 1616, the decree was issued by the Congregation of the Index, prohibiting, condemning, or suspending certain books which advocated the truth of the Copernican system.

In 1632 Galileo published his book, *Dialogue Concerning the Two Chief World Systems*, with formal authorization from the Inquisition for a book that presented a balanced view of both Copernican and Church theories. It was determined that the Copernican theory received better treatment and for this, Galileo was ordered in 1633 to appear before the Inquisition for trial "...for holding as true the false doctrine taught by some that the sun is the center of the world" against the 1616 condemnation, since "...it was decided at the Holy Congregation...on 25 February 1616 that...the Holy Office would give you an injunction to abandon this doctrine, not to teach it to others, not to defend it, and not to treat of it; and that if you did not acquiesce in this injunction, you should be imprisoned..." Galileo was found guilty and sentenced to house arrest for the rest of his life.

In 1758 the Catholic Church dropped the general prohibition of books advocating heliocentrism from the *Index of Forbidden Books*. It did not, however, rescind the decisions issued by the Inquisition in 1633 against Galileo.

On February 15, 1990, Cardinal Ratzinger, now Pope Benedict XVI, delivered a speech at La Sapienza University in Rome wherein he cited current views on the Galileo Affair as forming what he called "a symptomatic cast that illustrates the extent to which modernity's doubts about itself have grown today in science and technology." [39] As evidence, he presented the views of a few prominent philosophers including Paul Feyerabend, whom he quoted as saying: "The Church at the time of Galileo kept much more closely to reason than did Galileo himself, and she took into consideration the ethical and social consequences of Galileo's teaching too. Her verdict against Galileo was rational and just, and the revision of this verdict can be justified only on the grounds of what is politically opportune."

Cardinal Ratzinger did not indicate whether he agreed or disagreed with Feyerabend's assertions, but he did say, "It would be foolish to construct an impulsive apologetic on the basis of such views."

On November 4, 1992 the Catholic Church vindicated Galileo with Pope John Paul II's declaration:

"Thanks to his intuition as a brilliant physicist and by relying on different arguments, Galileo, who practically invented the experimental method, understood why only the sun could function as the centre of the world, as it was then known, that is to say, as a planetary system. The error of the theologians of the time, when they maintained the centrality of the Earth, was to think that our understanding of the physical world's structure was, in some way, imposed by the literal sense of Sacred Scripture…"

-Pope John Paul II, L'Osservatore Romano N. 44 (1264)

By the Editors; Sources: The Book Your Church Doesn't Want You to Read; Encyclopedia Brittanica; Inspired by Wikipedia (Retrieved June 5, 2010)

Galileo was tried on the suspicion of heresy, convicted and spent the rest of his life under house arrest.

University of Arizona, Vatican and Jesuits
Name New Telescope
'LUCIFER'
Housed at Mt. Graham, critics wonder are the 'evil ones' planning a staged end times scenario

The University of Arizona, together with the Vatican and Jesuit Order, announced that it had named its newest high-powered telescopic instrument 'Lucifer'.

There has been a great deal of speculation, among Vatican critics, why in the first place the Jesuit Order was allowed to build a huge stellar observatory on Mt. Graham in Arizona – on holy Indian ground – in cooperation with the state-run University of Arizona.

With the naming of Lucifer, critics claim the Vatican has shown its true colors, using God and Jesus as shills for their true master – Lucifer.

According to an article in Popular Science by Rebecca Boyle the "new instrument with an evil-sounding name is helping scientists see how stars are born."

The article went on to explain the name Lucifer stands for , "Large Binocular Telescope Near-infrared Utility with Camera and Integral Field Unit for Extragalactic Research."

"And yes," according to Popular Science, "it's named for the Devil, whose name itself means "morning star." However, according to a spokesman for the University of Arizona, it wasn't meant to evoke any connotations of evil.

Lucifer has three interchangeable cameras for imaging and spectroscopy in different resolutions. It has a large field of view and high-re capabilities, which allow a wide range of observations.

Critics are now shaking their heads even more, wondering why the Vatican would have its own stellar observatory, and why they would name a telescope after the Devil himself.

According to Mitch Battros, some people believe "it is for the purpose to monitor a warning present in the Bible."

Could it be named "Wormwood" coming from the New Testament book of Revelation, saying:

> "And the third angel sounded, and there fell a great star from heaven, burning as it were a lamp, and it fell upon the third part of the rivers, and upon the fountains of waters; And the name of the star is called Wormwood: and the third part of the waters became wormwood; and many men died of the waters, because they were made bitter." (Revelations 8:10,11 – King James Bible).

Battros added this reference to the end times as well as Mayan prophecy:
"Is it possible the Vatican has the same information as the Mayans? Both speak of an event coming from the center of our galaxy Milky Way. Both indicate a powerful celestial event. But the most important question of all is "when".

"I do not believe any scientist or focused individual can argue that all of space science and cosmology appears to have a certain urgency for discovery. From galactic 'charged particles' to new found asteroids, there is a sense of 'let's find it as soon as we can'."

Here is an article that appeared in the Native American Roots web site, explaining how the Vatican violated Native Holy ground:

For many Native American Nations there are certain geographic places which have special spiritual meanings. These sacred places are often portals to the spirit worlds. For the Apache in Arizona, one of these sacred places is Mount Graham. This place is called "Dzil Nchaa Si An" (Big Seated Mountain), and is mentioned in 32 of the sacred songs which have been handed down through the oral tradition for many generations. It is here that the Ga'an, the guardian spirits of the Apache, live.

In 1873, Mount Graham was removed from the boundaries of the San Carlos Reservation and placed in public domain. The spiritual value of Mount Graham to the Apache was not considered. This action set the stage for conflict a century later.

[Ojibwa: Mount Graham: Science and Apache Religion]

In 1984, the University of Arizona and the Vatican selected Mount Graham as a site for a complex of 18 telescopes. The fact that this is a sacred place for the Apache was not taken into consideration. to get around the legal barriers of the American Indian Religious Freedom Act, the University hired a lobbying firm to put pressure on Congress to remove this, and other roadblocks. The area in question is administered by the U.S. Forest Service.

The first Vatican observatory was established in 1774. The Vatican now has an observatory staff which is officially supported by the Vatican City State. The Vatican Observatory Foundation is supported by private donations. One of the important duties of the church is to maintain an accurate calendar and this requires astronomical observations. This accounts for the involvement of the Vatican with astronomy.

Congress passed the Arizona-Idaho Conservation Act in 1988. In response to lobbying by the University of Arizona and the Vatican, the Act included a provision to allow the construction of three telescopes on Mount Graham without having to comply with the American Indian Religious Freedom Act or with environmental laws.

The following year the Apache Survival Coalition was started by Ola Cassadore-Davis, the daughter of Apache spiritual leader Phillip Cassadore. The purpose of the Coalition was to save Dzil Nchaa Si An from desecration by a telescope

165

complex to be built by the University of Arizona and the Vatican.

In 1991, the San Carlos Apache Tribe passed a resolution stating that Mount Graham is sacred to them. Furthermore, the resolution stated that the tribe supported the efforts of the Apache Survival Coalition to protect the religious and cultural beliefs of the tribe.

Following the declarations of the sacredness of Mount Graham by the apache Survival Coalition and the San Carlos Apache Tribe, the Vatican in 1991 declared that Mt. Graham was not sacred because it lacked religious shrines. Jesuit Father George Coyne, director of the Vatican Observatory, indicated that he could not find an authentic Apache who thought the mountain was sacred. Father Coyne stated that to convince him that the mountain was sacred he would need to see evidence of shrines and that he would not accept Apache oral history or statements by Apache-speaking Euro-American anthropologists.

Father Coyne further declared that Apache beliefs were "a kind of religiosity to which I cannot subscribe and which must be suppressed with all the force we can muster."

The Arizona Republic (Phoenix, Arizona) reports that the Jesuit Father Charles W. Polzer calls opposition to the construction of the telescope complex on top of Mount Graham "part of a Jewish conspiracy" and comes from the Jewish lawyers of the American Civil Liberties Union who are out to undermine and destroy the Catholic Church."

In spite of opposition by the San Carlos Apache tribal council, Apache spiritual leaders, and environmental groups, construction of the project began in 1991.

With flagrant insensitivity to American Indians, the University of Arizona announced that it intended to name its new telescope on Mount Graham the Columbus telescope in honor of the European explorer. The University was apparently unaware that Columbus is not considered to be a hero by American Indian people. Ultimately, the University withdrew the name following public response against is.

The San Carlo Apache tribal council in 1993 reaffirmed resolutions opposing the construction of the telescope on Mount Graham. The council stated that the telescope "constitutes a display of profound disrespect for a cherished feature of our original homeland as well as a serious violation of our traditions religious beliefs."

166

After meeting with Apache elders and spiritual leaders at the San Carlos Apache Reservation, the National Council of Churches in 1995 passed a resolution calling for the removal of a telescope from Mount Graham.

The President's Advisory Council on Historic Preservation in 1996 declared the entire Mount Graham observatory a project to be in violation of the National historic Preservation Act because of the project's harm to Apache culture and spiritual life, but the telescope was not removed.

In 1997, the spokesman for the Apaches for Cultural Preservation was arrested for praying on Mount Graham. The Apaches for Cultural Preservation feel that the Forest Service, the University of Arizona and the Vatican developed the project on Mount Graham knowing that it would violate Apache religious beliefs. President Bill Clinton, using the line item veto, deleted $10 million in federal funds for the operation of the University of Arizona's Mount Graham telescope project. San Carlos Apache Chairman Raymond Stanley and the White Mountain Apache Cultural Resources Director Ramon Riley sent letters to the President thanking him for the veto.

Beginning in 1998 the University of Arizona began requiring Indians to obtain prayer permits before they crossed the top of Mount Graham near the University's telescopes. The University's prayer policy required that the permit be requested at least two business days before the visit and that it included a description of where on the mountain the prayers will take place. Only people who were enrolled members of federally recognized tribes were allowed to pray.

In 1999, the University of Notre Dame, a Catholic university, announced that it would also build a telescope on Mount Graham. the University president claimed that he was unaware that Mount Graham was sacred to the apache and that the Apache opposed the desecration of this sacred place in spite of the fact that the building of the telescope on this sacred mountain by the University of Arizona and the Vatican was a controversial issue and had been the subject to many news stories.

In 1999, the White Mountain Apache tribal council passed a resolution urging the U.S. Forest Service to "honor its duties to protect the physical integrity of Mount Graham and its long-standing and ongoing historical, cultural and religious importance to many Apaches."

Realizing that they were making little headway with the bureaucracies of the American government (Department of Interior and Department of Agricultural) and Congress, the Apaches took their cause to the United Nations in 1999. Ola Cassadore Davis testified before the Sub-Commission on Prevention of Discrimination and Protection of Minorities.

She stated:

"We Apache wish to bring to the people of this world a better understanding of Indian people, in order that we are able to preserve and freely live by our traditional cultural and religious beliefs."

Source:hhtp://www.envirolink.org/ext...

She asked that the special use permit by the Department of Agriculture Forest Service be terminated. She said:

"In conclusion, we Apache would respectfully urge this body of the United Nations to recognize and acknowledge that the disrespect and suffering caused by the nations and governments mentioned above be terminated forthwith. We Apache petition you for a resolution consistent with the National Congress of American Indians of 1993, 1995 and July 1999. They stated that the public interest in protecting Apache cultural is compelling, and that the U.S. Secretary of Agriculture should accordingly require the prompt removal of the telescopes from Mount Graham."

In 2004, the San Carlos Apache rejected an offer of $120,000 from the University of Arizona, calling it a bribe. Saying that the University had done nothing but tell lies to the Apache people, the San Carlos apache indicated that they would continue to honor their sacred mountain. One tribal council member indicated that if the University did not have a telescope on Mount Graham they would have no interest in the Apache people.

The conflict over this sacred site is still not resolved. on the one hand it can be viewed as a conflict between two different cultures. On the other hand, it can be seen as a conflict between science and religion.

The Mount Graham International Observatory is home to three telescopes: the Vatican Advanced Technology Telescope, the Heinrich Hetx Submillimeter Telescope, and the Large Binocular Telescope. On their website, their version of the history of Mount Graham focuses on James Duncan Graham and mentioned the Spanish Conquistadores. There is no mention of the Apaches. Their section on the legal actions necessary for the building of the complex mentions environmental concerns, but there is no mention of the Apache spiritual concerns.

The telescopes sit on land which has been leased from the Forest Service and the lease must be regularly renewed. Efforts by American Indian people and various environmental groups have so far been unsuccessful in convincing the forest Service to deny the renewal of the leases.
[Ref:http//www.nativeamericanroots.net/di...]

By Greg Szymanski, JD, investigative journalist, Arctic Beacon 2010

THE CATHOLIC CHURCH AND EVOLUTION

Since the publication of Charles Darwin's *On the Origin of Species* in 1859, the Catholic Church has been hedging its position on Darwin's work. There was no formal proclamation on the subject from the Holy See until Pope Pius XII agreed to allow academic freedom to study the scientific implications of evolution, as long as Catholic dogma was not violated but many clergy condemned it from the pulpit.

Darwin's work was published during the papacy of Pope Pius IX, who defined dogmatically papal infallibility during the First Vatican Council in 1869-70 and declared the following in the "Faith and Reason" section:

"Hence all faithful Christians are forbidden to defend as the legitimate conclusions of science those opinions which are known to be contrary to the doctrine of faith, particularly if they have been condemned by the Church; and furthermore they are absolutely bound to hold them to be errors which wear the deceptive appearance of truth" (Vatican Council I)

"Not only can faith and reason never be at odds with one another but they mutually support each other, for on the one hand right reason established the foundations of the faith and, illuminated by its light, develops the science of divine things; on the other hand, faith delivers reason from errors and protects it and furnishes it with knowledge of many kinds." (Vatican Council I)

Origin of the Species was never placed on the *Index Librorum Prohibitorum*; however, many Catholic writers who published works specifying how evolutionary theory and Catholic theology might be reconciled found themselves on the outs with the Vatican.

The Church's position is:
"Our first parents were formed immediately by God. Therefore we declare that the opinion of those who do not fear to assert that this human being, man as regards his body, emerged finally from the spontaneous continuous change of imperfect nature to the more perfect, is clearly opposed to Sacred Scripture of the Faith."

By the Editors

In Support of Creationism

•The Kolbe Center for the Study of Creation operates out of Jackson, Virginia, and is a Catholic lay apostate group.

•The "Faith Movement" was founded by Catholic Fr. Edward Holloway, in Surrey, England, and "argues from Evolution as a fact, that the whole process would be impossible without the existence of the Supreme Mind we call God."

CHURCH WARNS CELL SCIENTISTS
Not To Play God
From numerous press articles

Catholic Church officials have stated that the recent creation by researchers of the first synthetic cell can be a positive development if correctly used, but warned scientists that only God can create life.

The head of the Vatican Pontifical Academy for Life told the press, "We look at science with great interest. But we think above all about the meaning that must be given to life. We can only reach the conclusion that we need God, the origin of life."

The Catholic Church believes that human life is God's gift, created through natural procreation between a man and a woman.

At an Italian bishop's conference, Bishop Domenico Mogavero, expressed concern that scientists might be tempted to play God.

VATICAN ISSUES SWEEPING DOCUMENT OF BIOETHICS

The Vatican issued its most authoritative and sweeping document on bioethical issues, taking into account recent developments in biomedical technology and reinforcing the church's opposition to in vitro fertilization, human cloning, generic testing on embryos before implantation, and embryonic stem-cell research.

The Vatican says these techniques violate the principles that every human life –

even an embryo -- is sacred, and that babies should be conceived only through intercourse by a married couple.

The 32-page instruction, titled "Dignitas Personae" or the "Dignity of the Person", was issued by the Congregation for the Doctrine of the Faith, the Vatican's doctrinal office, and carries the approval and the authority of Pope Benedict XVI.

It bans the morning-after pill, the intrauterine device, and the pill RU-486, saying these can result in what amount to abortions.

The Vatican document reiterates that the church is opposed to research on stem cells derived from embryos. But it does not oppose research on stem cells derived from adults; blood from umbilical cords; or fetuses "who have died of natural causes."

The church also objects to freezing embryos, arguing that doing so exposes them to potential damage and manipulation, and raises the problem of what to do with frozen embryos that are not implanted. There are at least 400,000 of these in the United States alone.

"Vatican Roulette" or Natural Family Planning, is unnatural"

THE ROMAN CATHOLIC ALTERNATIVE TO CONDOMS: Vatican Roulette

Quite simply, the Catholic Church views contraception as immoral. The church teaches that contraception can never be a moral solution regardless of the enormity of any problem, which includes sustainable world population and the spread of HIV/AIDS.

The Catholic Church alternative to contraception is Natural Family Planning (NFP). Natural Family Planning requires a couple to track the woman's fertility cycle, using such methods as body temperature. If the couple does not want to conceive, it abstains from sex during the fertile days of the female's cycle, thus doing nothing immoral to prevent pregnancy.

The Catholic Church holds firm that NFP is a sustainable approach to over population, using inexpensive materials (the thermometer) rather than costly supplies, not always available to people living in poverty.

The Catholic Church believes contraception devices were invented for people who do not want to make the sacrifice of abstaining from sex because they want the instant gratification of the flesh.

However, on November 23, 2010, Victor L. Simpson of the Associated Press reported that "Pope Benedict XVI sought to 'kick-start a debate' when he said some condom use may be justified." This marked a curious departure from the Pope's previous stand: "Just a year after he said condoms could be making the AIDS crisis worse, Benedict said that for some people, such as male prostitutes, issuing them could be a step in assuming moral responsibility because the intent is to 'reduce the risk of infection.'"

Simpson went on to report that "The pope did not suggest using condoms for birth control, which is banned by the Church, or mention the use of condoms by married couples where one partner is infected."

Then, as reported by Victor L. Simpson and Nicole Winfield in the Associated Press on November 24, 2010, Pope Benedict XVI took another baby step by affirming that the use of condoms are "the lesser of two evils when used to curb the spread of AIDS, even if their use prevents a pregnancy." This baby step, however, has been called "a seismic shift" and a "game-changer" by observers.

So in a new twist of already twisted papal logic, the Pope has determined that it is OK for male prostitutes and others to use condoms to use condoms to prevent the spread of AIDS, even though the Church "condemns" prostitution and homosexuality as "intrinsically disordered."

But it is still forbidden to use condoms for the purpose of contraception.

By the Editors

Since the inception of birth control the population has risen from 4 billion to 6.5 billion. The only Pope to voice reform in the church for birth control because 40,000 children starve to death everyday was Pope John Paul I, who died mysteriously in September 1978.

Editor

Original Sin:
"Everyone is evil"

"Christians believe in guilty babies;
Catholics believe in guilty embryos."
William B. Lindley

BANNING

"Just think of the tragedy of teaching a child not to doubt."
Clarence Darrow

"People who don't read are no better off than people who can't read at all."
Thomas Jefferson

"Censorship always defeats its own purpose for it creates in the end a society that is incapable of exercising discernment."
Barry Steele Comminger

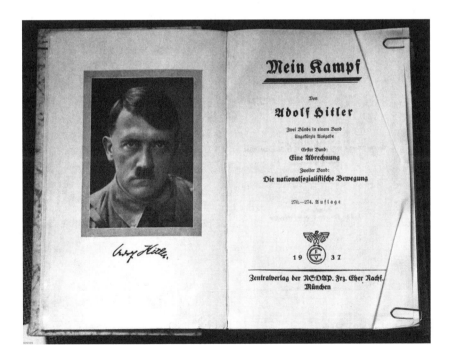

Mein Kampf

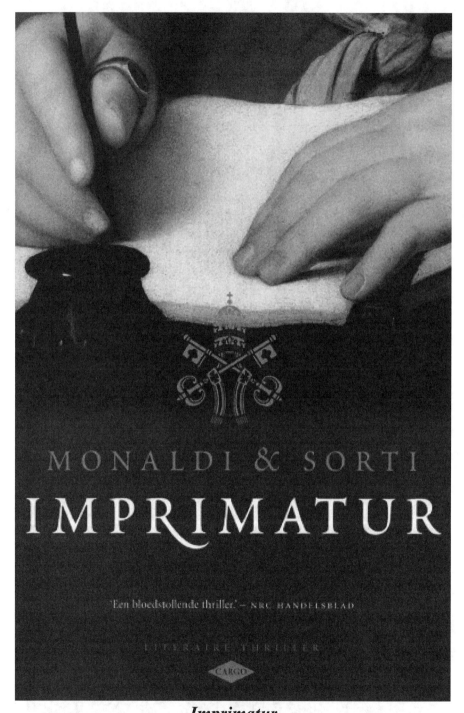

Imprimatur
**Getting on and off the list are dark episodes in the heretic paranoia
of the Church**

Banned Bible
The Church actually banned the Bible when it became popular with Protestants

TEN BOOKS BANNED BY THE CATHOLIC CHURCH

- *The Adventures of Huckleberry Finn by Mark Twain*
- *Harry Potter Series by J.K. Rowling*
- *Bridge to Terabithia by Katherine Paterson*
- *The Giver by Lois Lowry*
- *To Kill a Mockingbird by Harper Lee*
- *The Outsiders by S.E. Hinton*
- *James and the Giant Peach by Ronald Dahl*
- *The Face on the Milk Carton by Catherine Cooney*
- *Lord of the Flies by William Golding*
- *The Adventures of Tom Sawyer by Mark Twain*

Index Librorum Prohibitorum ("Index of Forbidden Books") is a list of publications the Catholic Church censored as dangerous to the church and the faith of its members.

The 20th and final edition of the list was published in 1948. The list was formally abolished on June 14, 1966 by Pope Paul VI.

NOTE: the Roman Catholic Church never banned Mein Kampf by Adolph Hitler.

NOTABLE AUTHORS WHO MADE THE LIST

Joseph Addison	Francis Bacon
Honore de Balzac	Simone de Beauvoir
George Berkley	Girodano Bruno
John Calvin	Gaicomo Casanova
Auguste Comte	Nicolaus Copernicus
Jean le Rond d'Alembert	Erasmus Darwin
Daniel Defoe	Rene Descartes
Denis Diderot	Alexandre Dumas, pere
Alexandre Dumas, fils	Anatole France
Galileo Galilei	Andre Gide
Graham Greene	Heinrich Heine
Thomas Hobbes	Victor Hugo
David Hume	Cornelius Jansen
Immanuel Kant	John Locke
Martin Luther	Niccolo Machiavelli
Karl Marx	Stuart Mills
John Milton	Blaise Pascal
Francois Rabelais	Jean-Jacques Rousseau
George Sand	Jean-Paul Sartre
Baruch de Spinoza	Jonathan Swift
Voltaire	Emil Zola

THE DEAD SEA SCROLLS COVER UP:
John Strugnell

John Strugnell was a pivotal person in the drama that developed after the Dead Sea Scrolls were discovered in 1947. Strugnell was educated at St. Paul's in London, became a professor at Harvard University, and was appointed to oversee the translation of the Dead Sea Scrolls. He worked on the Dead Sea Scrolls team for over forty years.

As a Catholic, Strugnell developed a working attitude toward the Dead Sea Scrolls project and those who could gain access to the Scrolls. Those renowned archeologists who did not share his Catholic view, such as John M. Allegro, were drummed off the team. Respected scholars such as Dr. Robert Eisenman and Theodore Gaster were blocked from accessing the scrolls in an effort to delay the progress and possibility of publishing the results of what was described as "the greatest archeological and historical find of our time."

During Strugnell's forty-year tenure, the team was more doctrinal than scholarly. Instead of consulting Aramaic and Hebrew language researchers, the team concentrated on the better-known Latin research. Finally in 1991 Dr. Robert Eisenman "liberated" the scrolls. The reason for forty years of delay became abundantly clear. Even more doctrinal than the team imagined, many of the scrolls were not compatible with the traditional Christian and Catholic story of Jesus. The scrolls tell of another teacher of righteousness in Jesus' brother James.

Strugnell sealed his fate in an interview with Haaretz Magazine when he stated, "Judaism is a horrible religion... and should not exist...it's a Christian heresy and we deal with heretics in different ways." Soon after the interview he was dismissed and, for a brief period, full access to the Dead Sea Scrolls was gained.

By Tim C. Leedom

John Strugnell
As the Catholic point man on the Dead Sea Scrolls team, he assembled a team that was ignorant of Hebrew and Aramaic languages. It took a banned Scroll and Biblical scholar, Dr. Robert Eisenman, to free the scrolls in 1991.

Pope Benedict says public figures who dissent from Church teachings should not receive
HOLY COMMUNION

Cardinal Joseph Ratzinger, now Pope Benedict XVI, went on record saying that public figures that openly dissent from Church teachings should not receive Communion.

In an official letter to the US bishops, the prefect of the Congregation for the Doctrine of the Faith wrote that Catholics who are "living in grave sin" or who "reject the doctrine of the Church," should abstain from the Eucharist.

The issue was brought to the forefront in the United States because of the presidential candidacy of John Kerry, a Catholic who was outspoken in his support for legal abortion and has opposed Church positions on issues such as euthanasia, stem-cell research, and homosexuality. Archbishop Raymond Burke of St. Louis said that he would deny Communion to Kerry; several other American bishops stated that politicians holding such views should not receive the Eucharist.

Some American bishops were reluctant to become involved in the public discipline of leading Catholic politicians for fear that they would be accused of violating the proper boundaries of Church-state affairs.

By the Editors

FREE SPEECH IS FREE SPEECH
Boston Bans Blogs

The Archdiocese of Boston blocked access to one of the websites from computers within the church's Braintree, Massachusetts headquarters.

The *Boston Catholic Insider* portrays Cardinal Sean P. O'Malley as a lax administrator and accuses his top aides of straying from Catholic doctrine and values.

Terrence C. Donilon, a spokesman for the archdiocese, said church officials blocked the site because it had become a distraction, not out of a desire to squelch debate. Its authors, he said, were "actively spamming the employees of the archdiocese with links to the site, interfering with their work day." He pointed out that employees could still visit it from their home computers.

The blogs contained the statement:

"Is the mere prospect of archdiocesan employees reading this blog concerning to Boston's archdiocesan leadership in a similar way that leaders of Communist China are concerned about Chinese citizens reading about the 1898 Tiananmen Square protests?" they wrote.

Bloggers told the press they consider themselves whistle-blowers and fear repercussions in their jobs and parishes if they identify themselves.

AFTER EDWARD (TED) KENNEDY'S DEATH
Brother of First Catholic President Ignored because of his Voting Record as a US Senator

U.S. Senator Ted Kennedy was the youngest brother of John F. Kennedy, first Catholic President of the United States. Upon Senator Ted Kennedy's death there was no response from Pope Benedict XVI.

According to press sources, "The niceties of international diplomacy do not require the Pope to issue a statement on the death of a non-head of state. However, earlier in the year when the Senator's sister Eunice was dying the Papal Nuncio to the U.S. delivered a letter to her family saying the Pope was praying for her, her children and her husband. One Vatican official told journalists, "Here in Rome, Ted Kennedy is nobody. He's a legend with his own constituency...If he had influence in the past, it was only with the Archbishop of Boston, and that eventually disappeared too."

Caroline Kennedy, daughter of the only U.S. Catholic President and one of history's most popular figures, was considered by President Obama to be the U.S. Ambassador to the Vatican but was considered too liberal and would be an outspoken person for change. The President caved in to political pressure and threats of condemning pro-life democrats who would withhold donations.

VATICAN DENOUNCES "AVATAR"
Numerous press articles

James Cameron's blockbuster **AVATAR** evoked criticism and warnings from Pope Benedict's Vatican.

Reviews by L'Osservatire Romano and Vatican Radio described the movie as "superficial" despite its ground-breaking effects. Vatican Radio said "it cleverly winks at all those pseudo-doctrines that turn ecology into the religion of the millennium."

Vatican spokesman, Reverend Federico Lombardi told the Italian press the movie reviews do reflect the views of Pope Benedict on the dangers of turning nature into a "new divinity". In his World Day of Peace remarks, Pope Benedict warned against ideas that equate human beings with other living things. He said such ideas "open the way to a new pantheism tinged with neo-paganism, which would see the source of man's salvation in nature alone."

ITALIAN COMEDIENNE FACED POSSIBLE IMPRISONMENT
For Insulting Pope
From numerous press articles

Sabina Guzzanti, an Italian comedienne, unwittingly violated the Lateran Treaty of 1929 with her joke about the Pope's anti-gay stance. The agreement between Italy and the Vatican says that an insult to the Pope shall carry the same penalty as an insult to the Italian president, five years in prison.

Paolo Guzzanti's father, a center Right MP, told journalists that the move was "a return to the Middle Ages. Perhaps my daughter should be submitted to the judgment of God by being made to walk on hot coals."

The Italian Minister of Justice decided not to proceed with prosecution against Ms. Guzzanti, "knowing the depth of the Pope's capacity for forgiveness."

The U.S. Amendment "Freedom of Speech and Press" is not a priority with the Roman Catholic Church.

"FATHER, MAY I?"

Permission to Publish

"Imprimatur" (translated from Latin: "Let it be printed") is the official declaration by the Vatican authorizing the publication of printed material.

"Nihil Obstat" (translated from Latin: "Nothing Hinders") is the first step in obtaining the imprimatur. The material must first be censored by a local ordinary in the jurisdiction of the author wishing to publish. If the censor finds no information damaging to the faith and morals of the Roman Catholic Church, he declares the material "nihil obstat."

The "nihil obstat" and imprimatur are declarations that printed material is free of doctrinal or moral error in the eyes of the Roman Catholic Church. These declarations do not indicate that the Church agrees with the contents, opinions or statements; only that the material is free of doctrinal and moral error.

The imprimatur is granted only for one work. Additional imprimaturs are required for later editions of the same work or translations of the work into another language.

AMERICA'S EDITOR RESIGNED
after Vatican Complaints

Thomas J. Reese, S.J. resigned as editor-in-chief of *America* magazine after repeated complaints from then-Cardinal Joseph Ratzinger, who objected to the magazine's treatment of sensitive church issues.

Jose M. DeVera, S.J., spokesman for the Society of Jesus (Jesuits) in Rome acknowledged that pressure had been coming from the Vatican for several years.

The articles that drew complaints included: "Dominus Iseus," the doctrinal congregation's document of Christ as the unique savior; same-sex marriage; stem-cell research and the reception of communion by Catholic politicians who supported legal abortion.

DeVera told the press, "The policy of Father Reese was to present both sides of the discussion. He wanted to present both sides within the Catholic community. But that did not sit well with Vatican authorities," Father DeVera said. Father DeVera said the tension had reached the point that Vatican officials had threatened to impose a board of censors on the magazine unless changes were made.

During Father Reese's tenure *America's* circulation grew and it was frequently quoted in other media. Father Reese, who has written books on how the Vatican and the U.S. Bishops operate, is frequently interviewed about church affairs by U.S. print and broadcast media.

This is not the fist time the doctrinal congregation influenced magazines run by religious orders.

In 1997 Pope John Paul II appointed an Italian bishop to oversee all Italian publications of the Pauline Fathers, including the weekly *Famiglia Cristiana*, which had a circulation of more than one million. It had run articles advocating Communion for divorced-remarried Catholics and arguing against censuring teenagers for masturbation.

The papal action came shortly after the order's superior general refused demands from Cardinal Ratzinger to rein in the magazine's editorial independence and to submit all articles to advance review by a panel of theologians appointed by the cardinal. The controversy ended with the removal of the magazine's director and, shortly after, his departure as a columnist.

By the Editors

ARCHBISHOP BANS MUSIC
No more rock...of ages

The Archbishop of Melbourne, Australia, banned the playing of pop music at funerals. According to his website: "Secular items are never to be sung or played at a Catholic funeral, such as romantic ballads, pop or rock music, political songs, football club songs."

The Archbishop told the press that funerals are not to be described as "a celebration of the life of the deceased."

THE LADY AND THE PITBULL

The Vatican's pit bull at the Catholic League slammed fellow Catholic Lady Gaga, who was educated at the elite Convent of the Sacred Heart in Manhattan and recently acknowledged as one of the world's most powerful women. Her offense was appearing in a white latex nun's habit and ingesting rosary beads as a symbol of spiritual cleansing. Lady Gaga's being on the Vatican's hit-list is similar to the condemnation of John Lennon's quote "We are more popular than Jesus," which was and is probably true considering 17% of the western population is atheist, 20% Islamic and Russia and China, where the Beatles had a solid following, are Communist.

By Tim C. Leedom

WOMEN AND THE CHURCH

The current abuses, denials, excuses, molestations and humiliations of women in the Catholic Church should come as no surprise if one simply looks at the history of the Catholic Church from the time of Constantine's overthrow of Rome and the Council of Nicaea.

"All women have been sexually abused by the Bible teachings, and institutions set on its fundamentalist interpretations. There would be no need for the women's movement if the Church and Bible hadn't abused them."

Father Leo Booth

ORDINATION OF WOMEN

Women: equal in the eyes of God but not in the eyes of the Pope

The official position of the Catholic Church, as expressed in the current canon law and the Catechism of the Catholic Church, is:

> "Only a baptized man validly receives sacred ordination."

The Church teaches this as a matter of divine law, thus doctrinal.

Today the issue of women's ordination is controversial and cutting a clear divide among members of the Catholic clergy as well as members. In a recent poll of Austrian priests, fifty-one per said women should be allowed to become Roman Catholic priests.

WOMEN PRIEST EXCOMMUNICATED
Mother Theresa, Virgin Mary, Mary Magdalene – could they have been priests?

Sister Bridget Mary Meehan was ordained in 2010 in Pittsburg, Pennsylvania by women bishops from Europe representing the global movement advocating the ordination of women.

She had been saying Mass at her home for two years until May, 2008 when the Vatican decreed that a women priest and those who ordained them are automatically excommunicated.

Meehan believes her excommunication was a good thing "…because we're really being recognized now as a movement within the church, even though they do not want to accept us quite yet."

She said "Women are excommunicated. Priests who are sexual abusers and the bishops who covered it up were not excommunicated. Now, does that really make sense?"

Women In The Catholic Church
No Women Need Apply

In opposition to the teachings of the Catholic Church, many scholars have written in favor of ordaining women.

TIMELINE OF WORLD RELIGIONS' ACCEPTANCE OF WOMEN'S ORDINATION

Early 1800s: In the U.S., in contrast with almost every other organized religion, the Society of Friends (Quaker) has allowed women to serve as minister since the early 1800's.

1815: Clarissa Danforth was ordained in New England by the Free Will Baptist denomination.

1853: Antoinette Brown Blackwell was ordained by the Congregationalist Church. Her ordination was not recognized by the denomination. She quit the church and later became a Unitarian. The Congregationalists later merged with others to create the United Church of Christ.

1861: Mary A. Will was the first woman ordained into the Weselyan Methodist Connection by the Illinois Conference.

1863: Olympia Brown was ordained by the Universalist denomination.

1865: Salvation Army was founded, which ordained both men and women.

1879: Mary Baker Eddy founded the Church of Christ, Scientist.

1880: Anna Howard Shaw was ordained in the Methodist Protestant Church.

1888: Fidelia Gillette was the fist ordained woman in Canada.

1889: Louisa Woosley was ordained in the Nolin Presbytery of the Cumberland Presbyterian Church.

1889: Ella Niswonger was ordained in the United Brethren Church

1892: Anna Hanscombe was ordained by the parent bodies that created the Church of the Nazarene in 1919.

1909: The Church of God (Cleveland, TN) began ordaining women.

1911: Ann Allebach was the first Mennonite woman to be ordained at the First Mennonite Church of Philadelphia.

1914: Assemblies of God was founded and ordained its first women clergy.

1917: The Church of England appoints female Bishop's Messengers to preach, teach and take missions in the absence of men.

1922: The Jewish Reform movement's Central Conference of American Rabbis stated that "Women cannot be justly denied the privilege of ordination."

1929: Izabela Wilucka is ordained in the Old Catholic Mariavite Church in Poland.

1936: The United Church of Canada starts to ordain women.

1947: Czechoslovak Hussite Church starts to ordain women.

1948: Evangelical Lutheran Church of Denmark starts to ordain women.

By the Editor from Church Sources; Inspired by Wikipedia (Retrieved July 23, 2010)

THE CATHOLIC CHURCH'S WAR ON NUNS

Nuns are struggling to find a meaningful role in Catholicism, but with Pope Benedict at the helm, the Church is doing everything it can to become more conservative – and force sisters back into lives of quiet obedience.

Since the reforms of Vatican II, and the dawn of mainstream feminism in the 1960s, many nuns have been trying to gain authority and redefine their positions within the Church. Now, Rome is launching an investigation into liberal American nuns. The goal: to find our whether nuns' movements into untraditional ministries (such as social justice work) and refusal to live in convents or wear religious robes is leading them astray.

"It's a witch hunt", says a Canadian religious sister who wishes to remain anonymous. "Women were just trying to build up the Church." She wants change, but it's almost impossible to push back – the Church has a history of punishing activist nuns, and religious sisters aren't allowed to be adversarial to men. It's hard to make big changes. We just don't have enough influence." Nuns are also frustrated by the Church's duplicity. While a recent ruling welcomes conservative Anglican priests fed up with female and openly gay clergy into the fold, religious sisters remain in handcuffs, their subjugation enforced.

Kenneth Briggs, a journalist and author of *Double Crossed: Uncovering the Catholic_Church's Betrayal of American Nuns*, says sisters deserve support, not questioning. "Priests aren't being investigated like this. There's a lot of people saying, 'Hey, aren't we investigating the wrong people?'"

During the reforms of the 1960s, there were many women working for change within the Church. But with an average age hovering around 70, today's nuns are often too tired for activism. Still, even a simple refusal to wear robes is seen as rebellion, and Briggs says Rome wants sisters silenced. "Nuns have a reputation of being more active, of picking up some of that feminist wave. The [traditionalist movement] is aimed at trying to oppose and eliminate that free spirit."

By Tom Henheffer, Canadian journalist.

CELIBACY

TIMELINE OF CELIBACY IN THE CATHOLIC CHURCH

Peter, depicted by the Roman Catholic Church as the first Pope, and the apostles were married men.

306 – The Council of Elvia, Spain, decreed "a priest who sleeps with his wife the night before Mass will lose his job."

325 – The Council of Nicaea decreed that after ordination a priest could not marry.

352- The Council of Laodicea decreed that women are not to be ordained.

385 – Pope Siricius left his wife to become Pope. He decreed that priests may no longer sleep with their wives.

401 – St. Augustine wrote: "Nothing is so powerful in drawing the spirit of a man downwards as the caress of a woman."

567- 2nd Council of Tours decreed any cleric found in bed with his wife would be excommunicated for a year and educed to a lay state.

580 – Pope Pelagius II made it a policy to not bother married priests as long as they did not hand over church property to wives or children.

590-604- Pope Gregory "the Great" said that all sexual desire is sinful in itself.

7-- - St. Boniface reported to the pope that in Germany almost no bishop or priest was celibate.

836- The Council of Aix-la-Chapelle admitted that abortion and infanticide took place in convents and monasteries to cover up activities of un-celibate clerics.

836 – St. Ulrich, argued that the only way to purify the church from the worst excesses of celibacy was to permit priests to marry.

1045- Benedict IX dispensed himself from celibacy and resigned in order to marry.

1074- Pope Gregory said anyone to be ordained must first pledge celibacy: "priests must first escape the clutches of their wives"

1095- Pope Urban II had priests' wives and children sold into slavery.

1123- First Lateran Council decreed that clerical marriages were invalid.

1300 – Bishop Pilagio complained that woman were still ordained and hearing confession.

1400s -50% of priests are married and accepted by the people

1545 – Council of Trent states that celibacy and virginity are superior to marriage.

1517 – Martin Luther

1530 – Henry VIII

1869 – First Vatican Council establishes infallibility of the pope

1930 – Pope Pius XI states sex can be good and holy

1951 – Pope Pius XII married a Lutheran pastor ordained catholic priest in Germany

1962: Pope John XXIII: Vatican council II states marriage is equal to virginity

1966 – Pope Paul VI: celibacy dispensations

1978 – Pope Paul VI puts a freeze on dispensations

1983 – New Canon Law

1980 – Married Anglican/Episcopal pastors are ordained as catholic priests on the U.S.

POPES WHO WERE MARRIED:

St. Peter the Apostle
St. Felix III (483-492) two children
St. Hormidas (514-523) one son
St. Silverus (536-537)
Hadrian II (867-872) one daughter
Clement IV (1265-1268) two daughters
Felix V (1439-1449) one son

POPES WHO HAD ILLEGITIMATE CHILDREN AFTER 1139:

Innocent VIII
Alexander VI
Julius
Paul III
Pius IV
Gregory XIII

Source: Religious investigation; Catholic Encyclopedia

Married Priests Now!

Married Priests USA and Married Priests Now! (MPN)) are organizations advocating changes in the rules of marriage for Roman Catholics priests. MPN is a Catholic organization lead by ex-Archbishop Emmanuel Milingo, a Zambian prelate.

According to Catholic Canon Law, the act of creating a bishop without permission of the Pope incurs automatic excommunication.

Milingo was excommunicated when he blatantly ordained four married men in the United States. The Vatican announced he was defrocked and referred to him as a layman.

Milingo stated: "There is no more important healing then the reconciliation of 150,000 married priests with the Mother Church…and the healing of a Church in crisis through renewing marriage and family."

By the Editors

WIDOW'S WALK
Reason For Priests Not To Marry

The real reason Catholic priests are forbidden to marry is that the Church historically wanted all their property and money to escheat to the Catholic Church upon their death.

BELGIUM BISHOPS QUESTION MANDATORY CELIBACY
A wave is coming and it's called the 21st Century

Two Belgian bishops openly declared that married men should not be excluded from the priesthood. Their comments came in the aftermath of the admission by the Belgian bishop that he sexually abused his nephew for years. However, the Vatican continues to insist that celibacy is not responsible for the molestations and that married priests in a non-negotiable issue.

Editor's Note: Pope Benedict XVI defends celibacy as a great sign of faith.

CATHOLIC INSURANCE

Are they in good hands?

The Catholic Church bans the right to coverage of birth control from health insurance coverage. The state of Wisconsin passed state legislature mandating that all health insurance companies that cover prescription drugs must cover contraceptive prescriptions. The Catholic Church is vehemently opposed to Wisconsin's law claiming it is immoral. Some Catholic hospitals are self-insured making them exempt from the ruling. Workers, including non-Catholics, could be terminated if birth control is used.

By the Editors

Section V

CRIMES OF THE CHURCH

PROTECTOR? OR PERPETRATOR?

LET US NOT CONFUSE THE DIFFERENCE BETWEEN "SINS" and "CRIMES."

RICO [Racketeer Influenced and Corrupt Organization Act] is on the books and has been used by federal prosecutors to jail many high profile members of the mafia since its passage in 1970. Simply put it targets organizations and businesses that show a consistent pattern of criminal activity. There has been a move in certain quarters by attorneys, members of congress and law enforcement to haul the Vatican, dioceses, cardinals and bishops in to court using the definitions laid out in the law. It makes sense to most people.

However, there is a huge roadblock to this common sense approach. The Roman Catholic Church, through intransigent strategy and questionable funding, has positioned itself in the halls of congress to virtually guarantee that justice will not prevail. There are now 131 Catholics in congress, 25 in the senate and most importantly on the U.S. Supreme Court there are 6 out of 9 justices who are Catholic. If for example a case such as the Brooklyn Poly Prep Country School Day School case worked its way to the Supreme Court it would never get a fair hearing with justices Sotomayor, Kennedy, Scalia, Thomas, Alito and Chief Justice Roberts sitting on the bench.

A prominent California state attorney lamented "The molested children of Catholic families will never have protection of the highest bodies in the land, nor the highest court. That is a crime in itself and I have seen with my own eyes the Vatican attorneys calling this and reduced statutes of limitations 'victories.'"

By Tim C. Leedom

Criminal History of the Papacy
How can the smallest country in the world cause so much world corruption?

Excerpted from Nexus Magazine, Volume 14, Number 1 (Dec. 2006- Jan. 2009)
By Tony Bushby, COPYRIGHT November 2006

The papal office has an unparalleled record of corruption and criminality over the centuries, and the true history of the popes is one of scandals, cruelty, debauchery, reigns of terror, warfare and moral depravity.

Most Catholics go through life and never hear a word of reproach for any pope or member of the clergy. Yet the recorded history of the lives of the clerical hierarchy bears no resemblance to its modern day portrayal, and the true stories of the popes in particular are among the most misrepresented in religious history. The Catholic historian and archbishop of New York, John Cardinal Farley (b.c. 1916) subtly admitted that the "old legends of their dissolute lives may be partly true...that they didn't sternly insist upon sexual virtue and injustice was a general license of the papal court, but it is probable that most improvement was at the vanguard of their thinking." (*Catholic Encyclopedia*, Pecci ed. 1897, iii, p. 207) Generally, the real character of the popes has been so falsely represented that many people don't know that so many popes were not only decadent but were also the most savage and perfidious of military strategists ever known. Cardinal Farley added this comment:

> " The popes were temporal rulers of the civil territory, and they naturally had recourse to force the re-establishment or extend the States of the Church until the conclusion of peace was confirmed...Their attempts to purify particularly the Duchy of Rome caused them considerable distress and the need to resort to violence, but always on the side of mercy...Lives were lost in the service of truth, but the legal basis for the Christian Church to hold and transmit properties for the benefit of revenues was given to them [the popes] by Emperor Constantine in 312." (*Catholic Encyclopedia*, Pecci ed., ii. Pp.157-169.)

The comments of the cardinal warrant our attention, for within them rests a little-known story of the leaders of the Christian religion and reveals that today's presentation of popes as incorruptible moral oracles is untrue. The hidden history of doctrinal foundations that permitted a papal alliance with conflict and licentiousness, and to what degree decadence among the clergy is "partly true," provides for an extraordinary story – one that has no precedent or parallel in the history of world religions. In the preface to an official papal record commissioned for publication by the Holy See, called *The Popes: A Concise Biographical History*, the Christian reader is tactfully prepared for some upcoming and unpleasant facts about popes with the apologetic admission:

> Some Catholics may find surprises when they read the papal biographies in this book. The part we are accustomed to think of the pope playing in the Church may need a little adjustment." (*The Popes: A Concise Biographical History*, Eric John, ed. Burns & Oates, Publishers to the Holy See, London, 1904. p. 19, published under the imprimatur of Georgius L. Craven)

This comment provides readers with a note of caution in dealing with papal history, but in this biographical history, the Holy See did not think it prudent to publish full details of the true nature of the papal court. Its real history is intermingled with "centuries of trafficking in ecclesiastical appointments, deceit, scandals, immorality, aggression, frauds, murder and cruelty, and the true disposition of the popes is knowingly falsely presented by the Church today." (*A History of the Popes*, Dr. Joseph McCabe [1867-1955] C.A. Watts & Co., London, 1939.)

For centuries, the Church maintained a comprehensive account of the lives of the popes who, up until the 11th century, called themselves "ecumenical patriarchs," and amazing excesses are recorded. Official Catholic records provide extraordinary confessions of wickedness in the whole Christian clergy, and the implications surrounding this knowledge begin to assume major new proportions when considered in light of the central Church claim of unquestionable piety in the clerical hierarchy.

The editorial committees of the Catholic Encyclopedia claim that their volumes are " the exponent of Catholic truth" (preface), and what is presented in this overview is assembled primarily from these records and without prejudice, in the same spirit, we also have available several papal diaries, letters and reports from foreign ambassadors at the Holy See to their governments, monastic documents, senatorial Roman records as well as access to the official and ancient registers of the ecclesiastical courts of London. Also of great help in this investigation was the availability of an original version of the Diderot's Encyclopedia, a tome that Pope Clement XIII (1758-69) ordered destroyed immediately after its publication in 1759. These documents uniformly report a condition of centuries of extraordinary debasement in the papal hierarchy and when considered in conjunction with the circumstances of their production, their contents can only be classed as astounding. The pretended holiness and piety of popes as publicly presented today is not represented in the records of history, and that provides proof of the dishonesty of the Church's own portrayal.

Pious Catholic historian and author Bishop Frotheringham extended this summary of Christian leaders up to his time:

"Many of the popes were men of the most abandoned lives. Some were magicians (occults); others were noted for sedition, war, slaughter and profligacy of manners, for avarice and simony. Others were not even members of the Church, but the basest of criminals and enemies of all godliness. Some were children of their father, the Devil, most were men of blood, and some were not even priests. Others were heretics. If the Pope be a heretic, he is ipso facto no pope."

(*The Cradle of Christ*, Bishop Frotheringham, 1877, see also *Catholic Encyclopedia*, xii. Pp. 700-703, passim, published under the imprimatur of Archbishop Farley)

And heretics they were, with many popes publicly admitting disbelief in the Gospel story, as we shall see. These facts are well known to Catholic historians who dishonestly tell their readers that the popes were virtuous and competent men with "soaring religious minds" (*The Papacy*, George Weidenfeld & Nicolson Ltd., London, 1964.) The reality of the matter is that they were intent on only upon their own interests, not those of God or Man, and cultivated a system of papal vice more assiduously than Catholic writers of Church history dare to reveal openly. The laity resented them and, when better economic conditions awakened the minds of a developing European middle class, there was widespread rebellion against them. Christian records show that popes were clearly a long way removed from the modern-day presentation of their character, and in trying to portray them with a pious past the Church developed a doctrinal façade that brazenly and deceptively presents them as devout.

With the late 20th-century model of the papacy in one's mind, it is difficult to imagine what it would have been like in the 16th or 14th centuries, let alone the 10th or the eighth. The now-called expounders of "Christian virtue" were brutal killers and "crimes against the faith were high treason, and as such were punishable by death" (*Catholic Encyclopedia*, Farley ed., xiv, p. 768.) Popes waded through rivers of blood to attain their earthly objectives and many personally led their Episcopal militia into the fields of battle. The Church ordered its "secular arm" to force its dogma upon humanity by "mass murder" (*The Extermination of the Cathars,* Simonde de Sismondi, 1826), and "the clergy, discharging in each district the functions of local state officials, seem never to have quite regained the religious spirit" (*Catholic Encyclopedia*, Farley ed., I p. 507) Apologetic contributors to Christian history vainly try to portray an air of sophistry about a papal past that scandalized Europe for centuries and one that is clearly unsophisticated and primitive.

As the line of popes began obscurely, we shall begin our assessment in the year 896 when "a body of nobles with swinish and brutal lusts, many of whom could not even write their own names" (*Annals of Hincmar*, Archbishop of Reims; pub. C. 905) captured the papacy and drew to a close 631 years later in 1527 when, under the subterfuges of Pope Clement VII (1523-1534), Rome fell to the army of Emperor Charles V.

In this brief evaluation of just a few popes, we read:

On the death of Pope Formosos (896) there began for the papacy a time of the deepest humiliation, such as it has never been experienced before or since. After the successor of Formosos, Boniface VI, had ruled only fifteen days, Stephen VII [VI] was raised to the papal chair. In his blind rage, Stephen not only abused the memory of Formosos but also treated his body with indignity. Pope Stephen was strangled in prison in the summer of 897, and the six following popes (to 904) owed their elevation to the struggles of the rival political parties. Sergius III (904-911" overthrew Christophorus, the last of them. (*Catholic Encyclopedia*, ii.p. 147)

Such periods of "deepest humiliation" to the papacy were quite recurrent, and have been even into the 21st century when the extent of priesthood pedophilia was publicly exposed (Apology of Pope John Paul II, March 2002).

It was Pope Stephen VII [VI] "a gouty and gluttonous old priest" (Bishop Liutprand of Cremona, c. 922-972), who ordered the rotting corpse of Pope Formosos to be exhumed from its grave of eight months, tied upright in a chair and put on trial for transgressions of the canon. In front of his putrefying body and dressed in purple and gold regalia stood the pope, his bishops, the nobles of Rome and Lamberto of Tuscany.

The "trial" was a grotesque and obscene farce. The pope paced backwards and forwards and shrieked at the corpse, declaring it guilty. A deacon, standing beside the decomposing body of the ex-pope, answered on its behalf. In this macabre incident, today piously called the "Cadaver Synod", the deceased pope was duly condemned, stripped of his vestment, three fingers cut from his right hand and his remains dumped into the River Tiber.

"In this disgusting business, he, Pope Stephen VII [VI] cannot be excused for what followed. In declaring the dead pope deposed he also annulled all his acts, including his ordination. His grim and grisly role provoked a violent reaction in

199

Rome, and in late July or early August Pope Stephen was imprisoned and later strangled". (*The Popes: A Concise Biographical History*, ibid. p. 160)

Morbid in its realism, the mental limitations of ancient popes are thus shown. From these and similar displays, we understand why the monks at the Eulogomenopolis monastery, today called Monte Cassino, described the Asinarian Station (later renamed the Lateran Palace) as an "abode of wrath, a charnel-house…a place of exotic vice and crime."

The Unholy "Rule of Whores"
Bishop Liutprand of Cremona, whose Antapodsis treats papal history from 886 to 950, left a remarkable picture of the vice of the popes and their Episcopal colleagues, maybe with a little jealously: "They hunted on horses with gold trappings, had rich banquets with dancing girls when the hunt was over, and retired with these shameless whores to beds with silk sheets and gold embroidered covers. All the Roman bishops were married, and their wives made silk dresses out of the sacred vestments". Their lovers were the leading noble ladies of the city, and "two voluptuous imperial women," Theodora and her daughter Marozia, "ruled the papacy of the tenth century" (Antapodsis, ibid.). Renowned Vatican historian Cardinal Caesar Baronius (1538-1607) called it the "Rule of the Whores", which "really gave place to the even more scandalous rule of the whoremongers". (*Annales Ecclesaistical*, folio iii, Antwerp, 1597). All that Bishop Liutprand reveals in detail about Theodora is that she compelled a handsome young priest to reciprocate her passion for him and had him appointed Archbishop of Ravenna. Later, Theodora summoned her archepiscopal lover from Ravenna and made him Pope John X (pope 914-928, d.928).

John X is chiefly remembered as a military commander. He took to the field in person against the Saracens and defeated them. He indulged in nepotism, or the enrichment of his family, and his conduct prepared the way for a deeper degradation of the papacy. He invited the Hungarians, who at this time were still half-civilized Asiatics, to come and fight his enemies and thus he brought a new and terrible plague upon his country. He had no principles in his diplomatic, political or private conduct. He spurned Theodora and enticed the charming young daughter of Hugh of Provence into his papal bedroom. Spurned, Theodora then married Guido, Marquis of Tuscany, and together they carried out a *coup d'etat* against John X. Theodora died suddenly by suspected poisoning, and John X entered into a bitter quarrel with Marozia and the leading nobles of Rome. John had brought his brother Peter to Rome, raised him to the rank of nobility, and heaped upon him the profitable offices which the elder nobles had come to regard as their preserve. In was an internal struggle for power. The nobles, led by Marozia, drove Peter, Pope John, and their troops from the city. The pope and his brother increased their army and returned to Rome, but a body of Marozia's men cut their way into the

Lateran Palace and murdered Peter before the pope's eyes. John was captured, declared deposed in May 928 and smothered to death in the Castel Sant' Angelo.

Marozia and her faction then appointed Leo VI (928) the new pope, but replaced him seven months later with Stephen VIII [VII]. He ruled for two years and then Marozia gave the papacy to her son, John XI (c. 910-936; pope 931-35). Pope Sergius III, illegitimately fathered him as "confirmed by Flodard, a reliable contemporary writer" (*The Popes: A Concise Biographical History*, ibid., p. 162). Sergius had previously taken the papacy by force with the help of Marozia's mother, Theodora. Both Theodora and Sergius took a leading part in the earlier outrage on the corpse of Formosus, and Sergius was later accused of murdering his two predecessors. The Church defended itself, but in doing so revealed that he wasn't the only pope sexually involved with Marozia:

> "It is commonly believed that Pope Sergius, although a middle-aged man, formed a union with the young Marozia and by her had a son, the future Pope John XI. Most of the information we have on the career of Marozia and the Roman scandals in which she and a series of popes were involved is derived from hostile sources and may be exaggerated". (*The Popes: A Concise Biographical History*, ibid.)

This rare painting is reproduced from a 17th century edition of Antapodosis, a 1,000 year old text written by Bishop Liutprand of Cremona who died c. 972. It purports to show Pope Stephen VIII [VII] overseeing the exhumation of Pope Formosus's corpse in readiness for its trial. An interesting aspect of this painting is the pope's headgear, reminiscent of the "crown of thorns" worn by the Caesar clan.

With sacerdotal dictatorship, Marozia ruled Christianity for several decades from the papal castle near St. Peter's, and dealt with everything Christian except routine matters. She could not sign her own name, yet she was the head of the Christian Church – a fact known to historians who have at least an elementary acquaintance with the papal record. She was amorously aggressive, callous, densely ignorant and completely unscrupulous. She appointed ruthless warrior-bishops to strengthen her factions, and she triumphed in her rule over oppositions. To translate the words of the Roman people literally, they called her "the Popes' whore" (plural) and she was directly responsible for selecting and installing at least four popes. Modern-day apologists say her promotions were "scandalous," but the Church now accepts those popes as "legitimate" successors of St. Peter. At the time, however, large bodies of good folk deeply resented the obscene farce the papal religion had become and turned upon it with disdain and anger. Later in his papacy, Pope John XI took ill and Marozia temporarily installed an elderly monk in the papal chair. He subsequently refused to resign and was forcibly removed to a prison cell to be starved to death. John XI then resumed his position and exhausted his remaining wealth hiring soldiers to restore order in Rome. The city was heavy with a feeling of revolt against the Church and the appalling clerical morals that existed throughout Italy. John XI then set out to recover and secure the rich temporal domains of the papacy, but in 936 he died. Thus, in this condensed description, we learn with amazement of the days when loose women ruled the Holy See and a Christian doctrine had not yet been developed.

The Papacy Sold Amidst New Depths of Wickedness

As incredible as it may seem, the papacy then sank to a lower depth of wickedness and remained in this condition for nearly a thousand years. Christian historians brush aside the true nature of the popes, saying that they never regarded them as "impeccable" and ignoring the fact that they committed outrages against every standard of human decency.

Pope John XII (Octavian, c. 937-964, pope 955-964, The Popes: A Concise Biographical History, ibid. pp. 166-7) was another in the succession of impious popes and he opened his inglorious career by invoking pagan gods and goddesses as he flung the dice in gambling sessions. He toasted Satan during a drinking spree and put his notorious mistress/prostitute Marcia in charge of his brothel in the Lateran Palace (Antapodosis, ibid.). He "liked to have around him a collection of "Scarlet women," said the monk-chronicler Benedict of Soracle, and at his trial for the murder of an opponent his clergy swore on oath the he'd had incestuous relations with his sisters and had raped his nuns (*Annals of Beneventum in the Monumenta Germaniae*, v) He and his mistresses got so drunk at a banquet that they accidentally set fire to the building. It would be difficult to imagine a pontiff who was farther removed from sainthood, yet in an age when the average life of a pope was two years, he held the throne for 10 years. However, his life came to a sudden and violent end when, according to pious chroniclers, he was killed by the Devil while raping a woman in the house in the suburbs. The truth is that the Holy Father was thrashed so severely by the enraged husband of the woman that he died of injuries eight days later. Emperor Otto then demanded that the clergy select a priest of respectable life to succeed John XII, but they could not find one. The new Pope, Leo VIII (963-965), was a layman drawn from "civil service who was put through all clerical orders in one day" (ibid.). Leo VIII is reckoned by the modern-day Church to be "a true pope." But his "election is a puzzle" – one that canonists have not cared to unravel (ibid.).

The Catholic Encyclopedia gives additional accounts of papal debasement:

"The Popes 'Benedict' from the fourth to the ninth inclusive (IV – IX) belong to the darkest period of papal history. Benedict VI (973) was thrown into prison by the anti-pope Boniface VII (d. 983), and strangled by his orders in 974. Benedict VII was a layman and became pope by force, and drove out Boniface VII. Pope Benedict IX (c. 1012-1055/1065/1087; pope 1032-45, 1047, 1048) had long caused scandal to the Church by his disorderly life. His immediate successor, Pope Gregory VI [1044-46], had persuaded Benedict IX to resign the Chair of Peter, and to do so bestowed valuable possessions on him." (*Catholic Encyclopedia*, I, p. 31)

Anti-Pope Boniface VII was described by Gerbert (to become Pope Sylvester II, 999-1003) as "a horrible monster that in criminality surpassed all the rest of mankind," but the "scandal" of Pope Benedict IX deserves special mention His name was Grottaferrata Teofilatto (Theophylact, in some records) and in 1032 he won the murderous scramble for the wealth of the papacy. He immediately excommunicated leaders who were hostile to him and quickly established a reign of terror. He officially opened the doors of "the palace of the popes" to homosexuals and turned it into an organized and profitable male brothel (*The Lives of the Popes in the Early Middle Ages*, Horace K. Mann, Kegan Paul, London, 1925). His violent and licentious conduct provoked the Roman people, and in January 1044 the residents of the city elected John of Sabine, under the name of Pope Sylvester III, to replace him. But Sylvester was quickly driven out by Benedict's brothers and fled for his life into the Sabine Hills.

Benedict IX then sold the papacy to his godfather, Giovanni Graziano, who assumed the papal chair as Pope Gregory VI, but in 1047 Benedict reappeared and announced he was reclaiming the papacy. The Church added that he was "… immoral…cruel and indifferent to spiritual things." The testimony to his depravity shows his disinterest in religious matters, and his disrespect for an ascetic life was well known. He was the worst Pope since John XII" (*The Popes: A Concise Biographical History*, ibid., p. 175.) Upon his death, the undertaker refused to build him a coffin. He was surreptitiously buried in a cloth under the cover of darkness. Four succeeding popes then briefly held the papal position, and the following paragraph from The *Catholic Encyclopedia* is pregnant with evidence of the moral depravity of the entire priesthood.

"At the time of Leo IX's election in 1049, according to the testimony of St. Bruno, Bishop of Segni, 'the whole Church was in wickedness, holiness had disappeared, justice had perished, and truth had been buried; Simon Magnus was lording it over the Church, whose popes and bishops were given to luxury and fornication. The scientific and ascetic training of the popes left much to be desired, the moral standard of many being very low and the practice of celibacy not everywhere observed. Bishops obtained their offices in irregular ways, whose lives and conversations are strangely at variance with their calling, who go through their duties not for Christ but for motives of worldly gain. The members of the clergy were in many places regarded with scorn, and their avaricious ideas, luxury and immorality rapidly gained ground at the centre of clerical life. When ecclesiastical authority grew weak at the fountain head, it necessarily decayed elsewhere in proportion, as the papal authority lost the respect of many, resentment grew against both the Curia and the papacy'"(*Catholic Encyclopedia*, vi, pp. 793-4; xii, pp. 700-03, passim)

Pope Leo IX (b. 1002, d. 1054) was an unscrupulous adventurer who spent his pontification touring Europe with a quota of armed knights, and left the world worse than he found it. The Church called him "Lapsi" (lapsed), coyly admitting that "he defected from the faith...he fell away by actual offering sacrifice to the false gods (thurificati) ...it is not known why he recanted his religion" *Catholic Encyclopedia*, Pecci ed., iii, p. 117).

St Peter Damian (1007-72), the fiercest censor of his age, unrolled a frightful picture of decay in clerical morality in the pages of his *Book of Gomorrah*, a curious Christian record that remarkably survived centuries of Church cover-ups and book burnings. He said "A natural tendency to murder and brutalize appears with the popes. Nor do they show any inclination to conquer their abominable lust, and many are seen to have employed into licentiousness for an occasion to the flesh, and hence, using this liberty of theirs, perpetrating every crime."

After a lifetime of research into the lives of the popes, Lord Acton (1834-1902), English historian and founder-editor of the Cambridge Modern History, summarized the militarist papal attitude when he observed:

"The popes were not only murderers in the great style, but they also made murder a legal basis of the Christian Church and a condition of salvation." (*The Cambridge Modern History*, vol.1 pp.673-77).

Maybe they took their example from Jesus Christ who, after being made the king, issued this murderous instruction: "Bring my enemies here that did not want me as king, and kill them in my presence" (Gospel of Luke, 19.27, Mount Sinai Manuscript of the Bible, British Museum, MS 43725, 1934). The Catholic Bible provides a softer approach. " But those, my enemies, which would not that I should reign over them, bring hither, and slay them before me" (Luke 19:27). Popes today do everything in their power to present Jesus as a harmless religious preacher and a prophet of peace, but carefully refrain from entering into discussion about this Gospel passage, one that nullifies everything that Christianity purports to represent.

Papal Warships and Rival Imperialist Popes

Around the time of St. Peter Damian, we find a reference to the existence of a papal navy crewed by Christian warrior-sailors. It was originally founded in 881 by Pope John VIII (pope 872-882; d. 882), but details of its size and missions do not publicly exist (Encyclopedia Britannica, vol. 6, 1973, p. 572) However, from a later solitary reference to "the Pope's fighting fleet" recorded in 1043 (Diderot's Encyclopedia, 1759). It was still operational at that time. This extraordinary record was found in documentation once belonging to the powerful Roman Crescenti family, who played an important part in papal coups from the middle of the 10th century to the beginning of the 11th century. The Pope's Navy was still operational in the 16th century, some 700 years after its inception. Pope Gregory XIII (b. 1502; pope 1572-85) commissioned Giorgio Vasan (1511-74) to paint a picture of the fleet while it was moored at the port of Messina in Sicily.

The true significance of records of such a military force nullifies the modern-day presentation of the "sweetness and light" that the Church today says Christianity brought to the world.

Further apologizing for centuries of pandemonium caused by popes, and giving a smear of whitewash to their actions, the Vatican has admitted that at the time of Pope Alexander II (1061-73) "the church was torn by the schisms of anti-popes, simony and clerical incontinence" (*Catholic Encyclopedia*, i. p. 541). The development of a multiplicity of popes simultaneously operating in conflict with each other is a little known episode in Christian history and provides clear evidence of the existence of powerful fractional opponents scheming to gain solitary control of the Papal States. "The Church was disturbed many times in her history by rival claimants to the papacy…the strife that originated was always an occasion of scandal, sometimes of violence and bloodshed" (*Catholic Dictionary*, Virtue & Co., London, 1954, p. 35).

In modern times, the Church labeled the anti-popes "devils of the chair of St. Peter," claiming that they were unlawfully appointed (*Catholic Dictionary*, ibid.). That distinction, however is purely arbitrary, for each multiple pope was canonically elected at Church conclaves. Here is an extraordinary confession from the Church:

"At various times in the history of the Church, illegal pretenders to the papal chair have arisen and frequently exercised pontifical functions in defiance of the true occupant. According to [Cardinal] Hergenrother (d. 1890), the last anti-pope was Felix V (1439-49). The same authority enumerates twenty-nine in the following order: [naming them]" (*Catholic Encyclopedia*, I, p. 582).

205

Each opposing papal hierarchy was supported by formidable military factions, and the subject of popes warring against each other is a topic too vast to summarize here. Their struggles for power were conducted with amazing bitterness, and the word "schism" is not strong enough for the depth of the fury that raged for centuries within the Christian religion. Catholic historians admit that "even now, it is not perhaps absolutely certain from the two lines of popes who was pope and who was anti-pope, or which anti-pope was a legal anti-pope" (*Catholic Encyclopedia*, Pecci ed,iii, 107; also *Catholic Dictionary*, ibid.).

This is luminous clerical reasoning, but there is more to this particular side of Holy See history and it is found in a book called Secrets of the Christian Fathers, written in 1685 by Roman Bishop Joseph W. Sergerus (d. c.1702). He provides evidence from Church archives at his disposal that at some periods in papal history there were four popes occupying the papal chair(s), each in a different building, city or country, operating independently with their own cardinals and staff and holding their own canonical councils. He names them, and one example from 12 quadruple sets of popes is that of the self-declared Pope Benedict XIV (1425) who, for years, rivaled popes Benedict XIII (1429), Clement VIII (!429) and Martin V (1431). In more recent times, Church historians have ingeniously referred to the fourth member of the quadruple set as "a counter anti-pope" (*The Popes: A Concise Biographical History*), and stated that "this is not the place [in Church reference books] to discuss the merits or motives of the multiple claimants" (*Catholic Encyclopedia*, Pecci ed., iii, pp. 107-8; *Catholic Dictionary*).

The introduction of the word "anti-pope" was a retrospective move by the Church to eliminate the reality of simultaneously serving popes and thus provide itself with a singular continuous ministerial succession of popes from St. Peter to Benedict XVI today. Investigation of the Church's own records, however, reveals that the claim of an unbroken papal continuity is false. Bishop Bartolomeo Platina (1421-81) a Christian historian and the first prefect (1475-81) of the embryonic Vatican Library, admitted that the direct lineage "was interrupted by repeated periods after Nicholas I (pope 858-867); an interregnum of eight years, seven months and nine days, etc., etc.,". those breaks are piously called "vacations" and are recorded by Bishop Platina as totaling "127 years, five months and nine days" (*Vitae Pontificum* ["Lives of the Popes"]. Bishop Platina, first pub. C. 1479; also *Catholic Encyclopedia*, xii, pp. 767-68). However, Platina failed to record the "vacations" that occurred in the nine centuries or so preceding Nicholas I, for "unfortunately, few of the records (of the Church) prior to the year 1198 have been released" (*Encyclopedia Biblica*, Adam & Charles Black, London 1899). Clerical insiders know writings purporting to record the lineage of popes are false, saying:

"As for the pretend catalogues of succeeding bishops of the different assemblies from the days of the apostles, exhibited by some ecclesiastical writers, they are filled up by forgeries and later inventions. Thus diocesan bishops came in, whose offices are considered as corruption or dishonest applications, as dictated by the necessities of the Church, or of instances of worldly ambition." (*The Authentic and Acknowledged Standards of the Church of Rome*, J. Hannah, DD., 1844, p. 414.)

However, humanitarian and biblical scholar Desiderius Erasmus (c. 1536) got it right when he frankly stated that "succession is imagery" (Erasmus in Nov. Test. Annotations, fol, Basel, 1542), simply because its modern day portrayal is contrary to recorded historical fact.

Around 50 years after the time of Pope Alexander II (s. 1073), an influential and opposing faction elected Lamberto of Bologna as Pope Honorius II (1124-30) and the church maintained its two rival popes, each bitter and warring opponents both living murderous and luxurious lifestyles. There is no doubt that Honorius was determined to buy or force his way into the papal chair and he succeeded, preserving his position for the term of his life. Upon his death, two new popes, Anacletus II (1130-38) and Innocent II (1130-43) were elected and consecrated on the same day by opposing clerical factions. Before the election, Pietro Pierleoni (anti-Pope Anacletus II) was military leader of a rival army whose family had fought for 50 years for control of the Holy See – a confrontation subtly called the "Fifty-Year War" by the Church today. If we can believe his enemies, he disgraced the papal office by his gross immorality and his greed in the accumulation of lucre. When Pierleoni died in 1138, his faction elected Victor IV to the papal chair (*Catholic Encyclopedia* I, p. 447). The church remained in bitter conflict, still under the divided control of two popes, neither possessing a Bible and each operating independently (*Confessions of a French Catholic Priest*, Mathers, New York, 1837).

The extent of papal transgression is expanded by the words of the Church through the Pecci edition (1897) of its *Catholic Encyclopedia*.

"At the time of Gregory VII's elevation to the papacy (1073-85), the Christian world was in a deplorable condition." During the desolating period of transition, the terrible period of warfare and rapine violence, and corruption in high places, which followed immediately upon the dissolution of the Carolingian Empire, a period when society in Europe seemed doomed to destruction and ruin, the Church had not been able to escape from the general debasement to which it has so signally contributed, if not caused. The tenth century, the saddest perhaps in Christian annals, is characterized by the remark of Cardinal Baronius (Vatican historian, 1538-1607) that "Christ was asleep in the vessel of the Church." (*Catholic Encyclopedia*, Pecci ed. Ii.pp 289,294, passim, also vi, pp.791-95).

Another peculiar event from the annals of Christianity takes us into the 12th Century and this piece of evidence makes us wonder just what was going through the minds of the popes. After an intriguing conclave lasting 10 weeks, Gherado Caccianemici was elected pope in 1144 and adopted the name of Lucius II. Modern Catholic historians look upon him as "a pillar of the Roman Church" (*The Popes: A Concise Biographical History*, ibid., p. 215) but the truth of the matter is much different. The Italians saw with dismay the new papal policy in which Pope Lucius II ordered a crusade against his own flock in Rome. Eleven months later, he personally led papal troops into battle and stormed the city. However, the residents, led by Giordano (Jordan) Pierleoni, rose up against him and the pope's army was defeated with great loss of life. Badly wounded in battle, Lucius II died of injuries on 15 February 1145 (*The Pope Encylcopedia: An A to Z of the Holy See*, Matthew Burson, Crown, New York, 1995).

The inquisition and the Crusades against the Cathars

The "glorious 12th century", which for some reason the faithful exalt proudly above all others of the Dark Ages of Faith, was ushered in with the horrific inquisition and the 35-year crusade against the Cathars (sometimes called the Albigenses). "By this term [inquisition] is usually meant a special ecclesiastical institution for combating or suppressing heresy" (*Catholic Encyclopedia*, viii, p. 26)- "heresy" simply meaning "holding a different opinion." Its introduction was the only time in Christian history when the Church was united in purpose and spoke with one voice. The Inquisition became a permanent office of Christianity and, to justify the tribunal's principles, the popes introduced a potent instrument in the form of an additional series of fictitious documents called the "Forged Decretals of Gratian".

The darker features of this period are not in dispute among authoritative historians, and here if ever, we must proceed with severe discrimination. In this period of Christian history, hundreds of thousands of people were butchered by the Church and the fairest half of France was laid desolate. In 1182, Pope Lucius III (1181-85, d. 1185) gained control of the official apparatus of the Church, and in 1184 declared the Cathars heretics and authorized a crusade against them. A crusade is a war instigated by the Church for alleged religious ends, and it was authorized as a papal bull.

Eighty-six years earlier, in 1096, Pope Urban II (1042-99; pope 1088-99) sanctioned the first of eight Church crusades that extended in time to a total of 19, and they continued unabated for 475 years (1096-1571). Heresy, said the Church, was a blow in the face of God and it was the duty of every Christian to kill heretics. Earlier still, Pope Gregory VII (1020-85; pope 1073-85) officially declared that "[the killing of heretics is not murder]" and decreed it legal for the Church and its militants to kill non-believers in Christian dogma. Up until the 19th century, popes compelled Christian monarchs to make heresy a crime punishable by death under their civil codes, but it was not heresy that instigated the crusade against the Cathars: its purpose was to "yield the papacy additional land and revenues, and the popes engaged in brutalities, threats and all kinds of stratagems to attain their ends." (*The Story of Religious Controversy*, Dr. Joseph McCabe, 1929, p. 40).

The Cathars, a peaceable and pious body of people, were now singled out by the Christian hierarchy for total destruction. We find it hard to realize the commotion raised by Christianity and the ardor of the popes' bitter campaign against the Cathars, and later against the progeny of Frederick II and then the Knights Templar.

Pope Celestine III (1106-98; pope 1191-98) supported the earlier decision of Pope Lucius III to annihilate every Cathar from the face of the Earth. To do this, now early in the 13th century, Pope Innocent III (Lotario di Segni, 1161-1216; pope 1198-1216), "one of the greatest popes of the Middle Ages" (*Catholic Encyclopedia*, viii, p. 13) ordered Dominic de Guzman (1170-1223) to deliver a troop of merciless followers called "the Catholic army" (*Catholic Encyclopedia* v. p. 107) and an initial force of 200,000 foot troops was established with assistance from 20,000 mail-clad, horse-mounted knights. The general populace labeled them the "Throat-cutters" but Dominic deemed them the "Militia of Jesus Christ" (ibid.), and he later increased the army by an additional 100,000 troops. The Catholic writer Bishop Delany (d.c.127) said that the Church's fighting force developed into 500,000 troops against a body of ordinary unarmed folk who saw that, in practice, the papal system of religion was frivolous and false.

This mosaic of Pope Innocent III, showing him around the time he became pope at the age of thirty-seven (c. 1198), is from the old basilica of St. Peter. Innocent III ruled "one of the most shameful episodes in Christian history" (The Papacy, ibid. p. 67). Because of his vehemence in dealing with "the menace of heresy" (*Catholic encyclopedia*, viii, p. 16), his name in later times became a synonym for cruelty (*Diderot's Encyclopedia*).

The crusade against the Cathars began on 22 July 1209, and it was a ruthless demonstration of the Church Militant Arnaud Amaury (d. 1225), the Abbey of C'teaux. He commanded troops bearing a banner with a green cross and a sword and members of the French nobility, including the Duke of Burgundy and the County of Nevers. The truth of the matter is that when the army was activated, it was directed and manipulated unequivocally under the control of the Church of Christ. With instructions of Abbey Amaury, the Church undertook one of the most gruesome massacres of human beings in world history.

What followed is horrific. The crusades started at Beziers, and some chroniclers say that all inhabitants of the city were massacred within one week. Some put the number of the dead at 40,000 men, women and children. It is said that during the first few days, 6,000 or 7,000 people were systematically taken to the Church of St. Magdalene and individually slaughtered. It is a great pity that we have no reliable records of the population of Beziers. One can only point out that it was one of the great cities of the prosperous and, for those days, highly populated Languedoc. What stands out with certainty about the massacre on 22 July 1209 is its appalling extent and its indiscriminate nature. But there was worse to come.

It is remarkable that until recent times, there has been little comment on the extent of the Church's horrors against the Cathars. With the increasing in Catharism in the last few decades, there have been attempts on the part of Catholics to minimize the extent of this outrage and conveniently downgrade the magnitude of the carnage to irrelevance. Such efforts suppress the truth of Christian history, while not wholly successful, seem to have strengthened the faith of those who wish to believe. The way in which Catholic writers now make light of this appalling outrage is shameful. The fact that popes carried out these murders in the name of Christ is especially unfortunate for Christians. If we accept the Church's excuses that the crusades were men in a mood of deep religious sentiment who set out to repress a body of people who did not believe their brand of Christianity, then we are accepting an untruth. What is beyond doubt is that when the Catholic army was mobilized, it was the most appalling killing machine Europe has ever seen.

The consequence of the sack of Beziers was stunning and was something analogous to the effect of the atomic bombing of Hiroshima in the Second World War. It was a horror of a magnitude exceeding anything in the memory of the people of the Midi. That popes could authorize such human tragedies to occur in a purportedly enlightened age is grim proof of the sightlessness that can be engendered by "blind faith." After Beziers, Church troops marched triumphantly to Carcassonne, the greatest fortress of the day. It could justifiably have been regarded as a prize which could only fall after months of siege, but it succumbed in less than a month after the sack of Beziers (the Great Heresy, Dr. Arthur Gorham, Neville Spearman, Jersey, 1977). Europeans shuddered when they heard that another 5,000 people were slaughtered at Marmande on 26 September 1209, and Guillaume de le Tud records a dreadful description of men, women and children being hacked to pieces by the Militia of Jesus Christ. That the supposed preaching of Christ ever came to be the basis of such exuberant aggressiveness against human beings is a matter for reflection. The records and literature of the Cathars were as ruthlessly destroyed by the Church as were the living exponents of the faith, and this evidence is provided in the *Catholic Encyclopedia* (iii,pp. 435-37) under a sterilized entry headed "Cathars".

Unable to achieve constant, crushing victories in battle because of the Cathars' fortifications, the popes embarked upon an official policy of systematic devastation of their farms, buildings, vineyards, wheat fields and orchards. The devastation caused by the Catholic army was immense and the loss to civilization is difficult to comprehend. Historians estimate that more than 500 towns and villages disappeared from the map as a result of its depredation. After three and a half decades of brutality, the disdain of Europe deepened and when the final battle against the Cathars took place their castle stronghold, (Montsegur, in 1244).

In later times the church naively confessed that the motive for its unprecedented butchery and devastation of the Cathars was "their wealth"…and their contempt for the Catholic clergy, caused by their ignorance and the worldly and the too-frequently-scandalous lives of the latter" (*Catholic Encyclopedia*, i. p. 268).

"The Inquisition", said Bishop Bruno of Segni, a 16th century Catholic writer, "was invented to rob the rich of their possessions. The pope and his priests were intoxicated with sensuality; they despised God because their religion had been drowned in a deluge of wealth" (*A History of the Popes*, McCabe, ibid.). Around the same time we have the complaint of the papal legate Elmeric, who said that the popes were relaxing their zeal to persecute because there were "no more rich heretics."

Is there a parallel to these motivations in the history of religion? We are thought to be offensive if we refuse to speak devoutly of a divinely guided "Holy Roman Church." Christian writers, with a habitual indifference to the truth, would have us forget these facts and accept their artifice that the "Holy Fathers" were men of pious integrity. But the worst was yet to come.

Author's Note:
Some of the dates for the popes and events in papal history are estimates; even the Church admits as much. The dates were further complicated by the changes made to the Julian calendar by Pope Gregory XIII (pope 1572-85) in 1582.

Excerpted from Nexus Magazine, Volume 14 Number 1 (December 2006-January 2009) by Tony Bushby, COPYRIGHT November 2006.

THE MURDERED POPE
Pope John Paul I, his legacy faded –
but the Church's lies live on

After the mysterious death of the "Smiling Pope" on September 28, 1978 there was a great skepticism about his demise. A vast majority of Catholics in Italy and Europe thought there was foul play. Newspapers and citizens demanded an official autopsy and investigation to no avail. The shroud of complete secrecy entombed his body, his works and his final hours. Gone was Pope John Paul I replaced by the curia's cover man, John Paul II – with his agenda of anti-communism and preservation of all dogma and doctrine at all costs. When asked about the inconsistencies of Pope John Paul I's death, John Paul II simply said, "I am not my brother's keeper." His obliteration of all history almost worked until 1984 when a respected English investigative author, David Yallop, wrote **IN GOD'S NAME**, which sold eight million copies. The book and his revelations have kept the issue alive but the crime is still unsolved until now as more evidence has come to light.

These pieces of the puzzle go well beyond the immediate obvious cover-ups about the time of his death, who discovered his body (John Villot or Sister Vincenzia) and the rushed embalming within twelve hours. Now come the post crime dominoes that shake the telling of the Vatican's lies even more.

The crime scenario is based on a Catholic source and a European intelligence official with residency both in Italy and Germany. The inside story contradicts none of what David Yallop assumed or proved as a conspiracy with members of the Curia, Masonic Lodge, Archbishop Paul Marcinkus, former president of the Vatican Bank, mafia kingpin Michele Sindona, Cardinal John Patrick Cody of Chicago, Lucio Gelli of the Rogue Masonic LodgeP2, Vatican Secretary John Villot and international financial criminal Roberto Calvi.

Soon after John Paul I was elected pope, warning bells went off in the halls of the Vatican, in vaults of the Vatican Bank, and in the dark caves of the mafia-mason underworld.

John Paul I was a grace-filled priest with a quiet missionary zest for reforming an archaic Church corrupted to the core, with stifling dogma and tired old men. John Paul's mission was to re-make the Church in the image of Christ – "the church of the poor" – but rich in spirit. Pope John Paul I was a determined man like Ralph Nader or Robert Kennedy, who was determined to right the wrongs no matter what obstacles he faced. The mistake he made was unwittingly revealing his mission to the enemies within, namely secretary John Villot. Thus, his undoing began.

In the bedtime hours of September 27, 1978, eyewitnesses saw a known resident of the Vatican lead into the sleeping Pope's residence by Vatican Bank head, Paul Marcinkus. The Opus Dei assassin remixed the Pope's nightly dosage of digitalis with an increased concoction and undetectable poison, pyrethrum. The poison was a derivative of the flower catheymn and deadly when exposed to the skin.

The deed was done. The crusader Pope was dead. Now the cover-up took hold: John Villot, mouthpiece for the Curia, and his fellow co-conspirators told conflicting stories of who found the Pope's body and when the body was found. It was too late to save the Pope – but the campaign to save the church was in full swing. The Pope's residence was cleaned up and sealed. The Pope's personal effects, reading material and medications disappeared. Access to his body was denied even to the Pope's personal physician until "things were in order."

A "secret autopsy" was ordered by Villot and performed within four hours by the Italian government doctors eight hours after the Pope's body was embalmed. All traces of poison were gone. The Opus Dei "hand" was packing to leave the employ of Paul Marcinkus on his way to Milan with the "secret autopsy". The Pope's autopsy was taken to Hospilter Seminary in the South of France. Several copies were made and delivered to the private archives of the King of Spain, John Carlos.

The ironclad trust still existed between the Vatican and remnants of the Catholic Franco fascist regime which hatched and protected Opus Dei and its founder Josemarie Escriva. The new Pope, John Paul II, was safely inducted a month later; the sensitive document was taken to the new pope's private archive, where it still sits today under the protection of Pope Benedict XVI.

No details were overlooked in the cover-up – the normal procedure of filing a death report with Roman police was NOT done – or at least the existence is denied. In addition, Pope John Paul I's own physician refused to sign the death certificate and was told never to reveal the existence of a certificate. Pressure and threats were delivered and enforced on nurses and nuns at the scene of the crime.

Nothing was left to chance – Italian Law states that the death certificate must return to the town of the decedent's birth... either this was not done, or more likely, the death information is under lock and key in the Italian town of Canale d'Agordo with denials religiously rehearsed and enforced.

Now, evidence and indication of foul play have surfaced through credible back-door sources, and public and private utterances in the Trier Seminary, Germany. A young Bishop told his seminarians in classes that John Paul I had been poisoned. He was severely reprimanded. The Bishop and his students were told of deadly consequences if the vow of total silence about the issue was broken. Some of the students have spoken and the retired Bishop, now in his 90's, lives in seclusion – too afraid to speak.

The protocols of Bishops in 1978 and 1979 discussed the Pope's premature death in detail. The predictable has happened – the transcripts and evidence may exist but are reportedly "lost."

Three other leaks have occurred which threaten the Vatican cover story to this day.

1.   A copy of the Pope's autopsy sits in the Archives of the German Benedictine Monastery, Maria Laach, outside Mayen.

2.   In an obscure location of the Pakistan Sufi Archive at Peshawar sits a comprehensive history of the Church that includes evidence of the murder of Pope John Paul I.

3.   The deep background and connecting of the dots will tell the story. Circumstantial evidence? Probably more weighty than that!

In the summer and fall of 1978 there were international pots boiling. In Europe communism was still somewhat monolithic. There was no Mikhail Gorbachev or hints that the Berlin Wall was to come down. The U.S. was concerned with keeping its intelligence agency wires; in addition, the mafia money dealings that collapsed the Franklin Bank in April, 1974, threatened several banks in Illinois, specifically the Illinois State Bank. These were top priorities. Known underworld characters such as Michelle Sindona and Lucio Gelli, whose corrupt money-laundering scheme including drugs and weapons, brought down the Franklin Bank. Also, a corrupted Catholic point man was Chicago's Cardinal, John Cody. The FBI, the DEA and the Italian Banking regulators, suspicious of the Vatican Bank and the Institute for Public Works, had their eyes open. The result was a wiretap on Cardinal Cody, Sindona, and officers at the Illinois State Bank. Cody was on John Paul I's clean up list. Cardinal John Cody, who publicly claimed "I don't own Chicago but I control it," said, if he were removed, "The top will be blown off of the Vatican."

The saga of the Curia's mafia and the Masonic Lodge P2 plot to remove the dangerous innovator, Pope Paul I, was about to take on a new dimension and lasting intrigue. The intrigue has yet to play out in the light of today, but is yet another dot to be connected. In a parking lot in wet, steamy Chicago, a new FBI agent set up his recording apparatus to snag evidence against Michelle Sindona, the Illinois State Bank and the corrupted Chicago Cardinal John Cody, who the new Pope vowed to remove ..."one way or the other".

The rookie FBI agent listened through tedious inconsequential conversations while gathering damning evidence against Michelle Sindona for a federal trial which eventually took place in New York. The trial ended in a conviction on money laundering and fraud charges that sent Sindona back to Italy where he was murdered in prison in 1986.

If nothing else had been collected, the assignment would have been ruled a success, but there was more. During the last week of September, 1978, there was a flurry of calls from not only the Vatican, but also from the Apostolic Palace, the Pope's private residence. The calls from Paul Marcinkus from the Vatican were to be expected, since Cody was a cardinal and the Vatican Bank was under investigation. Suddenly, a plot to poison the Pope was discussed. The poisoning had to happen before the end of the month, since the new Pope revealed he was going to make out the details of a complete house cleaning which included the Bank, Cody, Marcinkus and the Vatican Secretary, John Villot. Unfortunately, Pope John Paul I naively shared this information with Villot before hand.

Bells rang at all levels of the intelligence and law enforcement communities in the U.S. What to do with this information? Here an international crime was unfolding – the DEA was hot on the trail of international fugitives and a new powerful "unknown" entity was now on the world scene that could turn things upside down, politically and spiritually not all to the advantage of the establishment. Was this an FBI, CIA, Interpol or Italian issue? The problems caused by a disclosure could be counter productive to the powers that were. The decision: the discussions and revelations were to remain an internal top-secret affair, immediately deep-sixed by the FBI, into the swamp of Chicago and Church politics. Gone. Buried and tucked away in the U.S. archives filed under false title – well out of reach of the imperfect Freedom of Information Act.

Post Script: After all the criminality the Church sails on

•John Paul II is set to be beatified, never making public any information about his predecessor's death.

•Paul Marcinkus died quietly in Arizona in 2006 – far beyond the reach of Italian authorities, charges, petitions and the like.

•John Cody died, still the Cardinal of Chicago, being pursued to his death by state and federal law enforcement agencies.

•Josemarie Escriva, founder of Opus Dei, became a saint – beatified at record pace.

•Material not submitted at Sindona's trial sits out of reach. One of the deals reached was that no wiretap material concerning the Pope's death was to be submitted as evidence – thus the Church, the US government, (under Attorney General Griffin Bell), and the Italian government would not be dragged down the Alice in wonderland Rabbit Hole.

•Pope John Paul I's life was a blip on the radar screen. His writings on birth control, modernizing the Church and women's role have vanished from the shelves of the Vatican and his hometown. Even in an official book on the Popes, the location of his death is wrong.

•An investigative book done by a Roman priest on the murder of Pope John Paul I sits in the Vatican archives unreleased because Vatican Law states no book by a priest can be published without the Vatican's blessing.

•In 1986 the Vatican issued a press release absolving the Church, Marcinkus and the Vatican Bank of any wrong doing in the Vatican Bank scandals, stating the bank had been "set up."

•According to David Yallop in his best selling book, *In God's Name*, (pp. 210, 215, 220, 221) and other authors have reported that there is no doubt an autopsy was performed. There were no direct convictions in the plot to murder Pope John Paul I – Calvi was murdered; Sindona was murdered in prison; Marcinkus hid in Arizona until his death; Villot died in 1982 as did Cody; Gelli was on the run. The Opus Dei hand is a non-person.

•The mysterious Catholic worker Marie Laachi, who was said to have overheard murder plans disappeared without a trace, becoming another "non-person."

•"Early in the afternoon of March 15, 1978, eight men sat around a table in a sidewalk café in the mountain village of Vittorio Veneto in Northern

Italy. In casual clothes, they went unnoticed, even though one of them was the reigning Pontiff, Pope Paul VI, the second his Secretary of State, Cardinal Jean Villot, a third was the Patriarch of Venice, Cardinal Albino Luciano, soon to become Pope John Paul I, a fourth was the Primate of China, Cardinal Yu Pin, a fifth was the Metropolitan of Leningrad, Metropolitan Nikodim, a sixth was the Archbishop of Brussels, Cardinal Leon Joseph Suenens, and a seventh was their trusted confidant, Father John Champney, Luciani's long time personal assistant, friend, and theological ally. The eighth man was Aldo Moro, current political leader of the Christian Democratic Party. Together they comprised the leadership of the progressive movement in the Church, the rivals of the Roman Curia, that cluster of twenty or so right wing cardinals who shared the Vatican with Pope Paul VI. They left at four o'clock and Aldo reserved the table "for the same time next year." A year later, there was no point in Cardinal Leon Joseph Suenens traveling to Vittorio Veneto as his seven partners were all dead. And he, having just been removed as Primate of Belgium – no longer with pastoral influence – was also as good as dead, politically at least."

By. Tim C. Leedom. Sources: John Cornwall, Thief in the Night; Martin Malachi, Vatican: A Novel; Pedira Cuerta, Muerte y Figuraa de Juan Pablo I; Gregory Christano, The Mysterious Death of John Paul I; David Yallop, In God's Name; back story from R.

POPES MURDERED - A CHURCH TRADITION

•Stephen I (254-257), beheaded
•Stephen VI (896-897) strangled
•Stephen VII (939-942) mutilated
•John XII (955-964) murdered by his mistress
•Benedict VI (973-974) strangled
•John XIV (983-984) starvations, ill-treatment of direct murder
•Gregory V (996-999) poisoned
•Boniface VIII (1294-1303) ill-treatment

LIST OF POPES ALLEGED TO HAVE BEEN MURDERED

•John VIII (872-882) allegedly poisoned then clubbed to death
•Adrian III (884-885) allegedly poisoned
•Leo V (903) allegedly strangled
•John X (914-928) allegedly smothered with a pillow
•Stephen VII/VIII (928-931) allegedly murdered
•Sergius IV (1009-1012) allegedly murdered
•Clement II (1046-1047) allegedly poisoned
•Damasus II (1048) allegedly murdered
•Celestine V (1294) allegedly rumored to heave been murdered by his
  successor Boniface VIII after his resignation
•Benedict XI (1304-1305) allegedly poisoned
•John Paul I (1978) allegedly poisoned

Denial
Institutional denial runs deep.

In response to the editor's inquiry as to whether or not an autopsy had been performed on the body of Pope John Paul I, Father Bradley Autori responded:

"I honestly do not know. I have never looked into the question. I suppose if you go to GOOGLE or some such and make a search for that Pope's biography, you may find some information."

Pope John Paul I
Expendable and in the way of the Church's business

CHILD MOLESTATION

An Unspeakable Crime.
The Church's strategy: Crime? What Crime?

"Whoever causes one of these little ones who believe in me to sin, it would be better for him is a great millstone were hung around his neck and he were thrown into the sea."

Mark 9:42

TELL IT LIKE IT IS

Let's tell it like it is, Pope, these people are "employees" of The Church, which, after all, is a global business. These employees of yours who molest children are criminals by any definition of the word. Their collar does not make them innocent or forgiven or absolve them of accountability for their actions any more than other adults in the *real* world where <u>all</u> adults are held accountable for their actions, no matter what their religious denomination or rank.

Deceptive semantics and euphemisms no longer work in the world of full disclosure. It is for the world to see. They are criminals and you have enabled them and continue to do so.

"We convict here on earth. If God wants to forgive these predators in heaven, that's His business.

Los Angeles Victim Attorney

221

MURDER AND MOLESTATION IN HOMETOWN, U.S.A.:

According to national news reports on November 23 and 24, 2010, The Rev. John Fiala, a Roman Catholic priest in Texas, was arrested for offering to pay $5,000 to a "hit man" to kill a teenager whom he had sexually abused over an extended period. At the time of his arrest, Rev. Fiala was already out on bond for criminal charges and a lawsuit associated with his abuse of the boy, which included raping the teenager on church grounds, raping him on more than one occasion at gunpoint, and threatening to kill him if he spoke up about the crime.

While Fiala was a priest at Sacred Heart of Mary in Rocksprings, Texas, he began molesting the boy at the age of 16.

After an extended period of abuse, the teenager broke down and told a school counselor about the abuse, and the counselor called the authorities. The boy filed suits against Fiala, the Archdiocese of San Antonio the Archdiocese of Omaha, Nebraska, and the Society of Our Lady of the Most Holy Trinity, Fiala's order. All three, according to the suit, had tried to cover up the abuse.

It is particularly interesting to note that former San Antonio Archbishop Jose Gomez was, at the time of this writing (November 25, 2010), an assistant to Cardinal Roger Mahony, in the Archdiocese of Los Angeles, California. When Cardinal Mahony retires in 2011, Gomez will automatically assume Mahony's position. Mahony and Gomez are cited elsewhere in this book for his involvements in sex abuse cover-ups.

At about the same time, a neighbor of Fiala's tipped off Edwards County Sheriff Don Letsinger about what Fiala was up to, and Letsinger contacted The Texas Department of Public Safety, a division of which is The Texas Rangers.

An undercover agent, posing as the hit man, recorded Fiala on video and audio negotiating the deal to have the boy killed.

Meanwhile, the teenager (now 18 years old) had temporarily dropped out of college and gone into hiding for fear of his life.

Here is a transparent incidence of documented homosexual abuse by a priest, at gunpoint, threatening the life of the teenage victim if he talked. And the response to this unspeakable crime by the Archdiocese in which the abuse took place is, of course, cover-up. As if that were not enough, the speedy departure of the Archbishop of that Diocese to another Diocese headed by a soon-to-retire Cardinal linked to other sex abuse cover-ups is, of course, "coincidental."

For specific information on current cases of sexual abuse by priests, please see the following Bishop Accountability website: www.bishopaccountability.org

By Editors
(Sources: public statements in news media, Bishop Accountability, Newser's website)

BishopAccountability.org

Database of Publicly Accused Priests in the United States

Viewed by Diocese: Honolulu, HI
Total Individuals: 12

Return to main database page.   See abbreviations and posting policy. Send corrections.
The Database of Publicly Accused Priests does not state or imply that individuals facing allegations are guilty of a crime or liable for civil claims. The reports contained in the database are merely allegations. The U.S. legal system presumes that a person accused of or charged with a crime is innocent until proven guilty. Similarly, individuals who may be defendants in civil actions are presumed not to be liable for such claims unless a plaintiff proves otherwise. Admissions of guilt or liability are not typically a part of civil or private settlements. For more information, see our posting policy.

Last	First	Ord	T	Status	D/O	Notes	Diocese	Source/Assignments
Batoon	Roberto	1973	P	Accused	Diocesan	Extern priest from Philippines working in diocese since 1997. Removed 1//03 after he was accused of abuse of a minor while working in home diocese in Philippines. Supposed to return to Philippines but had not arrived there as of 2/21/03. By 5/03, he had agreed to be voluntarily laicized.	Honolulu, HI	**Source:** Honolulu Advertiser 1.27.03; Honolulu Star-Bulletin 1.28.03; Honolulu Advertiser 2.21.03; Honolulu Advertiser 5.22.03 ; Honolulu Star-Bulletin 2.27.04
Blazek	Eugene E.	1976	P	Sued	Diocesan	Man filed civil suit 3/08 accusing Blazek of sexually abusing him for over a year "during or after 1979." Suit also mentions abuse of other youngsters. Blazek, although still part of Honolulu Diocese, had been serving as a military chaplain for over 20 years. He retired 6/1/07 and lives in Houston, TX per Catholic Herald.	Honolulu, HI	**Source:** Honolulu Star Bulletin 3.10.08; Honolulu Advertiser 3.11.08; Hawaii Catholic Herald 4.4.08 **Assignments:** BA.org Assignment Record
Boumeister	Alphonsus	< 1915	P	Sued	Fathers of the Sacred Hearts	Accused in 2002 civil suit of abuse of 11 yr old boy in 1961. Case dismissed by Judge 3/05 who said Plaintiff had presented no evidence to support his claim. No other accusations known. Boumeister died in 1972 (30 yrs before suit) at age 84. He took his vows in Belgium and came to Hawaii in 1915.	Honolulu, HI	**Source:** Honolulu Star-Bulletin 8.1.02; Honolulu Advertiser 8.1.02; Honolulu Star Bulletin 9.17.02; Honolulu Advertiser 9.17.02 ; Honolulu Star-Bulletin 2.27.04; Honolulu Star-Bulletin 3.25.05

	Ronald					1987. Accused in 2005 of abuse of 1 boy beginning in 2002 when boy was 12 and lasting for 3 yrs. Placed on leave 2005. Pleaded guilty 5/06. Sentenced to 1 yr prison and 20 years probation 7/06.	HI	Honolulu Star Bulletin 7.24.05; KGMB 7.28.05; Honolulu Star-Bulletin 7.29.05; KGMB 8.1.05 ; Maui News 8.2.05; Honolulu Star-Bulletin 8.6.05; Honolulu Advertiser 8.9.05; Maui News 5.18.06; LA Times (AP) 5.18.06; Honolulu Advertiser 5.19.06; KHON (Hawaii) 7.20.06; Honolulu Advertiser 7.21.06; Honolulu Star Bulletin 7.21.06 ; Maui News 7.21.06; Maui News 7.21.06 (2nd article)
Henry	Joseph		P	Sued	Diocesan	In his 1991 petition against Bishop Joseph Ferrario, Plaintiff named Fr. Henry as the priest who first sexually abused him. Abuse occurred from 1964-1972 when Henry died. Plaintiff told Bishop Ferrario, who succeeded Henry as parish priest, and Ferrario than began abusing the Plaintiff.	Honolulu, HI	**Source:** Figueroa v. Bishop..; District of Hawaii; # 91-00453; Vanity Fair 12.91; Renew America 6.27.06
Jackson	James A.	1948	P	Accused	Maryknoll Missionary	In 6/02 Jackson (age 84, feeble and in poor health) was accused by at least three men of abusing them when they were children. Jackson worked in Hawaii from 1948-1992. No criminal charges were to be filed because of age of case and there were no records of complaints in Jackson's personnel file with the Order. Died 3/05.	Honolulu, HI	**Source:** Associated Press 6.17.02; Honolulu Advertiser 6.20.02; Honolulu Star-Bulletin 6.20.02; Associated Press 6.20.02 ; Honolulu Advertiser 4.24.03; Catholic New York 4.7.05
Mannetta	Andrew	1983	P	Sued	Capuchin	Sued 2003. Accused of abuse of 1 19 yr old, mentally-challenged youth in 1997-1998. Parents of 2 altar boys complained of his behavior in 1994 but Diocese said it was not sexual in nature. Reassigned in 2002 to NY prior to civil suit being filed. Civil trial settled for $375K in 1/07 just before trial. Underwent treatment for sexual issues and alcohol abuse. Admitted giving alcohol to minor boys. 2010	Honolulu, HI	**Source:** Honolulu Star Bulletin 5.22.03; Honolulu Advertiser 5.23.03; Honolulu Star-Bulletin 2.27.04; TheHawaiiChannel.com 1.03.07 ; Honolulu Star-Bulletin 1.06.07; Honolulu Advertiser 1.18.07; Honolulu Star Bulletin 1.19.07; Honolulu Advertiser 1.19.07; Pacific Daily News 1.19.07; KUAM 3.23.10; Marianas Variety 3.24.10; KUAM 3.25.10

| Bukoski, III | Joseph | 1979 | P | Sued | Sacred Heart | Placed on leave 5/02 after allegations of sexual abuse of 1 youth in 1970s. 2nd accuser also came forward. He was a brother in the Sacred Heart Order at the time. 2 civil suits filed in 2003. At least 1 suit says Order knew of the abuse but still allowed him to be ordained. This suit settled 11/05 after Bukoski admitted to the abuse. Immediately after settlement, criminal charges filed against this Plaintiff on behalf of woman who said she was assaulted by Plaintiff at age 14. He was acquitted 1/07. | Honolulu, HI | **Source:** Honolulu Advertiser 5.20.02; Honolulu Advertiser 5.24.02; Honolulu Advertiser 8.2.02; Honolulu Star Bulletin 8.3.02 ; Honolulu Star Bulletin 8.6.02; Honolulu Advertiser 4.24.03; Honolulu Advertiser 5.16.03; Honolulu Star Bulletin 5.16.03; Honolulu Star Bulletin 5.17.03; Honolulu Star Bulletin 7.25.03; Honolulu Star-Bulletin 2.27.04; Honolulu Star-Bulletin 4.8.05; Honolulu Star-Bulletin 11.09.05 ; Honolulu Advertriser 11.09.05; Honolulu Star-Bulletin 11.30.05 **Assignments:** Honolulu Advertiser 1.06.07 (add'l article); Honolulu Star-Bulletin 1.06.07 (add'l article) |
| de Otero | Roberto A. | 1977 | P | Settled | Diocesan | Accused in 5/17/02 suit of abusing 2 altar boys In late 1980s in Honolulu; settled 6/04. Accused in 8/30/04 suit of abusing boy at same parish in 1985. On leave 1987-89; Navy chaplain 1989-93. Admitted in 1993 to abusing a boy at a CA Marine base and resigned. After DiLorenzo came to Honolulu in 1993 he removed de Otero from public ministry. Had begun career in Portland OR archdiocese where in 1977-81 he had 2 parish assignments and sick leave before being loaned to then excardinated to Honolulu. | Honolulu, HI | **Source:** Honolulu Advertister 5.18.02; Honolulu Star-Bulletin 10.30.02; Arizona Republic 10.12.03; Honolulu Star-Bulletin 2.27.04 ; Honolulu Star-Bulletin 7.22.04; Honolulu Advertiser 7.23.04; Honolulu Advertiser 8.31.04 **Assignments:** BA.org Assignment Record |

225

Ferrario (Bp)	Joseph	1951	P	Sued	Diocesan	Accused of abuse. 1991 civil suit dismissed due to SOL. Allegations "found to be groundless by an internal church investigation." Became Bishop in 1982, retired 1993, and died 2003	Honolulu, HI	**Source:** Washington Times 11.06.89; Washington Times 8.14.91; Time Magazine 8.19.91; Houston Chronicle 9.27.92 ; Honolulu Star 12.14.03; Honolulu Advertiser 12.14.03; Honolulu Star-Bulletin 2.27.04; Freedom from Religion Foundation 10.07.04; Renew America 6.27.06; BA.org list of U.S. Bishops Accused of Abuse 4.14.08
Gonsalves	James		D	Convicted	Diocesan	Ordained as deacon articles allege abuse on Guam during seminary and 1st assignment.	Honolulu,	**Source:**
Sabog	Henry B.	1960	P	Sued	Diocesan	Sued 2005 by woman who accused her of molesting her when she was 12 and he was assigned to Our Lady of Good Counsel Catholic Church in 1964. Sabog denied the allegations.	Honolulu, HI	**Source:** KGMB Channel 9 12.22.05; Honolulu Star Bulletin 12.23.05
Stone	Dominic		B	Sued	Congregation of Sacred Hearts	Man filed suit 7/03 alleging that Stone, a religious Brother, molested him for over a year in 1970s. Same man alleged in the suit that he was also propositioned by abuser F. Joseph Bukoski. Died 4/06.	Honolulu, HI	**Source:** Honolulu Star Bulletin 7.25.03; Honolulu Advertiser 4.23.06

Information from BishopAccountability.org

BishopAccountability.org

Database of Publicly Accused Priests in the United States

Viewed by Diocese: Fairbanks, AK
Total Individuals: 44

Return to main database page.   See abbreviations and posting policy. Send corrections.

The Database of Publicly Accused Priests does not state or imply that individuals facing allegations are guilty of a crime or liable for civil claims. The reports contained in the database are merely allegations. The U.S. legal system presumes that a person accused of or charged with a crime is innocent until proven guilty. Similarly, individuals who may be defendants in civil actions are presumed not to be liable for such claims unless a plaintiff proves otherwise. Admissions of guilt or liability are not typically a part of civil or private settlements. For more information, see our posting policy.

Last	First	Ord	T	Status	D/O	Notes	Diocese	Source/Assignments
Astruc	Rene	1954	P	Accused	Jesuit	Native of France. Two or more pending claims against Astruc shown in bankruptcy reorganization documents for Fairbanks Diocese 1/25/10. Died 6/02.	Fairbanks, AK	**Source:** Northwest Jesuit, Spring 2002; Anchorage Daily News 6.30.02; Northwest Jesuit, Fall 2002; Excerpt from Bankruptcy Reorganization Documents for Fairbanks Diocese 1.25.10, p. 1 ; Alakanuk - Saint Ignatius Catholic Church Web site 1.25.10; Emmonak - Sacred Heart Catholic Church Web Site1.25.10
Bartles	Charles Arnold		P	Accused	Jesuit	One pending claim against Bartles shown in bankruptcy reorganization documents for Fairbanks Diocese 1/25/10. Believed to have taught at St. Johns-Jesuit-Loyola prep school in Shreveport, LA during 1960-1962 school years. Also worked in Brazil. Was working in New Orleans when he died 7/93.	Fairbanks, AK	**Source:** Times-Picayune 7.30.93; Excerpt from Bankruptcy Reorganization Documents for Fairbanks Diocese 1.25.10, p. 2
Beans, Sr.	Pat		D	Accused	Diocesan	Described as Eskimo Elder and Deacon per 3/03 Alaskan Shepherd, a newsletter from Fairbanks Diocese. Two or more pending claims against Beans shown in bankruptcy reorganization documents for Fairbanks Diocese 1/25/10	Fairbanks, AK	**Source:** Excerpt from Bankruptcy Reorganization Documents for Fairbanks Diocese 1.25.10, p. 1
Benish	Robert		B	Accused	Jesuit	Took vows as Jesuit brother in 1943. Came to Alaska in 1946 and left in 1989. Died in Spokane 4/91. Two or more pending claims against Benish shown in bankruptcy reorganization documents for Fairbanks Diocese 1/25/10.	Fairbanks, AK	**Source:** Seattle Times 4.26.91; Excerpt from Bankruptcy Reorganization Documents for Fairbanks Diocese 1.25.10, p. 1

BishopAccountability.org

Database of Publicly Accused Priests in the United States

Viewed by Diocese: Orange, CA
Total Individuals: 23

Return to main database page.　See abbreviations and posting policy. Send corrections.

The Database of Publicly Accused Priests does not state or imply that individuals facing allegations are guilty of a crime or liable for civil claims. The reports contained in the database are merely allegations. The U.S. legal system presumes that a person accused of or charged with a crime is innocent until proven guilty. Similarly, individuals who may be defendants in civil actions are presumed not to be liable for such claims unless a plaintiff proves otherwise. Admissions of guilt or liability are not typically a part of civil or private settlements. For more information, see our posting policy.

Last	First	Ord	T	Status	D/O	Notes	Diocese	Source/Assignments
Andersen	Andrew Christian	1982	P	Convicted	Diocesan	Convicted 1986 of 26 counts of felony molestation of 4 boys. Sentenced to 5 yrs probation after treatment at Servants of Paracletes. Continued to molest boys while in therapy. Arrested in New Mexico in 1990 for abuse of another youth. Sentenced to 6 yrs prison for violating Calif. probation. Laicized in mid-1990s. Current whereabouts unnknow. Prior to 2005 there were $4.62M in settlements regarding Andersen.	Orange, CA	**Source:** LA Times 4.26.86; LA Times 9.30.86; LA Times 11.25.86; Altoona Mirror (UPI) 11.25.86 ; OC Register 1.4.87; San Jose Mercury News 12.31.87 (Major Accounts); San Jose Mercury News 12.31.87; OC Register 5.3.90; OC Register 7.19.90; LA Times 1.11.04; OC Weekly 2.5.04; OC Weekly 4.12.04; OC Register 5.17.05 ; NY Times 5.19.05; LA Times 5.25.05 **Assignments:** OC Weekly 5.27.05 (add'l article); California Catholic Daily 10.12.07 (add'l article); Orange Diocesan Personal Record; Directory Listings Compiled by Arellano of OC Weekly
Aranda	Sofronio A. (Pon)	1963	P	Settled	Diocesan	In 2004 Diocese named him as one of six priests accused of the sexual abuse of minors. Allegations against all six were received during 2003 and deemed credible by Diocese. Per March 1996 obituary, he was born in the Philippines; came to the states in1975. Worked in Corona for 5 years and moved to Texas in 1992 or 1993. In Texas he served the Diocese of Galveston-Houston. Chaplain at county Hospital. Subject of	Orange, CA	**Source:** Press Enterprise 3.26.96; OC Weekly 7.09.04; OC Weekly 3.04.05; OC Register 5.17.05 **Assignments:** Orange Diocesan Personal Record; Directory Listings Compiled by Arellano of OC Weekly

			B	Sued	Servite			
Atherton	Gregory		B	Sued	Servite	Sued 1993. Accused of abuse of 3 boys.. LA archdiocese counts 5 accusers alleging abuse between 1967-1986. Also abused in Orange Diocese. 2 suits filed there 1/03. Orange made 2005 settlement for $4,169,325 but did not include him in list of abusive priests. Per 2002 article, he is still part of Order and works at the National Sanctuary of Our Sorrowful Mother in Portland, Ore. under close supervision.	Orange, CA	**Source:** LA Times 4.22.93; OC Register 4.23.93; OC Register 6.03.97; OC Register 5.05.02 ; LA Archdiocesan Report 2.17.04 (article); LA Archdiocesan Report 2.17.04 page 7; OC Weekly 3.04.05; OC Register 5.17.05 **Assignments:** Directory Listings Compiled by Arellano of OC Weekly; LA Times Database 4.20.06
Baird	Lawrence J.	1969	P	Accused	Diocesan	Spokesman for Diocese for many years. Accused in 2002 of abusing a girl who came to him for advice after being abused by Rev. John Lenihan. Baird countersued plaintiff 4/02 but his suit was dismissed in 2002 and he was ordered to pay atty fees for plaintiff. 2nd woman also alleged abuse as a child. Still active as of 8/07 per Diocese website.	Orange, CA	**Source:** NBC4 TV 4.1.02; LA Times 4.02.02; LA Times 4.05.02; Associated Press 4.11.02 ; LA Times 4.17.02; LA Times 11.07.02; LA Times 11.28.02; LA Times 10.06.03; LA Times 10.11.03; LA Times 3.05.04; Press Democrat 3.22.04; Orange County Weekly 1.12.09; OC Register 1.12.09 ; Orange County Weekly 1.13.09
Buckman	Franklin	1963	P	Sued	Diocesan	Accused of abuse between 1962-1981. LA archdiocese counts 3 accusers. Named in 1 civil suit. In 1984 he resigned from parish in Orange Diocese "because of the burden of administration." Later revealed that he resigned because of abuse allegation. Later transferred to Baker, Oregon Diocese. Woman in Calif. complained of abuse of son in 1989. Removed from ministry at some point and retired to Arizona in 2002. 2005 settlement in Orange for $1,959,700.	Orange, CA	**Source:** Diocese of Orange Press Release 1.10.04; LA Times 1.11.04; OC Register 1.13.04; LA Archdiocesan Report 2.17.04 page 3 ; LA Times 2.18.04; OC Weekly 7.09.04; Orange County Register 5.17.05; LA Times 5.18.05; Monterey Herald 5.25.05 **Assignments:** Directory Listings Compiled by Arellano of OC Weekly; LA Times Database 4.20.06
Casimano (Casamino)	Santino "Tony" A.	1975	P	Accused	Diocesan	Ordained in Gallup diocese in 1975. Moved to Orange Diocese in 1976 on	Orange, CA	**Source:** St. Bernard High School Alumni Page, 6.04.03; Diocese of Orange News

BishopAccountability.org

Database of Publicly Accused Priests in the United States

Viewed by Diocese: Chicago, IL
Total Individuals: 101

Return to main database page.   See abbreviations and posting policy. Send corrections.

The Database of Publicly Accused Priests does not state or imply that individuals facing allegations are guilty of a crime or liable for civil claims. The reports contained in the database are merely allegations. The U.S. legal system presumes that a person accused of or charged with a crime is innocent until proven guilty. Similarly, individuals who may be defendants in civil actions are presumed not to be liable for such claims unless a plaintiff proves otherwise. Admissions of guilt or liability are not typically a part of civil or private settlements. For more information, see our posting policy.

Last	First	Ord	T	Status	D/O	Notes	Diocese	Source/Assignments
Baranowski	Alexander Sylvester	1955	P	Accused	Diocesan	Newly identified as abuser in Chicago Archdiocesan report 3/06. Resigned from priesthood in 1975. Laicized 8/1976. No further information found.	Chicago, IL	**Source:** Chicago Archdiocesan Report 3.20.06 page 1; Chicago Sun-Times 3.21.06; Chicago Tribune 3.21.06; Chicago Archdiocesan Report 9.15.08page 1 ; Chicago Archdiocesan Report 8/16/09 **Assignments:** BA.org Assignment Record
Bartz	Richard Barry "Doc"	1974	P	Accused	Diocesan	In 1980s Bartz was on faculty of a seminary where he allegedly had sex with a minor male (may have been other victims as well). He went on leave indefinitely and was returned to duty at Columbus Hospital in 1988 under restrictions and monitoring. Served there until 2001. Left position at another hospital and resigned from priesthood 6/02 after Dallas Bishops' Conference.	Chicago, IL	**Source:** Chicago Tribune 6.20.02; Chicago Tribune 6.24.02; Modern Healthcare 7.1.02; USA Today 11.11.02 ; Chicago Sun-Times 1.17.03; Chicago Archdiocesan Report 3.20.06; Journal of Oak Park and River Forest 11.11.07 **Assignments:** BA.org Assignment Record
Becker	Robert Charles	1965	P	Settled	Diocesan	Canon lawyer who served on Metropolitan Tribunal for many years. At least 1 claim included in 10/03 settlement. New lawsuit filed 4/06 alleges abuse by Becker and another priest in late 1970s. Several other victims known to Plaintiff's counsel. Suit included in 5/07 $6.65M settlement with 14 people alleging abuse by 12 priests. At least 1 claim included in 8/08 $12.7M settlement	Chicago, IL	**Source:** Chicago Tribune 10.3.03; Chicago Archdiocesan Report 3.20.06 page 1; Chicago Tribune 4.25.06; Chicago Sun-Times 4.25.06 ; Daily Southtown 5.29.07; Earthtimes 5.29.07; Chicago Sun-Times 11.12.07; Chicago Tribune 8.12.08; WBBM 8.12.08; Chicago Tribune 8.13.08; Chicago Sun Times 8.13.08; Earth Times

BishopAccountability.org

Database of Publicly Accused Priests in the United States

Viewed by Diocese: New Orleans, LA
Total Individuals: 32

Return to main database page.   See abbreviations and posting policy. Send corrections.

The Database of Publicly Accused Priests does not state or imply that individuals facing allegations are guilty of a crime or liable for civil claims. The reports contained in the database are merely allegations. The U.S. legal system presumes that a person accused of or charged with a crime is innocent until proven guilty. Similarly, individuals who may be defendants in civil actions are presumed not to be liable for such claims unless a plaintiff proves otherwise. Admissions of guilt or liability are not typically a part of civil or private settlements. For more information, see our posting policy.

Last	First	Ord	T	Status	D/O	Notes	Diocese	Source/Assignments
Boudreaux	Claude P.	1955	P	Accused	Jesuit	Boudreaux, an 80 yr old teacher at Jesuit High, was placed on leave in Jan. 2005 after the Order received a complaint of abuse some 30 yrs previously. The Order found the allegations credible and he was sent out of state for treatment. In nearly 50 yrs as a priest, he served as a missionary in Sri Lanka and India, worked at the order's headquarters in Rome, worked in ministry to other Jesuits in Mobile and New Orleans, and taught at Jesuit high schools in Dallas and Shreveport	New Orleans, LA	**Source:** Times-Picayune 1.05.05 **Assignments:** Times-Picayune 9.27.96
Brueschere	Dave		B	Sued	order?	Named in 2005 civil suit. He is one of several religious accused of abuse at Madonna Manor, a Catholic home for troubled children. At least one claim included in almost $5.2M settlement with Archdiocese in Fall, 2009.	New Orleans, LA	**Source:** Times-Picayune 8.25.05; Times Picayune 3.11.10
Calamari	Paul	1980	P	Accused	Diocesan	Credible allegation of abuse. Believe abuse occurred prior to ordination. Name first appeared on list of abusive priests released by Bishop Saltarelli of Wilmington, Delaware on Nov. 16, 2006. Began working in Wilmington Diocese in 1997. Removed from ministry 2003. Was working as field supervisor for Penn State Univ's Center for Survey Research until	New Orleans, LA	**Source:** The Dialog 11.16.06; News Journal 11.16.06; WBAL 11.16.06; News Journal 11.19.06 ; Times Picayune 11.28.06 **Assignments:** News Journal 11.16.06

BishopAccountability.org

Database of Publicly Accused Priests in the United States

Viewed by Diocese: Boston, MA
Total Individuals: 206

Return to main database page.   See abbreviations and posting policy. Send corrections.

The Database of Publicly Accused Priests does not state or imply that individuals facing allegations are guilty of a crime or liable for civil claims. The reports contained in the database are merely allegations. The U.S. legal system presumes that a person accused of or charged with a crime is innocent until proven guilty. Similarly, individuals who may be defendants in civil actions are presumed not to be liable for such claims unless a plaintiff proves otherwise. Admissions of guilt or liability are not typically a part of civil or private settlements. For more information, see our posting policy.

Last	First	Ord	T	Status	D/O	Notes	Diocese	Source/Assignments
Acres	John H.	1983	P	Sued	Jesuit	Sued 2002. Accused of abuse of Students at Boston College High School. He has officially left the Order per 3/02 article.	Boston, MA	**Source:** Boston Globe 3.8.02; Boston Herald 3.8.02; Boston Globe 3.14.02 **Assignments:** BA.org Assignment Record
Atwater	John T.	1963	P	Accused	Diocesan	In 2002 it was revealed that in 1993 a student accused Atwater of abuse while he was director of Cardinal Cushing Academy in Scituate, MA in 1971 when boy was 14. Atwater denied allegations. Sent for therapy which said he "had no sexual conflicts." In 2/02 another man alleged he was abused by Atwater at same school some time after 1967. In 9/04 one man says he was abused by Atwater, then director of Cushing Hall Academy, at age 12 (approx. 1969) . Died 2006.	Boston, MA	**Source:** Boston Globe 9.13.02; Boston Globe 3.5.03; Patriot Ledger 10.20.08 **Assignments:** Boston Archdiocesan Assignment Record
Aubut	Charles E.	1941	P	Accused	Diocesan	Accused of abuse on unspecified date and location per diocesan records. He was also supervisor of Paul Desilets just before Desilets was transferred to Canada after parents complained to Aubut. Aubut was sued in at least one lawsuit because he was Desilets' immediate supervisor. Died 4/19/02	Boston, MA	**Source:** Boston Globe 1.31.03; Documents released by Boston Archdiocese; Boston Herald 1.31.03. **Assignments:** Boston Archdiocesan Assignment Record

BishopAccountability.org

Database of Publicly Accused Priests in the United States

Viewed by Diocese: New York, NY
Total Individuals: 58

Return to main database page.   See abbreviations and posting policy. Send corrections.

The Database of Publicly Accused Priests does not state or imply that individuals facing allegations are guilty of a crime or liable for civil claims. The reports contained in the database are merely allegations. The U.S. legal system presumes that a person accused of or charged with a crime is innocent until proven guilty. Similarly, individuals who may be defendants in civil actions are presumed not to be liable for such claims unless a plaintiff proves otherwise. Admissions of guilt or liability are not typically a part of civil or private settlements. For more information, see our posting policy.

Last	First	Ord	T	Status	D/O	Notes	Diocese	Source/Assignments
Albino	John C.	1990	P	Settled	Carmelite	Reportedly offered 16 yr old boy money for sex and verbally attacked him. Suit filed 2000 and settled by 2002. Has been "removed from ministry."	New York, NY	**Source:** USA Today 11.11.02; Staten Island Advance 6.22.06
Baisi	Linda		N	Settled		Accused in 2/8/96 suit of sexually abusing a boy for 5 years, starting at age 12 in 1987. The abuse included oral sex. In 1995, complainant mentioned the abuse to a counselor, who reported it to authorities. Baisi left her order in 1979 and was teacher when the abuse began. She was principal in 1996 when suit was filed and she was suspended. She admitted the abuse in taped conversations with the victim. Her attorney and the judge stated that she had effectively admitted to the charges.	New York, NY	**Source:** Daily News 2.25.96; Daily News 3.2.96; NY Times 9.15.00; NY Times 9.19.00 ; Daily News 9.19.00
Bazalar	Juan		P	Convicted	Diocesan	Peruvian. Indicted 1991 for sexually abusing a 15-year-old altar boy at St. Peter's Church in Monticello. He fled to Canada. Extradited and then convicted in 1993. Sentenced to 5-15 years in state prison. Conviction overturned. Found not guilty at 2nd trial. Returned to Peru.	New York, NY	**Source:** Dallas Morning News 2.27.93; River Reporter 8.10.95; Times Herald-Record 3.19.02; NY Post 4.06.02 ; USA Today 11.11.02; Times Herald-Record 2.28.04; Times Herald-Record 1.15.07
Bokulich	Dominic (Br Leopold		B	Convicted	Franciscan Friars of	Bokulich, also known as Br. Leopold, was arrested 10/07 and	New York, NY	**Source:** Journal News 3.21.08; Journal News 6.10.08;

THE BOOK NO POPE WOULD WANT YOU TO READ

BishopAccountability.org

Database of Publicly Accused Priests in the United States

Viewed by Diocese: Austin, TX
Total Individuals: 6

Return to main database page.   See abbreviations and posting policy. Send corrections.

The Database of Publicly Accused Priests does not state or imply that individuals facing allegations are guilty of a crime or liable for civil claims. The reports contained in the database are merely allegations. The U.S. legal system presumes that a person accused of or charged with a crime is innocent until proven guilty. Similarly, individuals who may be defendants in civil actions are presumed not to be liable for such claims unless a plaintiff proves otherwise. Admissions of guilt or liability are not typically a part of civil or private settlements. For more information, see our posting policy.

Last	First	Ord	T	Status	D/O	Notes	Diocese	Source/Assignments
Clogan	Paul	1999	P	Arrested	Diocesan	Clogan was older man from Texas who was ordained at age 66 after wife died. Spent 2 yrs Maine and then moved back to Austin TX. Had been working in Austin diocese since 1/01 He was arrested 2005 in Texas and charged with groping 16 yr old boy in movie theater. Criminal trial in 9/08 ended in mistrial before jury was seated. New trial will be held 12/08.	Austin, TX	**Source:** Austin American-Statesman 12.20.05; Portland Press Herald 12.21.05; Bangor Daily News 12.21.05; The Highlander News (Marble Falls, TX 3.16.06 ; KXAN 9.10.08
Delaney	Dan	1960s ?	P	Settled	Diocesan	In 11/03 R. Scamardo, the former chief counsel for Diocese of Galveston-Houston announced that he himself had been abused in 1975 by Delaney, former director for youth ministry for Austin TX Diocese. Plaintiff told Austin Bishop of his allegations and requested in-patient treatment. In 10/03, matter settled for $250,000 and counseling fees. Delaney laicized in 1987 "for behavior problems." Bishop admitted he had heard from other victims. 2nd suit filed 5/04.	Austin, TX	**Source:** New York Times 11.25.03; Austin American-Statesman 11.26.03; Houston Chronicle 11.29.03; Austin American-Statesman 12.3.03 ; Austin American-Statesman 12.24.03; Austin American-Statesman 1.6.04; Austin American-Statesman 5.12.04
Drinan	Dan	1977	P	Accused	Claretian	Removed 5/02 after complaint of inappropriate behavior with a minor. Per 7/02 article, he was charged with a misdemeanor assault that did not involve either sexual contact or injuries to a child. He paid a fine but no jail time. Bishop said he would not be allowed to return to ministry because of the incident and because of other issues and circumstances from the past discovered during	Austin, TX	**Source:** Austin American-Stateman 5.13.02; Austin American-Statesman 5.18.02; Austin American-Stateman 7.20.02; Austin American-Statesman 11.26.03 ; Austin American-Statesman 12.3.03; Austin American-Statesman 1.6.04; Reno Gazette Journal 1.16.05

BishopAccountability.org

Database of Publicly Accused Priests in the United States

Viewed by Diocese: Milwaukee, WI
Total Individuals: 61

Return to main database page.   See abbreviations and posting policy. Send corrections.

The Database of Publicly Accused Priests does not state or imply that individuals facing allegations are guilty of a crime or liable for civil claims. The reports contained in the database are merely allegations. The U.S. legal system presumes that a person accused of or charged with a crime is innocent until proven guilty. Similarly, individuals who may be defendants in civil actions are presumed not to be liable for such claims unless a plaintiff proves otherwise. Admissions of guilt or liability are not typically a part of civil or private settlements. For more information, see our posting policy.

Last	First	Ord	T	Status	D/O	Notes	Diocese	Source/Assignments
Adamsky	Raymond A.	1958	P	Accused	Diocesan	Adamsky's name appears on Archdiocese's 4/04 list of priests fully restricted from ministry because of credible allegations of abuse. Adamsky is retired per 2002 Catholic Directory. Case is being sent to the Vatican for review.	Milwaukee, WI	**Source:** Archdiocese of Milwaukee List 7.9.04; Associated Press 7.9.04; Milwaukee Journal Sentinel 7.10.04
Arimond	James L.	1965	P	Convicted	Diocesan	Placed on leave 1/90 when allegations of abuse of boy in 1988 surfaced; privileges suspended 7/90 when charges filed. Pleaded no contest 7/90. In 10/90 Arimond was sentenced to 18 mo. probation and 45 days in House of Corrections under work-release program. Laicized. In 1995 he began working as state-licensed professional counselor until State ordered him to surrender his license 7/03.	Milwaukee, WI	**Source:** Chicago Tribune 7.25.90; Milwaukee Journal Sentinel 4.17.02; Milwaukee Journal Sentinel 7.9.03; Archdiocese of Milwaukee List 7.9.04 ; Milwaukee Journal Sentinel 7.10.04; Archdiocese of Milwaukee website (updated 11.26.07)
Bandle	Ronald J.	1968	P	Accused	Diocesan	Bandle died 1/01 after suffered heart attack during evening Mass. Name appeared on Archdiocese's 7/04 list of priests fully restricted from ministry (or who would have been restricted if still living) because of credible allegations of abuse.	Milwaukee, WI	**Source:** Milwaukee Journal Sentinel 1.9.01; Milwaukee Journal Sentinel 1.10.01; Archdiocese of Wilwaukee List 7.9.04; Milwaukee Journal Sentinel 7.10.04

BishopAccountability.org

Database of Publicly Accused Priests in the United States

Viewed by Diocese: Wichita, KS
Total Individuals: 5

Return to main database page.   See abbreviations and posting policy. Send corrections.

The Database of Publicly Accused Priests does not state or imply that individuals facing allegations are gu
a crime or liable for civil claims. The reports contained in the database are merely allegations. The U.S. leg
system presumes that a person accused of or charged with a crime is innocent until proven guilty. Similarly
individuals who may be defendants in civil actions are presumed not to be liable for such claims unless a p
proves otherwise. Admissions of guilt or liability are not typically a part of civil or private settlements. For m
information, see our posting policy.

Last	First	Ord	T	Status	D/O	Notes	Diocese	Source/Assignment:
Blanpied	Robert D.	1948	P	Accused	Diocesan	Blanpied & Diocese sued in 1995 by a man who said Blanpied abused him from age 10-15 yrs. Suit dismissed on SOL and dismissal upheld by the state Court of Appeals in 1997. Blanpied admitted in 1994 meeting w/ man and his family that he improperly touched the man 30 years before. Worked in Wichita Diocese from 1948 until 1969. Worked in Pueblo 1969-1994. Removed 1994 but later reassigned since he received honors in 1998 upon retirement after 50 yrs as a priest. Died 10/03.	Wichita, KS	**Source:** Wichita Eagle 7.24.95 Wichita Eagle 7.26.95 Wichita Eagle (AP) 7. Durango Herald 4.6.0 Durango Herald 10.0: Lawrence Journal-Wc 6.23.10
Larson	Robert K.	1958	P	Convicted	Diocesan	Former Director of Catholic Charities. Removed/retired from active service in 1988 for "stress related problems." Accused of abusing >17 boys. Pled guilty in 2001 to abusing 4, including 1 felony count. Sentenced to 3-10 yrs prison; 5 others whom L denies abusing later committed suicide. Abuse included sodomy. Moved to St. John Vianney Renewal Center in MO. after 3/06 release from prison. Listed on MO sex offender registry.	Wichita, KS	**Source:** Links to Articles; KSD 5.6.10; Lawrence Jou World 6.23.10; Lawre Journal-World 6.23.10 **Assignments:** Detailed BA.org Reco

236

Metzinger	Agnesina		N	Sued	order?	Named in 1996 civil suit which alleged that Metzinger repeatedly had sex with a young boy who was a residence of St. Joseph's Home. Same suit alleges several of the boy's siblings were abused by priests at the home. Metzinger is dead as of 2010.	Wichita, KS	**Source:** Wichita Eagle 5.21.96; Lawrence Journal-World 6.23.10; Lawrence Journal-World 6.23.10
Mulvihill	**Daniel**	1953	P	Sued	Diocesan	Named in 1996 civil suit filed by 4 brothers. Men said that they were abused at St. Joseph's Children Home in KS and that they believed that another priest had molested their sister and that she had borne the priest a child. They say they found her diary after her death w/ picture of her & priest and a baby boy. Diocese investigated and said that Mulvihill denied that he was the father of the child. Said diary was the dreaming of a lonely young woman about a kid and handsome priest. He is deceased.	Wichita, KS	**Source:** Wichita Eagle 5.21.96; Lawrence Journal-World 6.23.10; Lawrence Journal-World 6.23.10
Wheeler	**William**		P	Sued	Diocesan	In 1996 civil suit, two men alleged that they were fondled by Wheeler several times in the mid-1950s at an El Dorado children's home. Same suit alleges that another brother was molested by nun and that a 2nd priest fathered a child on their sister. Died 1994.	Wichita, KS	**Source:** Witchita Eagle 5.21.96; Lawrence Journal-World 6.23.10; Lawrence Journal-World 6.23.10

nformation from BishopAccountability.org

A LETTER FROM FATHER THOMAS DOYLE
To Tim C. Leedom
No Good Deed Goes Unpunished
(one of "Murphy's Laws")

Tim,

I have not been excommunicated, though it has been threatened. I am basically isolated. No bishop will allow me to work in his diocese. I have been banned from speaking in every diocese where my talks have been scheduled in a church-owned building. I have been ordered by the bishop of the diocese where I live not to speak publicly, not to speak with the media, and not to exercise any ministry. I could have challenged all of it, but, rather, I ignored it. A few priests have spoken out and none as much or as publicly as I. Two bishops who have stood publicly with victims, Bishop Tom Gumbleton of Detroit (Assistant Bishop) and Geoff Robinson, Assistant Bishop of Australia, were both disciplined by the Vatican. Gumbleton was fired as an auxiliary bishop and removed as pastor. He must now get permission of the papal nuncio (ambassador) and the local bishop any time he wished to speak publicly. Three weeks after he spoke in favor of victims before the Ohio legislature, in the face of the Ohio bishops who were doing everything to stop legislative change, he received a letter from the Vatican telling him he was no longer an auxiliary bishop and giving him as the reason that he had "broken communion" with the other bishops...In other words, he stood up and did what was right. The same happened to Robinson. He spoke publicly and said that Pope John Paul II did not exercise or show any leadership in the abuse matter and shortly thereafter he was forced to resign. In 2007 he spoke in the U.S. in 15 states. The Vatican ordered him not to speak, and every bishop of every diocese in which he was to speak wrote and banned him from church property and ordered him not to speak. He ignored them. Both men are now isolated. But they forge on.

On the other hand, the Vatican was very instrumental in helping the Nazi party gain power by its efforts to shut down the Catholic Central Party in Germany. The Vatican entered into concordats (treaties) with Bavaria and Nazi Germany and then with Mussolini's government in Italy. Many of the Nazi leaders were Catholics, as was the case with the Italians. At no time did Pope Pius XII excommunicate any of them. Perhaps the most notorious is Msgr. Joseph Tiso. He was the leader of Slovakia and a collaborator with the Nazis throughout the war. After the war he was hanged for treason.

You might also look into the activities of Bishop Alois Hudal, a German bishop living in the Vatican who arranged for a number of the Nazis to get passage to

South America after the war. There are a lot of different sources that document all of this. The whole damn thing is totally sickening.
Tom

Source: Reverend Thomas Doyle

The Loss of My Endorsement
By Thomas Doyle

On April 29, 2004, Dan Wakin wrote a story in the New York Times about the loss of my endorsements as an Air Force Catholic Chaplain. The story made public what had been a fact since September, 2003.

In September, 2003, Archbishop Edwin O'Brien who was then archbishop for the Archdiocese for the Military Services, removed the official certification that was required for me to continue to act as a Catholic Chaplain for the Air Force. I learned of his action about two weeks after it had actually taken place. I had transferred from an assignment in Germany back to the US and was enroute to Seymour Johnson Air Force Base in North Carolina. In between, I was spending two weeks with my family. It was while I was staying with one of my sisters that I received an email from the Dominican provincial asking me why I had been removed. Since I had known nothing about it, I was understandably stunned.

This action meant that I could no longer function as a chaplain. According to Air Force regulations it also meant that my commission as an officer would expire within two weeks after the loss of the endorsement. The day I learned of it I received a call from Chaplain Charlie Baldwin, the Chief of Chaplains. Chaplain Baldwin, now retired, was a Major General and the Chief of all Air Force Chaplains. His call stunned me. When my sister told me who was on the phone I expected more bad news. Quite the contrary. Chaplain Baldwin was totally supportive, sympathetic and encouraging. He gave me the lift I so badly needed at the time. I loved the air Force and, in spite of O'Brien's negative view of my career, I had done very well.

Chaplain Baldwin assured me that he had done everything he could to prevent the loss of endorsement. He also assured me that the Air Force highly valued my contribution to the mission and wanted to keep me on board. To that end he told me that he and his staff were working at doing an end-run around the nearly obligatory departure from the service. On this they were successful. I was told to proceed to my next assignment and continue on as an Air Force officer. The actual "job" I would hold would be worked out.

239

The key question is "why did it happen?" Archbishop O'Brien needed a tangible reason to remove my endorsement. He used a memo I had written to the head chaplain at Ramstein Air Base as his excuse. It was not possible to misinterpret this memo because it was written in clear and concise language. Instead O'Brien lied about the contents and about my motivation. He claimed that I had denied the centrality of the Eucharist, and that I had also disobeyed one of its directives.

Neither of these accusations was at all true, and there is nothing in the memo that came close to such conclusion.

The obvious reason was retaliation for my outspoken criticism of the U.S. hierarchy over their mishandling of the clergy sex abuse issue. One of the most serious "sins" a priest can commit is to challenge a bishop, much less a collection of bishops. Bishops believe that they are right in all things. They believe this is grounded in God's will. This is magical thinking. The Catholic bishops of the US and elsewhere have been proven wrong on many issues, but the worst in my experience is the way they have responded to the victims of sexual abuse by the clergy. But apparently it was more important to the bishops to be in control than to right the wrongs of the lifelong traumas of the young people in their flock betrayed and abused by the very men – "men of God" – in whom they had total trust. Such betrayal is nothing short of monstrous.

The memo in question was intended for the chaplain only, but it was inadvertently left in a meeting room. It was found by a female staff member who was, and probably still is, a religious fanatic. She literally panicked and somehow thought the memo meant that I was trying to eliminate Mass from the Catholic program. This was obvious nonsense. She faxed the memo to the archbishop. I still remember her last words to me: *"we need the hierarchy to tell us what is right and what is wrong."* That sentence alone deserves a response but this is not the venue.

The date of the letter of removal was the day after the fax was sent. Archbishop O'Brien lost no time. Neither I nor anyone on the Ramstein chapel staff was contacted. In fact, other than two letters I sent to my superior, the Dominican provincial, who passed them on to O'Brien, I was never offered any opportunity to explain, rebut, revise or remove the memo by Archbishop O'Brien. My religious superior spoke with O'Brien and asked if he or I or both of us could meet with him, and this request was refused.

Archbishop O'Brien had been looking for a way to get rid of me for at least 4 years prior to this incident. In 1999, he took issue with a statement I had made in a private email which ended up being published on a Canadian website. In 2002, he took serious issue with the speech I gave at the Voice of the Faithful

Convention in Boston. Apparently he didn't have the ammunition on either occasion to make a move. I was strongly supported by my Air Force superiors, especially the Command Chaplain, who was the highest-ranking chaplain in the European Command.

The air Force wanted me to stay. For bureaucratic reasons my commission was very vulnerable for a short period of time because I did not have a specific job assignment. At the time Congress had also declared a "Reduction in Force" and I was notified that I would be discharged unless I received some form of chaplain endorsement within a matter of days. I wanted to stay in the Air Force. The endorsement would have eliminated the immediate threat of discharge and allowed me time to complete the process of changing my basic status from a chaplain to a regular officer. A close friend suggested that I get a temporary endorsement from another denomination or designation as any kind of chaplain.

The Archbishop's office learned of this and it gave them more fuel. One of their auxiliaries, the late Bishop Kaising, called me and told me I was going to be excommunicated for schism. I responded that I knew what schism was and I didn't qualify. But what really enraged him was when I told him to go ahead and excommunicate me because it meant nothing to me anyway. In the end they never excommunicated me and my career as a phantom non-Catholic chaplain ended after a week.

I was told by some other Catholic chaplains that O'Brien let the word out that they were not to communicate with me. I could have gone to the press at that time but I did not because I wanted to avoid media focus. Any media attention about anything related to sexual abuse by clergy needs to be on the victims and not their supporters. Even though O'Brien's actions robbed me of some significant Air Force benefits including the possibility of a retirement pension, I retained the conviction that this is not about me but about the victims of abuse by the clergy. Most of those victims have suffered far worse than I could ever expect to suffer at the hands of those bishops.

When the whole issue went public in April 2004, I was deluged with media calls. I was determined to maintain dignity and to avoid any angry responses. I chose the high road, and I do not regret it. I do regret, however, saying anything that sounded as if I was apologizing for what I did or how I did it. I do not regret one bit of it. Dan Wakin correctly reported that I considered the endorsement by a non-Catholic denomination a mistake. I said this only to avoid more publicity. It was not a mistake. The only problem was the narrow, prejudicial and paranoid outlook of Catholic bishops, O'Brien and Kaising included, towards other denominations. To them, it is "their way or the highway."

I used to have a close friend who worked in Archbishop O'Brien's office, the headquarters of the Archdiocese for the Military Services. He assured me more than once that O'Brien was gunning for my, constantly scouring the internet for anything that could be used against me. For O'Brien to publicly claim that my removal was not retaliatory is ridiculous. Of course it was. Had the same scenario happened with any other Catholic chaplain, a phone call of explanation would have ended the matter.

I have neither regrets nor anger. I knew that sooner or later one of the mud balls the bishops had been throwing at me would stick. This one may have ended my ministry in the Air Force, but it surely did not end my ministry to the countless people seriously abused by the bishops.

Above all, O'Brien's actions did not scare me into silence. On the contrary, his actions towards me were just one more clear sign that the bishops and archbishops of this country and probably others as well are seriously threatened by the increasing exposure of the truth.

Pope Benedict XVI asks for immunity.

Lawyers for Pope Benedict XVI asked then President Bush to declare the Pontiff immune from liability in lawsuits that accuse him of conspiring to cover up the molestations of three boys by a seminarian in Texas.

President Bush, in a move to solidify his political position with the Vatican, met the Pope at the airport (most unusual) and placed a lid on the freedom of information material covering the last forty years.

"Silence gives consent."
Pope Boniface VII (1235-1303)

CRIMEN SOLLICITATIONIS

Crimen Sollicitationis (Latin: *the crime of soliciting*) is the title of a 1962 document of the Holy Office (which is now called the Congregation for the Doctrine of the Faith) codifying procedures to be followed in cases of priests or bishops of the Catholic Church accused of having used the sacrament of Penance to make sexual advances to penitents.

The 1962 document, approved by Pope John XXII , was addressed to "all Patriarchs, Archbishops, Bishops and other Local Ordinaries, including those of the Eastern Rite." It gave specific instructions on how to carry out the rules in the Code of Canon Law on dealing with such cases, and directed that the same procedures be used when dealing with denunciations of homosexual, pedophile or zoophile behavior by clerics. Dioceses were to use the instructions for their own guidance and keep it in their archives for confidential documents they were not to publish the instruction nor produce commentaries on it.

Inspired by Wikipedia (Retrieved May 13, 2010)

The following is a copy of the actual document:

INSTRUCTION OF THE SUPREME SACRED CONGREGATION OF THE HOLY OFFICE
ADDRESSED TO ALL PATRIARCHS, ARCHBISHOPS, BISHOPS AND OTHER LOCAL ORDINARIES "ALSO OF THE ORIENTAL RITE" ON THE MANNER OF PROCEEDING IN CAUSES OF SOLICITATION
Vatican Polyglot Press, 1962

INSTRUCTION
On the Manner of Proceeding in Causes involving the Crime of Solicitation
TO BE KEPT CAREFULLY IN THE SECRET ARCHIVEOF THE CURIA FOR INTERNAL USE.
NOT TO BE PUBLISHED OR AUGMENTED WITH COMMENTARIES
PRELIMINARY MATTERS

1. The crime of solicitation occurs whenever a priest – whether in the act itself of sacramental confession, or before or immediately after confession, on the occasion or under the pretext of confession, or even apart from confession [but] in a confessional or another place assigned or chosen for the hearing of confessions and with the semblance of hearing confessions there – has attempted to solicit or provoke a penitent, whosoever he or she may be, to immoral or indecent acts, whether by words, signs, nods, touch or a

written message, to be read either at that time or afterwards, or he has impudently dared to have improper and indecent conversations or interactions with that person (Constitution *Sacramentum Poenitentiae*, §1).

2. Bringing this unspeakable crime to trial in first instance pertains to the *local Ordinaries* in whose territory the Defendant has residence (see below, Nos. 30 and 31), not only by proper right but also by special delegation of the Apostolic See;

and it is enjoined upon them, by an obligation gravely binding in conscience, to ensure that causes of this sort henceforth be introduced, treated and concluded as quickly as possible before their own tribunal. Nevertheless, for particular and grave reasons, in accordance with the norm of Canon 247, §2, these causes can also be deferred directly to the Sacred Congregation of the Holy Office, or called to itself by the same Sacred Congregation. The Defendants retain the right in any grade of trial to have recourse to the Holy Office; but such recourse does not, except in the case of an appeal, suspend the exercise of jurisdiction by a judge who has already begun to hear the cause. The judge can therefore continue to hear the cause up to the definitive sentence, unless he has ascertained that the Apostolic See has called the cause to itself (cf. Canon 1569).

3. The term "local Ordinaries" here means, each for his own territory: residential Bishops, Abbots or Prelates *nullius*, Administrators, Vicars and Prefects Apostolic, as well as all those who, in their absence, temporarily take their place in governance by prescription of law or by approved constitutions (Can. 198, §1). The term does not, however, include Vicars General, except by special delegation.

4. The local Ordinary is judge in these causes for Religious as well, including exempt Religious. Their Superiors are in fact strictly prohibited from involving themselves in causes pertaining to the Holy Office (Canon 501, §2). Nonetheless, without prejudice to the right of the Ordinary, this does not prevent Superiors themselves, should they discover that one of their subjects has committed a crime in the administration of the Sacrament of Penance, from being able and obliged to exercise vigilance over him; to admonish and correct him, also by means of salutary penances; and, if need be, to remove him from any ministry whatsoever. They will also be able to transfer him to another place, unless the local Ordinary has forbidden it inasmuch as a complaint has already been received and an investigation begun.

5. The local Ordinary can either preside over these causes himself or commit them to be heard by another person, namely , a prudent ecclesiastic of mature age. But he may not do so habitually, that is, for all such causes; instead, a separate written delegation is needed for each individual cause, with due regard for the prescription of Canon 1613, §1.

6. Although, for reasons of confidentiality, a single judge is ordinarily prescribed for causes of this sort, in more difficult cases the Ordinary is not prohibited from appointing one or two consulting assessors, to be selected from among the synodal judges (Canon 1575), or even from committing a cause to be heard by three judges, likewise to be chosen from among the synodal judges, with a mandate to proceed collegially in accordance with the norm of Canon 1577.

7. The promoter of justice, the advocate of the Defendant and the notary – who are to be prudent priests, of mature age and good repute, doctors in canon law or otherwise expert, of proven zeal for justice (Canon 1589) and unrelated to the Defendant in any of the ways set forth in Canon 1613 – are appointed in writing by the Ordinary. The promoter of justice, however (who can be different from the promoter of justice of the Curia), can be appointed

for all causes of this kind, but the advocate of the Defendant and the notary are to be appointed for each individual case. The Defendant is not prohibited from proposing an advocate acceptable to him (Canon 1655); the latter, however, must be a priest, and is to be approved by
the Ordinary.

8. On those occasions (to be specified below) when the intervention of the promoter of justice is required, if he was not cited, the acts are to be considered invalid unless, albeit not cited, he was in fact present. If, however, the promoter of justice was legitimately cited, yet was not present for part of the proceedings, the acts will be valid, but they are later to be subject to his full examination, so that he can observe and propose, either orally or in writing, whatever he judges necessary or appropriate (Canon 1587).

9. On the other hand it is required, under pain of nullity, that the notary be present for the proceedings in their entirety, and record them in his own hand or at least sign them (Canon 1585,§ 1). Due to the particular nature of these procedures, however, the Ordinary has the right, for a reasonable cause, to dispense from the presence of the notary in receiving denunciations, as will be specified below; in carrying out the so-called "*diligences*"; and in questioning the witnesses who have been called.

10. No lesser personnel are to be employed save those absolutely necessary; these are to be chosen, insofar as possible, from the order of priests, and in any case they are to be of proven fidelity and above all exception. It should be noted, though, that, when needed, non-subjects living in another territory can also be appointed to receive certain acts, or the Ordinary of that territory can be asked to do so (Can. 1570, §2), always duly observing the precautions mentioned above and in Canon 1613.

11. Since, however, in dealing with these causes, more than usual care and concern must be shown that they be treated with the utmost confidentiality, and that, once decided and the decision executed, they are covered by permanent silence (Instruction of the Holy Office, 20 February 1867, No. 14), all those persons in any way associated with the tribunal, or knowledgeable of these matters by reason of their office, are bound to observe inviolably the strictest confidentiality, commonly known as the *secret of the Holy Office*, in all things and with all persons, under pain of incurring automatic excommunication, *ipso facto* and undeclared, reserved to the sole person of the Supreme Pontiff, excluding even the Sacred Penitentiary. Ordinaries are bound by *this same law* , that is, in virtue of their own office; other personnel are bound in virtue of the oath which they are always to swear before assuming their duties; and, finally, those delegated, questioned or informed [outside the tribunal], are bound in virtue of *the precept* to be imposed on them in the letters of delegation, inquiry or information, with express mention of the *secret of the Holy Office* and of the aforementioned censure.

12. The oath mentioned above, whose formula is found in the Appendix of this Instruction (Form A), is to be taken – once for all by those who are appointed habitually, but each and every time by those who are deputed only for a single item of business or cause – in the presence of the Ordinary or his delegate, on the Holy Gospels of God (including priests) and not in any other way, together with an additional promise faithfully to carry out their duties; the aforementioned excommunication does not, however, extend to the latter. Care must be taken by those presiding over these causes that no one, including the tribunal personnel, come to knowledge of matters except to the extent that their role or task necessarily demands it.

13. The oath to maintain confidentiality must always be taken in these causes, also by the accusers or complainants and the witnesses. These persons, however, are subject to no censure, unless they were expressly warned of this in the proceedings of accusation, deposition or questioning. The Defendant is to be most gravely admonished that he too must maintain confidentiality with respect to all persons, apart from his advocate, under the penalty of suspension *a divinis*, to be incurred *ipso facto* in the event of a violation.

14. Finally, as to the drawing up of the acts , the language used, and their confirmation, safekeeping and possible nullity, the respective prescriptions of Canons 1642-43, 379-80-81-82 and 1680 are to be fully followed.

TITLE ONE
THE FIRST NOTIFICATION OF THE CRIME

15. The crime of solicitation is ordinarily committed in the absence of any witnesses; consequently, lest it remain almost always hidden and unpunished with inestimable detriment to souls, it has been necessary to compel the one person usually aware of the crime, namely the penitent solicited, to reveal it *by a denunciation* imposed by positive law. Therefore:

16. "In accordance with the Apostolic Constitutions and specifically the Constitution of Benedict XIV *Sacramentum Poenitentiae* of 1 June 1741, the penitent must denounce a priest guilty of the crime of solicitation in confession to the local Ordinary or to the Sacred Congregation of the Holy Office within one month; and the confessor must, by an obligation gravely binding in conscience, warn the penitent of this duty." (Canon 904).

17. Moreover, in the light of Canon 1935, any member of the faithful can always denounce a crime of solicitation of which he or she has certain knowledge; indeed, there is an urgent duty to make such a denunciation whenever one is compelled to do so by the natural law itself, on account of danger to faith or religion, or some other impending public evil.

18. "A member of the faithful who, in violation of the (aforementioned) prescription of Canon 904, knowingly disregards the obligation to denounce within a month the person by whom he or she was solicited, incurs an excommunication *latae sententiae* reserved to no one, which is not to be lifted until he or she has satisfied the obligation, or has promised seriously to do so" (Can. 2368, § 2)

19. The responsibility for making the denunciation is a personal one, and it is normally to be discharged by the person himself who has been solicited. But if he is prevented by very grave difficulties from doing so himself, then he is to approach the Ordinary or the Sacred Congregation of the Holy Office or the Sacred Penitentiary, either by letter or through another person whom he has chosen, describing all the circumstances (Instruction of the Holy Office, 20 February 1867, No. 7).

20. Anonymous denunciations are generally to be disregarded; they may however have some corroborative value, or provide an occasion for further investigations, if particular circumstances make the accusation plausible (cf. Can. 1942, §2).

21. The obligation on the part of the penitent who has been solicited to make a denunciation does not cease as a result of a possible spontaneous confession by the soliciting confessor, or his transfer, promotion, condemnation, presumed amendment or other such reasons; it does cease, however, upon the death of the latter.

22. Whenever it happens that a confessor or another churchman is deputed to receive

some denunciation, together with instructions about the proceedings to be carried out in judicial form, he is to be expressly admonished that he is thereafter to forward everything immediately to the Ordinary or to the person who deputed him, keeping no copy or record of it himself.

23. In receiving denunciations, this order is normally to be followed: First, an oath to tell the truth is to be administered to the one making the denunciation; the oath is to be taken while touching the Holy Gospels. The person is then to be questioned according to the formula (Formula E), taking care that he relates, briefly and fittingly, yet clearly and in detail, everything whatsoever pertaining to the solicitations he has experienced. In no way, however, is he to be asked if he consented to the solicitation; indeed, he should be expressly advised that he is not bound to make known any consent which may have been given. The responses, not only with regard to their substance but also the very wording of the testimony (Canon 1778), should immediately be put in writing. The entire transcript is then to be read back in a clear and distinct voice to the one making the denunciation, giving him the option to add, suppress, correct or change anything. His signature is then to be demanded or else, if he is unable or does not know how to write, an "x". While he is still present, the one receiving the testimony, as well as the notary, if present, are to add their signatures (cf. No. 9). Before the one making the denunciation is dismissed, he is to be administered the oath to maintain confidentiality, as above, if necessary under pain of excommunication reserved to the local Ordinary or to the Holy See (cf. No. 13).

24. If, on occasion, this ordinary procedure cannot be followed for grave reasons always to be expressly indicated in the acts , it is permitted for one or another of the prescribed forms to be omitted, but without detriment to the substance. Thus, if the oath cannot be taken on the Holy Gospels, it can be taken in another way, and even only verbally. If the text of the denunciation cannot be written down immediately, it can be set down at a more suitable time and place by the recipient or the one making the denunciation, and later confirmed and signed by the accuser in the presence of the recipient. If the text itself cannot be read back to the accuser, it can be given to him to read.

25. In more difficult cases, however, it is also permitted for the denunciation – with the prior permission of the accuser, lest the sacramental seal appear to be violated – to be received by a confessor in the places of confession itself. In this case, if the denunciation cannot be made immediately, it is to be written down at home by the confessor or the accuser himself, and on another date, when the two meet again in the place of confession, it is to be read back or handed over to be read, and then confirmed by the accuser with the oath and his own signature or the mark of a cross (unless it is completely impossible to affix these). Express mention of all of these things must always be made in the acts, as was stated in the previous number.

26. Finally, if a most grave and absolutely extraordinary reason demands it, the denunciation can also be made through a report written by the accuser, provided, however, that it is later confirmed by oath and signed in the presence of the local Ordinary or his delegate and the notary, if the latter is present (cf. No. 9). The same must be said for an informal denunciation, made by letter, for example, or orally in an extrajudicial manner.

27. Once any denunciation has been received, the Ordinary is *bound by a grave obligation* to communicate it as soon as possible to the promoter of justice, who must declare in writing whether or not the specific crime of solicitation, as set forth in No. 1 above, is present in the particular case, and, if the Ordinary disagrees with this, the promoter of justice must defer the matter to the Holy Office within ten days.

28. If, on the other hand, the Ordinary and the promoter of justice are in agreement, or, in any event, if the promoter of justice does not make recourse to the Holy Office, then the Ordinary, if he has determined that the specific delict of solicitation was not present, is to order the acts to be put into the secret archive, or to exercise his right and duty in accordance with the nature and gravity of the matters reported. If, on the other hand, he has come to the conclusion that [the crime] was present, he is immediately to proceed to the investigation (cf. Can. 1942, §1).

TITLE TWO
THE PROCESS
Chapter I - The Investigation

29. When, as a result of denunciations, notice of the crime of solicitation is had, a special investigation is to be carried out, "so that it may be determined whether the accusation has any basis and what that may be" (Canon 1939, §1); this is all the more necessary since a crime of this type, as was already stated above, is usually committed in private, and direct testimony regarding it can only rarely be obtained, other than from the aggrieved party.

Once the investigation has been opened, if the accused priest is a religious, the Ordinary can prevent him from being transferred elsewhere before the conclusion of the process. There are three major areas which such an investigation must cover, namely:
a) precedents on the part of the accused;
b) the soundness of the denunciations;
c) other persons solicited by the same confessor, or in any event aware of the crime, if these are brought forward by the accuser, as not infrequently happens.

30. With regard to the first area (a), then, the Ordinary, immediately upon receiving a denunciation of the crime of solicitation, must – if the accused, whether a member of the secular clergy or a religious (cf. No. 4), has residence in his territory – inquire if the archives contain any other accusations against him, even regarding other matters, and to retrieve them; if the accused had previously lived in other territories, the Ordinary is also to inquire of the respective Ordinaries and, if the accused is a religious, also of his religious superiors, whether they have anything in any way prejudicial to him. If he receives any such documents, he is to add them to the acts, either in order to make a single judgment thereupon, by reason of common content or the connection of causes (cf. Canon 1567), or else to establish and evaluate the aggravating circumstance of recidivism, according to the sense of Canon 2208.

31. In the case of an accused priest who does not have residence in his territory, the Ordinary is to transmit all the acts to the Ordinary of the accused, or, if he does not know who that might be, to the Supreme Sacred Congregation of the Holy Office, without prejudice to his right in the meantime to deny the accused priest the faculty of exercising ecclesiastical ministries in his diocese, or to revoke any faculty already granted, if and when the priest should enter or return to the diocese.

32. With regard to the second area (b), the weight of each denunciation, its particulars and circumstances must be pondered gravely and attentively, in order to clarify if and how much credence they merit. It is not sufficient that this be done in any way whatsoever;

rather it must be carried out in a certain and judicial form, as is customarily signified in the Tribunal of the Holy Office by the phrase "carry out the diligences" (*diligentias peragere*).

33. To this end, once the Ordinary has received any denunciation of the crime of solicitation, he will – either personally or through a specially delegated priest – summon two witnesses (separately and with due discretion), to be selected insofar as possible from among the clergy, yet above any exception, who know well both the accused and the accuser. In the presence of the notary (cf. No. 9), who is to record the questions and answers in writing, he is to place them under a solemn oath to tell the truth and to maintain confidentiality, under threat, if necessary, of excommunication reserved to the local Ordinary or to the Holy See (cf. No. 13). He is then to question them (Formula G) concerning the life, conduct and public reputation of both the accused and the accuser; whether they consider the accuser worthy of credence, or on the other hand capable of lying, slander or perjury; and whether they know of any reason for hatred, spite or enmity between the accuser and the accused.

34. If the denunciations are several in number, there is nothing to prevent employing the same witnesses for all of them, or from using different witnesses for each, yet care must always be taken to have the testimony of two witnesses with regard to the accused priest and each accuser.

35. If two witnesses cannot be found, each of whom knows both the accused and the accuser, or if they cannot be questioned about the two at the same time without danger of scandal or loss of good repute, then the so-called *divided diligences* (Formula H) are to be carried out: in other words, questioning two persons about the accused alone, and another two about each individual accuser. In this case, however, prudent inquiries will have to be made from other sources as to whether the accusers are affected by hatred, enmity or any other sentiments against the accused..

36. If not even *divided diligences* can be carried out, either because suitable witnesses cannot be found, or for a just fear of scandal or loss of good repute, this [lack] can be supplied, albeit cautiously and prudently, through extrajudicial information, set down in writing, concerning the accused and the accusers and their personal relationships, or even through subsidiary evidence which may corroborate or weaken the accusation.

37. Finally, with regard to the third area (c), if in the denunciations, as not infrequently happens, other persons are named who may likewise have been solicited, or for some other reason can offer testimony about this crime, these are all to be questioned as well, separately, in judicial form (Formula I). They are to be questioned first with regard to *generalities*, then gradually, as the matter develops, descending to *particulars*, whether and in what way they themselves were in fact solicited, or came to know or hear that other persons had been solicited (Instruction of the Holy Office, 20 February 1867, No. 9).

38. The greatest discretion is to be employed in inviting these persons to the interview; it will not always be appropriate to summon them to the public setting of the chancery, especially if those to be questioned are young girls, married women, or domestics. In such cases it will be more advisable to summon them discreetly for questioning in sacristies or elsewhere (e.g. in the place for confessions), according to the prudent estimation of the Ordinary or judge. If those to be examined live in monasteries or in hospitals or in religious homes for girls, then they are to be called with great care and on different days, according to particular circumstances (Instruction of the Holy Office, 20 July 1890).

39. Whatever was stated above regarding the way of receiving denunciations is also to be applied, with due adaptations, to the questioning of other persons [whose names were] brought forward.

40. If the questioning of these persons produces positive results, namely that the priest under investigation or another turns out to be implicated, the accusations are to be considered true denunciations in the proper sense of the word, and all else prescribed above with regard to the definition of the crime, the bringing up of precedents, and the *diligences* to be performed, is to be carried out.

41. When all these things have been done, the Ordinary is to communicate the acts to the promoter of justice, who is to review whether everything was carried out correctly or not. And if [the latter] concludes that there is nothing against accepting them, [the Ordinary] is to declare the investigative process closed.

Chapter II – Canonical Measures and the Admonition of the Accused

42. Once the investigative process has been closed, the Ordinary, after hearing the promoter of justice, is to proceed as follows, namely:

a) if it is clear that the denunciation is completely unfounded, he is to order this fact to be declared in the acts, and the documents of accusation are to be destroyed;

b) if the evidence of a crime is vague and indeterminate, or uncertain, he is to order the acts to be archived, to be brought up again should anything else happen in the future;

c) if, however, the evidence of a crime is considered grave enough, but not yet sufficient to file a formal complaint – as is the case especially when there are only one or two denunciations with regular *diligences* but lacking or containing insufficiently solid subsidiary proofs (cf. No. 36), or even when there are several [denunciations] but with uncertain *diligences* or none at all – he is to order that the accused be admonished, according to the different types of cases (Formula M), by a *first* or a *second* warning, *paternally*, *gravely* or *most gravely* according to the norm of Canon 2307, adding, if necessary, the *explicit threat of a trial* should some other new accusation be brought against him. The acts, as stated above, are to be kept in the archives, and vigilance is to be exercised for a period with regard to the conduct of the accused (Canon 1946, §2, No. 2);

d) finally, if certain or at least probable arguments exist for bringing the accusation to trial, he should order the Defendant to be cited and formally charged.

43. The warning mentioned in the preceding number (c) is always to be given in a confidential manner; nevertheless it can also be given by letter or by a personal intermediary, but in each case this must be proved by a document to be kept in the secret archives of the Curia (cf. Canon 2309, §§ 1 and 5), together with information about the manner in which the Defendant accepted it.

44. If, following the first warning, other accusations are made against the same Defendant regarding acts of solicitation which occurred prior to that warning, the Ordinary is to determine, in conscience and according to his own judgment, whether the first warning is to be considered sufficient or whether he should instead proceed to a new warning, or even to the next stage (Ibidem, §6).

45. The promoter of justice has the right to appeal these canonical measures, and the accused has the right to have recourse to the Sacred Congregation of the Holy Office within ten days from their issuance or notification. In this case, the acts of the cause are to be sent to the same Sacred Congregation, in accordance with the prescription of Canon 1890.

46. These [measures], however, even if they have been put into effect, do not extinguish a penal action. Consequently, if any other accusations are received

thereafter, the matters which prompted the aforementioned canonical measures will also need to be taken into account.

Chapter III - The Arraignment of the Accused

47. Once sufficient evidence is at hand for instituting a formal accusation, as was mentioned above in number 42 (d), the Ordinary – after having heard the promoter of justice and observed, to the extent that the particular nature of these causes allows, everything laid down in Book IV, Title VI, Chapter II, of the Code [of Canon Law] concerning the citation and intimation of judicial acts – shall issue a decree (Formula O) citing the Defendant to appear before himself or before a judge whom he has delegated (cf. No. 5), in order to be charged with the crimes of which he has been accused; in the tribunal of the Holy Office this is commonly referred to as "subjecting the Defendant to the charges" [*Reum constitutis subiicere*]. He is to see to it that the decree is communicated to the Defendant in the manner prescribed by law.

48. When the Defendant, having been cited, has appeared, before the charges are formally brought, the judge is to exhort him in a paternal and gentle way to make a confession; if he accepts these exhortations, the judge, having summoned the notary or even, if he considers it more appropriate (cf. No. 9), without the presence of the latter, is to receive the confession.

49. In such a case, if the confession is found, in light of the proceedings, to be substantially complete, once the Promoter of Justice has submitted a written opinion, the cause can be concluded by a definitive sentence, all other formalities being omitted (see below, Chapter IV). The Defendant however is to be given the option of accepting that sentence, or requesting the normal course of a trial.

50. If on the other hand the Defendant has denied the crime, or has made a confession which is not substantially complete, or even rejected a sentence summarily issued on the basis of his confession, the judge, in the presence of the notary, is to read him the decree mentioned above in No. 47, and to declare the arraignment opened.

51. Once the arraignment has been opened, the judge, in keeping with Canon 1956, having heard the promoter of justice, can suspend the Defendant either completely from the exercise of sacred ministry or solely from hearing sacramental confessions of the faithful, until the conclusion of the trial. If he suspects, however, that the Defendant is capable of intimidating or suborning the witnesses, or otherwise hindering the course of justice, he can also, having again heard the promoter of justice, order him to retire to a specific place and to remain there under special supervision (Canon 1957). There is no legal remedy given against either such decree (Canon 1958).

52. After this, the questioning of the Defendant takes place in accordance with Formula P, with the greatest care being taken on the part of the judge lest the identity of the accusers and especially of the denouncers be revealed, and on the part of the Defendant lest the sacramental seal be violated in any way. If the Defendant, speaking heatedly, lets slip something which might suggest either a direct or indirect violation of the seal, the judge is not to allow it to be recorded by the notary in the acts; and if, by chance, some such thing has been unwittingly related, he is to order it, as soon as it comes to his attention, to be deleted completely. *The judge must always remember that it is never permissible for him to compel the Defendant to take an oath to tell the truth* (cf. Canon 1744).

53. When the questioning of the Defendant has been completed in every detail and the acts have been reviewed and approved by the Promoter of Justice, the judge is to issue the decree concluding this phase of the cause (Can. 1860); if he is a delegated judge, he is to forward all the acts to the Ordinary.

54. Should, however, the Defendant prove contumacious, or, for very grave reasons the Charges cannot be brought in the diocesan Curia, the Ordinary, without prejudice to his right to suspend the Defendant a divinis, is to defer the entire cause to the Holy Office.

Chapter IV - The Discussion of the Cause, the Definitive Sentence, and the Appeal

55. The Ordinary, upon receiving the acts, unless he wishes to proceed himself to the definitive sentence, is to delegate a judge (cf. No. 5), different, insofar as possible, from the one who conducted the investigation or the arraignment (cf. Canon 1941, §3). The judge, however, whether he be the Ordinary or his delegate, is to give the Defendant's advocate, according to his prudent judgment, a suitable period of time in which to prepare the defence and to file it in duplicate, with one copy to be given to the judge himself and the other to the promoter of justice (cf. Canons 1862-63-64). The promoter of justice, too, within a time period likewise established by the judge, should present in writing his prosecutory brief (*requisitoriam*) as it is now called (Formula Q).

56. Finally, after a suitable interval (Canon 1870), the judge, following his conscience as formed by the acts and the proofs (Canon 1869), shall pronounce the definitive decision, either of condemnation [*sententia condemnatoria*], if he is certain of the crime, or of acquittal [*sententia absolutoria*], if he is certain of [the Defendant's] innocence; or of release [*sententia dimissoria*], if he is invincibly doubtful due to lack of proof.

57. The written sentence is to be drawn up in accordance with the respective formulas appended to this Instruction, with the addition of an executory decree (Canon 1918), and communicated beforehand to the Promoter of Justice. It is then to be officially communicated in the presence of a notary to the Defendant, summoned to appear for this reason before the judge in session. If, however, the Defendant, refusing the summons, does not appear, the communication of the sentence is to be done by a letter whose receipt is certified by the public postal service.

58. Both the Defendant, if he considers himself aggrieved, and the promoter of justice have the right to appeal [this sentence] to the Supreme Tribunal of the Holy Office, in accordance with the prescription of Canons 1879ff., within ten days of its official communication; such an appeal has a suspensive effect, whereas the suspension of the Defendant from the hearing of sacramental confessions or from exercising sacred ministry (cf. No. 51), if one was imposed, remains in force.

59. Once an appeal has been properly made, the judge is to transmit to the Holy Office as quickly as possible an authentic copy, or even the original itself, of all the acts of the cause, adding whatever information he judges necessary or appropriate (Canon 1890).

60. Finally, with regard to a complaint of nullity, should one be lodged, the prescriptions of Canons 1892-97 are to be scrupulously observed; as to the execution of the sentence, the prescriptions of Canons 1920-24 are to be observed, in accordance with the nature of these causes.

TITLE THREE
PENALTIES

61. "One who has committed the crime of solicitation... is to be suspended from the celebration of Mass and from the hearing of sacramental confessions and even, in view of the gravity of the crime, declared incapable from hearing them. He is to be deprived of all benefices, dignities, active and passive voice, and is to be declared incapable for all these, and in more grievous cases he is even to be subjected to reduction to the lay state [*degradatio*]". Thus states Canon 2368, §1 of the Code [of Canon Law].

62. For a correct practical application of this canon, when determining, in the light of Canon 2218, §1, fair and proportionate penalties against priests convicted of the crime of solicitation, the following things should be taken into particular account in evaluating the gravity of the crime, namely: the number of persons solicited and their condition – for example, if they are minors or specially consecrated to God by religious vows; the form of solicitation, especially if it might be connected with false doctrine or false mysticism; not only the formal but also the material turpitude of the acts committed, and above all the connection of the solicitation with other crimes; the duration of the immoral conduct; the repetition of the crime; recidivism following an admonition, and the obdurate malice of the solicitor.

63. Resort is to be had to the extreme penalty of reduction to the lay state – which for accused religious can be commuted to reduction to the status of a lay brother [*conversus*] – only when, all things considered, it appears evident that the Defendant, in the depth of his malice, has, in his abuse of the sacred ministry, with grave scandal to the faithful and harm to souls, attained such a degree of temerity and habitude, that there seems to be no hope, humanly speaking, or almost no hope, of his amendment.

64. In these cases, the following supplementary sanctions are to be added to the penalties proper, to ensure that their effect is achieved more fully and securely, namely:

a) Upon all Defendants who have been judicially convicted there are to be imposed salutary penances, befitting the kind of faults committed, not as a substitute for penalties proper in the sense of Canon 2312, §1, but as a complement to them, and among these (cf. Can. 2313) chiefly spiritual exercises, to be made for a certain number of days in some religious house, with suspension from the celebration of Mass during that period.

b) Upon Defendants who have been convicted and have confessed, moreover, there should be imposed an abjuration, according to the variety of cases, of the slight or strong suspicion of heresy which soliciting priests incur due to the very nature of the crime, or even of formal heresy, if by chance the crime of solicitation was connected to false teaching.

c) Those in danger of relapsing and, even more, recidivists, are to be subjected to special supervision (Canon 2311).

d) As often as, in the prudent judgment of the Ordinary, it seems necessary either for the amendment of the delinquent, the removal of a near occasion [of sin], or the prevention or repair of scandal, there is to be added an order to live in a certain place or a prohibition from the same (Canon 2302).

e) Finally, since, by reason of the sacramental seal, there can never be any account taken in the external forum of the crime of absolving an accomplice, as this is described in the Constitution *Sacramentum Poenitentiae*, at the end of the sentence of condemnation there is to be added an admonition to the Defendant that, if he has absolved an accomplice, he should provide for his conscience by recourse to the Sacred Penitentiary.

65. In accordance with the norm of Canon 2236, §3, all of these penalties, inasmuch as imposed by law, cannot, once they have been applied by the judge ex officio, be remitted except by the Holy See, through the Supreme Sacred Congregation of the Holy Office.

TITLE FOUR
OFFICIAL COMMUNICATIONS

66. No Ordinary is ever to omit informing the Holy Office immediately upon receiving any denunciation of the crime of solicitation. If it happens to concern a priest, whether secular or religious, having residence in another territory, he is at the same time to send (as already stated above, No. 31) to the Ordinary of the place where the denounced priest currently lives or, if this is unknown, to the Holy Office, an authentic copy of the denunciation itself with the *diligences* carried out as fully as possible, along with appropriate information and declarations.

67. Any Ordinary who has instituted a process against any soliciting priest should not fail to inform the Sacred Congregation of the Holy Office, and, if the matter concerns a religious, the priest's General Superior as well, regarding the outcome of the cause.

68. If a priest convicted of the crime of solicitation, or even merely admonished, should transfer his residence to another territory, the Ordinary *a quo* should immediately warn the Ordinary *ad quem* of the priest's record and his legal status.

69. If a priest who has been suspended in a cause of solicitation from hearing sacramental confessions, but not from sacred preaching, should go to another territory to preach, the Ordinary of that territory should be informed by his Superior, whether secular or religious, that he cannot be employed for the hearing of sacramental confessions.

70. All these official communications shall always be made *under the secret of the Holy Office*; and, since they are of the utmost importance for the common good of the Church, *the precept to make them is binding under pain of grave* [*sin*].

TITLE FIVE
CRIMEN PESSIMUM

71. The term *crimen pessimum* ["the foulest crime"] is here understood to mean any external obscene act, gravely sinful, perpetrated or attempted by a cleric in any way whatsoever with a person of his own sex.

72. Everything laid down up to this point concerning the crime of solicitation is also valid, with the change only of those things which the nature of the matter necessarily requires, for the *crimen pessimum*, should some cleric (God forbid) happen to be accused of it before the local Ordinary, except that the obligation of denunciation [imposed] *by the positive law of the Church* [does not apply] unless perhaps it was joined with the crime of solicitation in sacramental confession. In determining penalties against delinquents of this type, in addition to what has been stated above, Canon 2359, §2 is also to be taken into consideration.

73. Equated with the *crimen pessimum*, with regard to penal effects, is any external obscene act, gravely sinful, perpetrated or attempted by a cleric in any way with pre-adolescent children [*impuberes*] of either sex or with brute animals (*bestialitas*).

74. Against clerics guilty of these crimes, if they are exempt religious – and unless the crime of solicitation takes place at the same time – Religious Superiors also can proceed, according to the sacred Canons and their proper Constitutions, either administratively or judicially. However, they must always communicate a sentence rendered, or an administrative decision in those cases which are more grave, to the Supreme Congregation of the Holy Office. The Superiors of a non-exempt religious can proceed only administratively. In the case where the guilty party has been expelled from religious life, the expulsion has no effect until it has been approved by the Holy Office.

FROM AN AUDIENCE WITH THE HOLY FATHER, 16 MARCH 1962

His Holiness Pope John XXIII, in an audience granted to the Most Eminent Cardinal Secretary of the Holy Office on 16 March 1962, graciously approved and confirmed this Instruction, ordering those responsible to observe it and to ensure that it is observed in every detail.
Given in Rome, from the Office of the Sacred Congregation, 16 March 1962.
L.+S. A. CARD. OTTAVIANI

CATHOLIC SEX ABUSE SCANDALS

The Catholic sex abuse scandals are a series of lawsuits and criminal prosecutions related to the sex crimes committed by Catholic priests and members of religious orders that drew widespread public attention in the last two decades of the 20th century.

The scandals also focused on members of the Catholic hierarchy who did not report the crimes to civil authorities and in many cases reassigned the offenders to other locations where they continued to have contact with minors.

In defending the Church's widespread sheltering of pedophiles, some bishops and psychiatrists contended that the prevailing psychology of the times suggested that people could be cured of such behavior through counseling. In response to the widening scandal, Pope John Paul II failed to declare firmly that sex crimes are a criminal as well as spiritual offense. Instead, he declared in 2003, "…there is no place in the priesthood and religious life for those that would harm the young."

With the approval of the Vatican, the hierarchy of the Church in the United States instituted reforms to prevent future abuse including requiring background checks for Church employees and volunteers. The Church also prohibited the ordination of men with "deep-seated homosexual tendencies."

Members of the church hierarchy compared the church with the secular world, arguing that media coverage has been excessive, considering that abuse occurs in other institutions.

In 2002, the John Jay report tabulated a total of 4,392 priests and deacons in the U.S. against whom allegations of sexual abuse were considered by their dioceses to have been "substantiated". In 2001, major lawsuits emerged in the United States and Ireland, alleging some priests had sexually abused minors and that their superiors had conspired to conceal and otherwise abet their criminal misconduct.

Although the scandals in the U.S. and Ireland unfolded over approximately the same time period, there are some significant differences between them. In the United States, most of the abusers were parish priests under diocesan control. While there were also a significant number of abuse cases involving parish priests in Ireland, another major scandal involved criminal abuse committed by members of religious orders working in Catholic-run institutions such as orphanages and reform schools. In the United States, the abuse was primarily sexual in nature and involved mostly boys between the ages of 11 and 17; in Ireland, the allegations involved both physical and sexual abuse, and children of both sexes were involved, although a large majority was male.

Source: Bishop Accountability; SNAP; Inspired by Wikipedia (Retrieved March 24, 2010)

It has been estimated that three times as many rape cases by clergy may have occurred than cases of the non-clerical rape or spousal abuse.

Source: Bishop Accountability; John Jay Report; Inspired by Wikipedia (Retrieved August 27, 2010.

THE JOHN JAY REPORT

The 2004 John Jay Report commissioned by the U.S. Conference of Catholic Bishops was based on surveys completed by the Roman Catholic Church dioceses in the United States. The filtered surveys provided to the research team information from diocesan files on each priest accused of sexual abuse, and on each of the priest's victims, in a format which did not disclose the name of the accused priest or the dioceses where they worked. The dioceses were encouraged to issue reports of their own based on the surveys that they had completed.

The report found that 10,667 people had made allegations of child sexual abuse between 1950 and 2002. Of these, 3,300 were not investigated because the allegations were made after the accused priest had died: 1,021 survived at the date of the report.

After investigating the remaining 7,700 allegations, the diocese were able to substantiate 6,700 accusations against 4,392 priests in the USA, about 4% of all 109,694 priests who served during the time period covered by the study. The known number of abuses increased in the 1960s, peaked in the 1970s, declined in the 1980s and by the 1990s had returned to the levels of the 1950s.

Source: Bishop Accountability

"Honesty is the first chapter in the Book of Wisdom."
Thomas Jefferson

THE HOLY SEE'S REACTION
by: Matt Taibbi

The Holy See's reaction to both stories has been swift. An unsigned editorial this week in the Vatican newspaper L'Osservatore Romano attacked the New York Times by name, accusing the paper of willfully ignoring the "truth" of Ratzinger/ Benedict's record and of attempting "to instrumentalize, without any foundation in fact, horrible episodes and sorrowful events uncovered in some cases from decades ago." The media, it continued, showed a "despicable intent of attacking at whatever cost, Benedict XVI and his closest collaborators."

> *"Doctor Asserts Judges (or Police, Lawyers, district Attorneys, Therapists, Parole Officers) Ignored Abuse Warnings."*

Since we now know the sober fact that no one in the healing and law enforcement professions knew back then the depths of the scourge of abuse, of the now-taken-for-granted conclusion that abusers of young people can never safely work closely with them again.

The most revolting part of this response is the last bit about how "no one knew… back then" the depth of the scourge of abuse, or the fact that child molesters cannot be allowed near children ever again once caught. Dolan is trying to get us to focus on the 1962 case, but the truth is that as recently as this last decade, the Church's doctrinal office elected to proceed with church trails for less than 10% of the 3,000 cases of abuse reported to them between the years 2000 and 2010.

And just a few days after this blog of Dolan's, the *Times* would come out with another story indicating the current Pope, then a Cardinal named Joseph Ratzinger, seems to have quashed an effort to bring a serial child abused named Lawrence Murphy to a church trial. The inaction of Ratzinger's office resulted in Murphy being allowed to die "in the dignity of the priesthood", which was his wish as expressed in a letter to then-Cardinal Ratzinger in January 1998.

So while schools, parole officers, judges, lawyers and therapists may have been deficient in their understanding of child abuse back in 1962 (although, I'm sorry – it could have been 1562, if someone molested my child and was allowed back in the priesthood, I'd be reaching for an axe), the Catholic church is alone among all of them in continuing to not get it since then. Despite massive public scandal over the course of what now is decades, they continue to deflect and shield child molesters as a matter of institutional routine. The ugliest part of the *New York Times* story wasn't even the involvement of Ratzinger in this mess but the fact that three successive archbishops failed to do anything about Murphy, a man who apparently molested upwards of 200 children.

(And not only did he molest these children, but he clearly was not forthcoming about his crimes when examined by experts in sexual abuse. In the notes of one such expert there in telling notation: "...denies sexual contact with anyone named in outside complaints, i.e. admits to sexual contact only with those accused of!" The expert included that exclamation point, too.)

So this monster was known to the highest authorities in the church to be a monster was allowed to die an active priest who was allowed to work with children for 24 years even after he was exposed until the end of his life. For Dolan then to lay all this off on 1962 mores is disgusting all by itself and totally disingenuous.

But even worse – what does Dolan's whiny deflecting and excuse-making say about the church as an arbitrator of ethical values? These pompous assholes run around in their poofy robes and dresses shaking smoke-filled decanters with important expressions on their faces and pretending to great insight about grace and humility, but here we have the head of the largest diocese in America teaching his entire congregations that when caught committing a terrible sin, the appropriate response is to blame the media and pull the "All the other kids were doing it, too!" stunt!

I was raised Catholic but stopped going to church at the age of 12. I was a complete idiot at that age with regard to almost every other area of human knowledge, but even I knew back then that the church was a scam. There are good and decent people working as individual priests, but the institution as a whole is a gang of cheap charlatans preying on peoples' guilt feelings (which of course are cultivated

258

intentionally by the church, which teaches children to be ashamed of their natural sexuality) in order to solicit a lifetime of contributions.

When I see a Catholic priest chanting his ridiculous incantations and waving his holy smoke over someone's gravesite or at a wedding, the vice I get is exactly the same as the one I get watching a plumber groan and moan and babble gibberish about all the different things wrong with your kitchen pipes, when in reality all he had to do was replace a washer. It's the same as picking up your car after an oil change and listening to the mechanic rattle off a list of charges totaling thousands for the nineteen extra items he looked at under your hood, just out of concern for your safety…And when you protest, no, there was nothing wrong with my alternator, I'm not paying for that, he tries to bullshit you – oh, yes there was, trust me, if we hadn't fixed that, your car would've died on the highway within a week.

That's all the church is. They're a giant for-profit company using predatory salesmanship to sell what they themselves know is a defective, outmoded, basically unnecessary product. They'll use any means necessary to keep their market share and if they have to lie and cheat and deflect and point fingers to keep the racket going, they'll do it, just like any other sleazeball company.

But I think it's time we started considering that what the church is, is even worse than that. It's possible we should start wondering if **the church is also a criminal organization that in this country, anyway, should be broken up using RICO statutes.**

One of the few areas where I agree with George Bush was in the notion that a country providing safe haven to terrorists should itself be treated as a terrorist organization. Morally, this isn't a difficult one to figure out; a country that keeps house for a bin Laden and doesn't assist other countries in trying to catch him is a rogue state, one that should be booted out of the community of nations.

We don't permit countries that harbor terrorists to participate in international society, but the Catholic Church – an organization that has been proved over and over again to systematically enable child molesters, right up to now to the level of the Pope – is given a free pass. In fact, the church is not only not sanctioned in any serious way, it gets to retain its outrageous tax-exempt status, which makes its systematic child abuse, in this country at least, a government-subsidized activity.

Somewhere underneath all of this there is a root story that has to do with celibacy. The celibate status of its priests is basically the Catholic Church's last market advantage in the Christian religion racket, but human beings are not designed to be celibate and so problems naturally arise among the population of priests forced to live that terrible lifestyle. Just as it refuses to change its insane and criminal stance on birth control and condoms, the church refuses to change its horrifically cruel policy about priestly celibacy. That's because it quite correctly perceives that should it begin to dispense with the irrational precepts of its belief system, it would lose its appeal as an ancient purveyor of magical-mystery bullshit and become just a bigger, better-financed, and infinitely depressing version of a Tony Robbins self-help program.

Therefore, it must cling to its miserable celibacy in order to keep its sordid business scheme going; and if clinging to its miserable celibacy means having to look the other way while children are serially molested by its sexually stunted and tortured employees, well, so be it.

If you look at it that way, the Church's institutional behavior is far worse than is commonly believed. It's not just a matter of an intractable bureaucracy responding too slowly or too insensitively to some scattered accidents of fate. This is more like the situation of a car company that continues selling a cheap but faulty brake system because it has calculated that it stands to make more money selling the cars than it does to lose in lawsuits. The only difference is, a car company can fix the brakes is it wants to. What the Catholic Church is selling is by definition faulty. It can't change, or it will be out of business. So even if not changing means kids will continue to be molested, it doesn't change.

By Matt Taibbi, True/Slant March 27, 2010. Matt is an American journalist currently working at Rolling Stone where he authors the columns "Road Rage" and "The Low Post." and a blogger at True/Slant.

CRIES NOT HEARD ROUND THE WORLD
The Global Village Soiled

Argentina: Over forty-seven seminarians reported sexual abuse.

Australia: Priests were convicted of sexual abuse in over twelve dioceses.

Austria: Cardinal Hans Groer resigned as archbishop of Vienna over allegations of abuse.

Bavaria: Over 170 allegations of child abuse by German Catholic priests have been reported. The Bavarian scandal includes allegations against Pope Benedict

XVI for allowing accused clergy to continue pastoral duties.

Canada: More than 300 orphans from Mount Cashel Orphanage in St. John's Newfoundland came forward with reports of sexual abuse against them. The orphanage filed for bankruptcy.

Chile: Bishops recently asked for forgiveness for past abuse cases.

Colombia: Cardinal Dario Castrillon Hoyos defended the Church's practice of not reporting sexual abuse cases to authorities.

Ireland: The famous Ferns Report tells the Irish story along with the notorious Brendan Smyth whose extradition to Northern Ireland influenced the collapse of the Fianna Fail/Labour coalition government.

Mexico: The founder of the Legion of Christ in Mexico is accused by his alleged illegitimate son of molestation; for decades, abused members were unsuccessful in persuading the Vatican to take action against Rev. Marcial Maciel.

Netherlands: Hundreds of abuse cases have been reported. The victim's group Mea Culpa is advocating a class action lawsuit against the Dutch Catholic Church.

Norway: Bishop Georg Muller confessed to the police to sexually abusing altar boys. The abuse was reported to the Norwegian Catholic Church twenty years ago but never to police.

Philippines: Over 200 of the country's 7,000 priests are alleged to have committed crimes of sexual abuse over the past two decades.

Spain: Franciscans of the White Cross are under investigation for sexually abusing disabled residents in Cordoba.

Switzerland: The Swiss Bishop's Council is now investigating all reported abuses cases.

By Maryjane Churchville

Instead of weeding out the offenders, the Catholic Church's policy has been "geographic cure" – or moving offenders out of the area. Very few times has the Church lived up to its responsibility of punishment, removal or counseling for the Church and God's representatives…"

Jason Berry

"It would have been like testifying against a family member at trial.

Cardinal Dario Castrillon Hoyos

Kevin Annett

THE CANADIAN HOLOCAUST

(The following is an edited extract from the report, "Hidden From History: The Canadian Holocaust – The Untold Story of the Genocide of Aboriginal Peoples by Church and State in Canada – A Summary of an Ongoing, Independent Inquiry into Canadian Native 'Residential Schools' and their Legacy", by Rev. Kevin D. Annett, MA, MDiv. The report is published by the The Truth Commission into Genocide in Canada, a public investigative body continuing the work of previous Tribunals investigating abuse in native residential schools; The Justice in the Valley Coalition's Inquiry into Crimes Against Aboriginal People, convened in Port Alberni, British Columbia, on December 9, 1994; and The International Human Rights Association of American Minorities Tribunal into Canadian Residential Schools, held in Vancouver, BC, from June 12-14, 1998.

Editor

"Jasper Joseph is a sixty-four year old native man from Port Hardy, British Columbia. His eyes still fill with tears when he remembers his cousins who were killed with lethal injections by staff at the Nanaimo Indian Hospital in 1994.

I was just eight, and they'd shipped us down from the Anglican residential school in Alert Bay to the Nanaimo Indian Hospital, the one run by the United church. They kept me isolated in a tiny room there for more than three years, like I was a lab rat, feeding me pills and giving me shots that made me sick. Two of my cousins made a big fuss, screaming and fighting back all the time, so the nurses gave them shots, and they both died right away. It was done to silence them. (November 10, 2000)

Unlike post-war Germans, Canadians have yet to acknowledge, let alone repent from, the genocide that we inflicted on millions of conquered people: the aboriginal men, women and children who were deliberately exterminated by our racially supremacist churches and state.

As early as November 1907, the Canadian press was acknowledging that the death rate within Indian residential schools exceeded 50% (see Appendix, Key Newspaper Articles). And yet the reality of such a massacre has been wiped clean from public record and consciousness in Canada over the past decade. Small wonder: for that hidden history reveals a system whose aim was to destroy most native people by disease, relocation and outright murder, while "assimilating" a minority of collaborators who were trained to serve the genocidal system.

This history of purposeful genocide implicates every level of government in Canada, the Royal Canadian Mounted Police (RCMP), every mainstream church, large corporations and local police, doctors and judges. The web of complicity in this killing machine was, and remains, so vast that its concealment has required an equally elaborate campaign of cover-up that has been engineered at the highest levels of power in our country: a cover-up that is continuing, especially now that eyewitnesses to murders and atrocities at the church-run native residential "schools" have come forward for the first time.

For it was the residential "schools" that constituted the death camps of the Canadian Holocaust, and within their walls nearly one-half of all aboriginal children sent there by law died, or disappeared, according to the government's own statistics.

These 50,000 victims have vanished as have their corpses – "like they never existed", according to one survivor. But they did exist. They were innocent children, and they were killed by beatings and torture and after being deliberately exposed to tuberculosis and other diseases by paid employees of the churches and government, according to a "Final solution" master plan devised by the Department of Indian Affairs and the Catholic and Protestant churches.

With such official consent for slaughter from Ottawa, the churches responsible for annihilating natives on the ground felt emboldened and protected enough to declare full-scale war on non-Christian native people through the 20th century.

The casualties of that war were not only the 50,000 dead children of the residential schools, but the survivors, whose social condition today has been described by United Nations human rights groups as that of "a colonized people barely on the edge of survival, with all the trappings of a third world society." (November 12, 1999)

The Holocaust is Continuing

This report is the result of a six-year independent investigation into the hidden history of genocide against aboriginal peoples in Canada. It summarizes the testimonies, documents and other evidence proving that Canadian churches, corporations and the government are guilty of intentional genocide, in violation of the United Nations Convention of Genocide, which Canada ratified in 1952 and under which it is bound by international law.

The report is a collaborative effort of nearly 30 people. And yet some of its authors must remain anonymous, particularly its aboriginal contributors, whose lives have been threatened and who have been assaulted, denied jobs and evicted from their homes on Indian reserves because of heir involvement in this investigation.

As a former minister in one of the guilty institutions named in our inquiry – the united Church of Canada – I have been fired, blacklisted, threatened and publicly maligned by its officers for my attempts to uncover the story of the deaths of children at that church's Alberni residential school.

Many people have made sacrifices to produce this report, so that the world can learn of the Canadian Holocaust, and to ensure that those responsible for it are brought to justice before the International Criminal Court.

Beginning among native and low-income activists in Port Alberni, British Columbia, in the fall of 1994, this inquiry into crimes against humanity has continued in the face of death threats, assaults and the resources of church and state in Canada.

It is within the power of the reader to honor our sacrifice by sharing this story with others and refusing to participate in the institutions which deliberately killed many thousands of children.

This history of official endorsement of, and collusion in, a century or more of crimes against Canada's first peoples must not discourage us from uncovering the truth and bringing the perpetrators to justice.

It is for this reason that we invite you to remember not only the 50,000 children who died in the residential school death camps, but the silent victims today who suffer in our midst for bead and justice."

(Rev.) Kevin D. Annett
Secretary
The Truth Commission into Genocide in Canada
Vancouver, British Columbia, February 1, 2001

Excerpts from: PART ONE: *Summary of Evidence of Intentional Genocide in Canadian Residential Schools*, Article II: The intent to destroy, in whole or in part, a national ethnic, racial or religious group; namely, none-Christian aboriginal peoples in Canada.

The foundational purposes behind more than one hundred residential schools established in Canada by government legislation and administered by Protestant and Catholic churches was the deliberate and persistent eradication of aboriginal people and their culture, and the conversion of any surviving native people to Christianity.

This intent was enunciated in the Gradual Civilization Act of 1857 in Upper Canada and earlier church-inspired legislation, which defined aboriginal culture as inferior, stripped native people of citizenship and subordinated them in a separate legal category from non-Indians. This Act served as the basis for he federal Indian Act of 1874, which recapitulated the legal and moral inferiority of aboriginals and established the residential school system. The legal definition of an Indian as "an uncivilized person, destitute of knowledge of God and of any fixed and clear belief in religion," (Revised Statues of British Columbia, 1960) was established by these Acts and continues to the present day.

Then, as now, aboriginals were considered legal and practical non-entities in their own land and, hence, inherently expendable.

This genocidal intent was restated time and again in government legislation, church statements and the correspondence and records of missionaries, Indian agents and residential school officials (see Documentation Section). Indeed, it was the very raison d'être of the sate-sanctioned Christian invasion of traditional native territories and of the residential school system itself, which was established at the height of European expansion in the 1880s and persisted until 1984.By definition this aim was genocidal, for it planned and carried out the destruction of a religious and ethnic group, all those aboriginal people who would not convert to Christianity and be culturally extinguished. Non-Christian natives were the declared target of the residential schools, which practiced wholesale, ethnic cleansing under the guise of education.

Excerpts from Article II (a): Killing members of the group intended to be destroyed

That aboriginal people were deliberately killed in the residential schools is confirmed by eyewitness testimonies, government records and statements of Indian agents and tribal elders. It is also strongly suggested by the bare fact that the mortality level in residential schools averaged 40%, with the deaths of more than 50,000 native children across Canada (see Bibliography, inc. the report of Dr. Peter Bryce to Department of Indian Affairs Superintendent Duncan Campbell Scott, April 1909).

The fact, as well, that this death rate stayed constant across years, and within the schools and facilities of every denomination which ran them – Roman Catholic, United, Presbyterian or Anglican – suggests that common conditions and policies were behind these deaths. For every second child to die in the residential school system eliminates the possibility that these deaths were merely accidental or the actions of a few depraved individuals acting alone without protection.

Exposure to Disease

In 1909, Dr. Peter Bryce of the Ontario Health Department was hired by the Indian Affairs Department in Ottawa to tour Indian residential schools in western Canada and British Columbia and report on the health conditions there. Bryce's report so scandalized the government and the churches that it was officially buried and only surfaced in 1922 when Bryce – who was forced out of the civil service for the honesty of his report – wrote a book about it, entitled The Story of a National Crime (Ottawa, 1922)

In his report, Dr. Bryce claimed that Indian children were being systematically and deliberately killed in the residential schools. He cited an average mortality rate of between 35% and 60%, and alleged that staff and church officials were regularly withholding or falsifying records and other evidence of children's deaths.

Further, Dr. Bryce claimed that a primary means of killing native children was to deliberately expose them to communicable diseases such as tuberculosis and then deny them any medical care or treatment – a practice actually referred to be from top Anglican Church leaders in the Globe and Mail on May 29, 1953.

In March 1998, two native eyewitnesses who attended west coast residential schools, William and Mabel Sport of Nanaimo, BC, confirmed Dr. Bryce's allegations. Both of them claim to have been deliberately exposed to tuberculosis by staff at both a Catholic and a United Church residential school during the 1940s.

"I was forced to sleep in the same bed with kids who were dying of tuberculosis. That was at the Catholic Christie residential school around 1942. They were trying to kill us off, and it nearly worked. They did the same thing at Protestant Indian schools, three kids to a bed, healthy ones with the dying". (Testimony of Mabel Sport to IHRAAM officers, Port Alberni, BC, March 31, 2998).

Homicides

More overt killings of children were a common occurrence in residential schools, according to eyewitnesses. The latter have described children being beaten and starved to death, thrown from windows, strangled and being kicked or thrown down stairs to their deaths. Such killings occurred in at least eight residential schools in British Columbia alone, run by all three mainline denominations.

Bill Seward of Nanaimo, BC, age 78, states:

"My sister Maggie was thrown from a three-story window by a nun at the Kuper Island school, and she died. Everything was swept under the rug. No investigation was ever done. We couldn't hire a lawyer at the time, being Indians. So nothing was ever done. (Testimony of Bill Seward, Duncan, BC, August 13, 1998)

Diane Harris, Community Health Worker for the Chemainus Band Council on Vancouver Island, confirms accounts of the murders.

" We always hear stories of all the kids who were killed at Kuper Island. A graveyard for the babies of the priests and girls was right south of the school unit until it was dug up by the priests when the school closed in 1973. The nuns would abort babies and sometimes end up killing the mothers. There were a lot of disappearances. My mother, who is 83 now, saw a priest drag a girl down a flight of stairs by her hair and the girl died as a result. Girls were raped and killed, and buried under the floorboards. We asked the local RCMP to exhume that place and search for remains but they've always refused, as a recently as 1996. Corporal Sampson even threatened us. That kind of cover-up is the norm. Children were put together with kids sick with TB in the infirmary. That was standard procedure. We've documented thirty-five outright murders in a seven year period." (Testimony of Diane Harris to the IHRAAM Tribunal, June 13, 1998)

Evidence exists that active collusion from police, hospital officials, coroners, Indian Agents and even native leaders helped to conceal such murders. Local hospitals, particularly tuberculosis sanatoriums connected to the United and Roman Catholic churches served as "dumping grounds" for children's bodies and routinely provided false death certificates for murdered students.

Arnold Sylvester, who attended Kuper Island School between 1939 and 1945, corroborates this account:

"The priests dug up the secret gravesite in a real hurry around 1972 when the school closed. No one was allowed to watch them dig up these remains. I think it's because that was an especially secret graveyard where the bodies of the pregnant girls were buried. Some of the girls who got pregnant from the priests were actually killed because they threatened to talk. They were sometimes shipped out and sometimes just disappeared. We weren't allowed to talk about this." (Testimony of Arnold Sylvester to Kevin Annett, Duncan, BC. August 13, 1998)

Particular schools, such as the Catholic one at Kuper Island and the United Church's

Alberni School, became special centers where extermination techniques were practiced with impunity in native children from all over the province, alongside the usual routine of beatings, rapes and farming out of children to influentials.

Specially constructed torture chambers with permanent electric chairs, often operated by medical personnel, existed at the Alberni and Kuper Island schools in British Columbia, at the Spanish Catholic School in Ontario and in isolated hospital facilities run by the churches and Department of Indian Affairs in northern Quebec, Vancouver Island and rural Alberta, according to eyewitnesses.

Mary Anne Nakogee-Davis of Thunder Bay, Ontario, was tortured in an electrical chair by nuns at the Catholic Spanish residential school in 1963 when she was eight years old. She states:

"The nuns used it as a weapon. It was done on me on more than one occasion. They would strap your arms to the metal arm rests, and it would jolt you and go through your system. I don't know what I did that was bad enough to have that done to me." (From The London Free Press, London, Ontario, October 22, 1996)

Former employees of the federal government have confirmed that the use of "inmates" of residential schools was authorized for government-run medical experiments through a joint agreement with the churches which ran the schools.

According to a former Indian Affairs official:

"A sort of gentleman's agreement was in place for many years: the churches provided the kids from their residential schools to us, and we got the Mounties to deliver them to whoever needed a fresh batch of test subjects: usually doctors, sometimes Department of Defense people. The Catholics did it big time in Quebec when they transferred kids wholesale from orphanages into mental asylums. It was for the same purpose: experimentation. There was lots of grant money in those days to be had from the military and intelligence sectors: all you had to do was provide the bodies. The church officials were more than happy to comply. It wasn't just the residential school principals who were getting kickbacks from this: everyone was profiting. That's why it's gone on for so long. It implicates a hell of a lot of people. (From the Closed Files of the IHRAAM Tribunal, containing the statement of confidential sources, June 12-14, 1998)

Such experiments, and the sheer brutality of the harm regularly inflicted on children in the schools, attest to the institutional view of the aboriginals as "expendable" and "diseased" beings. Scores of survivors of 10 different residential schools in BC and Ontario have described under oath the following tortures inflicted on them and other children as young as five years old between the years 1922 and 1984:

- Tightening fish twine and wire around boy's penises;
- Sticking needles into their hands, cheeks, tongues, ears and penises;
- Holding them over open graves and threatening to bury them alive;
- Forcing them to eat maggot-filled and regurgitated food;
- Telling them their parents were dead and that they were about to be killed;
- Stripping them naked in front of the assembled school and verbally and sexually degrading them;
- Forcing them to stand upright for more than 12 hours at a time until they collapsed;
- Immersing them in ice water;
- Forcing them to sleep outside in winter;
- Ripping the hair from their heads;
- Repeatedly smashing their heads against concrete or wooden surfaces;
- Daily beating without warning, using whips, sticks, horse harnesses, studded metal straps, pool cues and iron pipes;
- Extracting gold teeth from their mouths without painkillers;
- Confining them in unventilated closets without food or water for days;
- Regularly applying electric shocks to their heads, genital and limbs.

Perhaps the clearest summary of the nature and purpose of such sadism are the worst of Bill Seward of Nanaimo, a survivor of the Kuper Island School:

"The church people were worshipping the devil, not us. They wanted the gold, the coal, the land we occupied. So they terrorized us into giving it to them. How does a man who was raped every day when he was seven make anything out of his life? The residential schools were set up to destroy our lives, and they succeeded. The whites were terrorists, pure and simple." (Testimony of Bill Seward to Kevin Annett and IHRAAM observers, Duncan, BC, August 13, 1998)

Kevin Annett Rips the Mask from Power, by Henry Makow, Ph.D., May 14, 2008

"When Kevin (what an exquisitely Canadian name) took up his next position as Minister in a British Columbia logging town, he opened his sanctuary to the poor and the non-White. He bean to hear stories from his Aboriginal parishioners about ethnic cleansing at government funded church-run "residential schools.""

Native children were abducted by the RCMP and forced to attend these "schools," which were concentration camps in disguise. Here helpless children were physically and sexually abused, sterilized and exposed to deadly viruses. Many were subjected to medical experimentation from Illuminati doctors. The death rate was 50%. Annett estimates over 50,000 children died at these schools.

The blurring of class and color lines strained relations with the church "Old Guard," but the deal breaker was when Kevin publicly opposed the lucrative sale of Aboriginal lands the church held in trust to a large logging company.

Kevin was stripped of his Ministry, the only United Church Minister ever to be defrocked. His supporters were expelled from the church, and his wife was pressured to divorce him and take their two children.

Recently, the Canadian government absolved the Church of any liability for is crimes. Kevin Annett wrote: "Yes, all the churches have been granted effective immunity; Indian Affairs announced so last February when they said there will be no criminal prosecuted for anything that went on in the rez schools. Disgusting. Natives cannot sue the churches after the settlement – that was part of the deal the AFN (Assembly of First Nations) did on behalf of all the survivors, without consulting them once. It's as bad a crime as the original atrocities.

By Rev. Kevin D. Annett, MA, MDiV, C 2001, The Truth Commission into Genocide in Canada.

Copies of Kevin Annett's historic book *Hidden from History: The Canadian Holocaust*, which documents the evidence of the deliberate genocide of native people in Church-run Indian residential schools across Canada, disappeared from libraries at McGill and Concordia Universities, the Vancouver Public Library and the University of British Columbia during October, 2010. Librarians have not provided any clear reason how the books vanished so easily and quickly.

Note: To obtain a copy of "Hidden From History: The Canadian Holocaust", contact The Truth Commission into Genocide in Canada, c/- 6679 Grant Street, Burnaby, BC V5B 2K9, Canada, telephone 1+ (604) 293-1972, email **kevinannett@yahoo.ca** or **kevin_annett@hotmail.com**, or visit the website: **http://annett55.freewebsites.com**. See review NEXUS 9/01. Watch Kevin's award winning documentary file UNREPENTANT on the website.

> *"Kevin Annett is more deserving of the Nobel Peace Prize than many who have received it in the past."*
>
> **Dr. Noam Chomsky, Institute Professor Emeritus, Massachusetts Institute of Technology.**

URGENT ACTION ALERT

From Kevin Annett and
The Friends and Relatives of the Disappeared (FRD) – Canada
www.hiddenfromhistory.org
May 19, 2010
Occupied Squamish Nation territory

Five of the aboriginal members and activists have died since December, and a sixth is missing and presumed dead.

All of these people were public critics of the Roman Catholic Church's killing of residential school children and had participated in protests against the church and the Anglican Church and the United Church of Canada.

Their names are:

Johnny "Bingo" Dawson, died December 8, 2009 after a severe beating by three Vancouver policemen.

Mike Wickson, died February, 2010, cause unknown.

Elder Phillipa Ryan, died April 26, 2010 from "cancer" in less than a month.

Norma Jean Baptiste, died early May 2010, apparent heart attack.

Chief Louis Daniels, died May 16, 2010 in a Winnipeg hospital, cause unknown.

Missing: William Combes, presumed dead after receiving poisoned crack cocaine.

Chief Louis Daniels was on the Executive Committee of the FRD. He was about to lead a major protest against the government's whitewashing "Truth and Reconciliation Commission" forum in Winnipeg on June 15, 2010; and he was scheduled to conduct an aboriginal delegation to Rome this September to heighten pressure on the Vatican for its murder of native children.

Elders Phillipa Ryan and Norma Jean Baptiste led the drumming in (and) our group when we occupied Holy Rosary Church in Vancouver in March 2008 that grabbed headlines across the world and forced an "apology" from the government of Canada.

Johnny Dawson had led several church occupations in Vancouver and publicly accused police of being involved in the present day disappearance and murder of aboriginal women. He was also scheduled to be part of the recent April protest in Rome led by our FRD group.

William Combes was an eyewitness to killings at the Catholic residential school in Kamloops and Mission, BC, and a regular speaker on our weekly radio program *Hidden from History*.

We believe that these activists and eyewitnesses were murdered, now that the Catholic Church especially is potentially facing criminal charges for the Pope's personal complicity in the rape and torture of children – and Canada and its churches may be censured and investigated by European politicians and human rights groups.

We ask you to help us stop more of these killings, by supporting our campaign to bring the churches and government of Canada to trial for their crimes against humanity – and to confront the Pope in London and Rome next September (2010).

Don't let the sacrifice of our people be in vain.

Which of us will be next to die?

Please share this Alert with your network and media – and join us this September in Europe!

Written by Kevin Annett and The Surviving Members of the Executive, The Friends and Relatives of the Disappeared (FRD) - Canada

THE NATIVE AMERICAN HOLOCAUST
Ken Bear Chief

Investigating Clergy Sexual Abuse of Native American Children at the Indian Mission Residential Schools in the United States

Ken Bear Chief is a 58 year-old Native American of Gros Ventre, Nez Perce, and Nooksak tribal decent. He has been working under contract with Tamaki Law Offices as an independent paralegal since 1994.

Since January, 2008, he has been working with Bonnilee Ball, paralegal/victim liaison, investigating the sexual abuse of Native American children who attended Indian Mission Residential Schools in Indian country throughout the Northwestern and Midwestern United States. Together they have visited almost every reservation in Eastern Washington, Idaho, Montana and South Dakota interviewing victims of abuse and investigating the residential mission schools that operated on or near reservations. They have interviewed more than 300 Native Americans who were physically, sexually, and emotionally abused as children while attending the mission and residential schools from the 1950s through the mid-1970s and beyond.

In 2009, Blaine Tamaki, lead attorney representing the victims, had this to say about the abuse of Native American children who attended the Jesuit operated Indian Mission Schools: "No one has ever heard the sexual predatory horrors we have heard firsthand. This is the first story that must be told. It is a universal violation of human rights and the ultimate in crimes. Yes, priest abuse of trusting white peoples' children has been revealed, and some compensation has been paid. But the particular hostage pedophilia at Indian boarding schools is the closest evil to the Holocaust in U.S. history. Children, helpless children of Indian blood, were systematically raped and sexually exploited for decades by pedophile Jesuit priests under the guise of their own Catholic God. Yes, cultural genocide occurred, but something much worse happened than anybody imagined. And that is the story that must be told, so that people around the world with universally held values can get sick to their stomach. Like the Holocaust, evil, the purest evil in its worst form, was perpetrated on the children of the Natives of our country. And no one was punished, no one was convicted. It was covered up for decades. And Jesuits have become rich with their great cathedrals and universities as the one of the most respected institutions in this country. That's the story I want told and am committed to tell."

The historical genocide that occurred at the residential schools, in particular the clergy operated mission schools where sexual abuse of Native American children was so rampant from the 1880s to the mid-1970s, is now being exposed in all its ugliness. Ken Bear Chief, Blaine Tamaki and others will not let the Churches and the U.S. Government continue to cover up and deny that this happened.

At present, the Oregon Province Society of Jesus which operated Jesuit Mission Schools throughout Washington, Idaho, Montana and Alaska settled 500 Native American sexual abuse claims in the Oregon BK Ct. for $166.1 million. This case really began when Tamaki Law Offices filed a lawsuit in the Eastern Washington Federal District Court on behalf of 19 Native Americans who were victims of childhood sexual abuse at the Jesuit operated mission schools in the Pacific Northwest, and less than four months later the OP, SoJ filed bankruptcy in Portland Oregon Federal Bankruptcy Court, which was an admission of guilt, but seeking financial protection under the bankruptcy laws. This is a historical settlement on behalf of Native American victims of abuse. A victory has finally been won holding those responsible for committing acts of genocide and sexual abuse of Native American children in the United States.

The Jesuit, Catholic, Franciscan, Ursuline, Oblate and other societies that operated residential Indian mission schools were charged by the U.S. Government to take away the Native American language, customs, traditions, dress and religion "to kill the Indian and save the man." This was a U.S. policy that the religious operated Indian mission schools embraced and enforced by using physical, verbal, emotional and even sexual abuse to break the spirits of captive, helpless, vulnerable Indian children sent to them under color of the law to assimilate into white society by any means necessary.

This was the beginning of the cycle of abuse that continues to tear apart our Indian communities from within to this day. The trauma to those that were so abused at the residential school resonates in our communities today; suicide, alcohol and drug abuse, depression, anger, shame, domestic violence, child abuse, all these are directly related to the affects of childhood sexual abuse. Sadly, this trauma was then passed onto those generations that were not even part of the residential school experience, but are affected by the abuse of those that were.

This is our dilemma, a part of history. We must all take actions necessary to being this to the door of those that were responsible for it, the Federal Government and the Churches that were their *fete accompli*.

By Ken Bear Chief, *private investigator*

BELGIAN ABUSE
The Church is hung up on its dogma of protecting the unborn but has failed miserably in protecting the born

Bishop Roger Vangheluwe of Brugge resigned in April, 2010, two weeks after his unnamed nephew met with retired Cardinal Danneels about the sexual abuse he had endured from his uncle for thirteen years.

During the meeting, Cardinal Daniels suggested a cover-up plan which the victim had secretly taped. Belgian newspapers published the tapes in August. In response to the publishing, Cardinal Danneels' spokesman, Toon Osaer, told the media, "There was no intention of any cover-up...the cardinal realizes he was rather naive..."

In a statement to Belgian newspapers, Osaer, said Cardinal Danneels "condemned and profoundly regretted" the abuse but also regretted taping of the April meeting without the knowledge of those present.

In June, 2010, Brussels police seized 475 files compiled by a church commission on clergy sexual abuse. Police detained bishops for hours and removed their cell phones. Police also seized a laptop computer in the possession of Cardinal Danneels.

As a result of the raid, all members of the commission immediately resigned. Belgian Justice Minister Stefaan DeClerck urged the Catholic Church to "continue assuming its responsibilities."

Source: Numerous press articles

PEDOPHILES AND PRIESTS:
Doing the Vatican Shuffle
by Michael Parenti

When Pope John Paul II was still living in Poland as Cardinal Karol Wojytla, he claimed that the security police would accuse priests of sexual abuse just to hassle and discredit them (New York Times,3/28/10). For Wojtla, the Polish pedophilia problem was nothing more than a Communist plot to smear the Church.

By the early 1980s, Wojtyla, now ensconced in Rome as Pope Paul II, treated all stories about pedophile clergy with dismissive aplomb, as little more than slander directed against the church. That remained his stance for the next twenty years.

Today in post-communist Poland, cleric abuse cases have been slowly surfacing, very slowly. Writing in the leading daily Gazeta Wyborcza, a middle-aged man reported having been sexually abused as a child by a priest. He acknowledged however that Poland was not prepared to deal with such transgressions. "It's still too early...Can you imagine what life would look like if an inhabitant of a small town or village decided to talk? I can already see the committee of defense for the accused priests."

While church pedophiles may still enjoy a safe haven in Poland and other countries where the clergy are above challenge, things are breaking wide open elsewhere. Today we are awash in a sludge of revelations spanning whole countries and continents, going back decades – or as some historians say – going back centuries. Only in the last few weeks has the church shown signs of cooperating with civil authorities. Here is the story:

As everyone knows, for decades church superiors repeatedly chose to ignore complaints about pedophile priests. In many instances, accused clerics were quietly bundled off to distant congregations where they could prey anew upon the children of unsuspecting parishioners. This practice of denial and concealment has been so consistently pursued in diocese after diocese, nation after nation, as to leave the impression of being a deliberate policy set by the church authorities.

And indeed it has been. Instructions coming directly from Rome have required every bishop and cardinal to keep matters secret. These instructions were themselves kept secret; the cover-up was itself covered up. Then in 2002, John Paul put it in writing, specifically mandating that all charges against priests were to be reported secretly to the Vatican and hearings were to be held "in camera" (in private), a procedure that directly defies state criminal codes.

Forgive No One else

The tender tolerance displayed by the church hierarchy toward child-rapists does not extend to other controversial clergy. Think of those radical priests who have challenged the hierarchy in the politico-economic struggle for liberation theology, or who advocate lifting the prohibitions against birth control and abortion, or who propose that clergy be allowed to marry, or who preside over same-sex weddings, or who themselves are openly gay, or who believe women should be ordained, or who bravely call for investigations of the pedophilia problem itself.

Such clergy often have their careers shut down. Some are subjected to hostile investigations by church superiors.

A Law unto Itself

Church leaders seem to forget that pedophilia is a felony crime and that, as citizens of a secular state, priests are subject to its laws just like the rest of us. Clerical authorities repeatedly have made themselves accessories to the crime, playing an active role in obstructing justice, arguing in court that criminal investigations of "church affairs" violated the free practice of religion guaranteed by the US Constitution – as if raping a child were a holy sacrament.

Church officials tell parishioners not to talk to state authorities. They offer no pastoral assistance to young victims and their shaken families. They do not investigate to see if other children have been victimized by the same priests. Some young plaintiffs have been threatened with excommunication or suspension from Catholic school. Church leaders impugn their credibility, even going after them with countersuits.

Responding to charges that one of his priests sexually assaulted a six-year-old boy, Cardinal Bernard Law asserted that "the boy and his parents contributed to the abuse by being negligent." Law himself never went to prison for the hundreds of cover-ups he conducted. In 2004, with things getting too hot for him in his Boston archdiocese, Law was rescued by Pope John Paul II to head one of Rome's major basilicas, where he now lives with diplomatic immunity in palatial luxury on a generous stipend, supervised by no one but a permissive pontiff. He is truly "above the Law."

A judge of the Holy Roman Rota, the church's highest court, wrote in a Vatican-approved article that bishops should not report sexual violations to civil authorities. And sure enough, for years bishops and cardinals have refrained from cooperating with law enforcement authorities, refusing to release abusers' records, claiming that the confidentiality of their files came under the same legal protection as privileged communications in the confessional – a notion that has no basis in canon or secular law.

Bishop John Quinn of Cleveland even urged church officials to send incriminating files to the Vatican Embassy in Washington, D.A., where diplomatic immunity would prevent the documents from being subpoenaed.

With Ratzinger's accession to the papal throne as Benedict XVI, the cover-ups continued. As recently as April 2010, at Easter Mass in St. Peter's Square, dean of the College of Cardinals, Angelo Sodano, assured Benedict that the faithful were unimpressed "by the gossip of the moment." One would not know that "gossip of the moment" included thousands of investigations, prosecutions and accumulated charges extending back over decades.

It is remarkable how thoroughly indifferent the church bigwigs have been toward the abused children, their "flock." When one of the most persistent perpetrators, Rev. John Geoghan, was forced into retirement (not jail) after seventeen years and nearly 200 victims, Cardinal Law could still write him, "On behalf of those you have served well, in my own name, I would like to thank you. I understand yours is a painful situation." It is evident that Law was more concerned about the "pain" endured by Geoghan than the misery he had inflicted upon minors, misery of the most degrading sort.

In 2001, a French bishop was convicted in France for refusing to hand over to the police a priest who had raped children. It recently came to light that a former top Vatican cardinal, Dario Castrillon, had written to the bishop, "I congratulate you for not denouncing a priest to the civil authorities. You have acted well, and I am pleased to have a colleague in the episcopate, who in the eyes of history and of all the bishops in the world, preferred prison to denouncing his "son and priest." (The bishop actually got off with a suspended sentence.) Castillon claimed that Pope John Paul II had authorized the letter years ago and had told him to send it to bishops around the world. (New York Times, 4/22/2010)

Circling the Wagons

The Catholic hierarchy managed to convince itself that the prime victim in this dismal saga is the church itself. In 2010 it came to light that, while operating as John Paul's uber-hit man, Pope Benedict (then Cardinal Ratzinger) had provided cover and protection to several of the worst predator priests. The scandal was now at the pope's door – exactly where it should have been many years earlier during John Paul's reign.

In the midst of all this some courageous clergy do speak out. At a Sunday mass in a Catholic Church outside Springfield, Massachusetts, the Rev. James Scahill delivered a telling sermon to his congregation (New York Times, 4/12/2010): "We must personally and collectively declare that we very much doubt the veracity of the pope and those of church authority who are defending him. It is beginning to become evident that for decades, if not centuries, church leadership covered up the abuse of children and minors to protect its institutional image and the image of priesthood.

The abusive priests, Scahill went on, were "felons." He had "severe doubt" about the Vatican's claims of innocent ignorance. "If by any slimmest of chance the pope and all his bishops didn't know – they all should resign on the basis of sheer and complete ignorance and incompetence, and irresponsibility."

How did Father Scahill's suburban Catholic parishioners receive his scorching remarks? One or two walked out. The rest gave him a standing ovation.

Michael Parenti (Ph.D., Yale University). Dr. Parenti is an internationally known, award winning author, scholar and lecturer who addresses a wide variety of political, historical and cultural subjects. Among his recent book are: *God and His Demons* (2010) which deals with all sorts of theocratic misconduct and misbelief; *Contrary Notions* (2007); *The Culture Struggle* (2006), *The Assassination of Julius Caesar* (2003), *Democracy for the Few*, 9th Edition (2010) and *The Face of Imperialism* (2011). For further information, visit his website: **www.michaelparenti.org**.

TOD D. BROWN
The advocate of complete transparency kept his own life secret.

Scott Hicks, 54, the man who accused the bishop of Orange County, California, Tod D. Brown, of sexually abusing him when he was a boy, decided to go public to lend credibility to his accusations.

Brown adamantly denied the accusations. In a court deposition Brown said he was "shocked by the accusations" when Church officials brought it to his attention in 1997.

Mr. Hicks told the press he had no desire to take legal action against Brown or the Church but believed the public should be aware of his story.

By Tim C. Leedom

POPE ACCUSED OF LETTING PAST ABUSE CASE LAY DORMANT

Yet another sexual abuse case from the past has come back to haunt the Vatican, and this time, Pope Benedict XVI is being scrutinized for decisions made about the case in his prior position at the Holy See.

The Associated Press released the detail of an exchange between then-cardinal Joseph Ratzinger and Bishop John Cummins of Oakland, Calif., whose diocese alerted the Vatican in 1981 about a San Francisco Bay area priest who was put on probation in 1978 after being accused of molesting two boys. It took Ratzinger a little while to respond, and his answer didn't matter quickly.

Pope Benedict XVI resisted pleas to unfrock an American priest with a record of sexually molesting children, arguing that the negative publicity would damage the church in a 1985 letter bearing his signature.

The 1985 letter typed in Latin and signed by the then Cardinal Ratzinger said any decision to remove Stephen Kiesle, a San Francisco priest from the priesthood must take into account the "good of the universal church."

The letter, obtained by the Associated Press news agency, is the first direct evidence to undermine the Vatican's insistence that the Pope was never involved in blocking the removal of pedophile priests during his two decades as head of the Catholic Church's Congregation of the Doctrine of Faith, the department that deals with molestations.

Source: Truthdig Posted April 9, 2010

"The first and second collections this morning are for:"

SETTLEMENTS AND BANKRUPTCIES IN CATHOLIC SEX ABUSE CASES

Payments to Victims:

1994, May	Lincoln, NB	$40,000
1997,	Dallas, TX	$31 million
2003,Jun	Louisville, KY	$25.7 million
2003, Sept	Boston, MA	$85 million
2004 Jul	Portland OR	$53 million
2004 Sept	Tucson, AZ	$22.2 million
2004, Dec	Spokane, WA	$48 million
2005, Jan	Orange, CA	$100 million
2006, Oct	Davenport, IA	Filed for Chapter 11 bankruptcy
2006, Dec	Phoenix, AZ	$100,000
2006, Dec	Los Angeles, CA	$60 million
2007	Los Angeles	$16 million
2007, Jan	Charleston, SC	$12 million

2007, Jul	Los Angeles	$660 million
2007, Feb	San Diego, CA	$198 million
2008, May	Fairbanks, AK	Filed for bankruptcy
2008, May	Sacramento, CA	$100,000
2009, Feb	Memphis, TN	$2 million
2009, Oct	Savannah, GA	$4.24 million

TOTAL: (You do the math)

BANKRUPTCIES:

Portland, OR: Citing monetary concerns arising from impending trials on sex abuse, the Archdiocese of Portland Oregon filed for Chapter 11 bankruptcy on July 6, 2004, hours before two abuse trials were set to begin, becoming the first Roman Catholic diocese to file for bankruptcy.

Tucson, AZ: Filed for bankruptcy in September 2004. The diocese reached an agreement with its victims which the bankruptcy judge approved.

Spokane, WA: Filed bankruptcy and agreed to pay at least 48 million dollars as compensation to those abused.

Davenport, IA: Filed for Chapter 11 bankruptcy.

San Diego, CA: Filed for Chapter 11 bankruptcy protection on February 27, 2007, hours before the first of about 150 lawsuits was due to be heard.

Fairbanks, AK: Filed for bankruptcy on March 7m 2008.

Wilmington, DE: Filed for bankruptcy on October 18, 2009 the day before eight lawsuits were scheduled to go to trial.

Source: Bishop Accountability website

BOSTON COLLEGE
Fallout from the Crimes of Bernard Law

It is more a crime than a coincidence that after Boston College purchased disgraced Cardinal Bernard Law's property at an inflated price that tuition rose accordingly and will do so since the value of the property has depreciated and there is a large balance owed to the depleted Boston Diocese.

Tim C. Leedom

The best defense is a moving target.

Ex-Cardinal Law aide to be Indy auxiliary bishop

By Associated Press | Friday, January 14, 2011 | http://www.bostonherald.com | Local Coverage

INDIANAPOLIS — Pope Benedict XVI named a former aide to disgraced Cardinal Bernard Law of the Archdiocese of Boston as auxiliary bishop of Indianapolis on Friday, making him the heir apparent to the ailing, aging archbishop of Indiana's largest Roman Catholic diocese.

The director of a group representing people who had suffered sexual abuse by priests immediately labeled the appointment of Rev. Christopher Coyne "irresponsible and callous."

The 52-year-old was Law's spokesman in 2002, when the sexual abuse scandal erupted in the Boston diocese.

He will be the first auxiliary bishop of the Archdiocese of Indianapolis in nearly 77 years and the presumed successor to Archbishop Daniel Buechlein, a native of Jasper who will turn 73 in April and has battled cancer of the lymph system.

Church rules require bishops to submit their resignations to the pope when they turn 75, although they often serve beyond that age.

Coyne has served as a priest in the Archdiocese of Boston for nearly 25 years, Cardinal Sean O'Malley of Boston said in a statement Friday. He currently is pastor of a parish in Westwood, Mass.

"Archbishop Daniel M. Buechlein is indeed blessed to receive one of Boston's finest priests," O'Malley said.

However, as Law's primary spokesman for Law at the height of the clergy sex abuse scandal, Coyne became a symbol of the crisis that rocked the Roman Catholic church.

Executive Director David Clohessy of SNAP, the Survivors Network of those Abused by Priests, condemned Coyne's impending elevation to bishop.

"It's irresponsible and callous for the Pope to promote one of disgraced Cardinal Bernard Law's top aides to be a bishop. It's thumbing your nose at the hundreds of men, women, and children who were sexually assaulted by Catholic clergy in Boston and Indianapolis," Clohessy said.

Law resigned months after a judge unsealed court records in January 2002 that showed he had allowed priests with confirmed histories of molesting children to continue working in parishes.

Coyne will be the first auxiliary bishop of the 226,000-member Archdiocese of Indianapolis since Joseph Ritter, a future cardinal from New Albany was installed as auxiliary bishop in 1933. He became bishop of Indianapolis on March 24, 1934, and was named archbishop 10 years later.

The appointment is the latest in a series of moves at the top of Indiana's five Roman Catholic dioceses. Evansville diocese Bishop Gerald Gettelfinger offered his resignation to the pope after he turned 75 on Oct. 20. Fort Wayne Bishop Kevin Rhoades was installed a year ago, and Bishop Timothy Doherty took over the Lafayette Diocese last summer. Gary Bishop Dale Melczek recently turned 72.

Article URL: http://www.bostonherald.com/news/regional/view.bg?articleid=1309541

SNAP
(Survivors Network of Those Abused by Priests)
Press Release Statement by Barbara Dorris

We are sad every time a deeply wounded loses a chance to expose wrongdoers – both predatory clerics and complicit officials – in court, whether criminal or civil. Victims need and deserve more opportunities, not fewer, to expose criminals, protect kids, disclose documents and start healing.

It is of course ridiculous and disingenuous for the Vatican's lawyers to claim there was "no evidence" of Vatican involvement in clergy sex crimes and cover-ups in this case. Because the Catholic hierarchy fights tooth and nail in court, exploiting every possible legal maneuver (however far fetched or immoral) many clergy cases never get near the discovery process. Unless there are depositions and interrogatories and records turned over, the cover up of horrific child sex crimes remains covered up. That's what has happened here: the Vatican has "won" by successfully taking advantage of legal technicalities, not on the merits. So at best it's premature, and at worst it's deceitful, to claim there's "no evidence of Vatican involvement."
See the SNAP Website: **www.snap.com**

NUNS TOO

The abuse crimes are not male dominated. Thousands of nuns have been accused of sexual and physical abuse around the world. The infamous Magdalene schools in Ireland, the Boston School for the Deaf are notorious for abusive crimes by nuns. The nuns seem to keep beneath the radar in the press but their victims suffer nonetheless. In consistent shows of denial the Leadership of Conference of Women Religious (Catholic nuns) has refused to allow survivors of sexual abuse to address their annual conferences for the past few years. Critics have accused nuns of being behind the times in addressing the abuse issues.
Source: Bishop Accountability; SNAP

OC DIOCESE LAWYERS SEEK TO SEAL BISHOP BROWN DEPOSITION

Attorneys of the firm of Manly, McGuire & Stewart deposed former Catholic Diocese of Orange Bishop Norman McFarland and current bishop Tod D. Brown as part of the firm's ongoing lawsuit against the Orange Diocese, Mater Dei High School, and former boy's basketball coach Jeff Andrade. Now sources tell the Weekly that lawyers for the Orange diocese successfully convinced a judge to stop Brown's deposition midway through his testimony and obtained a temporary sealing order. On Thursday, they'll seek to turn the "temporary" label in the deposition into "permanent". All of this begs the obvious question: what did Bishop Brown reveal that would make him break No. 5 of His Excellency's much-ballyhooed Covenant with the Faithful? For those of you who forgot the theses, here it is:

"We will be open, honest and forthright in our public statement to the media, and consistent and transparent in our communications with the Catholics of our diocese."

We'd love to include a quote here from either diocesan lawyers or normally loquacious lead plaintiff attorney John Manly, but both sides are under a gag order until the Thursday at 9:00a.m., when they argue for and against the permanent seal in Judge Gail Andler's courtroom in complex Civic Center 102. See you there!

By Gustavo Arellano, award winning columnist (What publication and date??)

"ACTION IS THE ONLY TRUTH"
Alan Watts

ACCUSED PRIEST'S PLAQUE REMOVED
AFTER 7 YEARS
Press Release June 17, 2007

The efforts of many Church members, and Balboa Island residents has resulted in the removal of a controversial plaque dedicated to alleged child predator Catholic Priest Joseph F. Sharpe. Sharpe was hounded by many accusations during his career as a Priest, administrators and finally as the Msgr. Joseph F. Sharpe at the St. Vianney Chapel on Balboa Island. As a result, Sharpe moved many times in face of investigations by outside authorities as well as the Church and Vatican. Sharpe was never convicted, owing in great part to Church attorneys and internal cover-ups that were the modus operandi of the Catholic Church at the time.

The Plaque was taken down hours before several dozen leaf letters were to converge of the Chapel Saturday afternoon.

"I am in great hopes this action is the final chapter here and not just a ploy to avoid further probing into Sharpe's life. In addition the decisions of O.C. Dioceses Bishop Tod Brown and Sharpe's successor Lawrence Baird to dedicate the Plaza to a man with such a dark and questionable record is certainly irresponsible." stated Tim C. Leedom, the main organizer of the campaign.

"All of us hope that this sign is of a positive change to make their stated Covenant of Faith, a doctrine of action and not just lip service," Leedom said. He added: "The Church and its leaders must learn that forgiveness is earned through candor and action not just given, especially in light of the horrendous record of the O.C. Diocese and the men who have overseen it in regards to molesting Priests in their recruited ranks."

Source: Balboa Island Citizens Plaque Removal Committee

Sharpe Plaque

THE PEDOPHILES OF
ORANGE COUNTY AND LOS ANGELES
The Billion-Dollar Men:
Bishop Tod D. Brown,Cardinal Roger Mahony

As the attendance in Catholic Churches in Los Angeles dwindled due to the presence of Cardinal Roger Mahony with dismal record not controlling predator priests and orchestrating their cover-ups, Mahony cleverly championed illegal Mexican immigrant rights hoping to draw them to the Church to make up for his negative cash-flow. This ploy was put on the back news pages by the $600 million molestation settlement and the building of a $350 million dollar Mahony Cathedral in downtown Los Angeles, which reportedly suffered uncontrolled cost overruns. During Mahony's several decades' rule, he was never penalized or removed by the Vatican, although he had been accused of molestation himself. Reaching 75, the unrepentant retired to "go fishing" on a nice pension, leaving his diocese nearly bankrupt, and with unresolved predator lawsuits pending."

The diocese paid over $500,000 to settle the sexual case against Daniel Murray, pastor of Our Lady of Mount Carmel Church. Murray denied the charges and Bishop Tod Brown called him "very highly regarded." As part of the settlement, Murray was to have been terminated, but Brown kept him on secretly for a year. His whereabouts today is unknown.

By Tim C. Leedom

THE REPORT ON CLAUDY
(Northern Ireland)

The Report on Claudy, published in 2010 by Al Hutchinson, the Northern Ireland Police Ombudsman, follows an eight-year investigation into the bombing incident on July 31, 1972 on the Main Street of Claudy, County Londonderry, Northern Ireland. The attack known as "Bloody Monday" killed nine, including an eight year-old girl.

The Vatican responded to the report with its usual well-rehearsed denials and accusations against the press. In the words of Bishop Edward Daly, "I am not at all convinced that Father Chesney was involved in the Claudy bombing. I may be mistaken about that, but I do not think so." A Vatican spokesman accused journalists of competing to write the "most lurid headlines."

Irish Cardinal Sean Brady said "It is shocking that a priest should be involved in such violence," and insisted that "the Catholic Church did not engage in a cover-up of this matter." He did accept the findings of the report but to date has issued no statement of apology.

The report included the following:

- •Father James Chesney, a Roman Catholic priest, was the IRA's director of operations in County Londonderry and a prime suspect in the Claudy bombing.

- •A detective's request to arrest Fr. Chesney was refused by an Assistant Chief Constable of RUC Special Branch who insisted that "matters are in hand".

- •The same officer wrote to the government about what action could be taken to "render harmless a dangerous priest," and asked if the matter could be raised with the hierarchy in the Catholic Church.

- •In December 1972, William Whitehead met with Cardinal William Conway, head of the Roman Catholic Church in Ireland. According to a Northern Ireland Office official, "the cardinal said he knew the priest was a very bad man and would see what could be done."

- •Fr. Chesney was moved to a parish in Ireland where British prosecutors had no jurisdiction to investigate him.

A Channel 4 News Home Affairs correspondent has some unanswered questions posted about this affair:

"It is now clear that in the aftermath of the Claudy bombings, the senior leadership of the RUC rejected calls from junior officials within the Special Branch to arrest Father Jim Chesney on suspicion of involvement."

- •Why had they done so in the face of what appeared to be such a powerful intelligence picture of his alleged links to the bombings?

- •Why did the British government and a senior Catholic cleric, who had apparently been visibly involved, not press charges or at least question him?

- •Why did they prefer instead to see the priest moved quietly across the border rather than questioned like other terrorist suspects?

•Could this have been a state gesture to help the Church avoid the acute embarrassment of having one of its clergy linked to such an atrocity?

The Vatican mantra: "Remove the accused – Deny the accusation – Accuse the press."

Sources: The Report on Claudy; Channel 4 News; Northern Ireland Police; Vatican News Releases; RUC

THE SAME MODUS OPERANDI:
New is Old, Transparency is Cover-up and Protection of the Church is Paramount

Archbishop Diarmuid Martin told the press that the Vatican rejected the resignations of his two auxiliary bishops following their reported involvement in the Roman Catholic Church's cover-up of child abuse.

The Vatican's rebuff dealt a blow to Martin, a veteran Vatican diplomat, who was appointed in 2004 to lead Ireland's most populous diocese through a growing storm of child-abuse scandals. From the start he has clashed with predecessors who suppressed reports of child molestation and transferred abusive priests to new parishes in Ireland, Britain and the United States.

A Vatican spokesman refused to confirm that the resignations had been rejected or to offer reasons why bishops allegedly involved in covering up abuse would be kept in their posts.

An Irish government-authorized investigation into Dublin Archdiocese cover-ups published in November named more than a dozen current and former bishops responsible for failing to tell police about more than 170 suspected pedophiles in the priesthood from the mid-1970s to mid-1990s.

Martin supported the state investigation by releasing thousands of secret church documents that demonstrated detailed church knowledge of crimes committed against several hundred Irish children. It found that Dublin church leaders began providing information to police only in 1995, but continued to keep secret, until Martin's appointment in 2004, many files and other records of reported abuse.

The Pope did accept the resignations of Donal Murray of Limerick and James Moriarity of Kildare, both of whom were former Dublin auxiliary bishops, and both of whom were criticized in the report. A third, Martin Drennan of Galway, has insisted he will not quit.

The two current Dublin auxiliaries, Walsh and Field, initially rejected criticisms but relented after failing to receive public backing from the outspoken Marten.

Their resignation offers were read out to Dublin worshippers at Christmas Mass.

In their joint Christmas statement Walsh and Field said they hoped their resignations "may help to bring the peace and reconciliation of Jesus Christ to the victims and survivors of child sexual abuse. We again apologize to them."

"All this abuse was covered up by successive Dublin archbishops and in the full knowledge of every auxiliary bishop until Martin's arrival. On those grounds, every single bishop involved in the governance of the Dublin Archdiocese until 1004 ought to have resigned by now," said Andrew Madden, a former altar boy who became the first Irish victim to go public with an abuse lawsuit against the church in 1995.

Sources: Bishop Accountability; Dublin Archdiocese; Statement issued by Archbishop Martin; Joint Statement by Walsh and Field.

Sinead O'Connor
AN OPEN LETTER TO THE POPE

Sir,
Your remarks made last week concerning church authorities' handling of child rape complaints give the impression that neither John-Paul II nor yourself knew of how these complaints were being managed.

Can you please make clear who has been running the church since 1979?

You have said church authorities did not act quickly or decisively in dealing with allegations. This is entirely dishonest.

In fact church authorities acted extremely quickly and decisively, but in protection of rapist priests and the church, not of children.

In your letter to Irish mass-goers you stated that the Irish hierarchy, in covering up rape and transferring known rapists to other parishes, where many more children were raped, had done so out of "a well-intentioned desire to protect the reputation of the church."

If there is any such well-intentioned desire on your part then why have you not in outrage fired every employee of the church who contributed even in the remotest of ways, consciously or unconsciously, to the attack on Christ himself as made manifest in those children who were raped?

It looks extremely bad that you have not done so, and that you continue to set up lies and smoke screens and treat us as if we are stupid.

Spokespeople on your behalf keep saying, falsely, that hierarchies acted independently of the Vatican, when countless pleading letters from bishops to the Vatican show that is not the case, as do the specific instructions issued by the Vatican in 1962 to all bishops in the world for dealing with allegations of rape and abuse.

As you are aware, those instructions required the cleric taking complaints, as well as the victim making the complaint, to sign an oath of silence under threat of excommunication.

Your letter of 2001 to all bishops in the world confirms the 1962 instructions were in operation until 2001.

Why do you allow your representatives to lie?

All reports carried out in the four corners of the earth have found, independently of each other, that the church's main concern in dealing with abuse was the preservations of its assets and reputation and that the welfare of children was not a consideration.

As an example I refer you to the fact that in 1987 the church in Ireland took out a series of insurance claims in every diocese in order to protect the church from claims they foresaw would be made. The church then sat back and did nothing until 1995 when complaints became public knowledge.

The reports show that without exception each diocese in the world behaved in exactly the same manner when dealing with allegations.

If hierarchies had been acting "independently of The Vatican" there would have been differences in their behavior.

We deserve better than lies and insults to our intelligence.

The Holy Spirit deserves better.

291

As long as the house of the Holy Spirit remains a haven for criminals the reputation of the church will remain in ruins.

Finally, your statement that you hope the church's "humiliation will help the victims" is deplorable on two levels.

One: not one member of the Vatican has publicly displayed an iota of humility over this issue. Instead each person who has spoken has done so most arrogantly and dismissively.

Two: how dare you use the word humiliation to describe what you and the church are going through? Hope and pray, and thank God that you will never know the abject humiliation of children who were raped by monsters in the employ of your church. That is true humiliation.

Sinead O'Conner, musician and mother of four, lives in Dublin. She is a respected voice on child abuse issues and has appeared on BBC's "Newsnight", CNN's Larry King Live.

PRIEST CHARGED IN U.S.
STILL SERVING IN INDIA

According to Catholic Church documents, a Catholic priest who has been criminally charged with sexually assaulting a 14-year-old girl in Minnesota six years ago is still working in his home diocese in India despite warnings to the Vatican from an American bishop that the priest continued to pose risk to children, according to church documents made public on Monday.

The documents show that the American bishop warned the Vatican that the priest was accused of molesting two teenage girls whose trust he gained by promising to discuss their interest in becoming nuns.

In 2006 the Vatican recommended that the priest simply be monitored, a document shows. A lawyer for the Holy See said in a statement that the Vatican had recommended that the priest be defrocked, but that canon law specifies that the decision rests with the local bishop. The bishop in India sentenced the priest to a year of prayer in a monastery rather than seeking his removal from the priesthood, according to documents and interviews.

The priest, the Rev. Joseph Palanviel Jeyapaul, was working temporarily in the Diocese of Crookston, Minn.. Father Jeyapaul ministered to three parishes simultaneously in Crookston, where he was accused of misappropriating church funds was well as sexual abuse.

Sources: Bishop Accountability; CNN Special Report "What the Pope Knew"; Vatican Press Release

There are literally hundreds of enabling cardinals and bishops who are still at their posts along with priests who have committed crimes – they can still be seen at your local church every Sunday.

SUPREME COURT ALLOWS SEX-ABUSE CASE TO PROCEED AGAINST THE VATICAN
Holy See vs. Doe

The US Supreme Court declined to examine whether an Oregon resident who allegedly was sexually molested by a Roman Catholic priest as a teenager in the 1960s can sue the Vatican for his abuse. The move allows the litigation to move forward to trial.

A federal judge and a federal court had ruled earlier that the lawsuit could go forward. Lawyers for the Vatican asked the high court to take up the case and dismiss it. They argued that the Vatican could not be held legally responsible for alleged criminal acts undertaken by a priest when those illegal acts were unrelated to his work for the Roman Catholic Church.

At issue was whether the Vatican, a foreign sovereign nation, can be forced to pay money damages to a US citizen for the alleged illegal acts of one of its employees.

Foreign nations are generally immune from lawsuits. But under Foreign Sovereign Immunities Act, Congress said a foreign nation can be sued in a US court if the harmful act was carried out by an official or employee of the foreign state "while acting within the scope of his office or employment."

Source: Bishop Accountability

MAKING DISTINCTIONS:
A Bishop Defends His Actions

Attorney John Manly illustrated the hierarchy's attitude toward sex by paraphrasing a June 19, 2001 deposition he took from Bishop Norman F. McFarland, now retired bishop of Orange (County CA).

"I asked the bishop, "Would you ever put a predator who had molested a child back in a parish?" 'No'. 'Would you ever put a predator who had molested a child back into a parish with a school?' 'No.' 'Would you ever put a predator back in parish circulation knowing he was a predator?' 'No.'

"Your Excellency, could you please explain why John Lenihan was a pastor at St. Edward's?"

"'Well,' he said, 'that's different.'

"'What do you mean, sir?'

"'You said child molester. As I understand it, these victims were adolescents. And you know many adolescents are fully developed and precocious.'"

Said Manly to the meeting, "Ladies and gentlemen, that is a view of the soul of the hierarchy of our church. That is what is a stake here."

NCR asked McFarland how he remembered the exchange. The bishop sent the deposition. Excerpts follow:

Q: (Manly) "Was it your policy while bishop that someone who you believed was a child molester would not be a priest in the diocese of Orange?"

A: "Of course, of course."

Q: "Your Excellency, can you explain why John Lenihan has administered the sacraments and is functioning as priest if this was the case?"

A: "There was a charge brought against him by a Mary Staggs. That's while I was bishop here. That was early in 1990-91. In fact, she entered a court case against him, and the allegation was that some 15 years earlier a Fr. John Lenihan, who was a young priest not long ordained, at St. Norbert's, had sexually molested her and this was pursued. I gave a deposition. Also there was a request of the plaintiff and her lawyer that he receive therapy, and also there was payment of money... And he's now the pastor of St. Edward's and I appointed him there about 1995 at the recommendation of the priest personnel committee.

When he went down to St. Edward's he informed them... Anyway, to answer your question directly, he had served well. There was no indication even approaching this kind of conduct, improper sexual contact..."

Q: "Has anybody from the National conference of Catholic Bishops, the Holy See or any other Roman Catholic institution ever provided your Excellency with data on the recidivism rate of child molesters?"

A: "Yes. I think the in the national meeting...but you used the term "child molesters", and they make a distinction between those of , like youngsters. Those that are adolescents."

Q: "Does it make any difference to you in terms of how you handle priest matters where a priest abused a 3-year old or sexually abused a 17-year old?"

A: "Yes, there is a difference."

Q: "What is the difference?"

A: "From what I have learned, the experts say that I don't think it's recoverable."

Q: "How about a 15-year old girl?"

A: "Well that is also very wrong. But I think there is more a chance for a person, first of all, being an isolated incident...I can understand the temptation of that more. It can't even occur to me with a child or a baby. Does one make a distinction that's 15 or 17? She may be very, very precocious or adult-looking, and there would be temptation."

(In addition to the Staggs case, Lenihan was later accused of molesting and impregnating another teenage girl in the 1980s and forcing her to have an abortion. Lenihan resigned from the priesthood in 2002 after the church paid our [$1.2] million in a settlement. The Los Angeles archdiocese paid $200,000, the Orange diocese $1 million.)

During this case, another enabler, Lawrence Baird, was accused of molesting the victim when she went to him for comfort. Baird was responsible for bringing molesting priests to the Orange County Diocese. He and Tod Brown worked hard to cover up their personal and pastoral failings.

Source: Orange County, California court records

Cardinal says He Erred in Meeting with Victim

The former head of Belgium's Roman Catholic Church has acknowledged that he should not have held a meeting with a victim of serial sexual abuse or suggest a cover up until the offending bishop retired.

The meeting that retired Cardinal Godfried Danneels held was secretly taped by the victim, and the conversation were published.

In the conversation that the victim secretly taped, Danneels said: "In fact, the monsignor steps down next year. It would be better that you wait" to go public. He then suggested measures about how to keep it quiet.

Later Danneels said: "I don't know whether it would be to your advantage to make a lot of noise about it. Neither for you, nor for him." He also urged the victim to forgive his uncle for the 13 years of abuse.

Source: Bishop Accountability

POPE PROTECTED CRIMINALS FROM LAW

In 2002 Cardinal Joseph Ratzinger spoke these words to an audience in Spain: "I am personally convinced that the constant presence in the press of the sins of Catholic priests, especially in the United States, is a planned campaign...to discredit the church."

On April 10, the New York Times – the apparent center of this "planned campaigned"- reprinted a letter signed by Ratzinger in 1985. The letter urged lenience in the case of the Rev. Stephen Kiesle, who had tied up and sexually tormented two small boys on church property in California. Kiesle's superiors had written to Ratzinger's office in Rome, beseeching him to remove the criminal from the priesthood. The man who is now His Holiness the Pope was full of urgent moral advice in response. "The good of the Universal Church," he wrote, "should be uppermost in the mind. It should be understood that 'particularly regarding the young age of Father Kiesle, there might be great 'detriment' caused 'within the community of Christ's faithful' if he were to be removed.

Kiesle went on to ruin the lives of several more children and was finally jailed by the secular authorities on a felony molestation charge in 2004. All this might have been avoided if he had been handed over to justice right away and if the Oakland diocese had called the police rather than written to the office in Rome, where it was Ratzinger's job to suppress such distressing questions.

Contrast this to the even more appalling was of the school for deaf children in Wisconsin, where the Rev. Lawrence Murphy was allowed unhindered access to more than 200 victims. Again, the same pattern: repeated petitions from the local diocese to have the criminal "unfrocked" met with stony indifference from Ratzinger's bureaucracy. Finally, in a letter to Ratzinger, Murphy complained of his frail health and begged to be buried with full priestly honors in his frock. He was.

All the letters from dioceses to Ratzinger and from Ratzinger to dioceses were concerned only with one issue: the public image of the Holy Mother Church? The traumatized children were merely irrelevant and inconvenient. Remember that there was a written and enforced policy of avoiding contact with the law. And remember that there was a Ratzinger propaganda program blaming the press if any of the criminal conduct or obstruction of justice ever became known. The pattern repeated itself time after time.

The obscene culmination of all this occurred on Good Friday, when the Pope sat through a sermon by an underling in which exposes of his church's crimes were likened to persecution and even to the pogroms against the Jews.

I have never been accused of taking part in a pogrom, let alone joining a mob that is led by raped deaf children, but I'm proud to take part in this one.

By what power is the fugitive cardinal shielded from the law? By the agreement between Benito Mussolini and the papacy that created the pseudo-state of Vatican City in the Lateran Pact of 1929, Europe's last remaining monument to fascism. This would be bad enough, except that Ratzinger is now exposed as being personally and institutionally responsible for obstructing justice and protecting and enabling pederasts.

Where is it written that the church is the judge in its own case? Above or beyond the law? Able to use private courts? Allowed to use funds donated by the faithful to pay hush money to the victims or their families?

There are two choices: We can swallow the shame, roll up the First Amendment and just admit that certain heinous crimes against innocent citizens are private business or are not crimes if they are committed by priests or excused by popes.

Or we can shake off the complicity that reports this crime a "problem" for the church and not as an outrage to the victims and to the judicial system.

Isn't there one district attorney or state attorney general in America who can decide to represent the children?

Source: Blog from suntimes.com member of Sun-Times Media, Unknown Author. The views expressed in the blog are the views of the author and not of the Chicago Sun-Times

Ex-cardinal Roger Mahony

Kept on despite a $650 million dollar predator priest payout by the Los Angeles Diocese; he followed in the footsteps of Nazi sympathizer Timothy McIntyre and replaced by José Horacio Gómez, whose record includes criticizing the decision of St. Mary's University in Texas allowing Hilary Rodham Clinton to hold a campaign event on campus, and another Catholic university's invitation to a high profiled nun who supports female ordination as a keynote speaker.

Cathedral of Our Lady of the Angels,
not the church of the poor that Jesus wanted but the church of accused
molester Roger Mahoney's final crimes –
a $350 million dollar monument to himself.

GET OUT OF JAIL FREE CARD
Go Directly to Club Ped

Roman Catholic pedophile priests have a "get out of prison early card," according to David Clohessy of SNAP (Survivors Network of Those Abused by Priests), referring to the Vianney Renewal Center in Dittmer, Missouri.

Vianney is a retreat facility for Catholic priests guilty of sexual abuse. Reyma McCoy, former therapeutic program coordinator, told investigative journalists "it is home to the nation's most dangerous pedophile priests". Many of them served no prison time. They were sent by courts, probation boards and diocese nationwide for intense therapy under strict supervision.

The center is operated by the Servants of the Paraclete, an order of Catholic priests. Supervision is not by guards but by other priests. Residents enjoy satellite TV, maid services, a cooking staff and access to the internet. According to McCoy they also have unsupervised access to pornography via the internet, cell phones and mail. She told the press "It's not that they're allowed it. It's that there's nobody checking."

Viewing pornography is a clear violation of parole. The Missouri Probation and Parole Board launched a formal investigation into the practices at Vianney.

David Clohessy of SNAP calls the center a "get out of prison early card." He told journalists: "Defense lawyers for the church and the predator priests go to the judges and prosecutors and say, 'Listen, we're going to make sure he's off the streets. He'll be supervised. It won't cost the state anything and everybody wins here...' Do you know any other profession that can say something similar? Can a superintendent say, 'Don't send that pedophile teacher to prison because we have a special facility that will treat and house him?'"

Archbishop Robert Carlson of St. Louis would not comment about the allegations explaining that Vianney is run by a separate Catholic order that does not fall under his jurisdiction.

By Tim C Leedom; Sources: Missouri Probation and Parole Board; SNAP

BERNARD FRANCIS LAW
Sexual Abuse Scandal in the Archdiocese of Boston

The actions of omissions and commissions of Cardinal Bernard Francis Law's brought down the oldest Catholic Diocese in the United States.

Widespread accusations and reports of sexual misconduct among the clergy in the Archdiocese of Boston soon spawned similar investigations across the United States.

Documents presented in numerous cases revealed Law's role in covering-up incidents of sexual misconduct against his priests. Despite substantial amounts of documentation demonstrating his deep involvement, Law refused to step down as Archbishop of Boston.

Under the non-watchful eye of Cardinal Law, St. John's Seminary, in the neighborhood of Boston College, had the distinction of spawning over 150 predator priests and bishops.

As a result of lawsuits, the Archdiocese of Boston lost millions of dollars in fines and settlements. It also funded the defense of accused priests. The archdiocese slipped into large financial deficits. In response to the scandal, over fifty priests signed a letter declaring no confidence in Cardinal Law and asking him to resign – something that had never happened in the history of the Roman Catholic church in America. The *Boston Globe,* the *Boston Herald* and the *Manchester-Union Leader* called for his resignation.

The Archdiocese closed sixty-five parishes before Cardinal Law stepped down.

Cardinal Law remains a cardinal in Rome in charge of the prestigious Basilica di Santa Maria Maggiore and has not lost his membership in any of the congregations or councils on which he served as Cardinal of the Archdiocese of Boston. At the Vatican he is referred to as "archbishop emeritus of Boston."

Sources: Bishop Accountability; SNAP; Inspired by Wikipedia (Retrieved May 13, 2010)

SEXUAL ABUSE IN ARIZONA
Insuring crimes and cover ups

Arizona State lawmakers approved a measure to get rid of the statute of limitations for victims of child abuse filing lawsuits except in the cases against churches and school districts. Church and school child abuse suits still have only two years to file.

Catholic Church lobbyist Ron Johnson says the exception is needed to allow the Church (as well as businesses and schools) to buy insurance.

Sorry About All This

It is estimated that within the Catholic Church between 2.5 and 5% of all priests are predators, although many cases are not reported. The Catholic Church always lied and covered up the dangers of priests in its churches until investigators, journalists and lawyers got to the truth and public awareness. The Church has had throughout history damages and run up millions of dollars to defend itself. The Catholic Church is now spending millions for a public relations campaign with the message "Oh, sorry but things weren't that bad, try this..."

The Editor

VICTIM JUSTICE

Italian victims of pedophile clergy are demanding that sexual abuse be declared a crime against humanity and have launched an international appeal during its first public gathering of Italian victims.

Organizer Salvatore Domolo, a former victim and a former priest, said the group is looking abroad for solidarity because justice in the shadow of the Vatican is next to impossible. "Here in Italy, and especially in Rome, there is no hope. By the time the victim arrives at the awareness of having been victimized legal intervention is not possible." Because of direct pressure by the Vatican, Italy has one of the shortest statues of limitations for crimes against its children. The statue of limitations is a mere ten years.

Another meeting will be held in Rome at the end of October. Verona was chosen for the first gathering because it is the home of one of the most hideous mass crimes of pedophilia in Italy where 67 former students of a school for the deaf have alleged sexual abuse and corporal punishment from the 1950s to the 1980s.

The Vatican, in its own back yard has turned a blind eye to crimes committed less than two miles from St. Peter's Cathedral. The Vatican has not commented on any of the group's demands.

Source: Bishop Accountability; SNAP

> " You can't put into words what this guy did to me.
> He stole my innocence and destroyed by life."
>
> **William Lynch**

MAKE MY DAY

William Lynch, a victim of sexual abuse, was arrested in Santa Clara, California after allegedly assaulting his abuser, Jesuit priest Jerold Lindner. Lynch was the victim of unspeakable sexual crimes at the hands of Lindner when he was five years old. Lynch and his brother were taken to a national park on a camping trip, and forced to have sex with each other while Lindner watched.

For 35 years William Lynch has suffered with depression, nightmares and suicide attempts.

Lindner now resides at a Roman Catholic retirement home.

Dontee D. Stokes, a 26 year-old Baltimore victim, shot his abuser three times when he demanded an apology and the priest told him to go away. He was acquitted of attempted murder.

The infamous Boston molester John Geoghan was strangled in his cell while serving a 10 year sentence for molesting more than 150 boys.

Source: Bishop Accountability; SNAP

VATICAN FAILS TO FILE REPORT ON CHILD RIGHTS
What would Jesus say?

The Vatican has failed to send the United Nations a report on child rights that is now almost 13 years overdue.

Like all countries that have signed the 1989 Convention on the Rights of the Child, the Vatican is required to submit regular reports on its efforts to safeguard child rights.

But the UN Committee on the Rights of the Child, despite sending repeated reminders, has received no explanation for the Holy See for why it missed a 1997 deadline, in years since the Vatican has come under scrutiny over its handling of child sex abuse allegations around the world.

A Vatican representative told the United Nations last year that the report was being "finalized as we speak." He told the Human Rights Council "...a paragraph will be dedicated to the problem of child abuse by Catholic clergy."

The Vatican representative, Hubertus Van Megen, told the council that the church was "very conscious of the seriousness of the problem" but insisted critics had misrepresented the situation.

While the Vatican delivered an initial report in 1995, the second, third and fourth reports are now overdue.

Source: UN Committee on the Rights of the Child; SNAP

Section VI

THE
CHURCH TODAY

CHALLENGES, BAGGAGE AND
CONFUSION

Milwaukee Priest Admits He's Gay
Don't ask, don't tell

The former Roman Catholic archbishop of Milwaukee, who resigned in 2002 in a sex and financial scandal, admits in an upcoming memoir that he is gay.

Archbishop Rembert Weakland, who preceded New York Archbishop Timothy Dolan as head of the Milwaukee archdiocese, said he wanted to be candid about "how this came to life in my own self, how I suppressed it, how it resurrected again."

"Some people will be angry about the book, others will support it," the archdiocese said.

Estimates of the number of gay priests vary from 25% to 50% reported Rev. Donald Cozzens, author of the *Changing Face of the Priesthood*.

Sample Rants from Different Slants

"It goes without saying that if it weren't for the news media, even less than what has been done by the Catholic Church of cleaning the chapels, cathedrals and Vatican of the sick criminals disguised as priests the trusted protectors of God's children would ever have been accomplished."

"The molesters have been harbored by Catholic dioceses across the country. The defense is always well scripted, the denial rehearsed and the cover-ups deep and complex. Asking for forgiveness from an unknown God and earning it from its victims, the families and society are two different things, but the church doesn't comprehend or acknowledge that."

"The actual number of sexually abused by the Catholic church are most likely far greater than the 3 to 5% numbers talked about. According the FBI numbers in regard to rape and physical abuse, only a smaller percentage get reported, much less litigated and tried. The Church has settled many non-public cases out of view, which would add to the list of victims, but I think about the numbers and think about it in the context of your own family, office or business. If five percent or more of your bowling team were pedophiles would you go to the lanes? If 5% of your hiking club were predators, would you take your son or daughter on an overnight? And, finally, if you found a person in your company who was a child molester, wouldn't your first call be to the police, not the Better Business Bureau. Then why do we have the tolerance of the Church, and why do we have the tolerance by the Sunday worshippers of the Church's culpability. I honestly don't get it."

"SNAP (Survivors Network of Those Abused by Priests) has offices in many major cities in the United States. Their sole purpose is to protect children, get justice, and rid the Church of the predators and enablers. The Church, who professes the same goals, has fought them tooth and nail, humiliating the victims, threatening the victims who are Catholics themselves. The molested are treated like lepers while the priest predators are protected by parishioners' money and high-priced attorneys, and when they are finally turned out, they are given in some cases a monthly stipend or sent to a club ped!"

By the Editors

CNN asked "What the Pope Knew?"

The CNN special "What the Pope Knew" asked the rhetorical questions that many people have been asking, "What about the bishops who failed miserably in their responsibility to their children by not rooting out the known predators? Why are they still there?" The inaction of these bishops led directly to the hideous crimes against children and cost the Vatican billions of dollars. We ask that question again, "Why are they still there? Many accused themselves." The Church still has much unfinished business and until this is done it will be the same as before...in denial, corrupt and sinful.

Come Home Again
Branding for Catholics

Two years ago, the Catholic Church launched a campaign targeting lapsed Catholics to return to the Church. Branded as "Catholics Come Home." the church is on a mission, according to Boston Cardinal Sean O'Malley, "To let them know that we want them to be a part of our family and are anxious for them to come back and participate in the Sunday Eucharist and be a part of our local community."

National Director of SNAP (Survivors Network of Those Abused by Priests), David Clohessy, told the press "It's like putting the cart before the horse...rather than spending time on advertising, they need to make real changes. Real changes to heal victims."

Boston College Professor Thomas Groome said in an interview with the press "Getting the flock back into the fold will take a lot more than slick marketing."

But Cardinal O'Malley claims it will take "... a lot of prayer and hard work and strategizing...what we have is the greatest product in the world, the Gospel."

The Catholic League

According to its website, the Catholic League is "the nation's largest Catholic civil rights organization, founded in 1973 by Father Virgil C. Blum, S.J. The Catholic League defends the right of Catholics – lay and clergy alike – to participate in American public life without defamation or discrimination.

Motivated by the letter and the spirit of the First Amendment, the Catholic League works to safeguard both the religious freedom rights and the free speech rights of Catholics whenever and wherever they are threatened."

"When slanderous assaults are made against the Catholic Church, the Catholic League hits the newspapers, television and radio talk shows defending the right of the Church to promote its teachings with as much verve as any other institution in society."

"When Catholics are the victims of a bigoted portrayal by the media, the Catholic League issues news releases bringing the matter to the attention of the public. It may also encourage a boycott of the program's sponsors."

Recent Catholic League Activism

On August 26, 2010 the empire State Building in New York City, NY was lit-up in red, white and blue to honor the anniversary of the 19th Amendment to the US constitution, granting women the right to vote.

Earlier in the summer, The Catholic League demanded that the owners of the Empire State Building light the building in blue and white in honor of the 100 birthday of Mother Teresa. When the owner, Anthony E. Malkin refused, the Catholic League launched a three-month campaign against the Empire State Building and Malkin personally. It held a protest outside the building on the night of the lighting.

By the Editors

Jesuit priest, Bill Cain, wrote and produced *"Nothing Sacred,"* a television series about the daily life of a Roman Catholic parish priest in today's world. It was aired on ABC to favorable reviews until a Catholic League spokesman declared the series "propaganda". Advertisers pulled out and the series was cancelled.

Dignity USA

Dignity USA envisions and works for a time when gay, lesbian, bisexual and transgender Catholics are affirmed and experience dignity through the integration of their spirituality with their sexuality, and as beloved persons of God participate fully in all aspects of life within the Church and Society.

Statement of position and purpose:
We believe that gay, lesbian, bisexual and transgender Catholics in our diversity are members of Christ's mystical body, numbered among the People of God. We have an inherent dignity because God created us, Christ died for us, and the Holy Spirit sanctified us in Baptism, making us temples of the Spirit, and channels through which God's love becomes visible. Because of this, it is our right, our privilege, and our duty to live the sacramental life of the Church, so that we might become more powerful instruments of God's love working among all people.

We believe that gay, lesbian, bisexual and transgender persons can express their sexuality in a manner that is consonant with Christ's teaching. We believe that we can express our sexuality physically, in a unitive manner that is loving, life giving, and life affirming. We believe that all sexuality should be exercised in an ethically responsible and unselfish way.

Source: Dignity USA Website

Luigi Cascioli Lawsuit

Luigi Cascioli, after having irrefutably demonstrated in his book "The Fable of Christ" that the facts presented as true and historical in the "Holy Scriptures" are in reality false, first of all, in regard to the figure of Jesus, called the Christ, which has been based on a certain John of Gamala, son of Judas the Galilean of the cast of Hasmoneans, acknowledged as descending directly from the house of David, concludes his studies with a DENUNCIATION-LAWSUIT against the Catholic Church, in the person of Don Enrico Righi, parish-rector of the ex. Diocese of Bagnoregio (VT), for abuse of the popular credulity (Art. 661 C.P.) and for impersonation.

The formal complaint was lodged at the Court of Viterbo on the 11th of September, 2002. Thanks to the intervention of the Court of Perugia regarding the absurd request of dismissal by Public Prosecutor Dr. Renzo Petroselli, Don Enrico Righi has been added into the registry of inquiry (See lawsuit: account of facts at the Court of Perugia 24/03/2004). After the request of dismissal received from the Court of Viterbo, the lawsuit has been transferred to the Court of Strasburg following the petition presented by Luigi Cascioli to the European Court of Human Rights.

Source: Luigi Cascioli website: **http://www.luigicascioli:eu/traduzioni/en_1.htm**

Righi claims there is substantial evidence to support the credibility of the historical Jesus including historical text.

Cascioli claims his book, *The Fable of Christ*, proves that Jesus did not exist as a historical figure.

"It is not permissible to say or even think that any of the evangelists might have lied. We must believe that contradictory statements are actually in agreement, even if we do not see how this can be true."
Saint Augustine

LIST OF EX-CATHOLICS

H. Tristram Englehardt, Jr., philosopher and bioethicist
Tom Hanks, American actor
Madeline Albright, former, U.S. Secretary of State
Jim McGreevy, former Governor of New Jersey
Alberto Cutir, priest
Kevin Rudd former Prime Minister of Australia
Josette Sheeran, director of the United Nations World Food Program and former editor of the Washington Times
Sinead O'Connor
Godfrey Silvester Shiundu, Kenyan priest
John Calvin, French religious reformer
Hugh Hewitt, law professor, author, radio talk show host, blogger
Dorothy Lucey, news reporter on Good Day LA
Tom Tancredo, U.S. Representative (CO)
Marie Cavallier, now Princess Marie of Denmark
Martin Luther, excommunicated by papal bull
Marcelo Crivella, senator in the federal government of Brazil
Edir Macedo, founded the Universal Church of the Kingdom of God
Efrain Rios Montt, a former de facto President of Guatemala

Marianne Thieme, Dutch politician
Stephen Baldwin, American actor
Bob Enyart, Christian talk show host
Sarah Palin, former Governor of Alaska
Tim Pawlenty Governor of Minnesota

Daily Missal iPad app Launched for Catholics

An Italian priest has developed an iPad application that will let priests celebrate Mass with an iPad on the altar instead of the regular Roman missal. The free application will be launched in July in English, French, Spanish, Italian and Latin.

The People Speak but the Church Hears Not

According to a GfK Austria poll, 80 per cent of the 500 interviewed parish priests supported calls for an abandonment of mandatory celibacy.

Fifty-one per cent said women should be allowed to become Roman Catholic priests.

GfK Austria revealed the new study showed that younger priests had more conservative mindsets than their elder colleagues.

The number of Austrian men deciding to become Catholic priests is meanwhile in decline.

The reputation of the Roman Catholic Church suffered dramatically as hundreds of people came forward to report violent and sexual abuse at its institutions over the past few months.

More than 30,000 Austrians left the Church in the first three months of 2010, up by 42 per cent compared to the same time span of 2009 when more people than ever cancelled their membership.

It is estimated that up to 80,000 Austrians will leave throughout the year.

Sources: Bishop Accountability; GfK Poll

St. Christopher

Remember the "dashboard saint," the pink and blue ribbon pins tied on the baby's crib, the holy pictures of the strong man with a child on his shoulders? All gone, down the road. St. Christopher is no longer recognized as a saint in the Catholic Church. However, those engraved images of the traveling protector are still best sellers in Catholic Paulis book stores and gift shops.

The Catholic Church reformed the Roman calendar in 1969. St. Christopher was dropped on the grounds there was not enough evidence to prove he actually lived. He was originally said to have been a martyr in the third century and his feast day was celebrated on July 25.

by Maryjane Churchville

Vatican Secret Archives

The Vatican Library contains books on one subject, while the archives are actually a working file of the Vatican's important documents.

The Vatican's Secret Archives contains over fifty-two miles of files. These files contain all of the Vatican's correspondence, contracts, diplomatic papers, papal bulls and encyclicals, dogmas and various petitions, along with records from the Sacred Rota, the congregations and all papal conclaves.

According to the Vatican official website, the archives today consist of "two reading rooms, an index room, an internal library, a laboratory for preservations, restorations and bookbinding, a laboratory for photographs and digital reproduction, a data processing centre and a computer laboratory."

The name "secret archives" came from the 100-year rule that keeps most of the Vatican's documents closed for one hundred years, to protect them from being released during the lifetime of those in the files.

The Vatican says there are no documents deliberately hidden. But the archives may still hold some unexpected secrets, as more and more scholars, working on their own research, uncovered previously overlooked texts.

Galileo and the Vatican
Not all historical mysteries have been resolved. In the archives, people have only been able to locate one of the known three volumes of documents pertaining to the inquisition and trial of Renaissance scientist Galileo Galilei.

The volumes of documents were collected after Galileo's conviction by the Vatican's Index Congregation, in order to explain and justify banning the publication and sale of his books.

Buried also is the full story of Pope John Paul I's death.

Sources: Vatican Archives Website; Catholic Encyclopedia

The Future Of The Roman Catholic Church

In any prescription for an ill patient there are two dynamics at play. First, the patient has to realize there is something wrong. Denial has killed more people than disease and bad medicine. This first step is usually the hardest, especially in religion. Believers in their brand of god worship can't stand the thought that anything they have ever done is wrong. Added to this is the territorial force of having a critic who is not one of faith by right.

Well, the Mother Church is going to have to get over these hurdles very quickly in the face of a despicable performance protecting god's children and making it worse by covering up their crimes.

As a result of this and other acts of omission and commission, the church is facing an increasing number of exit visas (as of 2009, 40% of Catholics considered themselves inactive). Of the remaining flock, only 40% attend mass on any regular basis, donations to the church are down in some cases by more than 30%, dozens of churches have been closed, and the church's charities have been shut down even in places like one of America's strongest Catholic centers: Boston, Massachusetts.

At least seven American dioceses have declared bankruptcy, while dozens of others are simply out of money. For a business, which the church is and always has been, this is not a good situation.

Added to this is the fact that there are few new priests coming up through the ranks. In the U.S., many of the priests are from Vietnam and the Philippines. New restrictions on sexual orientation and character issues have been added to the negative public perceptions of the priesthood. Recruiting is not easy...a problem created by the church and no one else.

The future of the Church does not necessarily rest with the press, the watchdogs or the general public. The Church must be rescued from within. As in any organization there are big differences: the liberal reformers, who seemingly have been most disgusted by the Pope and the molestation scandal and the conservatives who demand stricter adherence to the pronouncements of the Pope who, is still the "infallible" vicar of God on earth.

However, the main battle may be between the Vatican and its own parishioners, as individuals and some dioceses who want more of a say on certain issues. The church is still structured like a military organization. The private doesn't deal with the general...nor the lesser ranks communicate or instruct the higher ups. This is not a democracy, as has been seen. This is one of the dynamics that will decide the viability of a faith and the institution.

The internal battles will play out the picture on the world scene in finance, social policies, education and political influence. As the smallest country in the world, the Church still has a global presence...

The Church also faces a huge perception problem, not just because of the molestation crises and its shameful handling of its crimes. In order for the Vatican and the Pope to move the church on into the 21st century they will have to cleanse it and go into the world confessional for its past sins, but add action to their pious pronouncements. A church that talks about equality and keeps women unequal – would not the Mary's be eligible for priesthood?

Is the Pope worthy of adoration when he promotes a very flawed Nazi Tainted Pope Pius XXII for sainthood, when Copernicus is still condemned for his heretic findings about the sun being the center of the universe, when the church does not acknowledge the inclusion of pre-Christian rights in their teachings and symbols? Does a Pope who holds onto Cardinals and bishops who covered up and in many cases stand accused of child molestation deserve respect? The question here is why are they still there? Does a Vatican that brings back enablers of molesters and a bishop who still denies the holocaust deserve respect? Not in the eyes of the world if you believe opinion polls.

Will the church evolve or dissolve? Who will control its destiny? Only time will tell.

By Tim C. Leedom

Section VII

WHAT THEY ARE SAYING ON THE STREET

A SERENDIPITOUS COLLECTION OF COMMENTS

"I'm mad as hell and I'm not going to take it anymore."
Howard Beal, newscaster, in the movie Network

The Evil Catholic Church's History
by Karl Frank

The Philadelphia Inquirer (Sunday, September 25, 2005) contained a front-page story about the scathing grand jury report incriminating priests, and providing evidence of cover up by high-ranking officials. The gist of the article, called "*Faith strong despite scandal*," was that "Area Catholics are angry, but some call the idea of leaving the church unfathomable". Many Catholics, the article stated, are disappointed, and even mad, but with a faith in God that is still strong, many would never think of leaving the Catholic Church.

I've got news for the many Catholics in the world. The Catholic Church, not to mention other churches as well, has had scandal and blood on its hand since its beginning. This recent sex abuse scandal is just another in a long line of embarrassing, illegal, and inhumane atrocities of men who call themselves Christians, Roman Catholics, and "men of God."

Remember the Crusades? Remember the Inquisition? Remember the silence and even support of Hitler? Remember he many peoples conquered by the Catholic Church in the name of God? And now, think of the many children abused by the Catholic Church.

Is there anyone with the remotest acquaintance with the Gospels who would say that Jesus Christ would have condoned the torture and murder of individuals who disagreed with his teachings? Would he have condoned the extermination of whole populations of native people? Would he have condoned the repeated sexual molestation of innocent children? Would he have condoned the cover-up of all these crimes?

The answer is obvious.

I do not understand how a "strong faith in God" equates to support of the Catholic Church, or any church that commits such heinous atrocities. God is God. If we believe the Scriptures, He is not a man-made artifact for any one denomination. I have to say I know my Bible pretty well, but tell me where it says that God is the Roman Catholic Church? The Nicaean Creed, recited by Protestants, says "I believe in the Holy Catholic Church." But the word "Catholic" does not mean "Roman Catholic." It means "of or including all Christians."

Where is this "once a Catholic, always a Catholic" thing written? The God I believe in doesn't require me to belong to any particular church group. Would a God-fearing Christian continue to hold fast to any other organization that conducted illegal activity because he was told that it was "the work of God?" Even if it were contradictory to the teachings of the Gospels? If one belonged to a civic organization that decided to engage in criminal activity to increase its budget, would one think twice about leaving that organization? If a group of God-fearing Christians belonged to had several members routinely committing sexual child abuse, would those Christians continue to support that group?

Edited from a blog by Karl Frank, the internet Blogger at Karl's Corner (Sumpin' to Ponder)

Back to the future
Galileo was wrong!

A movement led by Robert Sungenis has hit the internet, claiming Galileo was wrong and the Catholic Church was right. As with the context of our whole book, do your research and, please let us know what you find out. We have our opinion, and Copernicus and Galileo are looking more brilliant all the time. The website does have a store where you can buy a pair of baby shirts and cups for the next dark ages.

By Tim C. Leedom

"Why Is Everybody Always Pickin' on Me?"
(Charlie Brown)

I think Chris Hitchens said this once, and I agree with him: If I were a person that made that kind of moral choice, I think I'd have to kill myself." But these guys not only don't kill themselves, they go out in public ranting about how wronged they are and how they've been fucked over by the evil *New York Times* for airing out their dirty laundry.

Again, I admire the balls, but seriously, they must know the game is almost up. Sooner or later people are going to catch on, the state is going to make a move, and there's going to be a hell of a lot of church property going up for auction along with the seized Escalades of DEA-busted drug dealers. Or maybe not in this lifetime – but one can only hope.

By Matt Taibbi, True/Slant March 27, 2010. Matt is an American journalist currently working at Rolling Stone where he authors the columns "Road Rage" and "The Low Post." and a blogger at True/Slant.

"The campaign against the Catholic Church is not one of hate...it is one of anger, disgust and a demand for justice."

Richard Dawkins

The Pope's New Clothes

"First of all, I never trust any one or organization that can't dress right – at least be stylish if not hip or with it – the Catholic Church people have been wearing the same clothes for 2,000 years – Heaven help us!"
Brian Burkhart

We stay because of the Mass

One word...the "Mass" is the reason Catholics like C. and I stay Catholics, despite what has happened in the Mass. At the Mass you have the presence of Christ, in flesh and blood, not just a symbol as Protestants believe. Being Catholic is not like being a member of a social club that you can switch on and off depending on which services fit you. At the end of the day, it is His church and every time we go to Mass and we partake of the Eucharist, we experience Heaven on earth through his real presence.

The Church has taken many steps...to make sure it does not happen again or if it does that the perpetrators are dealt with.

Y.

321

A Couple of Observations:

A woman called asking if the new priest in her grandchild's school was a predator (sadly not the first or only time we had that question) in the discussion I said something about her pastor and she replied "oh no we have a good pastor, he's only a drunk.

My parish has a very good grade school. When I asked friends why they were not angry about the scandals they replied they were only Catholic until their last child was out of school. They said the fight wasn't worth the effort since they just didn't care what the Church said or did. They attend Mass so their kids can go to school.

B.

Roman Catholic Boarding School Experience

My experience being in Catholic boarding schools since kindergarten was an interesting one. I became quite comfortable in boarding school. As I got older I noticed the lay teachers seemed preoccupied with the poor. They taught us to care for the unfortunate and to contribute money to missions. They preached they were poor and humble but they lived in plush housing and surroundings. After a while I became negative in my views in regard toward this double standard.

As I entered high school I became a non-interested catholic. As soon as I graduated from high school, I never went to Mass again.

I myself never experienced any personal abuse or observed any.

I did become aware of the countless incidents worldwide of sexual abuse of children by the clergy. This made me become even more distant from the church. I realized they protected their own at the cost of children's well being.

The church is now a huge corporation that through the centuries has become a more corrupt and greedy entity.

J.

Grievances and Accountability

I would like to see the Church set up a uniform process where victims of molestation can make their grievances known, and where accused priests can say their piece as well. I would like to see results of these procedures upheld and penalties enforced. I must be honest and say this kind of response to the molestations may actually already be in place and I am just unaware of them.

As a general comment, I must admit that I am not as aware of the magnitude of the molestations and cover ups within the Catholic Church worldwide. I am not condoning the fact that the molestations have occurred and church officials may not have always addressed them appropriately, I must confess that I have not followed these events closely outside of the events that happened in Massachusetts. While I was horrified by these incidents, they did not make me want to renounce my faith. I grew up in a very positive Catholic parish and went to a Jesuit Catholic college where the tradition of social justice made a deep and positive impression on my life. Lastly, I have never been that enamored by the hierarchy of the Catholic Church and it has been very removed from practicing my Catholic faith. Bottom line, I guess I am not that well informed about these things happening in the Catholic Church and it is hard to reconcile these events with the positive and meaningful experience I have had as a practicing Catholic. I think continuing to practice my faith as I have come to know it in the face of these terrible actions of individual priests and some officials of the church, might be the way to help the church come around to be a more open and welcoming place – I am not sure.

Again, the hierarchy of the Catholic Church is not something that I think about that often at all. I do not look to the leaders of the Catholic Church to guide my practice as a Catholic. I suspect that this is somewhat of a generational perspective as I believe my parents feel more allegiance to Pope and other senior officials of the church. I feel my experience growing up in my parish and continuing with Catholic education provided me with opportunities to look to the overall teachings and message of Jesus as a guide for how to live my life. I consider myself to be a "cafeteria Catholic" whereby I pick and choose what makes sense to me and I try to do my best to be a thoughtful and compassionate person. I do not look to the church hierarchy and institution as an integral part of what it means to be a Catholic and therefore, there is a major disconnect between the heinous acts that have happened and what it means to me to live as a Catholic in today's complex world. I also think it is human nature to block out what we don't want to deal with especially when it conflicts with how we understand what it means to be a Catholic. Again – I am not condoning this overriding passivity with respect to what has happened. I just think it is complicated and these crimes are horrendous as they are – do not negate all the wonderful teachings of the church and the positive actions that the Church as an institution has done and continues to so.

Again – I do not see so much evidence of the Catholic hierarchy in my life – especially from Rome. I do hear about what happens at the Boston Archdiocese level and this is where we continue to hear about positive works the Church in our area does. I also have seen certain protocols enacted in terms of the CCD and teaching program within the Catholic Church. New curriculum has been implemented to teach children what is appropriate in terms of their bodies and personal safety. There is also a full curriculum for all volunteers and employees of the Church to learn how to recognize pedophiles and other profiles of molesters. I think these are positive developments. On a somewhat different level, I also see that more parishes are instituting programs that are more welcoming of more diverse parishioners and tearing down barriers to people practicing in the church such as groups for divorced people etc. These are all steps in the right direction in my mind.

K.

Here's what I will say for now: 99.5% of all Catholic priests are not molesters, and 99.5% of Catholics have not been molested. The molestations stuff is not the first thing on my mind. However, the molestation revelations have served to educate all of us to be more aware of our surroundings and to take appropriate precautions. I am sure a molested person or relative or friend of a molested person will personalize this issue in a major way, but the answer is NOT zero tolerance, more rigid laws and punishments, etc. Those kinds of things just take more and more of our liberties away from us. The last 50 years in America have seen a huge erosion in our freedom and liberties. We need less laws and less regulation. If ½ of 1% of the people are affected negatively by keeping our freedom in tact, then that is a small price to pay. As a society we have a tendency to legislate everything down to the lowest common denominator and that is NOT GOOD. Lawyers can sue anybody for any reason, judges now have their hands tied to use their own good judgment about punishing individuals...it is a nightmare out there. As bad as I would feel if I had a loved one abused by a priest or killed by a drunk driver, I would feel even worse about doing something activist to destroy more individual freedoms in our country and world. MADD and SADD were well intended awareness groups, but now they are maniacs. You cannot even have a beer any more without worrying about the cops pulling you over and making you prove that you are innocent.

You rant and rave about Law and the Pope but I see nothing in your agenda except punishment. By and large the guilty ones are going to jail and paying for their transgressions, and victims are getting their day in court and financial compensation for their injuries. What more do you want? Do you punish every politician or corporate executive or school board member under whose watch a problem occurs? Certainly not. They are not guilty because of mistakes they made trying to deal with a situation even if they handled it in a way that you disagree with, or if they botched it. As a society we are spending way too much time trying to punish those in charge and not nearly enough time praising the good things they do.

H.

"There is something inherently wrong with a Church and the people who attend it. They donate money to it so that they can be in denial about so many things."

T.

Musings of a Catholic School Girl
Dedicated to the Very Most Irreverent Lady Gaga

Teens Expected to Ejaculate Before Rising.

In the Catholic lexicon, the word "ejaculation" refers to a short prayer. Every morning I was awaken by a black garbed "Mother" sprinkling "holy water" on my forehead while canting "Jesus, Mary and Joseph"…to which I responded "I give you my heart" as the holy water trickled down my nose. Sounds weird, but it sure trumped the bugle for getting you up and out. By 6:45 AM, I was on my way to Mass with the banned book *Belle de jour* meticulously placed between the hard covers of my Daily Missal.

Religion v. Reason.

Logic classes were terribly confusing because I knew anything worth knowing was all based on FAITH.

Speak only the Truth.

English, French and Latin were secondary to the ardent study of words and phrases from the four-letter vernacular.

Teenaged girls privileged to kiss a wizened old man's jewels.

Annually, His Eminence, the Archbishop, made a visit to the school. This visit promised an opportunity to accumulate an abundance of "grace." I donned the requisite white dress symbolizing my purity and was invited to approach His Eminence for the very important privilege of kissing his ring. The ritual was bothersome in light of my instruction to adore God, not material things, but I obediently knelt in front of this paramount of godliness awaiting the nod. I remember taking a quick peek at his face hoping for a glimpse of Our Lord, instead my gaze met his beady eyes and all I could think was: WTF?

Lesson in the Ladies Room.

I came upon Mother Huron in the ladies room with her arm stuck in the tampax machine. My stare in disbelief prompted her rapid explanation that she was investigating reports of "girls STEALING from this machine." Lesson learned: Catholics don't believe in handing out anything for free that pertains to the reproductive system.

A Mourning in May.

My epiphany came during the annual adoration of the Our Lady, Queen of the May. This celebration confirmed our love of the Virgin Mother and commitment to our own virginity. We assembled before her decked out in the RWD and, for those worthy, carried a lily, as the symbol of our virginity. This was the year I did not carry a lily, having been soiled by phone conversations with a *Jewish* boy. As I stood lily-less looking at my very best friend who was two months pregnant, holding her lily close to her breast singing "O Mary we crown thee with blossoms today….." it struck me that something was very wrong here. I looked heavenward and through the sunlight I swear I saw God wink.

M.

The Pew Forum on Religion & Public Life: Catholics Rank Last

website: **http://pewforum.org**

According to a recent poll conducted by the Pew Forum on Religion & Public Life, atheists and agnostics, Jews, and Mormons are among the highest scoring groups on a new survey of religious knowledge, outperforming evangelical Protestants, mainline Protestants and Catholics on questions about the core teachings, history and leading figures of major world religions.

On average, Americans correctly answered 16 of the 32 religious knowledge questions on the survey. Atheists and agnostics average 20.9 correct answers. Jews and Mormons do about as well, averaging 20.5 and 20.3 correct answers, respectively. Protestants on a whole average 16 correct answers; Catholics as a whole, 14.7.

Go to the website to take the sample test.

No Wiggle Room

The Catholic Church has finally attempted to put a protective wall around its children and the church to avoid future crimes such as those already committed by hundreds of its predator priests. The obvious question is why was this not done fifty years or a hundred years ago?

The program hatched in 1998 by Monsignor Kevin McCoy and Reverend Edward J. Arsenault, christened "Virtus," is a testing and screening system to try to prevent the crime wave of molestations from ever happening again. The system has many of the characteristics of a neighborhood watch by being aware of who has access to children, being aware of child behavior and warding signs of abuse.

Everyone is hopeful that the program will be successful, but a program is only as good as the people involved. People watching the watchers should be aware there is no czar on this project, or a strike force easily mobilized. The Church has taken, and is still taking, a long time to clear people out.

In a military organizational structure like the Roman Catholic Church, can a lowly do-gooder of Virtus report and get action on a molester with friends in high places? History has said no. Various policies such as Bishop Tod D. Brown's much touted Transparency were a smoke screen and a fiasco. Maybe that will change.

The other flaw may be that the foxes protecting the chickens have not purged the cardinals and bishops across the USA who have been accused of molestation, molested or at the very least been enablers. As the protecting God's Children Crusade in it's 13th year, it must have a house cleaning, zero tolerance policy, a system of swift removal of those accused of crime or covering up, a swift due process and one person in charge. As President Harry Truman said, "The buck stops here."

For a Church that is on double secret probation there should be no wiggle room. The Virtus program is a positive reaction to a self-created disgrace. It should be worldwide, but it is not.

The question is: Can the forces of awareness remove the entrenched habits, behavior, and escape hatches for the enablers who will simply wait until the heat dies down?

by Tim C. Leedom

POSTSCRIPT:
AND NOW...

Unfortunately, the documented stories told in this book do not yet have an end:

- Hundreds of priests and bishops who have been molesters and enablers are still working for the Church claiming to be "saving souls."

- Thousands of parents are unknowingly entrusting their children to the care of priests who have been transferred from other jurisdictions where they were being exposed as molesters and enablers.

- Nearly a dozen dioceses have declared bankruptcy in the U.S. They are still operating while leaving their victims without compensation, while the Vatican has not only done nothing to rectify this injustice, but it has also provided predator priests with comfortable retirements out of the reach of potential prosecution.

- Lay gays and lesbians are labeled heretics and sinners, while many priests are homosexuals.

- Women are still treated as "second-class citizens" in the Church. It is heresy to appoint a woman to the priesthood.

- NONE of the war criminals from World War II have ever been excommunicated, including Hitler, Mussolini, Mengele, and a host of others. But good Roman Catholics who championed the cause of the traumatized victims of predatory molestation and other persecution by the church have been ostracized from the Church.

- While pioneering scientists such as Galileo ("forgiven"), Copernicus (not "forgiven"), and Giordano Bruno (burned at the stake) have been persecuted for their scientific discoveries, the Church still resists medical and scientific progress.

- The Church has still refused to open its files on the murder of Pope John Paul I, and the Church continues its policy of denial and cover-up of all its crimes.

•The "Nazi Pope," Pius XII, is en route to beatification by the Church in spite of his collaboration with the Nazis, the best-known perpetrators of genocide in the history of the world.

•The Church still clings to its self-given super-human status of "Infallibility," which it bestowed on itself in the 19th Century.

How is it possible that what Steve Allen aptly described as "a crime wave through history" has been allowed to continue? The Church continues its policy of cover-up by depending on the effectiveness of two powerful psychological conditions: Denial, and Disbelief.

"Good Catholics" just cannot believe that the people they have entrusted with their souls could be capable of such atrocities as molestation of children and outright murder. Good Catholics just do not want to believe that such things could be true. And so the crimes continue *sub rosa*. The cover-ups continue. Church donations from hard-working ordinary believers, family men and women genuinely doing what they believe is right, are spent on heavy legal fees for the best lawyers money can buy to enable legal maneuvering to prolong the process of cover-up.

There are hundreds of lawsuits pending in the United States and in Europe for molestations, cover-ups, stolen gold and property. In the U.S. the Catholic Church is still lobbying legislators to shorten the liability exposure and decrease the statute of limitations on settlements. Dozens of bishops and priests have evaded legal action because of the Vatican attorney's limitation efforts over the years. And those cardinals and bishops are still on board living in comfort as though nothing happened.

But there is evidence of hope. There are signs that the overwhelming, inescapable mountains of evidence are being brought to light and at last being noticed by Roman Catholics themselves. The Church's membership has dwindled by over 40%, and less than 50% of the remaining Catholics attend Mass on a regular basis.

If we are ever going to come at all close to approaching justice, it will be up to the membership of the Roman Catholic Church to make it happen. How can they make it happen? By doing the two things that the Roman Catholic Church does not want them to do, and will do anything to prevent:

1. Ask Questions.
2. Insist on Answers.

The questions are there, and the answers are there. If the membership of the Roman Catholic Church insists on receiving complete answers, the truth will be brought to the surface. If the membership of the Roman Catholic Church does not insist on receiving answers, the truth will never be brought to the surface, because the church will succeed in its tactics of denial and cover-up.

Only because of a publisher's deadline did we interrupt our investigations and interviews and pouring through piles of records.

Now it is up to you to pursue the truth.

In Memoriam:
Steve Allen – 20ᵗʰ Century Renaissance Man by Tim C. Leedom (1997)

"It is a shame that so many people think of Steve Allen as a popular entertainer. Steve Allen is a true Renaissance man by every definition of that word. As a writer and lecturer in the history of religions and our human spiritual evolution, he is superb. His knowledge in comparative mythologies adds to his academic stature. Reading and listening to Steve Allen is time well spent. His contribution to religious literacy is monumental."- William Edelen

As one of the great talents of the 20ᵗʰ Century, Steve Allen can claim a spectacular list of accomplishments. He created and hosted the Tonight show, authored 44 published books, starred on Broadway in "The Pink Elephant," and starred in motion pictures, most notably Universal's "The Benny Goodman Story." He has written over 4,600 songs, including "This Could Be The Start of Something Big" and "South Rampart Street Parade," as well as the score for several musicals, including the Broadway production of "Sophie" and the CBS-TV version of "Alice in Wonderland." Allen produced some 40 record albums, including "Steve Allen Plays Jazz Tonight" for the Concord Jazz label, and he wrote the stirring Irish drama, The Wake, which won a L.A. drama critic's nomination as best play of 1977. Allen starred in the critically acclaimed NBC series "The Steve Allen Comedy Hour" and created, wrote and hosted the Emmy award-winning PBC-TV series Meeting of the Minds. He was inducted into the TV Academy's Hall of Fame and in 1993 became Abbot of the world-famed Friars Club, succeeding Milton Berle.

In the forward to "Dumbth and 81 Ways to Make Americans Smarter," published by Prometheus Books, Norman Cousins says: "The world knows Steve Allen as a musician and as an entertainer. In addition, his friends knew Steve Allen as someone whose thought processes are always working as a student of history and world affairs, as a philosopher, and finally as someone who takes pains to get the most out of his own capabilities. Certainly no one I know has thought more carefully about the use of his time and skills or relationships to other people. I first became aware of these special propensities when, in the middle of conversation, he whipped out a mini-tape-recorder and dictated notes to his secretary by way of following up on a point that emerged from our discussion. When I visited his office for the first time, I was enormously impressed with the organization of his files, which I learned he designed himself. I was consumed with envy at his ability to maintain access to, and stay in possession of, his past. I was to discover that he organizes his memories no less systematically than he does his papers."

As anyone who has attempted to write a book can tell you – much time is spent in preparation, study and research – but 44 books published! It's almost incomprehensible. From "Dumbth" here are just a few of the 81 ways or rules:

"Rule No. 1: Decide that in the future you will reason more effectively.

Believe it or not, this simple step, by itself, will produce positive results, however modest. It alone obviously cannot achieve the desired effect, bit it is a necessary beginning. The conscious act of will it requires narrows our concentration of the particular task. As much as anyone knows who has ever attempted to learn chess, table tennis, roller skating, to play the piano, or any other activity requiring special concentration and coordination, the simple decision, the will to master the ability, is always a necessary part of the process.

Rule No. 2: Do some casual studying about the brain, the mind, memory, the whole field of psychology.

For those who are still in school, this should be easy. Others can visit a used-book store and pick up a couple of good, recent college-level psychology texts. Engineers read about engineering, musicians read about music, athletes about sports, etc., anyone who decides to become something of a thinker should read about thinking.

Rule No. 19: Concede ignorance when you are ignorant.

Let's begin to apply the word "not." It may strike you as odd, even comic, but the truth is that one of the wisest things we can say is, "I do not know." I have not the slightest doubt that the drama of history, and the unknown prehistoric ages, would have been somewhat more peaceful if the honest concession of ignorance had been more common.

Rule No. 22: Know that reason need not be the enemy of emotion.

When some people hear reason being endorsed, they assume that, if the amount of rationality in the world is increased, it must inevitably follow that certain increments of sensation and emotion decrease. The supposition – or fearful concern – is, of course, groundless. Certain things will indeed be decreased if the domain of reason is enlarged, but they are such things as foolishness, fanaticism, brawling, fear, ignorance, bigotry, and racial, ethnic, and religious prejudice. As for the enjoyments of the senses, as for the warm, beautiful, endearing emotions, two things are possible: Either they will be unaffected by an increase in the reasoning faculty or – as seems more likely – they will be enhanced, since the increased exercise of reason will to a certain extent decrease those negative emotional factors that now limit the sensible joys of life.

Rule No. 34: Decide to continue your education until death.

Most of us think of education incorrectly. The word itself does not come properly into focus. We know readily enough, in a general sense, what it means, and we grasp the obvious, which is that education is a matter of acquiring knowledge. But when we think of the process, what comes to mind is a series of vague images of school buildings, books, teachers, classrooms, tests, and date. All of these have their relevance, but we should pass through them to the heart of the matter. The central item in the process of education is the individual human being. To you, the most important player in the ongoing drama of education is yourself.

Rule No. 37: Watch less commercial television

Novelist Walker Percy, among millions of others, is concerned about the great amount of time people spend watching television. Its influence? "Nobody has any idea," he has said. "It's the greatest, most revolutionary change in our culture since print. It has even more influence on our lives. People average five to six hours daily watching television. You can't tell me that five or six hours a day of feeding the mind is not having a profound influence." Percy is right.

Rule No. 53: When possible, spend time with people brighter than yourself.

It is a source of considerable sadness to me that I have spent so little of my time in the company of intellectuals. I hold no contempt for non-intellectuals. One would have to despise the human race if one did. But my soul and mind open up in the presence of highly intelligent people, in conversation with them, to a degree that rarely happens in other theaters of social contact.

Rule No. 58: Familiarize yourself with the commonly accepted scientific view of the universe.

Learning to think better also requires that we develop an at least rudimentary familiarity with the laws of physics; which is to say, the laws that govern the actual world. Doing so will make us less likely to be susceptible to superstition, to become the victim of pseudo-science, or to be guilty of common errors about the natural universe."

Steve Allen's varied interests range from the migrant farm worker to the 5000-year history of China. His most recent book, *Murder of the Atlantic*, published by Zebra Press, is the sixth in a series of murder mysteries. He is still an active thinker, and with his multi-talented wife, Jayne Meadows, he spends two-thirds of the time traveling.

As a contributing author to *The Book Your Church Doesn't Want You To Read*, published by the Truth Seeker Co., Allen has expanded his observations on abortion, crime, the press, war, virtue, sex, marriage, atheism and more in **Reflections**, published by Prometheus.

In Steve Allen on *The Bible, Religion and Morality*, he focuses his talents and critical intelligence on the Bible. In a work reminiscent of Voltaire's Philosophical Dictionary, Allen presents his ideas as a series of alphabetically arranged essays. Here are a few highlights:

"A Word to Believers: During many years as a churchgoer, I often heard or read Catholic or Protestant commentaries strongly critical of atheists or other persons who, it was said, "hated God." Only later did I come to realize that an atheist does not hate God; he simply is one who is unable to believe that a God exists. However, at that earlier time I embraced the implication that anyone who wrote critically of God would be intellectually depraved indeed. The strange thing is that it is not the atheist (many of them respected scientists, scholars, and philosophers) who has committed this offense. Rather, it is the mostly unknown authors of the Old Testament, who have, unwittingly or not, attributed to God hundreds of crimes as bad as, if not sometimes worse than, some of the enormities committed by humans.

A Word to Nonbelievers: Many atheists, agnostics, Free Thinkers, Secular Humanists, and other critics of organized religion have made the mistake of assuming that since some aspects of Judeo-Christian belief seem preposterous to them, they must also seem so to most defenders. Therefore, it is reasoned that the latter are brazen hypocrites pretending to have faith in a philosophy that they do not in fact respect. That Christian and Judaism on the one hand and hypocrisy on the other are not mutually exclusive is, alas, all too well established, but I believe that the majority of believers are sincerely convinced of the general reasonableness of their own versions of a faith.

Prayer: For me to appreciate is, in the same moment, for me to feel grateful. If I am appreciating a meal prepared for me, there is a sense of gratitude toward the preparer. In that sense, of course, it is not unusual that one reaction leads to another. We respond by thanking the person who hands us a cold drink on a hot day, something to eat when we are hungry, or who does even less important favors or services. But I feel the same pairing of emotions about gifts and splendors of nature, even though there is no way to determine whether they are available because of a creator's intent or are simply fortunate accidents.

At the moment I record these reflections, for example, my sense of gratitude has welled up because of a combination of physical circumstances: an ideal temperature in the low 80s, a clear sky, warm sun and, most pleasurable of all, a cooling breeze. Given the millions of individuals on other parts of the planet are at this moment dying of thirst and hunger, it can hardly be intelligently argued that a God has purposely ignored their prayer and entreaties while going out of his way, at the same moment to provide me with such pleasures. The sense of gratitude, nevertheless, is not only felt but also recognized.

Conclusion: No doubt some of my Christian friends, and a greater number of others whom I do not know, will wonder why I have written such a book. There are two factors alone which compromise the explanation.

The first is the Bible itself. During the years of my fervent belief, I simply had no idea how many sorry and embarrassing passages there are in the scriptural record. I had encountered a few instances of critical literature, but it had largely bounced off the armored shell of my bias and loyalty to the Catholic Church. I had unthinkingly accepted the argument that critics were atheistic and evil men who wished only to attack good, decent believers.

Now that I am older, at least somewhat wiser, and certainly better informed, I am deeply ashamed of having held opinions so unconnected to reality. I've known very few atheists but, without exception, they have been men and women of principle, and admirable as citizens. Of the few truly despicable human beings I have encountered, I regret to report that almost every one of them was at least a nominal believer in one religion or another."

Steve Allen

When we think of Steve Allen we think of great thinkers such as Thomas Paine, Thomas Jefferson and Voltaire, who were the people of their time. This is the time of Steve Allen. He was the 20th-Century man leading us into the 21st Century with his clear and witty style, which makes the difficult subject of today accessible to every reader.

By Tim C. Leedom

337

CONTRIBUTORS

Kevin D. Annett, M.Div., is an internationally known producer, lecturer and author of *Hidden from History: The Canadian Holocaust* and *Love and Death in the Valley*. His documentary film *Unrepentant: Kevin Annett on Canada's Genocide* won the 2006 Best Director award at the New York International Independent Film and Video Festival. Kevin is the founder of the Truth Commission into Genocide in Canada. for more information visit his website: **www.hiddenfromhistory.org**.

Gustavo Arellano is an awarding-winning columnist and staff reporter for OC Weekly, an alternative newspaper in Orange County, California. He is also a contributor to the Los Angeles Times Op/Ed Page. He has appeared on the Today Show, Nightline, NPR, and On the Media and is a frequent guest on both liberal and conservative talk shows. For more information visit him at his website: **http://www.askamexican.net**.

Ken Bear Chief, Gros Ventre, Nooksack, Nez Perce, is an investigative paralegal/victim liaison with Tamaki Law Offices in Yakima, Washington. Since 2008 he has been investigating clergy sexual abuse of Native Americans who attended the Catholic/Jesuit/Oblate operated residential schools during 1940-1980 and has interviewed over 200 victims of abuses throughout reservations in Washington, Idaho, Montana and South Dakota. For more information visit him **http://www.tamakilaw.com**.

Tony Bushby, an Australian, became a businessman and entrepreneur early in his adult life. He established a magazine-publishing business and spent 20 years researching, writing and publishing his own magazine, primarily for the Australia and New Zealand markets. Tony is a world traveler and has appeared on radio and television on all continents as an expert on religious deception and crime. He is the author of *The Bible Fraud* (2001); *The Secret in the Bible* (2003) and *The Crucifixion of Truth* (2005) published by Joshua Books and several new titles with Stanford House Publishing. Copies of these books are available from NEXUS offices and the Joshua Book website **http://www.joshuabooks.com**. Correspondence should be sent to him in care of NEXUS Magazine, PO Box 30, Mapleton, Qld 4560 Australia fax +61 (7) 5443-9381.

Daante is an accomplished master in many fields, from the physical, mental to the arts. Daante is a former security specialist in the U.S. Air Force and a martial arts black belt with college level athletic skills. His new manual of experimental work on overcoming fear is in the making. He is a certified teacher in the arts and drama and has published two volumes of poetry, with several singled out as "Best of the Year." Daante is writing his first novel while continuing his investigative research.

Reverend Thomas Doyle has spent twenty-five years advocating for the victims of clerical sexual abuse. Rev. Doyle holds a pontifical doctorate in canon law from Catholic University and five masters degrees in canon law, political science, church administration, theology and philosophy. As an Air Force major he held sixteen military awards and decorations for distinguished service. He has authored numerous commentaries on cannon law and was awarded the first *Priest of the Year Award* in 2002 by the Voice of the Faithful.

Karl Frank is a blogger at "Karl's Corner: Sumpin' to Ponder," a little place to come and share your thoughts. For more information visit his website: **http://www.karlscorner.blogspot.com**.

Tom Henheffer is a Canadian journalist, photographer and film critic, currently a staff reporter at Macleans Magazine. For more information visit his website: The Rye Diary or contact him at **Tom.Henheffer@macleans.rogers.com**.

Janja Lalich, PhD. is Associate Professor of Sociology at California State University, Chico. Her research and writing has focused on cults and controversial groups, with a specialization in charismatic authority, power relations, ideology and social control. *Take Back Your Life: Recovering from Cults and Abusive Relationships* (with Madeline Tobias – 2004) is a general introduction to cults with a focus on recovery. Other works include *Bounded Choice: True Believers and Charismatic Cults* (University of California Press – 2005); co-author of *"Crazy" Therapies: What Are They? Do They Work?* (Jossey-Bass, 1996); *Cults in Our Midst* (Jossey-Bass, 1995) and *Captive Hearts, Caprite Minds: Freedom and Recovery from Cults and Abusive Relationships* (Hunter House, 1994). She can be contacted at **JLalich@csuchico.edu**.

Michael D. Langone, PhD. is a counseling psychologist and Executive Director of International Cult Studies Association (ICSA). He was the founder editor of Cultic Studies Journal (CSJ), the editor of Cultic Studies Review and editor of Recovery from Cults. He is co-author of Cults: What Parents Should Know and Satanism and Occult-Related Violence: What You Should Know. Dr. Langone has spoken and written widely about cults. He received the 1995 Leo J. Ryan Award from the "original" Cult Awareness Network and was honored as the Albert V. Danielson visiting Scholar at Boston University. He can be contacted at **mail@icsamail.com**.

Dr. Jonathan Levy is licensed in the U.S. and several foreign jurisdictions as an attorney, advocate, barrister, and solicitor. His practice concentrates on international law, human rights, anti money laundering, asset recovery and related fields in banking, finance and administrative law. He is on the faculty of two graduate schools and instructs courses in law and counter terrorism. Dr. Levy is considered one of the world's leading experts on topics such as The Vatican and Exile Government. He is the author of a book on The Intermarium, a geopolitical plan for east central Europe. For more information visit his website: **info@brimstoneandcompany.com**

D.M. Murdoch/Acharya S. is an independent scholar of comparative religion and mythology and author of *The Origins of Christianity*; *The Christ Conspiracy: The Greatest Story Ever Sold*; *Sons of God: Krishna, Buddha and Christ Unveiled* (2004); *Who Was Jesus? Fingerprints of the Christ* (2007) *Christ in Egypt: The Horus-Jesus Connection and The Gospel According to Acharya S.* For more information visit her website *Truth Be Known* (**http://www.truthbeknown.com** and her blog site **http://www.tbknews@blogspot.com**)

Sinead O'Connor, the internationally acclaimed Irish singer, songwriter, musical artist, and mother of four lives in Dublin. She is a respected voice on child abuse issues and has appeared on BBC's "Newsnight" and CNN's "Larry King Live." For more information visit her website: **http://www.sinead-oconnor.com**

Michael Parenti, PhD., Yale University, is an internationally known award-winning author, scholar and lecturer who addresses a wide variety of political, historical and cultural subjects. Among his recent books are: *God and His Demons* (2010) which deals with all sorts of theocratic misconduct and misbelief; *Contrary Notions* (2007); *The Cultural Struggle* (2006); *The Assassination of Julius Caesar* (2003); *Democracy for the Few*, 9th Edition (2010) and *The Face of Imperialism* (2011). For further information, visit his website: **www.michaelparenti.org**.

Greg Szymanski, JD, is an investigative journalist, producer of the internet magazine *Investigative Journal*, radio host at Liberty Radio Live and Blog Talk Radio. Greg has made a life of uncovering crimes and truth. Greg has gained worldwide audiences on the church, war and government corruption. For more information visit his website: **http://www.blogtalkradio.com/gregbeacon**.

Matt Taibbi is an American journalist currently working at *Rolling Stone* where he authors the columns "Road Rage" and "The Low Post" and a blogger at *True/ Slant*. He has held editorial positions at the newspapers *The eXile*, *The New York Press* and *The Beast* and was a regular contributor to *Real Time with Bill Mather*. In 2009 Taibbi gained recognition for his article in *Rolling Stone* accusing

Goldman Sachs of helping engineer "every major market manipulation since the Great Depression." For more information visit Taibblog at **http://www.rollingstone.com/politics/matt-taibbi**.

Paul Tice is the author of *Shadow of Darkness, Dawning of the Light: The Awakening of Human Consciousness in the 21ˢᵗ Century and Beyond; Triumph of the Human Spirit; The Greatest Achievements of the Human Soul and How Its Power Can Change Your Life*; and *Jumpin' Jehovah: Exposing the Atrocities of the Old Testament God*. His work and other interesting books can be found at **www.thebooktree.com**.

To Our Contributors:

We have made every effort to credit and reach people who have added to ***The Book No Pope Would Want You to Read***. Some material has been deemed public domain or fair usage, some information comes from many sources, i.e. Wikipedia, newspapers, emails, internet, blogs, reviews, books, compilations, public announcements, etc.; thus the original source is difficult to determine and credit. If any contributor we have included believes they have not been acknowledged correctly, we will make the necessary adjustments in the next printing. We apologize in advance for this failing.

Please contact us at Manoa Valley Publishing Company, PO Box 5009, Balboa Island, CA 92662, USA or email: **timleedomintv@msn.com**.

ABOUT THE AUTHORS

Tim C. Leedom is the best-selling editor of the popular anthology *THE BOOK YOUR CHURCH DOESN'T WANT YOU TO READ*, now in its 11th printing, co-author of the right on book, *THE MAIN MAN*, correctly debunking the return of Jesus in 2000, and *THE LIGHT SIDE*, an award winning children's story.

Tim was an aide to both the Governor and Lt. Governor of Hawaii after finishing his college studies at the University of Hawaii, receiving three academic fellowships and scholarships.

Maryjane Churchville, B.S.ED, is an American investigative researcher, teacher, lecturer and former newspaper reporter. She has served on numerous task force teams investigating white-collar crime and legal issues. She is a former Catholic indoctrinated by the Madams of the Sacred Heart at the Convent of the Sacred Heart in Newton, Massachusetts.

ACKNOWLEDGMENTS

I want to pay tribute to those of you who have aided directly and indirectly in making ***THE BOOK NO POPE WOULD WANT YOU TO READ***. First and foremost my co-author who has been tireless in efforts to organize, evaluate and type endless articles, notes and research. Without her this book would be just an idea. Of course, the late Steve Allen, the consummate Renaissance Man. His writings on religion, humor and life should be on everyone's reading list; the contributors to our anthology who have spent countless and unappreciated hours digging, reading and asking questions that others were not brave enough to ask; Paul Tice who is an expert in his own right authoring many books of his own. He has helped revive classics which have sat on the shelf too long; Bonnie Lange a crusader who has dedicated her life to "getting the facts out so people can make up their own minds;" Journalists Gustavo Arellano and Matt Coker of the O.C. Weekly whom I witnessed take on the crimes of predator priests and enablers before it was fashionable or acceptable; Thomas Doyle, who relentlessly has pursued justice for the victims of the Vatican's crimes of commission and omission; Andrea Pandele, for her technical tutoring; two others who I will only refer to as R and H. who provided back story information that few have access to; and of course, the talent and imagination of our cover artist, Abigail Huchel, whose cover says it all. Thank you to Jordan Maxwell for making his extensive data base available and access to his library; also a thank you to D.K. for a very professional job editing and proofreading; and Yahaira at Eworld for her design and layout.

Life is a team effort...and this book is an example of that. We all hope our book will bring light to the dark corners of a Church that has thrived in its own shadows.

We would also sincerely like to thank those of you who have supported and encouraged us, and equally we would like to pay special acknowledgment to those who have told us that "we would never make it," and that "we were wasting our time." Those remarks have only strengthened our resolve and determination to complete our mission.

Illustrations and Photos

1. Junipero Serra 13
2. Father Edward Coughlin 15
3. Pope John Paul II 17
4. Opus Dei 20
5. Jose Escriva 22
6. The Vatican 25
7. The Mitre 30
8. Vatican Flag 30
9. Sol Invictus 45
10. Krishna 46
11. Jesus Mosaic 48
12. Vision of Constantine 50
13. Crusader 51
14. Pope Benedict XVI 63
15. Pope Benedict/Hitler Youth 64
16. Hanging Heretics 73
17. Burning Heretics 74
18. The Catholic Cross, Sword and Bible 74
19. Library at Alexandria 75
20. Children's Crusade 76
21. Knights Templar Shield 79
22. Joan of Arc 80
23. Giordano Bruno 83
24. Copernicus 84
25. Galileo 85
26. Platform of Jaguars and Eagles 86
27. Shroud of Turin 87
28. Anti-Catholic Coin 93
29. Nazi Flag at Catholic Church 96
30. Pope Pius XII 97
31. Pope Pius in Chair 103
32. Hitler with Archbishop 104
33. Bishops Saluting Hitler 105
34. Vaticans Triple Crown 107
35. Swastika 107

36. Andrija Artukovic 111
37. The Iron Fist. 114
38. Letter from Artukovic 1/5. 115
39. Letter from Artukovic 2/5. 116
40. Letter from Artukovic 3/5. 117
41. Letter from Artukovic 4/5. 118
42. Letter from Artukovic 5/5. 119
43. Letter from Artukovic's Brother-J. Artukovic. 120
44. Letter from Flaherty. 121
45. Letter from Dolan 122
46. Letter to Flaherty from Nixon. 123
47. Letter to Dolan from Nixon. 124
48. Letter from Croatian Union 1/2. 125
49. Letter from Croatian Union 2/2. 126
50. Dead prisoners of Holocaust. 127
51. Archbishop Saric and Andre Pavelic. 128
52. Catholic Bishops Nazi Salute. 129
53. Door at Auschwitz No.10 Block. 130
54. Sgt. Schultz. 130
55. Pope Benedict XVI. 131
56. Pope Pius XII. 132
57. Pope John Paul III 132
58. Alois Hudal. 138
59. Klaus Barbie. 140
60. Hermann Goering 140
61. Martin Bormann 141
62. Adolf Eichmann. 142
63. Eichmann Fingerprints. 143
64. Trial at Nuremburg. 144
65. Andrija Artukovic. 144
66. Benito Mussolini. 145
67. Adolf Hitler 145
68. Joseph Mengele. 146
69. Father Thomas Doyle. 147
70. The Power and The Glory Book. 148
71. Brimstone & Co. Letter pg.1/3. 153
72. Brimstone & Co. Letter pg.2/3. 154
73. Brimstone & Co. Letter pg.3/3. 155

74. John Patrick Cody. 157
75. Mein Kampf 173
76. Imprimatur Book 174
77. Banned Bible 175
78. John Strugnell. 177
79. Pope John Paul I. 220
80. Bishop Accountability-HI 1/4. 223
81. Bishop Accountability-HI 2/4. 224
82. Bishop Accountability-HI 3/4. 225
83. Bishop Accountability-HI 4/4. 226
84. Bishop Accountability-AK. 227
85. Bishop Accountability-CA 1/2. 228
86. Bishop Accountability-CA 2/2. 229
87. Bishop Accountability-IL 230
88. Bishop Accountability-LA 231
89. Bishop Accountability-MA. 232
90. Bishop Accountability-NY. 233
91. Bishop Accountability-TX. 234
92. Bishop Accountability-WI. 235
93. Bishop Accountability-KS 1/2. 236
94. Bishop Accountability-KS 2/2. 237
95. Kevin Annett. 262
96. Tod D. Brown. 280
97. Boston Herald Article. 283
98. Sharpe Plaque. 286
99. Ex-Cardinal Roger Mahony. 298
100. Mahony Cathedral 299

Index

A

Aaronite. *See* 98
Aarons. *See* 37,133,134,137
aboriginals. *See* 266,269
abortion. *See* 35,171,178,181,187,277, 295,336
Acta. *See* 70
Acton. *See* 204
Adam. *See* 58,206
Addison, Joseph. *See* 176
Ad extirpanda. *See* 71
AFN. *See* 271
Agnes. *See* 58
AIDS. *See* 171,172
Aix-la-Chapelle. *See* 187
Alberni. *See* 263,265,267,269
Albigenses. *See* 208
Albigensian. *See* 39,71
Aleksander. *See* 108
Alethes Logos. *See* 69
Alexander. *See* 5,15,44,61,88,189,205,207
Alexandre Dumas, fils. *See* 176
Alexandre Dumas, pere. *See* 176
Alezandria. *See* 68
Alito. *See* 195
Allegro. *See* 176
Allen, Steve. *See* 15,79,330,333,336,337,345
allusio Etruscanoracles. *See* 25
Alonso, Fernandez. *See* 20
Alpha. *See* 48
Amaury. *See* 209
ambassador. *See* 18,133,179,197,238
American Independent Party. *See* 148
Amorth, Gabriele. *See* 16
Anacletus. *See* 207
Anastasius Bibliothecarius. *See* 57
Andler. *See* 285
Andrade. *See* 285
Anglia. *See* 58
Anglicus. *See* ; *See* 56
Anich. *See* 112

Annett, Kevin. *See* 262,268,270,271,272,273,339
Announcement. *See* 3,342
Annu. *See* 49
Antapodsis. *See* 200
anti-popes. *See* 26,205
Anup. *See* 49
Apache. *See* 165-168
Aphrodite-Mari. *See* 50
apostle. *See* 39,42,49,73,187,189,207
Apostolic Vicar. *See* 14
Aquinas. *See* 70
Aramaic. *See* 32,33,177
archdiocesan. *See* 178
Archdiocese of San Antonio. *See* 222
Argentina. *See* 101,110,133,135-137,260
Arias. *See* 4
Arius. *See* 44
Arizona. *See* 163-168,217,301
Ar-jouan. *See* 47
Arjuna. *See* 47
Arsenault. *See* 327
artificial contraception. *See* 6
Artukovic. *See* 112-114,138
    Artukovic, Andrija.
    See also 111,112,127,136,144,148
Asimov, Isaac. *See* 15
Assembly of First Nations. *See* 271
assistants. *See* 21
Associate. *See* 21,340
Associated Press. *See* 172,280,281
Assumption. *See* 7
Athanasius. *See* 44
atheists. *See* 29,36,37,327,336,337
Athens. *See* 56,57
Attis. *See* 45
Atum. *See* 49
Audiencia. *See* 89
Augustine. *See* 72,187,311
Auschwitz. *See* 62,130,137,143
Australia. *See* 37,137,182,238,260,311,339
Austria. *See* 100,110,112,134,138,260,312

auto de fés. *See* 82
avatar. *See* 8,48,179
Avignon. *See* 26
Axis. *See* 108
Aztec. *See* 86,88

B

Babinsky. *See* 72
Babylon. *See* 30
Bacon, Francis. *See* 176
BAE. *See* 158
Baldwin. *See* 239,312
Ball, Bonnilee. *See* 273
Ballerini. *See* 31
bankruptcy. *See* 261,274,281,282,314,329
Baptism. *See* 5,6,44,88,310
Baptist. *See* 49,184
Baptiste, Norma Jean. *See* 272
barbarian. *See* 68
Barbie, Klaus. *See* 136-138,140
Barcelona. *See* 139
Baronius. *See* 200,207
Bartholomew. *See* 72
Bartolomé de las Casas. *See* 88
Barton, Clara. *See* 15
Basilica. *See* 26,58,60,209,301
Battros. *See* 164
Bavaria. *See* 64,138,238,260
Bavarian Concordat. *See* 100
Beatification. *See* 11,14,330
Beauvoir, Simone de. *See* 176
Becher. *See* 143
belief system. *See* 8,113,260
Bell, Alexander Graham. *See* 15
Benedict. *See* 11,14,58,59,61,63-65,81,131,
148,162,171,172,177,179,186,188,190,202,
203,206,214,219,242,246,257,260
        See also 278-281
Ben-Gurion. *See* 143
Berkley, George. *See* 176
Bernard Law. *See* 278,283
Berry, Jason. *See* 262
Bethlehem. *See* 40,49
Bierce. *See* 11
Bioethics. *See* 170
Birch. *See* 18,113,148

birth control. *See* 155,159,172,191,217,260,
277
bishop. *See* 11,12,26,31-4,44,57,62,64,88,89,
91,98,133,135,138,139,148,156,157,170,181,
185,187,188-190,198-201; *See* 203,206,209,
211,215,223, 238,240,241,256,257,261,275,
261,275,277-280,282,284-287,290,292-294,
296,301-303,312; *See* 315,327
Bishop Accountability. *See* 223,256,257,282,
284,290,293,296,301-303,312
Black. *See* 6,39,55,69,89,97,98,160,206,325,
339
black natives. *See* 6
Blackwell. *See* 185
Blanck. *See* 58
Blessed. *See* 4,11,12,14,20,31,32,111
blitzkrieg. *See* 108
Blondel. *See* 31,59
Bloody Monday. *See* 287
Blum. *See* 113,309
Bohemian. *See* 39,40,42,58
Bolshevik. *See* 111
Boniface. *See* 6,61,78,187,199,203,219,242
Book of Gomorrah. *See* 204
Bordeaux. *See* 58
Bormann. *See* 101,136-139,141
Boston. *See* 178,179,241,278,281,283,284,
300,301,303,308,309,314,324,340
Boureau. *See* 59
Boyle. *See* 164
Brahman priesthood. *See* 47
Braun. *See* 101
Brescia. *See* 5
Brewyn. *See* 60
Briggs. *See* 186
Brimstone. *See* 152-155
Brown. *See* 37,185,280,285-287,296,320,327
Brunner, Alois. *See* 134,136,137
Bruno. *See* 203,211
  Bruno, Giordano. *See* 15,83,176,329
Brussels. *See* 218,276
Bruys. *See* 5
Bryce. *See* 266,267
Buchenwald. *See* 106
Buddha. *See* 45,341
Buddhism. *See* 64
Burbank, Luther. *See* 15

Burgundians. *See* 81
Burke. *See* 178
burning. *See* 6,27,67,74,82,106,164
Bushby. *See* 37,63,68,196,211,339
Bush, George. *See* 259
Bythynia. *See* 43

C

Cabrini, Xavier. *See* 12
Caccianemici. *See* 208
Caccini. *See* 162
Cadaver Synod. *See* 199
cafeteria Catholic. *See* 323
Caggiano. *See* 133,135,136
calendar. *See* 44,165,211,313
California. *See* 12,13,49,90,112,113,138, 139,148,195,222,280,296,302,339,340
Calles. *See* 91
Calvin. *See* 6
    Calvin, John. *See also* 176,311
Camacho. *See* 92
Campbell, Joseph. *See* 15
camps. *See* 13,106,112,133,134,151,264, 265,270
Camus, Albert. *See* 15
Canada. *See* 18,133,137,185,261,263-267, 271-273,339
Canadian. *See* 28,186,240,263,264,265,270, 271,339,340
Canadian Holocaust. *See* 263-265,271,339
Canale d'Agordo. *See* 215
Canary Islands. *See* 6,82
canonization. *See* 11,103
canons. *See* 43,44,246,252,255
Carcassonne. *See* 210
Cardenas. *See* 92
Cardinal. *See* 11,14,20,27,34,42,56,59,98, 100,112,113,133,136,141,143,148,157,158, 162,163,177,178,181,182,196,200; *See* 205, 207,213,215-218,222,223,255,258,260-262, 275-281,283,287,288,296,297-301,308,309
Carlin. *See* 19
Carolingian. *See* 207
Carranza. *See* 91
Carson, Rachel. *See* 15
Casanova, Gaicomo. *See* 176

Cascioli. *See* 310,311
Cassadore. *See* 165,167
Cassetta. *See* 98
cassock. *See* 55
castration. *See* 44
catacombs. *See* 49
Catechism. *See* 183
catechumens. *See* 44
Cathars. *See* 198,208-211
catheymn. *See* 214
Catholic Action. *See* 129,135
Catholic Encyclopedia.
    See 6,11,12,14,20,25-27,47,59,60,78,79,81, 82,86,189,196-199,202-211,314
Catholicism. *See* 13,14,68,88-91,129,186
Catholic League. *See* 182,309,310
Cecelja. *See* 134
Celestine. *See* 209,219
celibacy. *See* 21,187,188,190,203,259,260, 312
celibate. *See* 21,67,187,259
Cephas. *See* 32,39
Chadwick. *See* 102
Chamberlain. *See* 61,62
Champagne. *See* 81
Chaplain. *See* 239-242
Charity. *See* 12,40,160
Charlemagne. *See* 11,68
Charles. *See* 5,15,33,34,81,82,89,101,102, 133,166,169,199,206
Chesney. *See* 287,288
Chief Louis Daniels. *See* 272
Chile. *See* 19,261
Chinon. *See* 78
Chomsky, Noam. *See* 271
Christ. *See* 4,5,18,31,32,37-39,45-47,49,50, 58,69,73,77,78,88,100,181,185,198,203,204, 207,209,210,214,261,290,291; *See* 296,310, 311,319,321,341
Christendom. *See* 43
Christian virtue. *See* 198
Christophorus. *See* 199
Chronica. *See* 55
Chronicles. *See* 55,161
Chronicon. *See* 55-58
Chrysostom. *See* 68

Church. *See* 5-7,11,14,16,18-20,23,25-29, 31-45,48,49,51,52,55-58,62,64,65,67-71,73, 77,79,81,83-93,95,96,98-103; *See* 105-107, 109-113,128,130,134,136-139,143,146,148, 149,157,159,161-163,165,166,169-172,174, 175,177,178; *See* 180, 181,183-187,190,191, 193,195-198,201-211,213-222,238,243, 254-273,275-281,286-301,303,305,307-315; *See* 319-325,327-331,336,337, 340,341,343, 345
Churchill. *See* 110
Church of England. *See* 185
Church of God. *See* 185
Church of the Nazarene. *See* 185
Cipriani. *See* 159
Cisteros. *See* 91
Clement. *See* 5-7,31,38,56,58,59,61,78,87, 189,197,199,206,219
cleric. *See* 31,44,90-92,187,254,276,288,291
Clinton. *See* 167,298
Clohessy. *See* 299,300,308
Clone. *See* 45
CNN. *See* 16,292,293,308,341
Codex Juris Canonici. *See* 71
Cody. *See* 157,158,213,215-217
coffee. *See* 87
Coliseum. *See* 56,60
College. *See* 27,134,222,278,283,300,309, 323,334,339,343
College of Cardinals. *See* 27,278
Colombia. *See* 261
colonization. *See* 13,73
Colossian. *See* 57
Colossus. *See* 57
Combes, William. *See* 272,273
Commandments. *See* 51
Commissary. *See* 12
commitment. *See* 8,326
Communion. *See* 5,64,177,178,181,238
Como. *See* 68
Comte, Auguste. *See* 176
concentration camp. *See* 110,137,151,152, 157
confessions. *See* 6,68,197,207,243,249, 251-254
Congo. *See* 73
Congregation. *See* 20,64,98,162,171,177, 181,243,244,246,248,250,254,255,279,281, 314
Congregationalist. *See* 185
conquistadors. *See* 86,88
Constance. *See* 5,40,41,58
Constantine. *See* 26,32,34,38,43,50,70,183, 196
Constantinople. *See* 4,79
contraception. *See* 6,171,172
Convention on the Rights of the Child. *See* 303
conversion. *See* 6,65,88,109,129,265
Conversos. *See* 81
Conway. *See* 288
Cooper. *See* 62
Cooperators. *See* 21
Copernicus. *See* 83,84,161,315,320,329
  Copernicus, Nicolaus. *See also* 176
Cordoba. *See* 43,261
Cornwall. *See* 97,102,218
Corpo Diplomatico. *See* 135
corporal mortification. *See* 21,22
corruption. *See* 26,28,36,41,196,207,341
Cortéz. *See* 88,89
Cosa Nostra. *See* 102
Coughlin. *See* 15
cover-ups. *See* 61,112,113,204,213,222,223, 278,284,286,287,289,307,330
Coyne. *See* 166
Cozumel. *See* 88
creationism. *See* 170
Creed. *See* 3,17,43,319
Crescenti. *See* 205
crimen pessimum. *See* 254
Crimen Sollicitationis. *See* 243
criminality. *See* 196,203,216
Croatia. *See* 14,102,109,110,112,128,138, 139,141,144
Croatian Ustashe. *See* 135
Cross. *See* 15-17,68,74,77,79,107,134,138, 209,247,261
Crucifixion. *See* 37,63,88,339
Crusades. *See* 38,68,71,77-79,208,210,319
cult. *See* 7,8,38,39,69,340
Cultic. *See* 7,8,340
cultural genocide. *See* 13,274
cultus. *See* 45

Cummins. *See* 280
cyanide. *See* 62
Cyprian. *See* 31,32

D

Daante. *See* 43,103,339,340
d'Alembert, Jean le Rond. *See* 176
Damascus. *See* 4
Damian. *See* 12,204,205
Danforth. *See* 184
d'Angelo de Scarparian. *See* 59
Daniels. *See* 272,275
Darboy. *See* 34
Dark. *See* 36-38,43,67,113,148,174,208,213, 286,320,345
Darrow, Clarence. *See* 15,173
Darwin. *See* 169,176
   Darwin, Charles Robert. *See also* 15
Darwin, Erasmus. *See* 176
Darwinism. *See* 100
Dauphin. *See* 81
Daye. *See* 133
deacons. *See* 44,256
Dead Sea Scrolls. *See* 176,177
Dean. *See* 27,40,98,278
Decian. *See* 69
DeClerck, Stefaan. *See* 276
Decretals. *See* 31,208
Defoe, Daniel. *See* 176
Deistic. *See* 48
DeMeo. *See* 68
de'Mussi. *See* 62
denial. *See* 95,112,113,139,141,156,220,277, 284,307,308,314,325,329-331
Denmark. *See* 186,311
Department of Indian Affairs. *See* 264,266, 269
Descartes, Rene. *See* 176
Devaki. *See* 47
DeVera. *See* 181
Devil. *See* 12,16,17,35,67,74,87,92,102,164, 198,202,270
Dewoitine. *See* 136
Díaz, Juan. *See* 88
Diderot, Denis. *See* 176
Didymus. *See* 39

DiFonzo. *See* 37
digitalis. *See* 214
Dignitas. *See* 171
Dignity USA. *See* 310
diocese. *See* 11,148,223,238,248,257,258, 277,280,282,283,285-287,289,291-300,310
Diocletian. *See* 69
Dionysus. *See* 45
Dirty Dozen. *See* 61
Disobedience. *See* 13
Divine Trinity. *See* 4
Doctrine of Faith. *See* 169,281
Dogma. *See* 1,3,4,7,12,27,36,86,169,198, 209,213,214,275
Dolan. *See* 114,257,258,307
Dominican Order. *See* 6,71
Domolo. *See* 302
Domremy. *See* 81
Donation. *See* 32,34
Donilon. *See* 178
Don Vasco de Quiroga. *See* 89
Door. *See* 27,100,130,215,275,279
Doyle. *See* 139,147,238,239,340,345
Draganovic. *See* 129,134,135,137,138
Drennan. *See* 290
Drexel. *See* 12
Dubner. *See* 35,37
Duchesne. *See* 12,60
Du Moulin. *See* 33
dung. *See* 58
Duomo. *See* 58
Duran. *See* 72
Dzil. *See* 165

E

Easter. *See* 44,46,65,71,98,278
Ebonites. *See* 39
ecclesiastical. *See* 33,44,59,63,68,98,99,197, 204,207,208,248
ecclesie. *See* 33
ecomiendas. *See* 88
ecumenical. *See* 197
   ecumenical council. *See also* 3-6,43,44
Eddy. *See* 185
Edwards County. *See* 222
Egypt. *See* 46,75,79,341

Eichmann. *See* 112,134,136,137,139,142, 143

Einstein, Albert. *See* 15

Eisenman. *See* 176,177

Ejidos. *See* 90

ekklesai. *See* 33

Elder Phillipa Ryan. *See* 272

Elizabeth. *See* 7,12

Elmeric. *See* 211

Emperor Constantine. *See* 26,38,43,196

Emperor Frederick. *See* 5

enablers. *See* 14,113,308,315,327-329,345

encyclical. *See* 6

England. *See* 7,40,78,79,92,99,137,170,184, 185

Ephesus. *See* 4

Epicurean Kelsos. *See* 69

epilepsy. *See* 34

Episcopal. *See* 34,188,198,200

equality. *See* 315

Erasmus. *See* 176,207

Erreur Poplulaire de la Papesse Jeanne. *See* 58

Errico, Rocco. *See* 7

Escriva, Josemaria. *See* 19-21

Etruscan. *See* 25

Eucharist. *See* 5,6,44,46,177,178,240,308, 321

Eugene. *See* 5,6,133,136

Europe. *See* 32,38,55,64,67,70-72,77,78,100, 111,113,133,141,184,199,204,207,210,211, 213,215,273,297,330,341

European Central Bank. *See* 151,152

European Union. *See* 64,151,159

Evolution. *See* 169,170,333

ex-cathedra. *See* 3,6

excommunicate. *See* 5,238,241

excommunicated. *See* 6,40,89,139,141,144, 184,187,189,203,238,241,311,329

excommunication. *See* 78,141,184,189, 245-247,249,277,291

Exorcist. *See* 16,17

F

Faith. *See* 3,5-7,18,20,28,31,32,35,36,47,49, 64,69,72,102,162,169,170,173,175,177,180, 190,198,204,208,210,243; *See* 246,281,286, 314,315,319,323,325,336

faithful. *See* 3,5,6,33,68,102,105,169,208, 240,246,251,253,278,285,296,297,340

Farben. *See* 62

Farley. *See* 196,198

Farrell. *See* 101

Feil, Johann. *See* 136

fellowship. *See* 6,111

Felzmann. *See* 19

feminism. *See* 186

Ferdinand. *See* 6,81,82,90,100

festival. *See* 46,339

Fiala. *See* 222

Final Solution. *See* 100,139,142,143,264

fish. *See* 49,50,270

Fisherman's Ring. *See* 27

Florence. *See* 5

Foemina. *See* 58

Formosos. *See* 199

foxholes. *See* 37

Frale. *See* 78

Francaise. *See* 133

France. *See* 5,26,38,71,78,79,81,102,108, 136,141,176,208,214,278

France, Anatole. *See* 176

Franciscan. *See* 12,35,71,73,88,98,109,134, 156,157,275

Franco. *See* 19,20,112,113,214

Franklin Bank. *See* 215

Franklin, Benjamin. *See* 15

Freakonimics. *See* 35,37

Freemasons. *See* 7

Free Thought Movement. *See* 36

Friar. *See* 14,73,88,162

Friedlander. *See* 101

Frotheringham. *See* 198

Fullman. *See* 101

fundamentalist. *See* 29,183

G

Galatha. *See* 43

Galileo. *See* 28,83,84,161-163,176,313,314, 320,329

Galileo, Galilei. *See* 85,161,176,313

Gandolfo. *See* 110

Gasparri. *See* 98
Gaster. *See* 176
Geneva. *See* 32
genocide. *See* 13,67,71,110,263-265,271,
274,330,339
Genosi. *See* 34
geocentrism. *See* 161
Geoghan, John. *See* 278,303
Gerbert. *See* 203
Gestapo. *See* 101,112,137
Gide, Andre. *See* 176
Gillette. *See* 185
Gline. *See* 110
Gnostic. *See* 39
godmen. *See* 45
Goebbels. *See* 143
Gomez. *See* 222
Goni. *See* 135-137
Goolvi. *See* 42
Gorbachev. *See* 215
Gorda. *See* 12
Gospels. *See* 16,38,245,247,319,320
Goupil. *See* 12
Gradual Civilization Act of 1857. *See* 266
Graham. *See* 135,163,165-168
  Graham, Father Robert. *See also* 135
Graziano. *See* 203
Greek. *See* 4,33,49,68,69
Greek Schism. *See* 4
Greene, Graham. *See* 176
Gregory. *See* 5,59,77,79,187-189,203,205,
207,208,211,218,219
Grings. *See* 139
Groome. *See* 309
Gros Ventre. *See* 273,339
Guadalupe. *See* 89
Guerin. *See* 12
Gumbleton. *See* 238
Guzman. *See* 89,209
Guzzanti. *See* 180

H

habit. *See* 51,182
Hanscombe. *See* 185
Hans Kung. *See* 36
Har-Khutti. *See* 49

Harris. *See* 268
Hasler. *See* 37
Hasmoneans. *See* 310
Hatuey. *See* 72
Hawaii. *See* 12,343
Hawking, Stephen. *See* 15
Heaven. *See* 11,32,39,47,62,72,73,77,96,148,
161,164,221,321
Hebrew. *See* 177
Hefele. *See* 34
Heim, Aribert. *See* 136
Heine, Heinrich. *See* 176
Helen Hermence Green. *See* 67
heliocentrism. *See* 161,162
Henheffer. *See* 186,340
Hepburn, Katherine. *See* 15
Hercules. *See* 45
heresy. *See* 4,5,16,81,82,84,163,177,208-210,
253,329
heretics. *See* 4,6,15,44,67,70,71,73-75,78,82,
177,198,208,209,211,329
Herriott. *See* 50
Hetx. *See* 168
Hicks. *See* 280
Hidden from History. *See* 263,271,273,339
Hinduism. *See* 47
Hitler. *See* 14,19,61,64,65,97,99-105,112,
129,130,137,145,175,319,329
HIV/AIDS. *See* 171
Hobbes, Thomas. *See* 176
Hoffer. *See* 15
Holloway. *See* 170
Holocaust. *See* 73,105,106,108,110,111,127,
136,137,139,143,148,151,152,156,157,
263-265,271,273,274,315,339
Holy Ghost. *See* 4,5,17,49
Holy Roman Rota. *See* 278
Holy See. *See* 14,26,64,156,169,197,202,
206-208,247,249,254,257,280,292,293,295,
303
homosexuality. *See* 64,172,178
Honore de Balzac. *See* 176
Honorius. *See* 6,79,207
Horus. *See* 45,49,341
Hosius. *See* 43
Hospilter. *See* 214
Hoyos. *See* 261,262

Hudal. *See* 133,134,138,139,148,238
Hugo, Victor. *See* 176
Huguenots. *See* 72
Humanae Vitae. *See* 6
Hume, David. *See* 176
Hungary. *See* 71,109
Hurons. *See* 12
Hus. *See* 38-43,58
Hussineez. *See* 39
Hussite. *See* 186
   Hussites. *See also* 41
Hutchinson. *See* 287
Huxley, Aldous. *See* 15
hybrid. *See* 45
Hypatia. *See* 68

I

Iconoclasm. *See* 4
ICRC. *See* 134,136
icthus. *See* 49
ideology. *See* 8,18,340
Iesous Christos Theou Uios Soter. *See* 49
Ignatius. *See* 16
Iguala. *See* 90
IHRAAM. *See* 267-270
images. *See* 6,313,335
immolated. *See* 67
immunity. *See* 135,151,242,271,278
Imperialism. *See* 88,279,341
Imprimatur. *See* 78,174,180,181,197,198
incest. *See* 40
India. *See* 46,292
Indian Act of 1874. *See* 266
Indian Mission Residential Schools. *See* 273
Indians. *See* 12-14,28,72,73,88,89-92,
166-168,266,268
Indulgences. *See* 6,40,41
infallibility. *See* 6,7,27,35,36,169,188,330
infallible. *See* 34-38,99,315
Ingersoll, Robert. *See* 3
Innocent. *See* 4-6,39,58,71,79,81,113,133,
141,189,207,209,221,264,279,297,319,324
Instituto. *See* 138
insufflation. *See* 17
Insurance. *See* 191,291,301
intercede. *See* 11

intercession. *See* 11,86
intercourse. *See* 67,88,171
International Criminal Court. *See* 265
interpretations. *See* 36,183
investigation. *See* 33,37,151,158,159,186,
189,197,206,213,216,244,248,250,252,261,
264,265,268,287,289,300
invocation. *See* 17
IRA. *See* 288
Ireland. *See* 18,112,256,261,284, 287-289,
291
Isabella. *See* 6,81,82
Islam. *See* 28,64,82
Iu-em-Hetep. *See* 49
Iznik. *See* 43

J

Jalisco. *See* 89,91
Jansen, Cornelius. *See* 176
Jasenovac. *See* 110,112
Jehovah. *See* 38,342
Jerome. *See* 31,40,41
Jerusalem. *See* 38,44,77,79
Jesuit. *See* 16,55,90,143,163,166,274,275,
302,310,323,339
Jesuit Mission Schools. *See* 274
Jesus. *See* 6,26,29,31,32-34,38,39,43,45,
48-50,52,55,61,65,73,77,86,92,164,177,181,
182,204,209,210,274,290,299; *See* 303,310,
311,319,323,325,341,343
Jews. *See* 6,19,28,65,70,71,81,97,100-103,
106,109,110,112,139,143,148,151,157,297,
327
Jeyapaul. *See* 293
Jihad. *See* 77
Joan. *See* 55-60,80,81
Jogues. *See* 12
Johannes. *See* 58,59
John Jay Report. *See* 256
Johnny "Bingo" Dawson. *See* 272
John of Gamala. *See* 310
John Paul II. *See* 11,14,17,62,63,65,106,132,
139,156,163,181,199,213,214,216,238,255,
276,278,279
Joseph, Jasper. *See* 263
Juan de San Martín. *See* 82

Juan de Zumarraga. *See* 89
Juárez. *See* 90,91
judicial astrology. *See* 7
Julius. *See* 5,189,279,341
jurisdiction. *See* 26,82,102,151,180,244, 288,300

K

Kaising. *See* 241
kalki. *See* 48
Kamber. *See* 134
Kant, Immanuel. *See* 15,176
Kastner. *See* 143
Kata Christianon. *See* 69
Ken Bear Chief. *See* 273-275,339
Kennedy. *See* 179,195,214
Kerry. *See* 178
Kiesle. *See* 281,296,297
King Charles. *See* 5
kingdom. *See* 29,108,311
Knights Templars. *See* 5
Kolbe. *See* 170
Kren. *See* 135
Krishna. *See* 45-47,341
Krisosztom Kruesz. *See* 34
kristallnacht. *See* 106
Krst. *See* 49
Kuper Island. *See* 268-270
Kuper Island School. *See* 268,270
Kythnos. *See* 139

L

Laach. *See* 215
Laachi. *See* 217
Lady Gaga. *See* 182,325
Lalande. *See* 12
Lalich, Janja. *See* 7,9,340
Lamberto. *See* 199,207
Lamentabili. *See* 36
Langone. *See* 7,9,340
Languedoc. *See* 210
Lansky. *See* 102
Laodicea. *See* 187
Lapide. *See* 102
Lapsi. *See* 204
Larue. *See* 49

Lateran. *See* 4,5,27,56-60,98,107, 180,188, 200-202,297
lawsuits. *See* 157,242,255,256,260,282,287, 293,301,330
Leavitt. *See* 35
Legatus. *See* 18,19
Le Monde. *See* 36
Lenihan. *See* 294,295
Lennon. *See* 182
Leo. *See* 6,36,57-59,61,82,99,183,201-204, 219,340
lepers. *See* 12,47,308
Lerdo. *See* 90
    Lerdo de Tejada. *See also* 91
Lescat. *See* 133
Letsinger. *See* 222
Levi. *See* 98
Levites. *See* 98
Levy. *See* 151,152,156,157,341
Liber Pontificalis. *See* 57
Library. *See* 57,75,114,206,271,313,345
Licinius. *See* 44
Lindner. *See* 302,303
List of Ex-Catholics. *See* 311
litany. *See* 16
Lithuania. *See* 71
liturgy. *See* 12,44
Liutprand. *See* 199-201
Llobet. *See* 133
Locke, John. *See* 176
Loftus. *See* 37,133,134,137
Logos. *See* 46,69
Lorraine. *See* 81
Los Angeles. *See* 112,113,138,221,222,281, 282,287,295,298,339
L'Osservatore Romano. *See* 163,257
Lothair. *See* 59
Loyola. *See* 16
Luciano. *See* 102,218
Lucifer. *See* 163,164
Lucius. *See* 208,209
Luke. *See* 29,204
Luther. *See* 6,39
    Luther, Martin. *See also* 6,39,176,188,311
Lutheran. *See* 186,188
Lynch. *See* 302,303
Lyon. *See* 137

M

Machiavelli, Niccolo. *See* 176

Macon. *See* 72

Mafia. *See* 37,102,195,213,215,216

Magdalene. *See* 39,184,210,284

Magi. *See* 46

magistrate. *See* 58

Magistris. *See* 20

Maglione. *See* 133

Mahony. *See* 148,222,287,298

Mailly. *See* 55,56

Mainz. *See* 56,57

Malathion. *See* 62

Mallorca. *See* 12

Mammon. *See* 62

Mandic. *See* 134

Manhattan. *See* 37,182

Manly, McGuire & Stewart. *See* 285

Manning. *See* 113,136,137,148

Marcia. *See* 202

Marcinkus. *See* 213,214,216,217

Marianne Cope. *See* 12

Marianus Scous. *See* 57

Mariavite. *See* 185

Marktl. *See* 64

Marmande. *See* 210

Marozia. *See* 200,201

marry. *See* 4,8,187,188,190,277

Martin. *See* 6,39,55,56,59,101,136,137,139,
141,176,188,206,218,289,290,311

Martins, Saravia. *See* 20

Marx, Karl. *See* 176

Masonic Lodge P2. *See* 216

Mass. *See* 5,6,21,65,71,112,148,184,187,198,
240,253,278,279,290,302,312,314,321,322,
325,330

mass murder. *See* 112,198

Mater Dei High School. *See* 285

Maternity. *See* 4

Matthew. *See* 32-34,208

Maxmilian. *See* 91

Maxwell. *See* 6,38,50,345

Mayan. *See* 164

Mayen. *See* 215

McCabe. *See* 69,70,72,197,209,211

McCoy. *See* 299,300,327

McFarland. *See* 285,294

McGarr. *See* 158

McIntyre. *See* 148,298

medical experiments. *See* 269

Mediterranean. *See* 45,78

Melbourne. *See* 182

Melchiades. *See* 31

Mengele, Josef. *See* 136,139

Mentz. *See* 57

Mercator,Isodorus. *See* 31

Messiah. *See* 8,46

Methodist. *See* 185

Metropolitan. *See* 44,218

Metz. *See* 31

Mexico. *See* 12,72,82,88-92,261

Mexico City. *See* 12,91

Michelangelo. *See* 86

Michoacán. *See* 89-91

Middle Ages. *See* 11,26,55,57,180,203,209

Midi. *See* 210

midwife. *See* 67

Migdal. *See* 39

Milingo. *See* 189,190

Mills, Stuart. *See* 176

Milton, John. *See* 176

Mirabilia Urbis Romae. *See* 58

miracle. *See* 11

missionary. *See* 6,12,213

Mithra. *See* 45,46

Mithras. *See also* 39,45,69

Mithraism. *See* 45

Mitre. *See* 30

molestation. *See* 61,139,148,221,222,261,
287,289,297,315,319,323,324,327,329,330

molestations. *See* 132,183,190,242,281,
323,324,327,330

Molokai. *See* 12

Monaghan. *See* 18

Montezuma. *See* 88

Moriarity. *See* 289

Morillo. *See* 82

Moriscos. *See* 82

Moro, Aldo. *See* 218

Mt. Graham. *See* 163,166

Mudd. *See* 135

Mulierbus. *See* 57

Muller. *See* 101,138,261

murder. *See* 12,37,40,61,67,102,103,106,

109,112,197,198,202,204,209,215,217,219,
222,263,272,273,303,319,329; *See* 330,336
Murder Incorporated. *See* 102
Murphy, Lawrence. *See* 258,297
Murray. *See* 287,289
music. *See* 182,334
Mussolini. *See* 27,107,108,145,238,297,329
mystical. *See* 37,310

N

Nakogee-Davis. *See* 269
Nanaimo Indian Hospital. *See* 263
Naples. *See* 41,102
Napoleon. *See* 91
Native. *See* 12,73,89,92,165,263-275,319,
339
navy. *See* 26,205
Nazi. *See* 19,64,100,101,103,106,107,111,
112,129,132,133,135-139,141,143,148,151,
156,238,298,315,330
Netherlands. *See* 82,261
Network. *See* 20,138,273,284,299,308,317,
340
Neumann. *See* 12
New York Times. *See* 239,257,258,276,279,
296,320
Nexus Magazine. *See* 196,211,339
Nez Perce. *See* 273,339
NFP. *See* 171
Nicaea. *See* 4,26,34,36,38,43,183,187
Nice. *See* 4,32,287
Nihil Obstat. *See* 180
Nikolai. *See* 41
Niswonger. *See* 185
Nixon. *See* 112,114
Nooksak. *See* 273
Norway. *See* 261
Nostra Aetate. *See* 65
Notre Dame. *See* 167
Novatianists. *See* 44
Nueva España. *See* 88,89
Numerary. *See* 21
Nuncio. *See* 100,179,238
Nuño de Guzmán. *See* 89
Nuremberg. *See* 140,144

O

Oaxaca. *See* 91
Obama. *See* 179
Oblate. *See* 275,339
Obregón. *See* 91
O'Brien. *See* 239-242
O'Connor. *See* 290,311,341
Octavian. *See* 202
ODAN. *See* 20,22
O'Donnell. *See* 101
OECD. *See* 160
Olivi. *See* 35
Olmedo. *See* 88
O'Malley. *See* 178,308,309
Omega. *See* 48
Ontario Health Department. *See* 267
Opava. *See* 56
Opus Dei. *See* 19-22,159,214,217
Orange. *See* 112,138,148,280,281,285,287,
294-296,339
　Orange County. *See* 112,148,280,287,296,
　339
　Orange Diocese. *See* 285,295
orders. *See* 6,90,91,143,156,160,181,202,
203,255,256
ordination. *See* 44,98,183-185,187,199,255,
298
Oregon Province Society of Jesus. *See* 274
original sin. *See* 4,172
Orleans. *See* 81
orthodoxy. *See* 43,81,129
Osaer. *See* 275
Osborne. *See* 134
Ostia. *See* 57

P

Pacelli. *See* 97-103,107
Pajic. *See* 129
Palestine. *See* 69
papacy. *See* 26,28,29,33,34,37,40,55,56,61,
62,68,98,169,198-205,207,209,297
Papal Bull. *See* 3,6,40,78,208,311,313
papal infallibility. *See* 7,27,35,36,169
Papess. *See* 39,58,60
pappas. *See* 26
Parenti. *See* 276,279,341

Paris. *See* 6,34,81,106

parliament. *See* 58,108

Pascal, Blaise. *See* 176

Pasquala. *See* 12

Pastoral. *See* 6,14,104,218,261,277,296

patriarch. *See* 4,218

  patriarchs. *See also* 44,197,243

Paulian. *See* 44

Pauline. *See* 181

Pavelic. *See* 108-112

  Pavelic, Andre. *See* 14,108,112,128,129,
  134-136,138,139,144

PAX. *See* 158

Payens. *See* 77

Pearly Gate. *See* 49

pedophiles. *See* 255,276,287,289,307,324

pedophilia. *See* 199,274,276,277,302

Pelagius. *See* 187

penance. *See* 57,243,244

Penitentiary. *See* 20,245,246,254

Pentecost. *See* 44

Peron. *See* 110,137

Persia. *See* 46

Peter. *See* 4,6,26,27,31-35,37,39,40,56,58,60,
68,187,189,200,201,203-206,209,266,267,
278,302

Petranovic. *See* 134

Pew Forum on Religion & Public Life.
See 326

Phayer. *See* 133,136

Philadelphia. *See* 12,185,319

Philippine Duchesne. *See* 12

Philippines. *See* 261,314

Phillip. *See* 34,38,165

Photius. *See* 4

physics. *See* 37,101,335

Piacenza. *See* 62

Pierleoni. *See* 207,208

'Pietre, Pater Patrum, Papisse Prodito
Partum'. *See* 56

Pilgrims. *See* 77,92

Pius. *See* 6,7,11,14,21,27,34,36,37,55,61,
97-103,107,110,112,132,133,138,139,141,
144,148,169,188,189,238; *See* 315,330

Place. *See* 11,29,34,35,49,56,57,59,60,77,81,
88,151,163,165,167,187,200,206,211,216,
222,239,243,244,247,249,251; *See* 253-255,

268,269,323,340

Platina. *See* 206

  Platina, Bartolomeo. *See* 57,206

Plymouth. *See* 92

Poelzl. *See* 100

Poggius. *See* 41,42

Polonius. *See* 59

Polzer. *See* 166

Pontiac. *See* 93

pontiffs. *See* 31,56

Pontifical Biblical Commission. *See* 36

Pope. *See* 3-7,11,14,17-19,21,26,27,29,31,
32,34-40,44,50,55-65,68,71,72,77-79,81,82,
84,86-88,92,93,97-103,106; *See* 107,110,112,
131,132,138,139,141,143,144,148,156,157,
160,162,163,169,171,172,175,177,179-181,
183; *See* 186-190,196-209,211,213-218,220,
221,238,242,243,255,258-260,273,276,
278-281,289,290,293,296,297,308; *See* 314,
315,321,323,325,329,330,342,345

Pope John Paul I. *See* 62,172,213-218,220,
314

popes alleged to have been murdered.
See 219

Popes Murdered. *See* 219

Prague. *See* 40,41,58

pray. *See* 11,167,292

Prayer. *See* 16,17,21,44,65,167,292,309,325,
336,337

predator priests. *See* 14,147,279,287,300,
327,329,345

predatory. *See* 259,274,284,329

Prefect. *See* 20,57,69,177,206

Presbyterian. *See* 185,266

presbyters. *See* 44

Priebke, Erich. *See* 136

Prohibition. *See* 44,162,253

Prometheus. *See* 37,45,333,336

Prophyry. *See* 69

Protestants. *See* 32,71,72,91,175,319,321,
327

Providence. *See* 12

provincial. *See* 44,239,240

Prussians. *See* 71

Psalms. *See* 16

Ptolemy. *See* 161

Puerto. *See* 12

purgatory. *See* 6,84
pyrethrum. *See* 214

Q

Quaker. *See* 184
Quinn, John. *See* 278
Qui quorundam. *See* 35

R

Ra. *See* 49
Rabelais, Francois. *See* 176
Raemond, Florimund de. *See* 58
Ramstein. *See* 240
Rand, Ayn. *See* 15
rape. *See* 256,273,290,291,307
Ratlines. *See* 106,112,129,133,137
Ratzinger, Joseph Alois. *See* 64
Rauff, Walter. *See* 136
Raushning. *See* 99
RCMP. *See* 264,268,270
redeemer. *See* 46,47
Reese. *See* 181
Reform. *See* 11,172,185,256
Reichsconcordat. *See* 107
Renaissance. *See* 38,57,313,333,345
Report on Claudy. *See* 287,289
residential schools. *See* 263-267,269-271,
273,274,339
resurrection. *See* 44,46,77
Revelation. *See* 3,164
RICO. *See* 12,195,259
Robbins, Tony. *See* 260
Roberts. *See* 195
Robinson. *See* 238
Rocksprings. *See* 222
Rodriguez, Manuel. *See* 12
Rogue Economist. *See* 35,37
Roma. *See* 109,151,157
Roman Catholic Church. *See* 7,16,25,26,28,
38-40,42,51,52,64,79,95,98-103,109,110,
128,143,159,175,180,187,195,256,272,288,
289,293; *See* 296,301,312,314,319,327,330,
331
Roosevelt. *See* 110
rosary. *See* 21,182,272
Roschmann, Eduard. *See* 136

Rose. *See* 12,40,46,112,113,208,283
Rothschilds. *See* 100
Rousseau, Jean-Jacques. *See* 176
Royal Canadian Mounted Police. *See* 264
RU-486. *See* 171
Rule of Whores. *See* 200
Russell, Bertrand. *See* 3,72
Russia. *See* 99,100,111,182

S

Sacraments. *See* 6,41,141,294
Sacrifice. *See* 5,20,46,104,171,204,265,273
Sagan, Carl. *See* 15
sainthood. *See* 12,19,20,98,128,202,315
Salem Massachusetts. *See* 67
salvation. *See* 6,35,47,88,102,179,185,204
Salvation Army. *See* 185
Sand, George. *See* 176
San Girolamo. *See* 134,135
Santa Barbara. *See* 138
Santo Domingo. *See* 88
Sapienza. *See* 162
Saric. *See* 109,128,129
Sartre, Jean-Paul. *See* 176
saved. *See* 5,46,86,92,93,102,148
Savior. *See* 46,47,49,60,69,73,92,181
Scahill. *See* 279
Scalia. *See* 195
Schiklgruber. *See* 100
Schism. *See* 4,5,38,79,206,241
Schmitz. *See* 113,148
Schweitzer. *See* 49
Science. *See* 161,162,164,165,168-170,335,
340
scientific. *See* 29,37,161,162,169,203,329,
335
scientist. *See* 164,185,313
scripture. *See* 3,5,29,36,41,161-163,169
Scrolls. *See* 37,176,177
Seat. *See* 6,27,28,37,58,59
sede vacante. *See* 27
sedia stercoraria. *See* 58
Seelos, Xavier. *See* 12
Segni. *See* 203,209,211
Seigel. *See* 102
Senator. *See* 179,311

Serbs. *See* 106,109,110,112,129,157
Sergius. *See* 61,199,201,219
Serono. *See* 159
Serra, Junipero. *See* 12,14
Servants of the Paraclete. *See* 300
Seton. *See* 12
Seward. *See* 268,270
Sharpe. *See* 286
Shaw. *See* 185
shepherd. *See* 46,47
Shroud of Turin. *See* 87,88
Siena. *See* 58
Sigismund. *See* 41
Sign. *See* 16,17,49,59,151,190,201,214,242, 245,286,291
Simon Bar-Jona. *See* 32
simony. *See* 40,198,205
Simpson. *See* 172
sin. *See* 4,7,42,47,172,177,221,253,254,258
Sindona. *See* 37,213,215-217
Sisters. *See* 12,186,202,239
Sistine Chapel. *See* 27,86
Sixtus. *See* 6,7,57
Skinner, B. F.. *See* 15
slavery. *See* 6,88,89,188
Smiling Pope. *See* 213
SNAP. *See* 256,284,299,300-303,308
Society. *See* 8,18,19,21,35,109,113,139,148, 173,207,222,259,264,275,307,309,310,324, 325
  Society of Friends. *See also* 184
  Society of Jesus. *See also* 6,55,181,274
Sodano, Angelo. *See* 278
sodomy. *See* 40
Sol Invictus. *See* 45
Solomon. *See* 38
solstice. *See* 47
Sonora. *See* 90
Sorbubor. *See* 137
Sotomayor. *See* 195
Soviet Intelligence. *See* 37
Spain. *See* 19,21,73,82,88,90,92,133,135, 187,214,261,296
Spanish Catholic School. *See* 269
Spanish Inquisition. *See* 71,81,82
Spinoza, Baruch de. *See* 176
spirituality. *See* 29,50,310

Squanto. *See* 92
SS. *See* 137,143
Stalin. *See* 110
Standish. *See* 92
Stangl, Franz. *See* 136,137,139
Stanislaw Jerzy Lec. *See* 52
Stannard. *See* 73
St. Christopher. *See* 313
Stedingers. *See* 71
stem-cell research. *See* 170,178,181
stem cells. *See* 171
Stephen. *See* 15,35,37,58,61,199,200,219, 281,296,312
Stepinac. *See* 14,111,112,141,144,148
  Stepinac, Alojzije. *See also* 14,111,144
Stevens. *See* 156
St. Joseph. *See* 12
Strugnell. *See* 176,177
Stuttgart. *See* 41
Sufi Archive. *See* 215
Sunday. *See* 44,46,98,279,293,308,319
Sungenis. *See* 320
Supernumerary. *See* 21
superstitious. *See* 7
survivors. *See* 151,152,156,157,264,269,271, 284,290,299,308
Swastika. *See* 107
Swift, Jonathan. *See* 176
Switzerland. *See* 112,156,261
Sylvester. *See* 32,62,203,268
symbol. *See* 46,49,50,182,315,321,326
Synods. *See* 43,44
Syria. *See* 69,79

T

Taibbi. *See* 257,260,321,341,342
Talmud. *See* 6
Tamaki,Blaine. *See* 274
Tamaki Law Offices. *See* 273,274,339
Tarascan. *See* 89
Tardini. *See* 134
Tarot. *See* 60
Tears. *See* 27,128,263
Tedeschi. *See* 159,160
Tentonico. *See* 138
Teofilatto, Grottaferrata. *See* 203

Testament. *See* 26,38,164,336,342
Thanksgiving. *See* 92
Theodora. *See* 200,201
Theodosian Code. *See* 70
theologian. *See* 36
Theology. *See* 3,36,64,169,277,340
Theophylact. *See* 203
The Story of a National Crime. *See* 267
Thirty Year War. *See* 72
Thomas. *See* 15,39,70,139,147,173,176,181,
195,238,239,257,309,337,340,345
Tice. *See* 37,38,40,342,345
Tiso. *See* 238
Tisserant. *See* 133,136
Tito. *See* 110,111
Tobias. *See* 9,340
Torquemada. *See* 82
torture. *See* 6,67,71,264,269,273,319
tradition. *See* 3,33,47,165,219,323
Transubstantiation. *See* 5,84
Treaty. *See* 27,98,100,107,180
trials. *See* 67,70,144,282
Tribunal. *See* 82,162,208,244,245,249,251,
252,263,268,269
Trier Seminary. *See* 215
Troppau. *See* 55
Troyes. *See* 77
Tunisia. *See* 79
Turkey. *See* 43,64
Tuscany. *See* 58,199,200
Twain, Mark. *See* 15,175
tzintzuntzan. *See* 89

U

Ulrich. *See* 187
UN Committee on the Rights of the Child.
See 303
Unholy Trinity. *See* 37,133,137
Unitarian. *See* 185
United Brethren. *See* 185
United Church. *See* 185,263,265,267,268,
271,272
United Church of Christ. *See* 185
Universal. *See* 5,21,31,47,274,281,296,311,
333
Urban. *See* 61,68,78,188,208

Ursuline. *See* 275
U.S.. *See* 35,36,64,102,111-113,134,137,138,
158,165,167,168,179-181,184,188,195,215,
216,238,240,256,274,275,292; *See* 311,314,
329,330,339,341
Usk. *See* 58
Ustase. *See* 108-112,128,129,134,135
usury. *See* 44,77
Utashi Army. *See* 14
Utt. *See* 113,148
Uzes. *See* 58

V

Vaclav. *See* 40,41
Valla, Lorenzo. *See* 34
Vangheluwe, Roger. *See* 275
Vannutelli. *See* 98
Vatican. *See* 6,11,16,20,21,25-29,31,32,34,
36,37,52,57,59,63-65,69,74,78,98,99,102,
105-107,110-112,133-135,137,138; *See* 141,
147,148,151,152,156-160,163-171,179-182,
184,186,188-190,195,200,205-207,213-218,
238,242,243,255; *See* 257,261,272,276-281,
284,286,287,289,291-293,297,301-303,307,
308,313-315,329,330,341,345
Vatican Bank. *See* 151,156,157,159,160,
213-217
Vaticaniis ferendis. *See* 25
Vatican's Secret Archives. *See* 313
vaticanus collis. *See* 26
vaticanus mons. *See* 26
Vaticinia. *See* 25
Vaticum. *See* 25
vernal equinox. *See* 44
vescia piscis. *See* 49
Vianney. *See* 286,299,300
Via Sacra. *See* 56
Virgin Mary. *See* 4,184
Virtus. *See* 327,328
Vishnu. *See* 47,48
Vitae Pontificum Platine Historici Liber de
Vita Christi ac Omnium Pontificum
Quihactenus Ducenti Fuere et XX. *See* 57
Vittorio Veneto. *See* 217
Voltaire. *See* 176,336,337
von Faulhaber. *See* 143

W

Wagner, Gustav. *See* 133,136,137
Wakin. *See* 239,241
Waldensians. *See* 71
Walker. *See* 67,69,335
Wallace. *See* 148
War. *See* 37,61,62,72,77-79,91,92,95,97,98,
100-102,104-106,108,109,111,112,128,129,
133-139,141,144,151,156,157; *See* 186,198,
207,208,210,238,239,263,264,329,341
Weakland. *See* 307
Webb. *See* 158
Weidenfeld. *See* 198
Welshman. *See* 58
Weselyan. *See* 185
Western Schism. *See* 5
Westminster. *See* 112,113,138
Wheless. *See* 70,71
Wickson, Mike. *See* 272
Wikipedia. *See* 6,11,12,14,20,27,45,60,65,
78,79,82,92,111,137,163,186,243,256,301,
342
Will. *See* 4,31,72,184,334
Williams. *See* 37
Williamson. *See* 139,148,156
Wilucka. *See* 185
Winfield. *See* 172
witchcraft. *See* 12,81
witch trials. *See* 67
Wojtyla. *See* 276
  Wojtyla, Karol. *See also* 62
Wolf. *See* 102,129
women. *See* 21,28,35,47,67,68,72,82,88,
182-187,200,202,210,217,249,263,273,277,
284,309,312,315,329,330,337
Woosley. *See* 185
World War II. *See* 95,97,98,101,102,104,
129,133,139,156,329
Wormwood. *See* 164
worship. *See* 12,91,314
Wycliffe. *See* 5,39-41,84,85

Y

Yadus. *See* 47
Yallop. *See* 37,213,217,218
Yoni. *See* 49,50

York. *See* 12,37,102,196,207,208,216,239,
257,258,276,279,296,307,309,320,339,341
Youth. *See* 64,65,108
Yugoslavia. *See* 108,110,112,113,139,151,
157

Z

Zachary. *See* 59
Zapotecán. *See* 90
zealous. *See* 8
Zola, Emil. *See* 176
Zoroaster. *See* 45
Zyklon. *See* 62